PREFACE

The world of cargo movements is constantly changing, especially in the maritime sector. Over 90% of trade into and out of the UK is carried by maritime means, and this infers that the UK relies on the maritime sector to maintain its livelihood. The trader, be it importer or exporter, relies on freight agents and shipping lines to ensure that goods are carried between the UK and other parts of the world, including the continent. And yet the practicalities of the maritime movement of goods are often overlooked and are not necessarily understood by all parties concerned.

There is a need for full communication between the trader, the freight forwarder and the shipping line, and that means a full understanding of the principles involved. The efficient movement of goods by sea is often compromised by delays or mishaps, often resulting in financial cost to the trader, without an understanding on the part of the trader as to why such issues occur.

This book has been written out of necessity, in order to address the issues concerning the maritime movement of goods, and its purpose is to introduce the reader to the principal elements of the maritime movement of goods and thus the management of marine cargo. It aims to cover most of the main elements of such movement, as well as to highlight the new initiatives affecting the sector. It is hoped that the reader will be able to understand the workings of the maritime freight sector, and that closer relationships can be forged between traders and those responsible for the maritime movement of goods.

The book has been designed for all aspects of freight management, from traders themselves through logistics practitioners, shipping lines, freight forwarders, professionals in the sector wishing to improve their knowledge of the business, and students of marine management and logistics, to those simply wishing to know more about how the maritime sector functions. The book is not intended as a panacea to the whole sector; there are too many facets to the industry, and each has its own specialist operators and practitioners. To this extent, the book is intended more as a detailed overview of the maritime cargo sector, in order to encourage the reader to explore various specific areas of the maritime sector depending upon their professional or commercial needs.

Although much of the book has been written based on UK practices and considerations, much of the basis of maritime trade is standard worldwide. It is accepted that there are somewhat different practices and considerations in the maritime sector for each country, but the basic principle of world maritime trade remains the same throughout. The reader is encouraged to learn more about their own national maritime sector, and thus to compare it with other similar systems elsewhere in the world. The reader is also encouraged to keep up to date with changes in national maritime policy and legislation, as these may change on a very frequent basis depending upon the requirements of the global maritime community, especially concerning security and safety of both vessels and cargoes. New global initiatives, particularly in the area of maritime controls, are requiring new legislation and practices, especially concerning the issue of maritime reporting and declaration of cargoes, and many changes lie ahead. It is important that the reader recognises these changes, and ensures that they are constantly updated with regard to such matters.

INTRODUCTION TO
MARINE CARGO MANAGEMENT

LLOYD'S PRACTICAL SHIPPING GUIDES

Other titles in this series are:

The Handbook of Maritime Economics and Business
by Costas Th. Grammenos
(2002)

Maritime Law
6th edition
by Chris Hill
(2004)

ISM Code: A Practical Guide
to the Legal Insurance Implications
2nd edition
by Dr. Phil Anderson
(2005)

Risk Management in Port Operations,
Logistics and Supply Chain Security
by Khalid Bichou, Michael G.H. Bell and Andrew Evans
(2007)

Port Management and Operations
3rd edition
by Professor Patrick M. Alderton
(June 2008)

INTRODUCTION TO
MARINE CARGO MANAGEMENT

BY

J. MARK ROWBOTHAM

informa

LONDON
2008

Informa Law
Mortimer House
37–41 Mortimer Street
London W1T 3JH
law.enquiries@informa.com

an Informa business

First published 2008

British Library Cataloguing in Publication Data
A catalogue record for this book
is available from the
British Library

ISBN 978–1–84311–756–8

Text set in 9/11pt Plantin
by Interactive Sciences Ltd, Gloucester
Printed in Great Britain by
MPG, Bodmin, Cornwall

Printed on paper sourced from sustainable sources

ACKNOWLEDGEMENTS

In writing this book, my grateful thanks go to many people who advised, encouraged and supported me, despite the daunting challenges this project presented.

I would especially like to thank colleagues in Informa Group, Lloyd's Maritime Academy, Imperial College London, the Chartered Institute of Logistics and Transport in the UK (CILT), HM Revenue & Customs (my former employers from some years ago, as HM Customs & Excise), the Maritime & Coastguard Agency, the port authorities of Clydeport, the Humber, the Tyne and the Mersey, and several shipping lines including P&O Ferries and CMA CGM. I would also like to thank Lloyd's MIU for their permission to access their AIS website, and enabling me to assess the value of electronic vessel monitoring systems.

I wish to thank personal colleagues, especially those who have mentored me through my advancement in the CILT, and those who have, at some stage or another, given up some of their valuable time to enlighten me in a variety of the finer issues concerning vessel and port management, thus giving me a wealth of knowledge and encouraging me to write this book. I also owe thanks to those of my distant relatives who are still in the maritime business, for their personal views of the business. Without all the support I have received, this book might never have been written. May it encourage all who read it.

CONTENTS

CHAPTER 1 THE MARITIME SECTOR

CHAPTER 2 CARGOES AND VESSELS

CHAPTER 3 CHARTERING AND BULK CARRIAGE

CHAPTER 4 ORGANISATIONS AND PROCESSES

CHAPTER 5 LEGAL, FINANCIAL AND INSURANCE ISSUES

CHAPTER 6 COMPLIANCES AND CONTROLS

CHAPTER 7 ROLES AND RESPONSIBILITIES

CHAPTER 8 AWARENESS & VIGILANCE

CHAPTER 9

ABOUT THE AUTHOR

Mark Rowbotham is an independent consultant and trainer in customs and marine security and control issues, especially concerning marine cargo management. He deals with compliance, control and procedural issues in both customs and marine matters, having originally been an officer in HM Customs & Excise, where his responsibilities involved import and export controls over maritime freight traffic into and out of several southern UK ports.

He graduated in Export Management and gained a Masters' degree in International Relations and Political Economy in 1995. He has written extensively on the subjects of customs, VAT, international supply chain and marine compliance issues for a wide variety of publications, including international trade and logistics magazines, and journals of the universities of Cranfield, Glasgow and Imperial College London.

He advises several Chambers of Commerce and Local Enterprise Authorities on customs, international trade and marine issues throughout Scotland and Northern England, and frequently delivers training courses and seminars on these issues. He is a tutor with Lloyd's Maritime Academy, and is also an adviser to UK Trade & Investment on customs and logistics procedures pertaining to trade with North and Latin America. In his capacity as a Chartered Fellow of the Chartered Institute of Logistics and Transport, he is co-chair of their Freight Forwarding, Ports and Maritime Forum, and has presented marine seminars to a variety of organisations. He is also fluent in French and Portuguese.

LIST OF FIGURES AND TABLES

Chapter 7

Chapter 8

INTRODUCTION

THE MARITIME COMMERCIAL ENVIRONMENT

Two-thirds of the surface of the globe is covered by either fresh or salt water. Fresh water only accounts for a small percentage of this total, as the vast majority is accounted for by salt water in the form of the world's seas and oceans. These masses of water separate continents from each other, as well as providing a source of livelihood to a wide variety of people and professions, from national defence services, through the fishing industry and the offshore oil and gas sector, to the carriage of commercial goods by sea.

In some ways, the nature of the sea may seem placid and even romantic: it has spawned some of the finest literature over the past centuries, from novels to poetry, as well as countless musical creations dedicated to its beauty, both classical and popular. But the nature of the sea can also be extremely wild, creating tempests so violent that coastlines are being steadily eroded, communities destroyed, and livelihoods shattered. Every year, there are many instances of shipwrecks, founderings and sinkings of vessels as a result of what may be best described as *force majeure*. Many lives have been lost as a result, despite the best efforts of rescue teams including the UK's Royal National Lifeboat Institution (RNLI) and its gallant volunteers, and such occurrences are a stark reminder to all of the sheer destructive power of nature, especially in its rawest form. Anyone who listens to the Shipping Forecast issued by the Meteorological Office on behalf of the Maritime and Coastguard Agency will equally be reminded of these natural conditions.

But behind the seemingly endless stream of lists of weather conditions around the British coastline delivered from the Meteorological Office, there lurks another major issue: that of the nature of shipping within the maritime framework and why it is so important to the national economy and its lifeblood. The issue of maritime transport covers a variety of circumstances, from cruise vessels designed for the large-scale maritime entertainment of the international public, through the international passenger and cargo ferry network plying regional maritime routes, to the huge container ships deployed in the carriage of long distance, deep-sea voyages around the globe.

This book seeks to address such issues and to examine and assess the nature of marine cargo management, from both a landward and a seaward perspective, as well as from both a legal and a commercial perspective. It also seeks to examine many topical and prevalent issues, as well as recommending ways in which such management may be rendered more efficient and compliant. It addresses some of the history of the present forms of maritime commercial activity, especially the rise of the use of the container for the carriage of maritime cargoes, and seeks also to highlight the pitfalls and problems associated with such transport, while attempting to address such problems and suggest ways of preventing or avoiding them. It is said that prevention is better than cure. It is better, therefore, to understand the nature of marine cargo management in order to avoid the problems which may arise as a result of a lack of understanding of the principles of the movement of cargoes by maritime means.

Over the centuries, the world of maritime cargo has changed concerning the types of vessels used and the quantities of cargo they carry. And yet, the basic principles of cargo management have remained the same throughout the centuries; namely the need for commerce to send goods by sea from the seller to the buyer, using some form of maritime vessel. Maritime trade has become the instrument of matching demand with supply, and being paid for the privilege. International trade trends have, however, changed over the decades, with raw materials being shipped in bulk in one direction, and finished products being shipped the other direction. There is, seemingly, a gigantic trade imbalance between the Far East and Europe and the Americas, with the latter two becoming reliant on products originating in the former. What is not appreciated is that the Far East relies on the import of bulk shipments of raw materials from the Americas and Europe to manufacture products for shipment elsewhere. To this extent, there is therefore an oblique trade balance, with bulk raw materials being exchanged for large quantities of finished products. And the vast majority of this is carried by maritime means.

The UK is an island. It relies on maritime means for its overseas trade. And yet, considering that it was once one of the prime maritime powers in the world, it has lost most of its maritime industry, sold to overseas bidders. The UK now relies on shipping lines based elsewhere in the world to satisfy its demands. One of the latest class of Maersk Line vessels, the 12,000 TEU (twenty-foot equivalent unit) *Emma Maersk*, called in late-2006 at the Port of Felixstowe for the first time on her way from the Far East to the Northern European Ports. As a member of the newest class of Maersk vessels, the PS-class, she is one of the world's largest container vessels in one of the world's largest shipping lines. At over 150,000 tonnes, she dwarfed the terminal where she was berthed, unloading a vast variety of cargoes destined for the retail shelves to satisfy pre-Christmas demand for stocks. In itself, this was a significant milestone in the sense that the Port of Felixstowe was able to handle such a leviathan of the seas, but it was very definitely a portent of things to come, as well as a measure of how international trade is managed in the present day.

The shipping magazine *Fairplay* warned in 1975 that if the situation of allowing the European ports of Rotterdam, Antwerp, Hamburg and Le Havre to overtake London (once seen as the maritime centre of Europe) prevailed, the Port of London, already relocated down the River Thames to Tilbury in

Essex, would slip down the "big league" of major ports, and would face the grim prospect of being relegated to the role of feeder port to the continent, whereas the port of Felixstowe would surge forward. In reality, this prediction has come true, and risks applying to the other southern UK major ports as well, as tonnages of container vessels rise further and the requirement for the use of hub European ports by the major global shipping lines becomes more prevalent.

Due to the introduction of containers as a means of maritime cargo trans-port in the 1960s, the port system had to change radically within its own confines, especially with the construction of new container terminals at several major UK ports, especially those in the South of England. But even as these new terminals were being completed for use, the maritime container market was also changing, with the arrival on the scene of ever-larger vessels capable of carrying twice the original capacity of containers. The volume of containers carried rose from 2,500 TEU to 5,000 TEU per vessel, then to 8,000 TEU and now to 12,000 TEU, with the latest vessels weighing in at in excess of 150,000 grt (gross registered tonnage). The latest question is not how large vessels will become as whether the ports they serve will be able to handle the sheer volume of containers they carry. The relative ease of construction of the present-day container vessel allows vessels of over 150,000 grt with a capacity of 11,000 TEU+ on the high seas with equal comparative ease. The constrain-ing factor remains the capacity of the port to deal with the sheer volume of containers carried by these leviathans of the high seas. In reality, the solution being considered is that of the "hub and spoke" network, where the shipping lines owning the large container vessels choose the ports where they can operate, such as Rotterdam/Europoort, transferring containers on to other feeder vessels for shorter voyages to regional ports such as those in the UK, Scandinavia or the Baltic. It will simply become impractical for the larger vessels to call at these ports, especially in the UK, on their way to the larger European ports where they can be handled more efficiently.

On the continent, this expansion in volume is not a problem. The Dutch port of Rotterdam/Europoort and the Belgian port of Antwerp have gained substantial government grants to improve their infrastructure, from container handling facilities to road and rail access to and from the ports, along with extensive dredging of the channels into and out of the ports. The channels of both the rivers Maas/Rijn (Rotterdam) and Schelde (Antwerp) have been extensively dredged to allow for such increasing tonnage, thus allowing for large increases in the volume of maritime container traffic into and out of the respective ports. New container terminals at both Rotterdam and Antwerp have also been constructed to allow for increased container movements, mainly with government assistance, and these are designed specifically to handle the new, larger container vessels.

In the UK, the issue of funding to facilitate such improvements is much less positive. Although in theory the ports of Southampton and Felixstowe are capable of accommodating the latest container vessels, the combined issues of the ability of the port structures themselves to handle the increasing flow of containers into and out of the ports and also their strategic importance as far as shipping line schedules are concerned are far more questionable. In effect, the UK port authorities are being required to fund their own expansion plans, a scenario less palatable to any such authority, especially as there is little will or initiative from the national government to engage in such funding strategies. It would appear that the days of nationalised ports in the UK are well and truly over. And even if the port authority in question were blessed with such abundant revenues as to allow it to immediately consider an expansion in its facilities and infrastructure, there is still the question of environmental issues and the availability of land close to the terminals for such development. Sooner or later, environmental issues come to the fore, and questions must be asked about sustainability and compromise to the environment as a whole, as well as the effects of increased road and rail traffic flows on the overall regional and domestic infrastructure. The stark reality is that much of the UK's port access networks were designed when such expansion in maritime container traffic had not been envisaged. Along with the increased tonnages of the deep-sea vessels, the tonnage of the short-sea feeder vessels is also increasing, with container capacity per feeder vessel rising to some 2,000 TEU. The increase in container traffic into and out of UK ports by road is severely compromising the regional and national road networks, with questions being asked in several lobbies, including the environmental lobby, as to what steps must be taken to reduce congestion. Increased numbers of containers through any of the major ports will only aggravate the problem. This argument also fuels the feeder strategy, where the cost of a container carried by feeder vessel from the South Coast to the North East of England or the Firth of Forth costs some £300, compared with some £500 by road.

Even the Port of Liverpool, located on the River Mersey in the North West of England, has admitted that it will have to seriously upgrade its road and rail access to the port, as well as build a completely new river terminal for increased container handling capability to flourish as a front-line seaport, especially given its regained importance in terms of transatlantic maritime cargo traffic. In 2006, several new container services were introduced from the port, including CMA-CGM, China Shipping, MSC (Mediterranean Shipping Company) and Italia Marittima/Zim, all serving the East Coast of the US. These services add to those already operated to Canada by OOCL and ACL, as well as feeder services to and from Ireland and other European ports. No other port north of the North-South divide can as yet come anywhere near achieving this. In Scotland, the container services out of the Clydeport and Grangemouth (Forth) terminals are feeder services to other UK and European ports. In this respect, the "hub and spoke" concept favours European ports such as Rotterdam, Antwerp, Bremerhaven and Hamburg, which are ideally suited to handling large numbers of containers destined for elsewhere in Europe, as well as serving the North Sea and Baltic Sea rims. The UK ports form just part of the spoke mechanism reaching out from these central hubs, as do the ports in Scandinavia and the Baltic.

Port congestion has become a major issue in the management of marine cargo. As the volume of inbound marine traffic increases, so the ports, especially those in South-East England, are finding it increasingly difficult to manage the movements of both container vessels and their cargoes. It is becoming more common to find vessels queuing up outside the port areas, waiting their turn to enter port and unload their cargoes, owing to the limited space available for berthing. The ports of Southampton and Felixstowe are two of those affected, and even the European ports are engaging in ambitious expansion initiatives to accommodate the increasing volumes of container traffic entering the European ports, such as Stage 2 of the Maasvlakte project at the western end of the port of Rotterdam/Europoort. Further initiatives are under way to expand the port facilities further north in the UK, namely at the ports of Liverpool, in North West of England, which primarily serves the transatlantic trade, and Teesport, in the North East of England, which is engaging in a £330 million project to expand the container facilities at the port as part of the Northern Gateway initiative. The purpose of the project at Liverpool is to construct a new riverside container terminal on the River Mersey itself, thus being able to accommodate the larger 8,000–10,000 TEU container vessels, which at present cannot enter the port owing to the restrictions of the lock leading into Gladstone and Seaforth Docks. This can only accommodate container vessels of some 35,000 grt, with a capacity of some 2,500 TEU, and thus restricts access to the Seaforth container terminal, as well as adding time to berthing and loading/unloading operations. Both these projects are also intended to relieve some of the congestion which at present besets the port sector in the southern part of the UK.

The doomsday scenario is that unless the congestion issue is resolved, major UK port authorities may ultimately lose out on maritime business as the larger vessels and the major shipping lines head automatically for the continental ports which can accommodate them. Besides which, the UK market by no means accounts for anywhere near the volume or demand for international trade of that of the rest of Europe, where the requirement for super-ports such as Rotterdam, now the largest port in Europe, is far more prevalent. Add to this the significance of overall voyage costs, taking into account a mixture of bunker fuel costs, port berthing charges, harbour and light dues, pilotage and tug costs and the practicability and viability of including the UK ports in the itinerary schedules of the new vessels becomes far less attractive and thus diminishes. The fewer ports served, the lower the overall voyage costs to the shipping line. It is inevitably cheaper to move a large container deep-sea vessel into a single destination port and then distribute the containers on a regional feeder basis than it is to have the deep-sea vessel call at several ports en route, adding to the voyage costs along the way, as well as adding time to the itinerary schedule of the vessel which could otherwise be avoided. These considerations support the strategy of the large shipping lines to use the "hub and spoke" system, where the large vessels only call at the large ports in continental Europe, and discharge their containers onto smaller feeder vessels which then serve the regional ports. The Port of Rotterdam does not hide its claim of being Europe's largest port, and its plans to expand the existing port area at Maasvlakte (Maas Plain), to the west of the existing port complex, will only increase its capacity further. In order to combat increasing levels of port congestion in the UK, the UK ports may simply become part of the feeder link network to the continent, into a "hub and spoke" container system, and the UK will become reliant on these feeder services to and from the continent for the vast majority of its maritime container traffic. In some ways, this trend may be seen as a more practical solution, as long as the continental ports do not exert significantly greater levies on traffic heading to and from the UK, especially in the form of trans-shipment charges, which would strain the rope further on the maritime economic lifeline the UK would have with Europe.

CHAPTER 1

THE MARITIME SECTOR

1 OVERVIEW OF THE UN CONVENTION OF THE LAW OF THE SEA

The UN Convention of the Law of the Sea (UNCLOS) was agreed in 1982 and was signed by 159 countries. It did not enter into force until a year after it had been ratified by 60 States. The 60th instrument of ratification was deposited on 16 November 1993, and the Convention entered into force on 16 November 1994. The UK, along with Germany and the United States, was not originally party to the Convention because of disagreements concerning the deep sea bed mining regime, but an agreement to resolve these difficulties was adopted by the UN General Assembly in July 1994. The Territorial Sea Act of 1987 extended UK territorial waters from three miles offshore to 12 nautical miles offshore. However, although the United States and Germany subsequently ratified the Convention, the UK delayed acceding to the Convention because of concern about the legality of the Rockall fisheries zone (the UK Exclusive Economic Zone encompassed by the 200-mile limit). However, it eventually acceded to the Convention on 25 July 1997 with effect from 24 August 1997.

The UNCLOS concerns all aspects of the management and regulation of worldwide maritime activities, including national and international jurisdiction over the high seas, and refers, *inter alia*, to the following issues:

- National territorial limits;
- Exclusive economic zones;
- The continental shelf;
- Contiguous zones;
- Rights of innocent passage;
- Movement of vessels;
- The marine environment;
- Marine pollution.

It is administered by the International Maritime Organisation (IMO), based in London, and covers not only the high seas themselves, but also shipping movements upon the high seas.

1.1 Definition of Territorial Maritime Limits

Territorial Maritime Limits can be defined at three specific levels:

- 200-mile exclusive economic zone (the continental shelf);

- The 12-mile limit;
- The three-mile limit.

Each of the above are considered as *baselines*, and demarcate the boundary between a measured area deemed to be *landward* and the area deemed to be *seaward*. The measurements of such areas are defined in *UNCLOS, Article 8*.

Internal waters are all waters on the landward side of the baseline from which the breadth of the Territorial Sea is measured, and within such areas (i.e. the three-mile limit), a national State enjoys absolute sovereignty, except insofar as it may have undertaken Treaty obligations to admit foreign vessels, whether commercial or naval, into its ports. Under such obligations, such a vessel will be required to report into the port in question at least 24 hours in advance.

The sovereignty of a national State also extends to its *Territorial Sea* (UNCLOS, Article 2), but this differs from internal waters in that it is subject to a right of "innocent passage" by foreign vessels (UNCLOS, Article 17). The right of innocent passage does not exempt the vessel from being required under certain rules, such as the requirement to report to either UK or French coastguards when passing through the Strait of Dover, and also stipulates requirements for such vessels to identify themselves by their national flag or flag of convenience. Certain other restrictions are placed on the passage of vessels, such as the requirement for all submarines of any nationality to remain surfaced while passing through the defined strait. In general, territorial sea limits are defined as being at a 12-mile limit from the national shore, although this may vary due to tidal fluctuations and the existence of islands or archipelagos controlled by that National State.

The *200-mile* Exclusive Economic Zone (EEZ) is patrolled by Fishery Protection Vessels, especially those of the Royal Navy, and serves to protect fishing rights within these waters and restrict them to EU vessels.

The *12-mile limit* refers to the absolute offshore limit pertaining to national territorial controls. Within this limit, waters are deemed as being under national territorial control, and are not deemed to be international waters.

The *three-mile limit* refers to the rights of Admiralty and HM Customs & Excise to control all shipping and maritime movements within these waters. All vessels operating within the three-mile limit are subject to Admiralty and Customs controls, and may be subject to boarding by Officers belonging to such authorities where required.

1.2 Contiguous Zones

Contiguous zones are those areas of water subject to national territorial controls which border straits of water between two national sovereign countries (e.g. the Strait of Dover between the UK and France, the Öresund between Denmark and Sweden, and the Strait of Gibraltar between Gibraltar/Spain and Morocco). Owing to the narrow nature of each Strait, normal rules concerning the application of the national 12-mile limit for each country cannot apply, and only the three-mile limit applies concerning national maritime territorial controls in each case. Thus, the three-mile territorial limits are deemed to be the Contiguous zones in each case.

A lesser degree of national territorial control is permissible in Straits used for international navigation between parts of the high seas or exclusive economic zones, such as the Straits of Dover and Gibraltar. In these, a new right of "transit passage" has been introduced by the Convention of the Law of the Sea, conferring freedom of navigation and overflight on foreign ships and aircraft for the purpose of continuous and expeditious transit (*UNCLOS, Article 38*). However, the vessel concerned must identify itself and show that it is bound for a port outside these areas, and its movement is still monitored by the national authorities concerned in order to comply with the applying rules. There is no requirement that the passage should be innocent, as defined in the rules pertaining to Territorial Seas, but ships must refrain from activities not incidental to normal transit (e.g. warfare, terrorism or aggression), and must comply with international regulations, procedures and practices for the safety at sea (SOLAS—Safety of Lives at Sea) and control of marine pollution (*UNCLOS, Article 39*). However, the scope of national legislation and regulation is limited, and at present the only available measures of control are as follows (*UNCLOS, Article 42*):

- prevention of fishing;
- international standards on maritime safety;
- international standards on pollution;
- customs and fiscal enforcement;
- immigration controls;
- sanitary and health controls.

It should be noted that with initiatives towards electronic Cargo Reporting and Declaration, combined with a downsizing in personnel employed by many national Customs Authorities, even Customs controls over such activities have become less evident, and in most cases, especially within parts of the European Union such as the UK, such maritime fiscal controls can no longer be exercised owing to the lack of human resources for such a task. In this case, the application and enforcement of Article 42 of the UNCLOS would appear to be less defined and practical.

1.3 The Continental Shelf

This was defined in the 1958 Continental Shelf Convention as the seabed and subsoil of the submarine areas adjacent to the national coastline but outside the Territorial Sea to a depth of 200 metres or, beyond that limit, to where the depth of the adjacent waters admits and permits the exploration and exploitation of their natural resources, be they mineral or otherwise. This definition has been replaced by the UN Convention of the Law of the Sea, which refers instead to the natural prolongation of the land territory to the outer edge of the continental margin or a minimum distance of 200 nautical miles from the territorial sea baselines (usually 12 miles), subject to a maximum of 350 miles from the baselines or 100 miles from the 2,500 metre isobath (UNCLOS, Article 76). These areas must also be specifically defined and must be charted and mapped for official purposes. However, for the purposes of most practical exercises, the Continental Shelf is generally still deemed to refer to the geographic maritime area generally bounded by the 200-mile limit, where the seabed closer to national shores is at a much shallower level than out in the main body of the ocean. It is this area which is used primarily for the exploration of oil and gas reserves. In the case of the UK, specific areas used for oil and gas exploration are the area to the West of the Shetland Islands, and the North Sea from the German Bight to the waters of the Norwegian Basin between the Shetland Islands and the Norwegian Coast.

A coastal state has sovereign rights over the continental shelf for the purpose of exploring it and exploiting its natural resources, but these are confined to mineral and other non-living resources (i.e. fish and crustaceans) together with sedentary species of living organisms (*UNCLOS, Article 77*). These rights may be exercised and enforced by the use of vessels deployed specifically for such purposes, often owned by the national Navy or the Fishery Protection Service.

The exploration of oil and gas has meant that a huge amount has been invested in the construction and installation of offshore production platforms, and these are protected by the UNCLOS in the form of an exclusion zone comprising a 500-metre radius around each platform. However, there is no reporting mechanism governing the safe passage of vessels within the areas containing such platforms, namely the various oil and gas fields in the North Sea and to the West of the Shetland Islands. The supply vessels serving these platforms must report to the relevant Harbour Authority of Departure, such as the Port of Tyne or Aberdeen, concerning their general destination (a designated oilfield), prior to sailing from the port in question. They must also be in possession of correct cargo manifests pertaining to all consignments loaded aboard the vessel prior to departure for the satisfaction of both port authority and customs control requirements. However, once the vessel has sailed, there is no specific way for the vessel to report its intentions, pertaining to its course and position other than by the AIS System (Automatic Identification System) or the VTS system (Vessel Traffic System).

The offshore oil and gas sector is an area which is vulnerable to maritime threats or incidents. Oil and gas production platforms are located well outside the 12-mile limit of UK territorial waters, and have little or no protection around them. To this extent, the provisions of the UN Convention of the Law of the Sea (UNCLOS) have afforded them an automatic 500-metre exclusion zone, prohibiting the incursion of any vessel other than those authorised to unload materials and supplies onto them.

We live in an era of political uncertainty, with the constant risk of threats and acts of international terrorism. Because of the lack of a major security initiative controlling these maritime areas, as well as the lack of a more secure marine reporting regime, there is always the great risk of sabotage or at worst a major disaster in one of the oilfields caused by acts of terrorism, or a collision in adverse weather conditions. A fictional scenario, far-fetched as it may have seemed at the time, depicted in the 1980s film "North Sea Hijack", illustrated such risks in graphic and chilling detail. Indeed, tragic events such as the 1980s *Piper Alpha* disaster show how easy it is for a simple error or cost-cutting exercise to become a major international disaster, as well as a menace to shipping in the vicinity. A huge area of the North Sea, and indeed much of the Northern European Continental Shelf, is now covered by oil or gas platforms. Some are operational, some are non-operational, but each poses its own hazard to shipping in the area. In fine weather, these platforms are clearly visible to ships in the area, whereas in less-clement weather conditions, they are only identifiable on radar screens when approached at close quarters. Given that each platform is surrounded by a 500-metre radius exclusion zone bestowed upon it by the UN Convention of the Law of the Sea, there is a great need for vigilance on the part of ships' masters to ensure that they will only approach the platform for legitimate supply purposes, and will otherwise avoid the area. This said, there is an increasing need for all vessels in the area of the North Sea Oil and Gas fields to make their positions known to the platforms located in these fields, to ensure complete maritime security and that their presence is monitored and accounted for.

The Continental Shelf is protected by international interests because of its environmental considerations and fishing grounds. In the European Continental Shelf, the waters are fished by several nations, each requiring large catches to satisfy national demand and to make a commercial living. But in recent years, the levels of fish in these areas have been severely depleted, mainly as a result of over-fishing by the fleets of several nations. As a result, strict quotas have been imposed by the European Commission on yearly catches by each of the maritime nations. However, this has not stopped illegal incursion into the fishing grounds by many vessels in direct violation of these quotas, and the net result has been that several nations, including the UK, have imposed controls on these areas using Fishery Protection Vessels. These vessels do not use conventional identification systems such as active AIS systems, so that they remain undetectable by fishing vessels, but by using passive AIS and other monitoring systems, they can detect other vessels conducting illegal activities and if required, can detain or arrest them. However, there are only limited resources available for the operation of these vessels, and they can only be in one location at once.

2 VESSEL TRAFFIC MONITORING

2.1 EC Directive 2002/59

An area of Maritime Law to be addressed, and one which defines the need for maritime reporting, especially of commercial cargo vessels, is EC Directive *2002/59/EC* of the European Parliament and the Council of 27 June 2002, establishing a Community Vessel Traffic Monitoring and Information System. This Directive repealed Council Directive *93/75/EC* [Official Journal of the EC L208 of 05/08/2002].

The Directive 2002/59/EC was the result of part of the action taken in line with the EC Commission's second communication on maritime safety following the disaster involving the tanker *Erika*, and was known as the Erika II package. The main purpose of the Directive was to establish a Community Vessel Traffic Monitoring and Information system (VTMS), which was designed to help to prevent accidents and pollution at sea and to minimise the impacts of such accidents on the marine and coastal environment, and consequently on the economy, health and well-being of local communities.

The VTMS Directive covers all vessels of 300 grt and upwards, whether or not such vessels carry dangerous or hazardous cargoes as defined by the IMO IMDG (International Movement of Dangerous Goods) Code, except for:

- warships;
- fishing vessels, traditional ships and recreational craft less than 45 metres in length;
- bunkers below 5,000 tonnes.

2.2 Ship Reporting and Monitoring

The operator of a ship bound for a port of a Member State must give the Port Authority of that port certain information at least 24 hours in advance, where this is feasible. The information concerned must include:

- name of the vessel;
- IMO identification number;
- type of vessel;
- total number of persons on board;
- port of destination;
- estimated time of arrival.

The Directive also stipulates that ships built on or after 1 July 2002 and calling at a port of a Member State must also be fitted with:

- an Automatic Identification System (AIS), plus
- a Voyage Data Recorder (VDR) system ("black box") to facilitate investigations following accidents.

Member States had until the end of June 2007 to provide themselves with appropriate equipment and staff to utilise the AIS and VDR information and until the end of June 2008 to co-ordinate their national systems with those of other Member States. The process of building up all necessary equipment and shore-based installations for implementing this Directive will have been completed by the end of 2007. More about the AIS structure is detailed later in this text.

2.3 Notification of Dangerous or Polluting Goods on Board Ships

In respect of the carriage of dangerous, hazardous or polluting goods on board ships, the shipper is required to deliver a declaration containing certain information (correct technical names of the dangerous or polluting goods and the address from which detailed information on the cargo may be obtained) to the master or operator prior to taking the goods on board vessel. The operator, agent or master of a ship must also notify general information, such as the identification of the ship and the information provided by the shipper, to the competent authority.

2.4 Monitoring of Hazardous Ships and Intervention in the Event of Incidents and Accidents at Sea

Member States which have been notified of the presence of hazardous ships (ships which have been involved in incidents or accidents at sea, have failed to comply with notification and reporting requirements, have deliberately discharged pollutants or have been refused access to ports) must transmit the information they have to the Member States concerned.

Member States must take all appropriate measures consistent with international law to deal with incidents or accidents at sea and to require the parties concerned (the operator, the master of the ship and the owner of the dangerous or polluting goods carried on board) to co-operate fully with them with a view to minimising the consequences of the incident.

In addition, the master of the ship must immediately report:

- any incident or accident affecting the safety of the ship;
- any incident or accident which compromises shipping safety;
- any situation liable to lead to pollution of the waters or shore of a Member State;
- any slick of polluting materials and containers or packages seen drifting at sea.

The Directive also provides for the possibility of ships being prevented from leaving or entering port in the event of poor weather conditions and obliges Member States to set up places of refuge to accommodate ships in distress, as in the case of the beaching of the container vessel *MSC Napoli* off the Devon coast in January 2007 following severe damage sustained as a result of encountering a violent storm in the Channel.

2.5 Accompanying Measures

Ships entering the area of competence of a vessel traffic service must comply with any IMO (International Maritime Organisation)-approved ships' routing systems, which cover sensitive areas, areas with a high maritime traffic density and areas dangerous for shipping, and must use the vessel traffic services provided. Member States must ensure that these facilities have the requisite human and technical resources to accomplish their tasks.

Member States will have to co-operate to ensure the interconnection and interoperability of their national information systems, in order to ensure that the requisite information on the ship or its cargo can be exchanged electronically at any time.

Each Member State must designate the competent national authorities, port authorities and coastal stations to which the notifications required by the Directive are to be made.

Full co-operation must be arranged between the Commission and the Member States with a view to the future development of the European monitoring, control and information systems for maritime traffic. It will cover the development of automatic communication links between coastal stations and port authorities, and the extension of the coverage of the European monitoring system. Efforts must also be made to improve the management of shipping information, which is one of the tasks of the European Maritime Safety Agency (EMSA).

In order to ensure that the Directive is being implemented successfully, Member States must make regular checks on the operation of their information systems and must introduce a system of financial penalties to act as a deterrent against failure to comply with the Directive's requirements regarding notification and the installation and carriage of the necessary equipment.

The Directive, although far-reaching, has met with differing levels of compliance throughout the European Community to date, with only some of the maritime nations involved able to show full implementation. Other states are still in the process of implementing VTS systems in their ports and waterways, as highlighted later in the book, and in general there are areas concerning compliance, especially in terms of maritime reporting requirements, which at present fall significantly short of the requirements set out by the Directive. Further vessel tracking and monitoring controls, namely AIS, are discussed later.

CHAPTER 2

CARGOES AND VESSELS

1 TYPES OF MARINE CARGO TRAFFIC

1.1 Deep Sea Traffic

Deep sea traffic is all traffic engaged in the maritime carriage of cargoes, be they bulk or containerised, over long maritime distances (e.g. transatlantic, transpacific, or from the Far East to Europe). Over the years, the vessels involved in such trades have increased in size, especially in the container sector. Thirty years ago, in the 1970s, the average size of a container vessel was some 50,000 grt (gross registered tonnes), with a container-carrying capacity of approximately 2,500 to 3,000 TEU (twenty-foot equivalent units). The present generation of containerships has increased those figures to a gross tonnage of 150,000 per vessel, with a container-carrying capacity of up to 11,000 TEU, exemplified by the "E" Class vessels of the A.P. Møller Maersk Fleet. The Maersk Line, originally founded in Denmark in 1904, is at present the largest operator of container vessel fleets and supply vessel fleets in the world, and hence accounts for a large proportion of the carriage of maritime containers and maritime cargoes worldwide.

Deep sea cargoes range through the following categories:

- containerised;
- general;
- bulk;
- hazardous;
- petroleum/hydrocarbon.

The subject of maritime container transport will be covered later in this text, but the other areas are detailed in this section.

All these cargoes are transported in large quantities across the oceans by vessels purpose-built for such activities. The need for the bulk carriage of such commodities is mainly because of the economy of maintaining such activities. The larger the vessel, the more cargo which can be carried, compared with a comparatively lower cost increase. Although the cost of operating larger vessels increases according to the size of the vessel, the value pertaining to the quantity of the increased volume of cargo carried outweighs the operating cost of the vessel. Hence the decision in the past few years to increase the size and tonnage of container vessels operating worldwide. Although the tonnage of vessels designed for the carriage of hydrocarbon commodities and products has increased over the years, the size of such vessels has more often been

9

governed by the worldwide price of oil as a commodity, coupled with the fluctuating demand for the commodity over the last several decades. Vessels carrying general cargoes have also increased in size and efficiency over the years, but not to the same extent as those deployed in the container-carrying business. The same is true of vessels designed for the carriage of hazardous cargoes such as chemicals, although vessels used for the carriage of liquefied gases have increased in size over the decades.

1.1.1 General cargoes

Once a common means of maritime transport, especially before the era of containerised transport, are less common today, although they are still a niche form of maritime transport. They are especially useful where specific cargoes are to be carried, such as oil and gas offshore field supply equipment, or non-standard size cargoes. Indeed, there are still many ports in the world where container vessels cannot operate, and these ports may only be accessed by general-purpose cargo vessels, often carrying a mixture of containers and general cargoes. These are loaded and unloaded by means of cranes mounted aboard the vessel for the easy and convenient transfer of cargoes from ship to shore and vice versa.

1.1.2 Bulk cargoes

These are very much part of the mainstay of the maritime freight sector. Ships specifically designed for the carriage of bulk cargoes ply the ocean waves in large numbers, with cargoes of coal, iron ore, other minerals, grain and other dry products. The world's largest vessel, the Norwegian-owned *Berge Stahl*, weighing in at a cool 364,768 grt, regularly plies between Terminal Maritimo de Ponta da Madeira in Brazil, and the port of Europoort/Rotterdam, the only ports large enough to accommodate the vessel, laden with vast quantities of iron ore. She makes the journey between the two ports some 10 times per year, including some trips to and from Saldanha Bay, South Africa, the only other port capable of handling her size.

In many cases, bulk carriers are often chartered by specific traders from their owners for specific voyages or a series of voyages, depending upon the nature and frequency of the international carriage of bulk commodities. These arrangements, known as charterparties, range from single voyage charters through multiple voyage charters to time charters, where a vessel may be chartered by a vessel management company, an agent or a trader for a specific length of time encompassing a series of voyages.

1.1.3 Hazardous cargoes

These range from explosives and nuclear waste through chemicals, liquefied gases and petrochemicals to petroleum itself. The carriage of petroleum is a separate item, and is described below. The carriage of other hazardous cargoes ranges from bulk shipments in specially designed and constructed cargo carriers to containerised transport alongside normal non-hazardous containerised cargoes aboard a conventional container vessel. Unlike normal non-hazardous cargoes, these must be specifically marked and described with specific documentation for dangerous cargoes, and must be stowed aboard the vessel in such a way that they will not prejudice the safety of the vessel concerned or its crew, let alone the safety of the ports of departure and destination of the vessel concerned. They also require special loading and unloading facilities at such ports, especially where they are carried in bulk by a specific form of carrier. The master of the vessel must notify the port of destination well in advance of arrival (at least 24 hours prior to arrival) to ensure that all necessary berthing and unloading facilities have been arranged in advance of the vessel's arrival in port, and in accordance with the port's legal requirements for such activities, especially where maritime law and regulations are concerned. There are specific regulations set out for the maritime carriage of dangerous cargoes, and these are contained in the IMDG (International Movement of Dangerous Goods) Code of the IMO (International Maritime Organisation). Every trader, agent and shipping organisation involved in the carriage of dangerous and hazardous goods must keep an up-to-date copy of the IMDG Code on their premises at all times, and must be fully aware of the main points contained within the Code.

1.1.4 Petroleum products

Mineral hydrocarbon oils, are carried by vessels specially designed and constructed for the purposes of the carriage of petroleum products. These VLCCs (Very Large Crude Carriers) operate between specific terminals at major ports, usually close to petroleum storage areas or refineries and can carry very large quantities of petroleum on any voyage. Refined products, such as diesel fuel or petrol/gasoline, are also carried by dedicated carriers, often smaller than the VLCCs, but equally specific in their role. As with the carriage of other dangerous and hazardous products and commodities, there are specific requirements laid down by the IMDG Code relating to the carriage of these products and how the vessel is to be managed and operated.

1.2 Short-sea Traffic

Where deep sea covers the worldwide maritime operational environment, short-sea transport concerns the maritime carriage of goods within specific, more geographically limited regions such as the North Sea, the Baltic Sea and the Mediterranean Sea. It comprises two distinct means of maritime transport:

- container/bulk/hazardous;

- Ro-Ro (Roll-on, Roll-off).

Figure 2.1: Cast container vessel

The container/bulk/hazardous market

This operates in much the same way as the deep-sea market, except that the vessels used are much smaller than their deep-sea counterparts. The container market is operated by the short-sea feeder vessels, plying between ports such as Felixstowe, Rotterdam, Antwerp, Bremerhaven and other North Sea ports such as Immingham, Teesport, Port of Tyne, Grangemouth, Clydeport, Belfast and Dublin. The ports of Belfast and Dublin are also linked by regular frequent feeder vessel services with transatlantic deep-sea services from the port of Liverpool to the ports of the East Coast of North America, namely Charleston, New York and Montréal.

1.3 Ro-Ro (Roll on–Roll off)

The Ro-Ro market caters for the carriage of trailers rather than containers. Where containers can be detached from the chassis of the road vehicle, trailers cannot. The average size of the Tautliner curtain-sided trailer equates with that of a 40-foot container box and, as with a container, can be loaded and unloaded at the trader's premises. The main difference in terms of international transport is that a trailer is driven aboard a Ro-Ro ferry, whereas a container is detached from the vehicle chassis and loaded by gantry crane aboard a container vessel. The Ro-Ro or Ro-Pax (Freight/Passenger) ferry operates between specific ferry ports such as Rosyth (Scotland) or Hull (England) and Zeebrugge (Belgium), Port of Tyne (North Shields, North-

East England) and IJmuiden (Netherlands), or Hull (England) and Euro-poort/Rotterdam (the Netherlands). Companies such as DFDS operate an extensive network of services across the North Sea, serving a variety of countries with both passenger and freight operations. They are not confined simply to maritime movements. Their inland operations extend well beyond the ports to inland destinations for the purpose of integrated maritime/inland trailer operations, with trailers loaded at an inland point, moved via road truck transport to a ferry port, then shipped across the North Sea to a port of destination, and thence by road to a customer at an inland destination. The operation of such vehicles is kept relatively simple, with a minimum of docu-mentation covering the integrated marine and road journey. A basic integrated booking reservation system is used to ensure that the vehicle can be loaded aboard the vessel of choice.

These areas are further elaborated upon later in the book, as each type of maritime transport has its own complexities as well as its specific applications with relation to the type of cargo carried. It should be pointed out that barges are also considered a waterborne means of carriage, but in general they are not sea-going, and only operate on certain waterways, mainly in Europe. However, they are equipped to carry bulk consignments, as well as containers, through the European inland waterway system. There are also the larger bulk and container carriers, the "Lakers", which operate throughout the freshwater Great Lakes system of North America, but these vessels are not sea-going or ocean-going vessels, hence their exclusion from this book, which deals pri-marily with international maritime cargo issues.

2 TYPES OF CARGO VESSEL

2.1 General Cargo Vessels

Maritime cargo vessels vary in their nature according to the kind of cargoes they carry, as well as the volume of cargo transported. Before the era of containerisation, most cargo was carried by general cargo vessels, equipped with their own cranes and derricks capable of loading and unloading cargoes at most docksides and wharves without the need for specialist cranes mounted on the quayside itself. This form of cargo carriage remained standard practice until the 1960s, when seafreight containers became a more efficient form of cargo transportation.

Figure 2.2: Hazmat carrier *Bro Juno*

The function of the general cargo vessel was that it could transport, load and unload cargoes of a variety of shapes, sizes and volumes and sail to any part of the world, either on regular "liner" sailings, or as a "tramp" vessel, transporting cargoes as required. All cargoes were packed and stowed in the vessel's holds, and inevitably the process of loading and unloading was time-consuming and laborious once the vessel was berthed alongside the quay.

General cargo vessels still exist, and have an important part to play in the international maritime carriage of goods, but their role is somewhat more limited in the present day, partly because of their size and function, and partly because of the heavy demands placed on the carriage of goods because of the container system. However, their onboard cranes and derricks enable them to serve international seaports which other vessels, such as the huge container vessels cannot, and this enables them to serve more niche maritime markets. They are also capable of carrying more specialist maritime loads, especially cargoes which may be considered too voluminous for other carriers and which require specific forms of transportation. A present example of such vessels is the MV *Apollogracht*, which is equipped with heavy-purpose cranes and capable of transporting heavy items such as oilfield equipment around the world.

2.2 Container Vessels

Although the issue of containerisation is covered later in this book, it is worthwhile considering the container vessel as a means of maritime transport in its own right. The container vessel has evolved over the past 50 years, with the first commercial vessel to carry containers being a converted oil tanker, the

Ideal X. She sailed in 1956 with her first cargo of some 30 containers mounted on her deck from Port Newark, New Jersey, around the US Coast to Port Houston, Texas. The container age was born, and soon other vessels were being equipped to carry this revolutionary form of cargo transport. The first dedicated container vessels were constructed in the early 1960s, primarily for the newly-formed US container line, Sea-Land, owned and founded by Malcom McLean, the man responsible for introducing the container.

Figure 2.3: Container vessel *Canadian Explorer*

As the concept of containers became more prevalent in the 1970s, the second generation of container vessels were capable of carrying larger numbers of containers, up to 2,500 TEUs (twenty-foot equivalent units), and could transport these loads around the world. By this time, several container shipping lines existed, including Sea-Land, ScanDutch (a consortium of several European Shipping Lines including Nedlloyd of the Netherlands and Wilhelm Wilhelmsen of Norway) and OCL (Overseas Container Lines, a subsidiary of the P&O Group).

The third generation of container vessels, constructed in the 1980s, increased both the size of the vessel and the number of containers carried, up to 4,000 TEUs. Named the Panamax vessels (so-called because they belonged to the 1985 Panamax standard) they were the largest vessels capable of negotiating the lock systems on the Panama Canal. The fourth generation of container vessels increased capacity yet further to 5,000 TEUs, and were known as the Post-Panamax vessels because they exceeded the size allowable to negotiate the Panama Canal. The Post-Panamax standard was introduced in 1988, and referred to container vessels of capacity up to 5,000 TEUs. These vessels were constructed in the period between 1988 and 2000, and became the main vessels to sail the seas, weighing in at some 100,000 grt and carrying huge numbers of containers, largely across the Pacific Ocean and from the Far East to Europe.

Figure 2.4: Maersk Line container vessel at terminal

The present range of vessels, the fifth generation, has taken the carrying capacity through 8,000 TEUs to 11,000 TEUs, with a displacement of 150,000 gross tonnes. These vessels are somewhat limited in the number of container ports they can serve, and it is already established that they will only serve a limited number of European ports because of their size and berthing requirements. There are also trans-shipment requirements for containers to be transferred to smaller feeder vessels for more regional voyages. The new Maersk Line vessels, introduced in 2006 and capable of handling up to 14,000 TEUs, are in this category, as are several new vessels belonging to the Chinese Shipping Lines. However, where the largest vessels are more limited in the number of ports which they can serve, the smaller container vessels are able to serve more ports and are thus more versatile. That said, the larger vessels are more convenient for the specific high-density markets, where the requirement exists to serve a limited number of ports, thus reducing laytime (the length of time a vessel spends berthed at port) and maximising the time the vessel spends at sea between ports. All other traffic can be maintained on a hub-and-spoke basis, with smaller feeder vessels serving the larger deep-sea vessels in a system of limited trans-shipment ports.

A variation on the design of the container vessel is that of the Ro-Ro container vessel. Several shipping lines have used these vessels over the past decades, with a notable present user being Atlantic Container Line (ACL), sailing out of Liverpool across the North Atlantic ocean. These vessels not only handle containers, but also can accommodate road trailers by way of an angled ramp located at the stern of the vessel.

2.3 Bulk Carriers

The bulk carrier is of itself a vital form of maritime cargo transport. Whereas container vessels and general cargo vessels carry all kinds of general cargoes, the bulk carrier specialises in the carriage of bulk cargoes, such as minerals, grain, liquefied gas or crude petroleum. Although owned by specific shipping companies, they are often chartered out to other companies for the purpose of the carriage of specific cargoes from one port to another, on either a voyage charter (single voyage) or time charter (multiple voyage) basis. In some cases, the vessel may be transferred from one owner to another in the middle of the voyage, an activity particularly prevalent with petroleum-carrying VLCCs (very large crude carriers). This practice is less common at present, but it still occurs from time to time depending upon the needs of the customer. In general, however, the petroleum carriers are owned by the large oil companies, and spend their time on the high seas carrying petroleum on behalf of those companies.

Some bulk carriers are equipped to carry different types of bulk cargo with little modification, whereas others are equipped solely for the carriage of a specific type of cargo. Those carriers which can be modified for the carriage of both mineral and petroleum loads are known as "OBO" (ore/bulk/oil) carriers, whereas other carriers, such as the 364,768 tonne Norwegian-owned *Berge Stahl* are equipped solely for the carriage of iron ore. The MV *Berge Stahl* operates between just three ports in the world—Europoort/Rotterdam (Europe), Terminal Maritimo de Ponta da Madeira (Brazil) and Saldanha Bay (South Africa). This vessel makes some 10 journeys per year, mainly between the ports of Ponta da Madeira and Europoort, carrying huge quantities of iron ore from Brazil to Europe.

As with the large container vessels, the large bulk carriers are only able to service certain ports worldwide owing to their immense size; the draft of the *Berge Stahl* at 15m means that she can only just negotiate the mouth of the Maas/Rhine estuary at Europoort which is not much deeper. This means that she can only enter the port safely at high tide, and even then the clearance between her keel and the seabed is extremely limited.

Another distinction between the various types of bulk carrier is that some are "geared" and others are not. A geared carrier is one which has its own cargo lifting gear mounted on board the vessel, enabling it to load and discharge at ports which may not have the correct lifting gear mounted on the quay. A non-geared vessel relies entirely on the lifting gear installed at the dedicated terminal at the port to load it and discharge its cargo. Vessels such as the *Berge Stahl* fall into this category, hence the limitations imposed upon her scope of activity.

The VLCC vessels require even more dedicated terminal facilities. Because they carry only petroleum commodities, which are classed as hazardous or dangerous hydrocarbons, they require a specific terminal for the purpose of loading and discharging their cargoes. There is a specific procedure for handling these vessels at each port, as well as a specific form of both documentation and controls. Every tanker is subject to a different set of rules and regulations from its more general commercial counterparts, and the carriage of such commodities is strictly controlled by the maritime authorities. This is not only because of the nature of the cargo itself, but also because of the inference of the impact of such commodities upon the environment, given the number of marine accidents and disasters involving tankers, especially where the tanker grounded on a coastline, or even where an oil spillage occurred at sea, thus damaging the marine environment to a significant degree.

Other examples of bulk carrier include the car carriers dedicated to the bulk carriage of cars on the high seas. These were particularly designed to serve the Far East markets, in order to transport cars from the Far East to Europe, but they are also used to transport cars from the European plants, especially those of Toyota and Nissan to overseas destinations. It is commonplace to witness such a vessel at the Port of Tyne loading with cars destined for overseas markets, and also at the Port of Liverpool, bringing in vehicles from the Far East for sale in the UK.

Figure 2.5: Bulk carrier at sea

2.4 Short-Sea and Ro-Ro Vessels

The short-sea business, although different from its deep-sea counterpart in the sense that the voyages are generally much shorter than a long-distance deep-sea voyage, are nevertheless as important to the commercial maritime sector as the deep-sea business. Short-sea vessels are divided into much the same categories as the deep-sea business, namely general cargo vessels, container vessels, this time of the feeder variety in that they only accommodate in general up to 1,000–1,500 TEUs, and short-sea bulk carriers such as petroleum or petrochemical carriers.

There is also the Ro-Ro vessel, capable of handling all kinds of road transport such as trailers, coaches and cars. Some Ro-Ro vessels are designed solely for the carriage of commercial traffic such as trailers or chassis-mounted containers (with or without the tractor) and the drivers of these vehicles, where the vehicle is accompanied. Such vessels operate on freight-only routes, chiefly across the North Sea and also in the Mediterranean Sea. They can accommodate several hundred trailers on any voyage, and operate on voyages classed as frequent regular sailings.

Other Ro-Ro vessels are designed for the carriage not only of road trailers, but also cars and coaches. From small beginnings after the Second World War, when a car ferry displaced some 2,000 tonnes, these huge ferries of the present day are also designed as semi-cruise vessels, with a displacement of up to 70,000 grt in some cases. There are two vessels of 59,000 tonnes each plying the route between Hull and Europoort/Rotterdam, owned by P&O North Sea Ferries, namely the *Pride of Hull* and the *Pride of Rotterdam*, but the biggest vessels in the category are the two new vessels in the Norwegian-owned Color Line fleet, the *Color Fantasy* (already in service) and the *Color Magic* (entered service mid-2007). Both are 70,000 tonnes, and ply the route between Oslo (Norway) and Kiel (Germany).

The purpose of these vessels is to carry both passengers and vehicles on overnight or daytime sailings between the major ferry ports on a mixture of commercial and leisure activities. Their operation has given rise to a certain extent to the phrase "Booze Cruise", where passengers use these vessels to make day or weekend trips to Continental ports in order to take advantage of the duty-reduced or duty-free prices on such commodities as alcoholic or tobacco goods. This is particularly prevalent on the cross-Channel services between Dover and Calais, where French prices are vastly lower than those in the UK. The ferries operating these routes have also increased over the last several decades, from some 2,000 tonnes to 35,000 tonnes at present. There are smaller ferries operating in other parts of the UK, especially between the Scottish mainland and the Scottish islands; these vessels range from approximately 2,500 tonnes to the largest vessel at 6,700 tonnes.

2.5 Oilfield Supply Vessels

The other category of vessel now increasingly common as far as the nature of maritime cargo carriage is concerned is the Oilfield Supply Vessel. This type of vessel is designed for the supply of offshore oil and gas field equipment to the offshore oil and gas platforms, located in areas of the globe such as the North Sea, the South Atlantic Ocean off the coasts of Brazil and Angola, and the seas off the coast of Australia. These vessels can carry a variety of equipment, and are equipped with their own handling gear such as cranes and derricks for the loading and offloading of such equipment on to other vessels or on to the platforms themselves. Most of these vessels are also equipped with a helicopter landing pad, where personnel may also be offloaded and loaded for deployment in such operations and areas. They are designed for deep sea operations as well as Continental Shelf maritime operations close to the European coastline, and can withstand the severe forces of mid-ocean conditions without problem.

Examples of such a vessel are the *Toisa Perseus* and *Toisa Polaris*, operated by the company Subsea 7, which undertakes to supply oilfield equipment from Europe to several offshore oilfields worldwide. They are often seen in the ports of Aberdeen and Tyne loading equipment to such locations, and can be away from her home ports for as much as six months at a time. This time is spent calling at overseas ports to load and unload cargo as well as directly serving the overseas offshore oil and gas fields, transferring equipment to the offshore platforms as well as laying sub-sea flowlines for the purpose of facilitating the undersea flow of oil or gas from the wellhead to a shore-based installation. At tonnages of some 6,000 grt, they are capable of operating in relatively-sheltered waters such as the North Sea, as well as in the deep-sea conditions of the North Atlantic and South Atlantic Oceans.

3 THE NATURE OF CARGOES

Cargoes vary in nature as much as do the vessels carrying them. The nature of cargoes has in some ways changed little over the past hundred years or so, although various commodities and products have changed significantly over the passage of time, along with the need to package and carry them correctly, speedily and efficiently. The sheer demand and indeed the insatiable desire of the world for consumer goods has resulted in the need to transport huge quantities of goods worldwide on a cost-effective basis, using the most up-to-date means available. Although some goods travel by air freight means, the vast majority of world trade—some 95%—is undertaken by maritime means.

As seen in the previous chapter, commercial vessels are designed for the carriage of a diverse range of goods, from basic commodities to manufactured products. These goods may be transported in bulk, or individually in either trailers or containers. The container, as explained in the following section, can be used to transport a wide variety of goods, from hazardous chemicals through foodstuffs to manufactured engineered goods. There is no end to the possibilities of how such cargoes may be carried, as cargoes may be packed or arranged in whatever way is required to transport them by sea. In some cases, and entire container may be used for one single load. This form of transport is known as a Full Container Load (FCL), as the cargo occupies the whole container. In other cases, there may be a series of cargoes bound for a specific destination. These cargoes are not large enough to occupy a single container, but when grouped together they will fill the container. This format is known as the Less-than-full Container Load (LCL), not so much because the container is only half-full, but because the loads filling it belong to different customers, and thus make it a consolidated cargo.

3.1 Basic Commodities and Raw Materials

Bulk loads tend not simply to fill an individual container, but may take up the full cargo capacity of a vessel. Such loads range from minerals such as iron ore or coal, through grain such as wheat or barley or even timber, to petroleum commodities such as hydrocarbon oil, fresh from the oilwells of the Middle East.

There are five main classifications of dry bulk cargoes. These are:

- iron ore;
- coal;
- grain;
- bauxite and alumina (aluminium);
- phosphate rock.

Iron ore and *Coal* are used in the steelmaking process, to produce high-quality steel, which is used in so many industrial processes.

Grain is used in the food-processing industry, for the purpose of baking and animal feeds, as well as the production of alcoholic products such as beer and whisky.

Bauxite and *alumina* are used are the raw materials used in the process of aluminium making, the second-most important structural metal in the present-day industrial society.

Phosphate rock is the principal bulk fertiliser used in crop production.

Because of their volume, the five major bulk trades are the prime driving force behind the dry bulk carrier market. In 1995, such trade accounted for more than one-quarter of the total maritime cargo market. The traffic of such bulk commodities is of great importance to the shipping industry, as it accounts, along with the transportation of petroleum products, for a significant proportion of maritime cargo, and of itself accounts for a significant degree of study for those involved in the maritime sector.

Such commodities require special handling treatment, often requiring separate terminals at any port, and often equally requiring specific forms of port and maritime security to avoid mishaps or disasters. The storage of such commodities also requires dedicated areas, removed from conventional storage or warehousing facilities. Where containers or trailers can be moved directly inland once unloaded from a vessel, bulk commodities require special temporary storage facilities at or close to the port prior being loaded aboard other forms of land transport for onward carriage to their final destination.

The vessels carrying such cargoes must equally be able to be accommodated at the dedicated facilities available, and able to leave the port without any impediment or obstruction in as short a time as possible. The documentation for such cargoes is equally of a specific nature, and is usually maintained with specific procedures relating to the commodity in question. This issue is addressed at a later stage in the text.

3.2 Containerised Cargoes

The following chapter deals exclusively with the history of containerisation, but it is worthwhile noting as an introduction that the container has become the primary form of transporting most cargoes by sea. Containers can be used for most cargoes which are not in bulk form, although certain semi-bulk cargoes such as timber and chemicals can be transported by container, with liquids and hazardous or dangerous goods transported in dedicated containers solely used for that purpose. Containers are carried by dedicated container ships, although containers can also be loaded aboard general cargo vessels and even Ro-Ro vessels where required. They are classified in two forms—the 20-foot container (one twenty-foot equivalent unit—1 TEU) and the 40-foot container (2 TEU), and are designed in such a way as to be carried on a road-based container chassis and on a container vessel, either stacked above deck or slotted into cells below deck.

3.3 Perishable Cargoes

Perishable cargoes are sensitive to both time and conditions of carriage. Therefore, they require specific forms of cargo handling and carriage. Such cargoes include the following foodstuffs:

- meat;
- fish;
- vegetables;
- fruit;
- dairy products.

They are generally packed into refrigerated or chilled containers (reefers), or can be loaded directly into the refrigerated holds of vessels specifically designed and built for the purposes of the carriage of such cargoes. Well-known examples of this are the so-called "banana boats", the vessels which serve the West Indies and Central America to load vast quantities of bananas and other tropical fruits, for shipment to the markets of Europe and North America.

3.4 Hazardous and Dangerous Cargoes

Hazardous and dangerous goods require specialist handling, owing to their unstable and volatile nature. They can be flammable, toxic or explosive, and often require dedicated and specialist handling facilities at the ports of loading and unloading. They must also be stowed aboard vessel in such a way that they do not incur the risk of prejudicing or compromising the safety of the vessel and its crew, and must be properly notified to the ports, the shipping lines and the shipping agents. There is a specific form of documentation pertaining to such cargoes set out in accordance with the rules determined by the International Maritime Organisation (IMO), and equally specific international codes of operation and practice, in particular the IMDG (International Movement of Dangerous Goods) Code applies to such cargoes and their movement. These codes have been formulated and implemented by the International Maritime Organisation (IMO) with the full co-operation of the governments of all subscribing member states, and these codes are applied rigorously concerning the carriage of such cargoes. In the case of the carriage of petroleum and other bulk cargoes of a hazardous or dangerous nature, such as chemicals or liquefied gas, there are specific vessels used for such purposes, and these also require specific handling requirements at the ports of loading and unloading. Where containerised cargoes of a hazardous or dangerous nature are concerned, the containers or tanks must be marked in such a way as to draw attention to the nature of the cargo and its classification. In this way, the stowage of the cargo aboard vessel can be determined in advance in order to ensure compliance with the international regulations as well as ensuring that all safety measures are adhered to at all times.

4 THE PORT SYSTEM

No marine cargo management system can operate without considering the port, its structure and its purpose. Ports have developed according to the needs of the economic community, as well as the nature of the shipping business, and to this extent, there is no such object as a typical port. Each port is developed according to the trade needs of the region and the types of vessel it is designed to accommodate, as the port is the interface between land and sea. The port structure has changed over the decades, with the original docks and basins having been abandoned in favour of long, riverside terminals with space for several large container vessels, as well as distant jetties and terminals for the purpose of accommodating bulk carriers or tankers, each terminal with its own dedicated equipment purpose-designed for the loading and unloading of such cargoes.

A port is a geographical area where vessels are brought alongside land to load and unload cargo. The area where a port is located is a sheltered deepwater area such as a bay or a river mouth. The Port Authority is the organisation whose responsibility encompasses the provision of the various maritime services required to bring ships alongside land and facilitate their loading and discharge. Ports can be public bodies, private bodies or even government-controlled organisations. Within the port, the terminal is a specific section of

the port comprising several berths devoted to a specific form of cargo handling, such as containers, general cargo, Ro-Ro, bulk, chemicals or petroleum.
Each terminal may be owned or operated by the port authority itself, or by a
shipping company operating the terminal for its own specific use.

As economic demands have required greater maritime efficiency, so ports
need to invest in new technology and facilities in order to meet these demands.
The greater the size of vessel, so the larger the facility is required to accommodate such vessels, meaning that the port must spend large sums of money
in investing in increased terminal facilities to accommodate these vessels.
Equally, the port must invest in more efficient cargo-handling facilities such as
cranes and other loading/unloading facilities, especially as all the forms of
maritime transport require different types of facility, including storage areas
for containers, trailers or bulk cargoes. Furthermore, there is the need to
integrate these facilities into the domestic infrastructural networks, thus
requiring efficient road and rail links with the land networks. To this extent,
port improvement plays a major role in the reduction of maritime transport
costs, although the cost of investment in such facilities may often be passed on
to the maritime operator, namely the shipping lines.

The facilities provided by a port depend on the type and volume of cargo in
transit. The ports change according to trade patterns, which is why there is no
such thing as a typical or standard port. The facilities in each port vary
according to the trade in the region it serves, or according to national and
international requirements, such as in the ports of Antwerp and Rotterdam,
which serve large international communities on a hub-and-spoke basis, by sea,
inland waterway, road and rail. However, port facilities may be categorised
according to their particular area, and these are as follows.

4.1 Type 1: Small Port

Worldwide, there are thousands of small ports serving local trade. They
handle varied cargo flows, often serviced by short-sea vessels. Since the
volume of trade is low, facilities are basic, generally comprising general-
purpose berths adjacent to which are warehouses ranged along the quayside.
Only small vessels can be accommodated, and the port handles a mixture of
cargoes, from containers, break-bulk cargo and shipments of commodities in
packaged form, such as fertilisers, grain or liquids in drums. Other cargoes can
be shipped loose in the vessel's holds, and unloaded for storage in the warehouses, or on the quayside until collected by the trader.

4.2 Type 2: Large Local Port

When volumes of cargo are higher, special investment becomes more economic and is often a basic requirement to accommodate such trade. In the
case of bulk cargoes, specific bulk terminals are constructed taking into
account the deep water facilities required for larger bulk carrier vessels of

35,000 dwt or more. Quaysides are equipped with grab cranes, apron spaces to stack cargo, rail and road access for trains and trucks. Furthermore, the break-bulk facilities may be expanded to handle regular container traffic, by installing container-handling equipment and strengthening and even lengthening the quayside to accommodate larger vessels, or several smaller vessels.

4.3 Type 3: Large Regional Port

Ports handling high volumes of deep-sea cargo require significant investment in specialised and dedicated terminal facilities. Unit loads such as pallets and containers are handled in sufficient volume to justify a unit load terminal with cargo handling equipment such as gantry cranes, fork-lift trucks and storage space for unit load cargo, in the form of large, purpose-built warehouses. In the case of high-volume commodity trades, special terminals are built (e.g. coal, grain, oil product terminals) which are capable of accommodating the larger ships of 60,000 dwt plus, employed in the deep-sea bulk trades.

4.4 Type 4: Regional Distribution Centre

Regional ports can have a wider and more varied role as distribution centres for cargo shipped deep sea in very large vessels, and requiring distribution to smaller local ports or to inland centres. This type of port, exemplified by the ports of Rotterdam, Antwerp, Hong Kong or Singapore, comprise a network of specialist terminals, each one dedicated to a specific cargo. Containers are handled in container terminals; unit load terminals cater for timber, iron and steel and cargo transported by Ro-Ro ferry means. Homogeneous bulk cargoes such as grain, iron, coal, cement and oil products are handled in purpose-built terminals, often operated and managed by the cargo owner. These terminals allow for the trans-shipment of cargoes by sea, barge, rail and road, thus facilitating hub-and-spoke international transport operations.

Each port has its own authority, and personnel qualified to run its operations. A well as the normal management team dealing with commercial and operational aspects of the port, there are other specialist managers such as harbourmasters, harbour pilots and terminal managers, whose job it is to control inward and outward vessel movements. Port operations are complex matters, and require specialist personnel to deal with specific activities. Port state control and vessel inspection is also a major area, requiring the specific skills of inspectors involved with health and safety activities, as well as port security issues.

Ports and terminals earn revenue by levying charges to ship owners and operators for the use of their facilities. Port charges such as harbour and light dues and berthing charges must cover unit costs, and these have a fixed and variable element. The ship owner can be charged in two ways, namely:

- an "all-in" rate, where, apart from a few minor ancillary services, everything is included in the rate; or

- an "add-on" rate, where the ship-owner or operator pays a basic charge on top of which extras are added for the various services used by the ship during its visit to the port.

The method of charging generally depends upon the type of cargo operation involved, but both methods vary according to volume and the tonnage of vessels visiting the port, with trigger points such as tonnage levels activating changes to tariff charge levels. These charges are reviewed every year in line with national and regional economic trends, such as inflation, and are notified to the ship owners and operators in advance of the revised tariff levels taking effect, usually at the beginning of each calendar year.

5 THE DEVELOPMENT OF CONTAINERISATION

The story of the sea container starts in November 1937, when a trucker from North Carolina, in the South of the United States, was waiting in his truck at a port in New Jersey, while the cargo of his vehicle, namely bales of cotton, was being offloaded from his truck and loaded in an extremely time-consuming process on to a vessel berthed at the quayside bound for Istanbul, Turkey. He was becoming more and more frustrated with the time spent waiting in his cab before he could leave the port and pick up another load. He thought, during this seemingly-interminable wait, that it would be far more sense to have cargoes loaded aboard vessel in larger quantities and not handled by so many people during this process. Indeed, he surmised, it would be far easier to have the whole truck unit detached from the tractor vehicle and loaded aboard vessel, then transported overseas and unloaded at the other end on to another tractor unit and driven directly to the customer's door. Some 26 years later, on 26 April 1956, that trucker had a chance to prove his point. His name was Malcom P. McLean, and he went on to become the Chairman of the mighty US Shipping Line, Sea-Land. The vessel which made history that day transported 58 new trailer trucks, emblazoned with the name "Sea-Land" on their sides, on her open converted spar decks from Port Newark, New Jersey, to Port Houston, Texas. Her name was the *Ideal X*, and she was a tanker with a converted deck, belonging to the Pan-Atlantic Steamship Company. As well as her pioneering cargo, she was loaded with ballast on her way to Houston, where she would reload with petroleum from Texas bound for the US North-East.

This voyage was hardly an auspicious start to what would become a revolution in maritime cargo transport, but it would pave the way for that revolution. The berth from which she departed, Berth 24 at the foot of Marsh Street, Port Newark, would eventually become part of the gigantic Port of Newark, the present port serving the whole of the North-East of the United States. The trailers would become the precursor of the present metal box system well-known today in its 20 foot and 40 foot capacity as simply the "Container", mainly because by this time McLean had decided that it was impractical to load full trailers aboard vessel, including their chassis. He decided to invest in a system whereby the box (i.e. the container) could be attached to a road chassis for the purposes of road transport, and then detached from the chassis for the purposes of loading aboard vessel. To ensure complete safety and security aboard vessel, the containers were fitted with corner castings, a method by which there was a casting on each corner of the box, top and bottom, into which a twist lock could be inserted. This would engage with the corner castings of the containers both above and below it, thus creating a single vertical cellular unit fixed to the deck of the vessel and capable of withstanding the most inclement of natural elements while at sea. The containers were manufactured out of aluminium by Brown Industries, based in Seattle, These could be mounted both on the existing Fruehauf trailers, and on the deck of the vessel. The bigamous marriage of container, road trailer and sea-going vessel has continued ever since. Eventually, this relationship was expanded to include rail wagons specially constructed to handle these containers, in the case of the USA to handle double-stacked container loads per wagon.

The reward for its inventor, Malcom McLean, was that some years later he would become the Chairman of Sea-Land, by then one of the most powerful Container Shipping Lines in the world. Today, Sea-Land no longer exists in its original form; it was eventually absorbed early in the 21st century by the A.P. Møller-owned Maersk Group of Denmark, having already been purchased by the transport conglomerate CSX in the 1980s. The *Ideal X* was joined by the *Almena*, and these vessels were soon followed by the *Gateway City*, seen as the world's first true container vessel, converted from a wartime C-2 cargo vessel, and owned by the Waterman Line, also to come under McLean's ownership. The previous two vessels mentioned were simply tankers mounted with additional spar decks for the purpose of the carriage of containers above deck. The *Gateway City* was converted to only carry containers, and had a series of vertical rails installed in the holds to accommodate containers stacked on top of each other in cellular form. Once the hatch covers were closed, further containers could be loaded on deck above the hatch covers and on top of each other, locked into place. Containers could be stacked four high in the holds of *Gateway City*, with a further two high on deck, allowing the carriage of 226 containers on board the vessel.

Soon after the initial forays by the Pan-Atlantic Steamship Company and the Waterman Line into the operation of carrying detachable trailers, the next entrant into the field was the Matson Line, primarily operating from the West Coast of the United States to Hawaii. The Matson Line vessel *Hawaiian Merchant*, a C-3 Class cargo ship constructed in 1945, slipped her moorings at San Francisco on 31 August 1958 and passed underneath the Golden Gate Bridge bound for Honolulu, Hawaii and thus inaugurated the first container service across the Pacific Ocean. She carried some 20 containers above deck, while below deck her holds were still configured for conventional cargo. Six days later, on 6 September, she docked at Honolulu, and her containers were unloaded on to rail flatcars and hauled away from the quay by a small diesel locomotive. The era of multi-modal or intermodal transport had begun. Matson converted five other C-3 cargo vessels to transport containers above deck, and in Spring 1960, it took delivery of its first all-container cargo ship on the San Francisco-Honolulu route, the *Hawaiian Citizen*. She started life as a conventional C-3 cargo ship, but after extensive rebuilding into a fully cellular container ship she was able to carry 356 containers. She was the first of a series of generations of container vessel which have progressively evolved into the super-giants presently plying the ocean waves. On 19 May 1960, she set sail from Alameda, California, bound for Honolulu with 237 containers on board, somewhat less than her full capacity but nevertheless a milestone in the history of container transport. Unlike the *Gateway City* and her five sister ships, the *Hawaiian Citizen* had no onboard cranes or gantries capable of unloading and loading the containers aboard ship. She relied on the dockside cranes at the port for that purpose.

Also in 1960, Malcom McLean, by now the owner of both Pan-Atlantic Steamship Company and Waterman Line, decided to replace the name of Pan-Atlantic with the official name used for his trucks, namely Sea-Land Services. Soon, other converted ships entered the container-carrying business. In September 1962, another vessel, a converted T-3 Tanker named *Elizabethport* and owned by McLean, became the first container vessel to transit the Panama Canal from the East Coast to the West Coast. Four years later, the first transatlantic container service was inaugurated by the vessel *American Racer*, a C-4 cargo ship belonging to United States Lines with 50 containers secured below decks, sailing on 18 March 1966 from New York bound for Europe. Sea-Land, not to be outdone, despatched the vessel *Fairport* across the Atlantic on 23 April 1966, 36 days after the departure of the *American Racer* and just three days short of the tenth anniversary of its first container sailing on the *Ideal X*, from New Jersey to Rotterdam. The global container business was well underway and here to stay, despite misgivings expressed by other shipping executives who doubted its viability.

By 1966, Sea-Land was also dispensing with cranes mounted aboard vessel, and purchased its first gantry cranes for the purpose of loading and unloading containers on and off the vessels, which would be installed on the quayside. It was at this time that purpose-built container vessels started to enter the arena, along with new container shipping lines such as Atlantic Container Line (ACL), based in Europe. Other container lines followed, as Europe and the Far East entered the container markets, with well-known names such as OOCL of Hong Kong, Overseas Container Lines (OCL) (owned by a consortium of Ocean Steamship Company, P&O and Furness Withy), a subsidiary of the P&O Group, Nedlloyd and Hapag-Lloyd, once renowned for its graceful and popular transatlantic passenger liners under the banner of Nord-

Deutscher Lloyd, prior to its merger with the Hamburg-America Line. Another milestone was reached with the construction in 1969 of the OCL-owned *Encounter Bay*, the world's first cellular container vessel capable of transporting over 1,000 TEUs, joined soon after by three sister ships. At first, there was stiff opposition to the use of containers at British ports, mainly because of the resistance of the trade unions representing the dockworkers, who were fearful of job losses because of the new form of cargo handling techniques. The new OCL container vessels were forced to unload their cargoes of containers at Rotterdam and have them transported to smaller UK ports by conventional ferries. It was this opposition to the container business which eventually saw the decline of many of the UK ports, and the rise of the European ports, which were far more flexible in their approach to the new form of marine cargo transport. It was during this period that the Port of London went into decline, with all major operations eventually transferred to the Port of Tilbury, well down river from the original Port of London. The ports of Liverpool and Glasgow suffered greatly too, and it is only in recent years that the Port of Liverpool has seen a dramatic renaissance in its maritime fortunes—it now handles a large proportion of container traffic across the North Atlantic to the United States and Canada. To accommodate the rise in container traffic into and out of the port, it has been decided to construct a new container terminal on the side of the River Mersey, which is able to accommodate the larger transatlantic container vessels. At present, these are limited in their access to the Port of Liverpool owing to the constraints imposed by the lock into the port's Seaforth Dock.

The impact of the use of containers and their vessels was demonstrated by Overseas Container Lines (OCL) in 1970, showing the productivity realised by the use of such vessels. While *Encounter Bay* spent 300 days of its first operational year at sea and only 65 days in port, over the same interval of 12 months, the most modern conventional break-bulk cargo ship operated by any of the OCL partners was in port for 149 days and at sea for merely 216 days (*Fairplay International Shipping Weekly*, 6 March 1975). This set of data reinforced the view previously stated by Malcom McLean that a ship was at its most profitable while it was at sea, not berthed in port. With the steady increase in maritime container traffic, he was proved correct. The demise of much of the Port of London was due to this impact, and the fact that the original docks located towards the metropolis were incapable of handling container vessels. In due course, they all closed, and container traffic centred upon the ports of Tilbury, Felixstowe (by this time developing from a small insignificant port to a massive container terminal) and Southampton. By 1969, 199 new container vessels were under construction throughout the world, mainly in the United States and Europe, of which 47 could accommodate more than 1,000 TEUs. It should be noted, however, that the container business had its casualties. OCL was eventually allowed to fold when its owners, P&O Group, decided to take over container operations using their own vessels. The *Encounter Bay* went to the breaker's yard in 1999, 30 years after her introduction into the container market. P&O itself was eventually merged with Nedlloyd of the Netherlands, and this merged conglomerate was in due course bought by the Maersk Group, which also purchased the Sea-Land Corporation, making it the largest container and vessel operator in the world at present. It has no intention of relinquishing that position.

Malcom McLean's vision has come a long way since the earliest days of the container being carried on the deck of a converted tanker. The container has taken over as the primary form of maritime transport for a variety of cargoes, other than bulk transport, and it has made conventional break-bulk cargo ships very much a thing of the past, although they are still used to service certain niche markets. So dominant is the container business that deep-sea vessels generally service the larger ports in Europe, while regional and local services are maintained by container feeder vessels serving these ports and linking them with other local European ports on a "hub-and-spoke basis".

The principle of the hub-and-spoke method is that major principal seaports act as centres for container handling and shipment, with large numbers of containers shipped inward and outward by the large deep-sea vessels, which connect with smaller feeder container vessels plying between these hub seaports and the smaller regional ports located elsewhere within the region. The port of Rotterdam is a classic example of this. The new Maasvlakte terminal at the western end of Europoort handles the large deep-sea vessels from the Far East, which discharge their containers at the container terminal. In turn, smaller feeder vessels load the containers destined for specific seaports such as the East Coast UK ports, and duly move those containers to their onward destinations somewhere in the UK. The same is true in reverse. A shipment may leave the UK on a container feeder vessel bound for Rotterdam, where the container is transferred to a large deep-sea container vessel for onward shipment to the Far East. The trans-shipment nature of this type of movement means that through container rates can be agreed between seller and buyer, thus resulting in an overall integrated pricing arrangement. The drawback is that such shipment methods may yet lead to a decline in the importance of some of the larger UK seaports, as the hub-and-spoke seaport such as Rotterdam, Antwerp and Bremerhaven strive to increase in size and gain even more international logistics trade.

It is increasingly likely that, as the size of deep-sea container vessels increases beyond the 10,000 TEU threshold, fewer major seaports will be able to handle such large vessels economically, with the result that the hub-and-spoke method of container operation will become more prevalent. This is especially the case in Europe, with the large Northern European Ports of Antwerp, Rotterdam and Bremerhaven dominating the system, and regional services spreading out to other parts of Europe from these ports, including the inland waterways of Belgium and the Netherlands. In mid-2007, the Maersk Group decided that it was no longer profitable for their largest vessels, especially the gigantic "E" class vessels, to call regularly at the Port of Felixstowe, on the East Coast of England. Instead, these vessels only serve the continental European ports. A sign of the times indeed, as the Port of Rotterdam is already proclaiming itself as the UK's largest port.

The problem arising from such a policy is that, if the size of the vessels keeps increasing, the size of the port container operations also has to increase in size, as well as providing landward access to such facilities. As things stand, the traffic in road-hauled containers is increasing to the point that there is congestion on many UK and European road systems because of the number of containers being hauled by road between the ports and inland destinations. Sooner or later decisions have to be made in how to handle such an increase in traffic, and ports are being forced to invest heavily in their land-based operations. In the UK, this is a problem, as it has been stated that the Government is not prepared to finance such development at the ports. On the continent, however, there is no such reluctance. Massive investment has been injected into the ports of Antwerp and Rotterdam by their respective governments in order to boost container traffic into and out of the ports, given that such a policy is seen to foster regional and national economic growth. It is because of the decision to invest in the new river terminal on the Mersey that the Port of Liverpool, owned by Peel Holdings, will be able to increase its own revenues through an increase in transatlantic container traffic. This will contribute in no small way to the regional economy. An increase in such traffic also has a knock-on effect for the regional container traffic heading into and out of the Port of Liverpool. This will undoubtedly increase as a result of the anticipated increase in deep-sea container traffic movements.

Containerisation has brought a complexity of issues concerning cargo movement and management. It has brought significant advantages, such as:

- a door-to-door service from the factory production location to the distributor's warehouse;
- full unit loads (FCLs) or consolidated groupage loads (LCLs);
- a reduction in intermediate handling at terminal trans-shipment points, namely rail/road depots or seaports;
- reduced risk of cargo damage and pilferage;
- less packing requirements;
- more efficient use of maritime container vessels;
- faster transit time;
- simplified documentation;
- simplified INCOTERMS;
- the provision of through door-to-door freight rates, either as a consolidation rate or as a full-box rate;
- reliability of transit and movement;
- dedicated port container facilities.

However, there are other complexities concerning how containers are used worldwide, particularly in terms of the relocation of containers owing to worldwide imbalances in international trade. The Far East is a huge export market, while North America and Europe have become huge import markets. Thus, containers are at a premium out of the Far East, while there is a glut of containers waiting to be shipped back from the Americas and Europe to the Far East for re-loading. This implies that a massive effort is required to relocate containers for this purpose. This is a very costly exercise for shipping lines, container operators and container leasing companies alike, and arises because of the worldwide imbalance in trade patterns. In general, trade from America and Europe to the Far East comprises raw materials and semi-finished goods, mainly components. In turn, the Far East exports finished consumer goods. For every full load exported from the Far East, an empty container is required for shipment in the other direction. The huge demand for finished goods from the Far East has pushed container rates ever higher (originally some US$2,700 for a 40-foot box, and around $1,800 for a 20-foot box, although as at 2007 these costs have risen to $3,800 for a 40-foot box), along with price adjustment and surcharges such as Bunker Adjustment Factors (BAF), whereas the cost of the shipment of a container from Europe or North America to the Far East is relatively low, standing at some $300–500 per box outbound from Europe. The shipping lines are doing their utmost to minimise prices in order to stimulate export shipments from Europe, as they know that the container returning to the Far East would be transported empty—hardly an ideal economic solution. However, owing to the sheer volume of containers being transported from the Far East to Europe and then languishing empty before being relocated back to the Far East, there is a major problem with container congestion at many ports, especially in the UK. The net result is an imposition of a congestion surcharge on all containers imported into the UK of $145 per TEU as from 1 December 2007. However, this surcharge was removed in February 2008.

Solutions to the problem are as follows:

- The container operator or owner moves the containers to points where they are most needed at the lowest cost available, often by renting them out at reduced rates or by arranging indirect routes so as to capitalise on existing export trade from elsewhere.
- The container operator or shipping line offers the containers to European exporters at vastly reduced costs, thus stimulating the export market wherever possible.
- The lease company requires the container to be returned to a strategic location, thus influencing shipping contracts on a longer-term basis and influencing the lease price by regularly shipping or relocating containers to specific destinations.
- The chartering of shipping space (slot chartering) to reposition the boxes, such as for traffic between Europe and the Far East.

The solution of shipping space on eastbound vessels to reposition boxes in the Far East has one major drawback—the shipping line requires payment for shipping containers on the vessel. Boxes cannot be moved free of charge, as the shipping line requires revenue for its eastbound journeys. A further problem arises in the costs associated with the movement of empty containers from within the country to the port. These may be considerable, depending on the location of the container in the country.

However, regardless of these measures, the trend is moving towards greater trade imbalances, resulting in a mass movement of empty containers from Europe and North America to the Far East, to satisfy the insatiable demand for finished goods produced in the Far East.

6 MULTIMODALISM

The term *"multimodalism"* has come into the English language as a result of the development of a specific form of transport, namely that of expediting a shipment between two points by the use of several forms of transport. It is referred to in North America as *intermodalism*, implying an intermodal form of transport using two or more modes of transport, but its implication is exactly the same as for multimodal transport. The term developed generally around the use of 20-foot and 40-foot containers, which could be loaded as unit devices aboard maritime vessels, road chassis, and specially-designed rail wagons. The introduction of the container in the late 1950s revolutionised freight transport, as discussed earlier in the text, and meant that there was no longer a need to physically handle a cargo from one form of transport to another, as it could be easily moved by different transport methods once it had been loaded into the container. The venture conceived in the mind of Malcom McLean could now be used to transport goods worldwide simply by loading a box and transporting it from one point to another without needing to open the doors on the box until it arrived at its ultimate destination.

6.1 Intermodalism

This became particularly prevalent on the North American continent. A container, or trailer, could be taken to a local consolidation point, or load centre, where it was loaded aboard a train, transported across the continent, and unloaded at a point local to the customer. Special trains were developed for the transportation of large numbers of containers, often in double-stacking mode, where one container is loaded on top of another on the rail wagon. However, the use of such forms of transport became particularly useful when dealing with large numbers of containers to be loaded on board a vessel, or unloaded from it. Because of the sheer distances between seaports and inland destinations, the container train became part of the means by which a container was transported from one part of the world to an internal American destination, and vice versa. The whole journey of the container from one point to another became known as an intermodal journey, because of the transfer for the container from one mode of transport to another during that journey.

As the container revolution spread, so the need to arrange inland transport for containers at both ends of the journey became necessary. As the size of maritime vessels used for the carriage of containers increased, so did the need for multimodal transport arrangements. The containerships of the 1970s and 1980s required dedicated facilities at the major seaports, and it became clear that ultimately there would only be a specific number of ports worldwide capable of handling such leviathans of the seas. The need arose to create huge load centres and clearance depots capable of handling the increasing numbers of containers carried by such vessels. The essence of moving containers from one place to another became one of arranging an integrated transport movement from the supplier's premises to the customer's premises by means of one container load, particularly in the case of the FCL (Full Container Load).

The purpose of the exercise was to ensure that all documentation and procedures related to the entire movement of the container, rather than a specific part of that journey, such as by sea alone. Whereas historically, the cargo would be transported to the port of loading by the seller, and then international transport and onward movement would be arranged by prior negotiation between the seller and the buyer, using the existing INCOTERMS, it was now possible for the seller and buyer to negotiate an integrated journey from door to door using specific INCOTERMS which only related to this form of transport. Although the original INCOTERMS still existed, they would be used much less than before as a result of such integration. It was also possible to arrange flexible solutions using internal rail or road transport as well as transport by sea, using a single document.

The point of the integrated solution was that it was designed to simplify the whole transport arrangement from door to door. As long as the information concerning the container load was accurate, the consignment could be accepted by the shipping company and the information concerning the load put on to the container manifest. This manifest would then accompany the container by sea until its arrival at the port of destination and the point of clearance through customs. As time progressed, such information was input on an electronic basis, and all controls, especially those of customs, were moved to a trader-driven basis, with all export and import declarations being made electronically. Thus, it was no longer necessary to examine a container load unless the computer flagged up the container for examination at the time the vessel's cargo manifest was being scrutinised. So important and widespread was the multimodal system as far as the process of international trade was concerned, that the United Nations agreed the *Convention on International Multimodal Transport of Goods* in May 1980. This Convention, adopted by the UNCTAD, set out the rules by which cargoes should be moved worldwide on a multimodal basis, and set out the procedures by which all national authorities should control such movements. This Convention set out provisions for the following:

- documentation;

- liability of the multimodal transport operator;
- liability of the consignor;
- claims and actions;
- customs matters.

It was designed to ensure that all goods moving under multimodal conditions were correctly documented, transported and accounted for during their movement, and that all steps were taken to ensure satisfactory transit during all aspects of the multimodal journey.

As the multimodal concept developed, so too did the need for the transport operators to specialise in such transport methods. The shipping lines, which had hitherto been involved simply with the shipment of goods by sea between seaports, found themselves dealing with not only the maritime sector of the journey but also the inland movement of the consignment as well. Indeed, the maritime sector became little more than a single cog in the whole wheel of the integrated transport movement. The documentation associated with such transport, in particular the Ocean Bill of Lading, became a more flexible document, dealing with trans-shipments and onward journeys, thus becoming a Combined Transport Bill of Lading or Through Bill of Lading, covering the inland element of the journey as well as the maritime element of the journey, with the transport document arranged by either the seller or the buyer from the point of despatch form the seller's premises. The original INCOTERMS such as FOB or CIF were dispensed with, in favour of the following INCOTERMS:

- EXW (Ex Works);
- FCA (Free Carrier . . .);
- CPT/CIP (Carriage Paid To . . . /Carriage and Insurance Paid . . .);
- DDU (Delivered Duty Unpaid . . .).

Further simplifications were made to the Terms of Delivery, with the Terms *Freight Collect* or *Freight Prepaid* being used instead of the previous Terms. The INCOTERMS stated above replaced the other, more individual, INCOTERMS, as they were more flexible, and could be used for a variety of freight methods within the multimodal framework. The company arranging such movements does not need to be a shipping line itself, but rather a Non-Vessel Operating Carrier (NVOC) or Non-Vessel Operating Common Carrier (NVOCC). Under such conditions, carriers such as NVOCs or NVOCCs issue Bills of Lading for the carriage of consignments on vessels which they neither own or operate, thus acting as agents for the carrier itself. Freight Forwarders usually issue the FIATA Multi-modal Transport Bill of Lading for a container or freight movement, or, in the case of a UK-European shipment, a CMR Consignment Note, which implies a movement by Ro-Ro ferry means.

As the concept has developed, there are now various forms of multi-modalism. These are:

- containerisation (FCL/LCL/road/sea/rail);
- Landbridge (trailer/truck—road/sea/road);
- Landbridge (pallet/container—road/sea/air/road);
- Trailer/truck (road/sea/road);
- Swap-body (road/rail/sea/road).

The *containerisation* method implies that the consignment is loaded into a container, either at the seller's premises, or at a convenient point of consolidation, and is then moved by either road or rail to the port of loading. There, the container is lifted off the road or rail means of transport, and is loaded aboard the ocean-going vessel. It is then transported to the seaport of destination, where it is unloaded off the vessel, and on to another road truck or rail wagon, for onward transportation to its final destination.

The *Landbridge* principle is that the consignment is transported by truck or by trailer from one point to another, often by Ro-Ro ferry means for the maritime sector. This form of transport is common within Europe, where consignments originate in Ireland, then cross the Irish Sea by Ro-Ro means to the UK, then move across the UK to a North Sea port, where they are loaded aboard another Ro-Ro ferry bound for a continental port, where they will be driven off the ferry and onwards to their final destination. In reality, under either *Landbridge* or *Trailer/Truck* movement conditions, a trailer movement is not strictly multimodal, insofar as the consignment does not leave the trailer while it is being moved by maritime Ro-Ro ferry means across the sea. Only where a container is being moved from a road or rail vehicle to a container vessel or vice versa under such circumstances would the movement be considered multimodal, even under *Landbridge* conditions.

Given that multimodalism has become a major influence in the present-day means of international transportation, the trader or the shipper is looking to the carrier or the logistics provider to provide the optimum route and transport solution for shipment of a consignment to their customers at a competitive cost and an acceptable overall transit time. Hence, the concept of multimodalism has developed for the following reasons:

- the development of the "just-in-time" strategy amongst sellers and buyers, requiring integrated schedules within warehousing and distribution arrangements;
- a requirement for continuous improvements in the distribution and supply-chain networks;
- simplified and integrated transportation documentation;
- the worldwide expansion of containerisation;
- customised and dedicated logistics departments within the major shipping lines dealing with multimodal shipments and networks;
- electronic transmission of information in the form of electronic data interchange (EDI), including customs clearance;
- larger, more efficient seaports and container handling facilities;

- greater integration, standardisation and harmonisation of international transport networks.

The development of multimodalism has led to a series of initiatives amongst the container lines towards taking greater control over inland services, with their logistics and customer service departments spending more time in dealing with aspects for freight movements outside the remit of simply maritime activities. Furthermore, the major seaports are competing to ever-increasing degrees for more multimodal-oriented business, while working alongside large global logistics operators. Furthermore, there is a greater need for the international harmonisation of regulations and competition rules, particularly with relation to international transport. As containerisation has encouraged container vessel and container operators to extend their hub-and-spoke systems, especially concerning their use of specific worldwide ports such as Singapore and Rotterdam, so the use of intermodal transport has become much more prevalent, thus necessitating an integrated structure in the overall transport industry, especially concerning road haulage operators whose function it is to transport the container to and from the seaport to connect with the arriving or departing vessel.

The intermodal framework:

- provides a dedicated door-to-door cargo service with each operator or carrier committed to a schedule;
- can function using NVOC or NVOCC arrangements;
- uses standard-size containers for transport, based on ISO-accepted standards;
- competes on price for a door-to-door service;
- provides the optimum transport modes for the benefit of the trader or shipper;
- uses the state-of-the-art electronic systems for information transfer;
- is increasing in size;
- uses a simplified documentary regime, using a single transport document rather than several;
- uses simplified INCOTERMS;
- encourages the growth of the principal seaports as hub-and-spoke port operations;
- favours both large and small shippers and traders by facilitating full loads or consolidated shipments;
- provides an integrated solution to the large-scale distribution and logistics sector, facilitating speedier and more efficient shipments.

As the use of the container developed through the 1960s, 1970s and 1980s, so too did the principle of intermodalism. It developed particularly in North America and Europe, as transport systems became progressively deregulated. However, it has generated its own problems and complexities, and has led to certain anomalies within the shipping business. These problems can be detailed as follows:

- abbreviation of documentary information;
- transparency of freight costs;
- use of INCOTERMS;
- development of specific seaports at the expense of other ports;
- anomalies in declarations and customs clearance;
- outsourcing of expertise by shippers leading to the deskilling of the logistics function;
- increasing demands on the container operator to meet deadlines;
- greater need for controls, especially concerning container security.

The abbreviation of documentary information has become a major issue, especially for consolidated LCL container loads. Often, the consolidator will only insert abbreviated information on a manifest or a Bill of Lading concerning a consolidated load, especially where each consignment relates to the others, as in the automotive sector. Furthermore, there may not have been sufficient information passed to the consolidator by the shipper, thus resulting in inadequate details of each consignment in the container.

The transparency of freight costs becomes an issue where Customs clearance is carried out at the port of destination, but where the container is heading inland to the customer as part of an integrated journey on a door-to-door basis. Customs authorities still require the declaration of a CIF (Cost Insurance Freight) Import Landed Cost for the purposes of import declarations, and this cost cannot include additional inland freight to the premises of the customer, especially on a DDU (Delivered Duty Unpaid) basis. Where the cost to the customer is arranged on an intermodal DDU basis, this additional inland freight cost may well have been included by the shipper in the first instance, so the customer must isolate this additional inland haulage cost and exclude it from the CIF cost for import declaration purposes.

The use of INCOTERMS has become a major issue. In many cases, an intermodal shipment will be undertaken on either an EXW (Ex Works) or DDU (Delivered Duty Unpaid) basis. In the case of the EXW (Freight Collect) arrangement, the buyer arranges the whole integrated shipment from the shipper's premises, and the shipper has little means of knowing how the consignment was shipped, especially where consolidations are undertaken. Thus, the shipper may have no substantial shipping documentation, especially where a consolidation is concerned. The documentation may comprise a Master Bill of Lading for the through shipment, without any form of Bills being issued to the shipper for compliance purposes. To counteract this problem, the use of the term FCA becomes more suitable, in that the shipper takes responsibility for the delivery of the consignment to a convenient place of loading into the container, or physically takes charge of the loading of the container at their own premises. In the case of DDU (Freight Prepaid) shipments, the documentation will have been raised entirely by the shipper and sent to the buyer, often without any specific details relating to the breakdown of shipping costs for the international leg of the journey separated from the onward domestic leg of the journey from the seaport of destination to the inland destination itself. For consolidated consignments, the term used by be CIP (Carriage and Insurance Paid) to a specified inland destination, where the consolidation is broken down from its groupage form to each individual consignment, with each consignment being cleared individually for its respective recipients. In this way, only the costs to the point of clearance are taken into account for declaration purposes, with the onward haulage to the customer's location being arranged separately.

Intermodalism has resulted in certain major seaports such as Rotterdam developing far more rapidly at the expense of other ports such as Southampton or Felixstowe. In some ways this is inevitable, as UK international trade only accounts for a fraction of the total trade being carried by deep-sea vessels serving the European port network. The hub-and-spoke system is becoming more prevalent, with the UK seaports reduced to the role of serving the continental EU ports, which provide the main facilities for the much larger deep-sea vessels. The other main factor for this trend is that, by its very nature, the port of Rotterdam serves not only the ports around the North Sea rim, but also the huge inland European networks of road, rail and inland waterway transport. By its sheer nature, size and multiplicity, the port of Rotterdam has become the largest port in Europe, serving a wide range of regions and networks on a hub-and-spoke basis.

Customs clearance has become more automated to cope with the number of import and export container clearances. Historically, the function of the Landing and Control Officer at the port or inland clearance depot was to examine the documentation, occasionally examine the container itself, and issue a report accordingly, as well as clearing the goods being declared. In an age of EDI and electronic submissions of data concerning import and export consignments, the customs computer does far more work, selecting certain containers for examination and scrutiny on a random basis while automatically clearing others by electronic means. In general, the customs officers located at the port do little more than answer enquiries, examine containers or trailers where absolutely required, and otherwise process documentation as the need arises. The rest of the customs function is carried out from inland regional centres on an audit basis, with examinations of company import and export transactions carried out on the basis of necessity rather than as a matter of course. In this way, information concerning container consignments may be overlooked, and certain anomalies and discrepancies may arise because of a failure on the part of the customs authority to address the issue at the time of clearance. In general, the trader is increasingly required to ensure that the information they submit to customs through their clearing agents is accurate at the time of submission, and in most cases this depends upon the nature of the information supplied to them by their overseas supplier. If that information is incorrect, it may only be picked up by customs at a much later stage, by which time the import has already occurred and clearance through customs has already been undertaken. With the increase in intermodal activities, the emphasis is on speedy clearance and delivery of the consignment to the customer, regardless of the accuracy (or otherwise) of the information provided on the shipping documentation. In many cases, the information used for export or import declarations is inaccurate, and is only found out by customs some time after the event. The intermodal nature of the shipment often compounds the problem, rather than resolving it.

Intermodalism has also resulted in the generation of specific logistics functions within the major shipping companies which act as third-party logistics providers, specialising in a mixture of maritime shipment, inland haulage, customs clearance and storage facilities. Many shippers prefer not to employ their own staff, and outsource the logistics function to these logistics providers. Intermodal traffic largely relies on this form of cargo management, where the shipper does no more than make the consignment ready for shipment. The rest is carried out by the logistics operator, including the freight forwarder. However, the logistics operator still relies on the correct information concerning the cargo being issued by the shipper in the first instance, and cannot be made responsible for any problems with the movement of that shipment due to the inaccuracy for the information provided by the shipper. In many cases, such inaccuracies can lead to costly delays in shipment owing to the rejection of documentary information by authorities such as customs, and it is the direct responsibility of the shipper to ensure that all information relating to any international shipment is correct at the time of loading of the container.

As intermodal traffic increases in volume, so too does the need for the container operator to meet deadlines imposed by traffic schedules, especially the loading of deep-sea vessels. There are deadlines for the receipt of containers at the port of loading in order to meet close-out requirements by the shipping line and port authority. This means that the container operator and haulage contractor must ensure that every container is cleared for loading and is received by the port authority in the specific time frame required prior to the loading of the vessel. In many cases, documentary inaccuracy or delays owing to traffic congestion can lead to delays in the container arriving at the port or being made ready for loading aboard the vessel, and this can lead to expensive demurrage charges or sudden panics while the necessary information is obtained to facilitate export clearance of the consignment.

Container security has become an increasingly important issue in an age of political uncertainty. In many cases, there is insufficient information concerning the container load to satisfy the authorities of the nature of the cargo, especially where security may be compromised. The ISPS Code has done much to tighten port and vessel security, but it has done little to identify the anomalies and shortcomings relating to the cargoes themselves. The responsibility for the security of the container load and the accuracy of the information pertaining to that load still lies with the shipper and the container operator. Intermodalism has done little to enhance this security, as once the load has been locked inside the container at the point of despatch, that load will not be intercepted until it arrives at its destination, unless there is an urgent need to do so. Security depends upon the accuracy of information, and it is vital that the shipper conveys all necessary information concerning the consignment to the container operator at the time of loading, to ensure that the container is shipped correctly and arrives at its destination efficiently and without damage or delay.

Multimodalism/Intermodalism has many advantages, but it also has its shortcomings. It is undoubtedly a major influence on international trade and the management of maritime cargoes, but it has generated its own complex features, not all of which are fully understood by its users and operators. However, it has become the major form of international movement of goods, especially by sea, and has resulted in more efficient means of delivery of consignments from the seller to the buyer. As the demand for more cost-effective forms of maritime shipment increase, so intermodalism appears to supply the solutions to such demand. However, in order for the concept to be used correctly and efficiently, it must be fully understood and applied in such a way that it benefits everyone, not just a select group of users. In some ways, it has limited the maritime carrier to one element of the whole transport movement rather than the prime influence in the international movement of goods, yet it has also enabled the major shipping carriers to consolidate their overall activities and concentrate on an ever-competitive, yet growing market.

6.2 Multimodal Information and the International Supply Chain

A key factor in deciding upon the transparency of information submitted through marine channels is the availability of information emanating from the supplier of a consignment of goods, or, in the case of passenger liners, the agency booking the voyage on behalf of individual passengers. If the supplier or the agency concerned does not convey accurate or detailed information to the carrier, then it cannot be expected that the carrier can in turn convey such information to the relevant authorities of the country of destination or even the port of arrival.

The basic process of the supply chain can be illustrated as follows:

Figure 2.6: The simplified international supply chain

In the case of sea cargoes, the information flow within the supply chain commences at the door of the exporter (the supplier). In order to facilitate such a flow of information, there are 13 recognised International Terms of Delivery—the INCOTERMS—which are occasionally revised to account for changes in international market conditions or to clarify the varying degrees of risk and responsibility incurred by either the seller (supplier) or the buyer (customer) in each of the stages of any international shipment. The very basic term used by the exporter is Ex Works (EXW), where the exporter does no more than make the consignment ready for collection by the buyer from its premises. The buyer takes total responsibility for the shipment right up to its own premises. It would be normal practice to expect the exporter to inform the buyer of the nature of the shipment by way of a commercial invoice or a packing list.

However, in cases where the consignment from the exporter is collected by a haulage company on behalf of the buyer and transported to a point of consolidation for loading into a container, such information may well be absorbed into a more general description pertaining to the overall contents of the groupage container on the basis of an LCL shipment. Under such circumstances, it is more common to find the terms "Said to contain . . . " or "Freight of all kinds" (FAK), or even a general term applicable to the purposes of the consignment (e.g. "Automotive Parts"). The fact that within such a consignment there may be a host of different commodities included does not figure in the description used on a Marine Bill of Lading. A more radical example is that of a consignment described loosely as "cosmetic products", which may contain commodities ranging from aromatic oils through soaps to lipsticks and nail varnish. However, the consignment may also include items such as nail varnish remover. This is classed as hazardous because of its flammable nature, but the overall groupage consignment description made no mention of this. The specific commodity was overlooked and no specific dangerous goods documentation was issued for the nail varnish remover, despite the evident risk involved in the shipment of the consignment.

Groupage or consolidation is one of the principal enemies of the accuracy of information pertaining to marine cargo reporting. Where the freight agent has accurate detailed knowledge of the consignment to be shipped, that information should be adequately transmitted via the carrier to the port of arrival, and any extra precautions required in the case of the reporting of hazardous goods should be taken. But if this information is not known, such precautions cannot be taken and the result is a compounding of risk pertaining to both cargo insurance and the provisions for the handling of hazardous goods under the IMO Codes, especially under the IMDG and FAL requirements. In this respect, there is a clear need for the freight agent to be absolutely aware of the nature of the consignment at the time that it is loaded into the container, so that the correct information concerning the cargo can be passed to the carrier (i.e. the shipping line) prior to the container being loaded aboard vessel.

Failure to provide such information could result in several compromises, as follows:

- failure to adhere to the requirements of the SOLAS, IMDG and FAL regimes laid down by the IMO;
- the nullification of the cargo insurance policy under the provisions of the Maritime Insurance Act 1906.

The nullification of the insurance policy would thus also compromise and prejudice the general average principle concerning both the safety of the vessel and the insurance of cargoes and their consequent indemnity if it were found that:

- neither the exporter nor the importer had properly insured the consignment in question;
- neither the insurance company nor the underwriters were made aware of the true nature of the consignment under the principle of *uberrimae fidei* (utmost good faith);
- neither the shipowners nor the shipbrokers nor the master of the vessel were correctly informed of the true nature of the consignment;
- The consignment (or the container in which it was placed) was not correctly stowed in accordance with IMO Regulations.

There is therefore the need for a fully transparent system for the transmission of cargo information to the carrier in the multimodal system long before the container or trailer is loaded aboard vessel. The nature of the international supply chain demands that information pertaining to cargoes is passed down the line from supplier to customer to ensure the smooth and efficient despatch and delivery of the consignment, and that all authorities and parties within the supply chain, are fully informed as to the nature and risk of the consignment in question especially from a transportation and national control perspective. Even where no international frontier controls are involved, such as within the European Union, there is still a significant need for such flows of information, especially where mixed forms of transport are involved, such as road and sea, either from a Roll-On/Roll-Off perspective or a short-sea container perspective. The demands of the short-sea marine motorway require that integrated information flows pertaining to the maritime carriage of goods exist long before the vessel is loaded and sails, as the timescales involved between one part of Europe and another, especially on Baltic Sea or North Sea routes, are minimal. These flows start at the point of the exporter or seller, and progress through the freight agents, the road trucking companies and shipping lines, the port authorities, the customs authorities, to the importer or buyer. Such information flows should show the full extent of the consignment as well as the risks involved in handling and transporting it between the seller and the buyer.

The timely and efficient arrival of the consignment at the buyer's premises should be reflected in the ability of all relevant parties and authorities to show that they were all party to the same accurate information pertaining not only to the method of transport involved in the movement, but also to the nature of the cargo itself. Any failure in the flow of information could result in at best a delay in the delivery of the consignment to the customer's premises, or at worst, the destruction of the consignment and the potential loss of a marine vessel as a result of an accident occurring while the vessel was at sea, because of a problem with the consignment.

This could attract the attention not only of the Marine Accidents Investigation Board (MAIB) but also those responsible for maintaining the integrity of, and compliance with, the regulations of the SOLAS Convention, especially where failure to report the true nature of the consignment insofar as it is hazardous or dangerous by the exporter or the freight agent resulted in a catastrophe occurring at sea and the safety of the vessel carrying the cargo being compromised or prejudiced. The International Maritime Organisation (IMO) is seeking to address the problem of container security in the context of global security initiatives, but this initiative is designed more to fit into the present ISPS (International Ship and Port Security) framework, and does not necessarily address the transparency of cargoes inside a container, especially in the case of consolidated loads, where the information contained on a Bill of Lading or a Cargo Manifest may be less than accurate.

CHAPTER 3

CHARTERING AND BULK CARRIAGE

1 CHARTERING

The term "chartering" refers to the arrangement of the use of vessels and containers for the purpose of the transport of cargo by sea. Several terms are used for the purpose of chartering:

- bareboat (demise);
- voyage charter;
- time charter;
- slot chartering (containers).

The chartering principle generally refers to the carriage of bulk cargoes by dedicated bulk carriers, but it can also refer to the carriage of general or specific cargoes on a general cargo carrier, as well as the carriage of containers on a container vessel. The carriage of general or specific cargoes as well as container carriage is covered under the slot chartering arrangement, to be covered later in this section.

A vessel is owned by a shipping line, but is not necessarily managed by it. The vessel may be managed by a separate vessel management company, which is responsible for crewing and maintaining the vessel, as well as ensuring that its operation remains profitable. The vessel management company (or the shipping line, whoever manages the vessel) then employs shipping agents to represent the vessel and the company when it arrives in port, and to ensure that its cargo is arranged, managed, loaded and unloaded correctly and efficiently. In many cases, the space on board the vessel is chartered by way of the slot chartering method (explained later in this section) but often the whole vessel is chartered by another trader wishing to arrange the transportation of a cargo or a series or group of cargoes from one port to another. In the main, this concerns the use of bulk carriers for the purpose of the transportation of raw materials such as minerals, grain, petroleum, fertilisers or timber from one place to another. Equally, bulk shipments of finished products such as road vehicles, steel, aluminium, heavy machinery and refrigerated cargoes can be transported in consignments large enough to fill a ship to capacity. The contract made for carrying these bulk consignments is known by the generic title of "charter party", a term derived from the Latin "charta partita", literally translated as "a letter divided". In the early days of such agreements, a contract was copied exactly, and the paper on which the two parts were written was then cut in half, so that each of the contracting parties kept one segment which agreed entirely with the other. The present-day charter party is a

45

maritime contract by which the charterer, a party other than the shipowner, obtains the use of a ship for one or more voyages (voyage charter), or for a specified period of time (time charter).

Vessels transporting cargoes under the terms and conditions set out in a charter party are known as "private carriers", in that they are operated to cater for the needs and schedules of the shipper and the vessel owner. In direct contrast to this arrangement, a carrier which offers transportation for all goods offered between the specific ports it serves is known as a "common carrier", given that it regularly operates on such routes, often as what is described as a "liner" service. The term "common carrier" can also be used to describe a company which owns or operates container services, but does not own its own vessels; it uses the services of vessels owned by other shipping companies for the transportation of its containers. Such an outfit is known as an NVOCC (non-vessel-owning common carrier), and it charters slots, or spaces for the loading of containers, on container vessels operating on specific routes on an agency basis. Certain NVOCCs act as liner or shipping agencies for shipping lines in several ports worldwide.

An important distinction can be made between a private carrier and a common carrier. A ship loaded with cargoes belonging to a single shipper is a private carrier, whereas a vessel carrying the property of two or more shippers is a common carrier. In this respect, if a bulk carrier, such as the *Berg Stahl*, is carrying a single load of iron ore (e.g. between Brazil and Rotterdam) and that cargo is destined for a single buyer, then that vessel is a private carrier. On the other hand, if a vessel such as the *Emma Maersk* is carrying several thousand containers from the Far East to Rotterdam, and each container load is destined for a variety of different importers, then she is seen as a common carrier. The same is true for a vessel such as the *Toisa Polaris* carrying a variety of cargoes on her deck from the UK and Norway bound for the Brazilian offshore oilfields. A private carrier undertakes the service specified by the owner of the cargo, in that it loads the particular cargo at the place designated by the shipper, transports it to the destination named in the contract, and delivers the cargo according to the conditions laid down in the contract or charter party, including the specific International Term of Delivery (INCO-TERM), usually FOB or CIF (the INCOTERMS will be covered later in this book).

There are three types of charter available:

- voyage charter;
- time charter; and
- bareboat charter.

1.1 Voyage Charter

This is a maritime contract under which the ship owner agrees to transport, for an agreed amount of money (technically known as *freight*) per tonne of cargo loaded, a stipulated quantity of a named cargo between two or more designated ports. The ship owner retains full responsibility for the operation of the ship and costs relating to its voyage (its *voyage costs*). The charter agreement lasts for the duration of the voyage or specific number of voyages determined in the terms of the charter agreement deemed necessary to transport the specific consignment or consignments from one port to another.

Under the terms and provisions of a voyage charter, the ship owner is obliged to provide a fully operational and seaworthy vessel, fit to carry the proposed cargo on the proposed route. The charterer in turn is required to provide a full load of the named and described items or commodities and to that end may demand that the ship owner stipulate, as warranties or verifiable facts, the following details:

- the name and classification of the vessel;
- the flag and nationality of the vessel;
- the IMO registration number of the vessel
- the deadweight tonnage and capacity (in cubic feet or metres) below decks;

Operational characteristics such as speed, fuel consumption and date of last drydocking do not concern the charterer, as these are issues for the shipowner, and would normally be omitted from the warranties (additional details not otherwise specified as terms or conditions) of the voyage charter. The charter party always stipulates the port in which the vessel is to be delivered or "tendered" by the owner. It also specifies the beginning and the ending of the period of days during which tender of the vessel may be made. This period is known as "lay days", as the vessel may well be lying idle while berthed at the quayside prior to being loaded in readiness for the voyage specified in the charter. In order to obtain maximum revenue from the voyage, the shipowner directs the master of the vessel to accept as much cargo as the safety of the vessel will permit, up to the level permitted by the load line (the Plimsoll line) marked on each side of the hull of the vessel. Once the vessel has been tendered or delivered, the charterer is expected to have the cargo waiting at the quayside so that no time is lost in loading once the vessel has been delivered to the charterer. Any delay incurred as a result of the cargo not being ready for loading is classed as "laytime" for the vessel, and may be incurred as costs against the charterer, known as "demurrage". The voyage charter must also specify and precisely state the responsibilities of the contracting parties for the loading, unloading and stowage of the cargo aboard the vessel, and which party is liable for costs incurred as a result of cargo handling by the port authority, in terms of the use of dockside cranes and quayside personnel. The "net form" of charter makes this task the responsibility of the charterer, whereas the "gross form" charter or "liner terms" contract simply states that the charterer is obliged only to provide the cargo at the loading port and to accept it at the port of destination, often under the terms of a CIF contract. The freight cost charged includes the cost of stevedoring and all other voyage expenses. The shipowner bears full responsibility for the proper loading, stowage and discharge of the cargo, and passes these costs on to the charterer as part of the overall freight cost.

1.2 Time Charter

This is a maritime contract setting out the terms under which a person or party other than the shipowner obtains the use of the vessel for a specified period of time to trade and transport cargoes within broad but defined limits, carrying any cargoes not positively barred or prohibited by the wording of the contract. Time charters normally contain restrictions concerning the types of cargo which may be carried aboard vessel. These restrictions range from any lawful cargo not deemed as being injurious or harmful to the vessel, to specific cargoes which may not be loaded aboard the vessel, such as toxic substances or livestock. Compensation, known as *charter hire*, may be defined at an agreed sum per deadweight tonne per month or at a fixed amount per day. The shipowner remains in all aspects the operator of the vessel. The charterer, among other obligations, assumes responsibility for loading and discharging the cargoes, especially where certain INCOTERMS such as FAS, FOB, C&F, CIF and DES are concerned. The charterer also pays the costs of vessel fuel (bunkering), pilotage, harbour and light dues, wharfage and dockage (berthing), among other operational costs such as port handling and conservancy charges.

The time charter (and, for that matter, the bareboat charter) directs where the vessel may sail. Because marine insurance underwriters are very definite as to the areas of the world where they will accept responsibility for damage sustained by vessels they insure, the time and bareboat charter parties provide a space in which the limits of the ship's voyaging are stipulated, including entry into sea areas vulnerable to icing up during winter months, for which an "ice clause" applies.

1.3 Bareboat Charter (or Demise Charter)

This is a maritime contract by which the vessel itself is transferred in all but title from the owner to a separate party for a specified period of time. It is the least used, for the reasons that it imposes the heaviest burden upon the charterer, who becomes the *de facto* operator of the ship. Among members of the legal profession, it is referred to as a "demise charter". The charterer pays compensation (charter hire), either at an agreed amount per deadweight tonne per month or at a fixed sum per day. All burdens and responsibilities of operation, including hiring officers and other crew and maintaining the vessel in good condition, are assumed by the charterer, who legally is said to be the owner *pro hac vice* (for this period).

The term "bareboat" refers to the fact that the fully-operational ship is delivered to the charterer in its "bare" state (i.e. it has no crew, no stores, little or no fuel, and no navigational charts). The term "demise" refers to the transfer of possession (but not ownership), command, and control of the chartered vessel from the owner to the charterer for the length of time covered by the contract. Although this type of charter is the least used out of all the charter types, it is still a common occurrence where vessels are chartered out by one shipowner to other shipowners for the purposes of temporary expansion of their fleets to satisfy the demands of specific markets, such as container transportation. Under the bareboat charter, the shipowner is required to provide to present a fully seaworthy and operational vessel that is fit and suitable for the service intended. Once the vessel is accepted by the charterer, the responsibility of seaworthiness no longer rests with the owner, but passes to the charterer. The charterer has the full right and responsibility of recruiting the officers and crew of the vessel, although they may be nominated by the shipowner if required. The vessel's entire crew thus become the employees of the charterer. All voyages undertaken by the vessel are specified by the charterer, and all associated costs per voyage are incurred by the charterer.

Documentation, such as marine bills of lading or sea waybills, for the cargo carried by the vessel in question may be issued by the charterer. If the master of the vessel is required to sign these bills, as well as the mate's receipt, the documents must indicate or state that the vessel's master is the agent of the charterers. The shipowner is not deemed responsible for loss or damage to the cargo, but the ship may be subject to liens (rights of possession) by cargo interests. Under the terms of the laws of Carriage of Goods at Sea, the carrier is deemed responsible for the cargo while it is on board the vessel. In this case, the party accepting liability for the carriage of the cargo is the charterer, who has undertaken to perform the contract of carriage in agreement with the shipper or owner of the cargo.

1.4 Slot Chartering

This is a term which refers to the chartering of space aboard a vessel for freight of various kinds. It is used to refer to containerised freight, as it concerns the "slotting" of a container on board a container vessel, and generally concerns the allotting of space on board a vessel of one shipping line for containers belonging to another partner, or other shipping or container line.

A container load may be a single consignment destined for one buyer (FCL), or may be a groupage or consolidated consignment comprising several loads, each destined for a different buyer (LCL). In each case, each cargo belongs to a different owner, and may be booked aboard the vessel separately from the other cargoes. However, the representative of each shipper or cargo owner, in this case a freight forwarder, arranges a space aboard the vessel by entering into a contact with the shipping agent. The shipping agent may be the liner agent representing the shipping line, or may be an NVOCC, as described earlier in this text.

In the case of the container business, the shipping agent or NVOCC arranges for a container to be despatched to the premises of the shipper or consolidator, where the individual or consolidated consignment is loaded into the container. The space for that container is then arranged aboard a specific vessel in the form of a "slot", or space, either above or below deck depending upon the nature of the consignments concerned. That slot is effectively chartered from the shipowner or operator of the vessel, depending upon whether or not the vessel is chartered out under the terms of a bareboat charter. In reality, shipping agents may charter slots on a series of vessels depending upon their relationship with the shipping lines. In the case of shipping conferences, where several shipping lines pool their maritime resources and fleets to operate on a specific set of routes, the shipping agents or container operators will be able to charter slots on several vessels, each of which belong to a different shipping line, but which operate collectively on the same set of routes (e.g. between the Far East and Europe). The shipping agent hires in the container at a fixed container (box) rate, which applies to any of the shipping lines operating on the specified routes, and then sells the space to the shipper either at a fixed-box rate for the container or at groupage or consolidation rates, based on the volumetric weight of each of the consignments consolidated inside the container.

The slot refers to a specific single voyage, as once the container has been offloaded at the port of destination the terms of the charter cease to apply. Another slot charter arrangement will be made for the return of that container to its point of origin. The same is true of any consignment loaded directly aboard vessel without being containerised. In cases where the cargo is of an outsize nature, or is being despatched to a specific destination outside the scope of container operations on a general cargo vessel, the slot applies to the space booked aboard vessel. An example of this is the transportation of oil and gas equipment destined for offshore operations. A vessel belonging to a shipping line can be chartered under a voyage or time charter arrangement for the purposes of the shipment of such equipment to a particular customer located in the area where the offshore activities are being undertaken, e.g. Angola or Brazil. However, the deck or hold space on board that vessel may also be booked on a slot charter basis (i.e. each cargo may be booked separately with the shipping agent by the supplier for loading aboard vessel). That slot charter only applies to the shipment of that consignment on a single specified voyage, and is completed once the vessel has been unloaded at its destination. Unless further shipments have been booked for the vessel's return voyage, it will return empty, although in reality, it may well be loaded with equipment for return to the UK or Europe. As with container loads, each cargo is covered by a specific document, usually a Bill of Lading, which refers to either the container in which the cargo is loaded and the details of the cargo itself, or to the cargo itself where a container is not utilised. That Bill of Lading refers to the details of the consignment and/or container details shown on the cargo manifest, which is produced once all the slots have been arranged aboard vessel.

2 BULK CARRIAGE

The carriage of cargoes in bulk is, in most cases, linked with the chartering of bulk carriers for such purposes. Bulk cargoes of either a dry or wet nature are generally carried as unit loads, with break-bulk operations being carried out at the port of unloading and discharge wherever necessary. Since the buyer requires a bulk load of a particular commodity, the decision is usually made to charter a vessel from a specific bulk shipping company for the express purpose of shipping that commodity.

Bulk trading is nothing new. It was evident at the time of the Roman Empire, when Rome imported huge quantities of grain from elsewhere in the Mediterranean region, and more recently it is evidenced by the examples of the famous tea and wool clippers, such as the *Cutty Sark*, which plied the ocean from the Far East and Australia to the UK in the 19th century. Other commodities which required shipping in bulk, especially around the UK coast, were coal and iron ore, especially during the days of the industrial revolution in the late 18th and early 19th centuries, to the point that between 1840 and 1887, the coal trade grew from 1.4 million tons to 49.3 million tons, as highlighted by Robin Craig in his book *The Ship: Steam Tramps and Cargo Liners 1850–1950* (HMSO, 1980). Since the 19th century, the volume of maritime trade has greatly increased, and this has been reflected in the increase in tonnage of bulk carrier vessels, in order to increase handling and carriage efficiency. Indeed, bulk transport has reduced shipping costs to the extent that various commodities can be shipped across the world for much the same price per ton as it would have cost over 125 years ago.

The term "bulk cargo" is used to describe commodities such as crude oil, iron ore, coal and grain, whose homogeneous physical character infers its movement by bulk handling and transport. Another definition of bulk cargo focuses on transport economics and is used to refer to any cargo which is transported in large quantities, such as cars in car carriers, or timber, usually a shipload, to reduce transport costs. Other cargoes included in this definition include refrigerated meat, chilled bananas and other perishable tropical fruits, which are generally transported in shiploads. Because many of these cargoes do not stow easily in conventional bulk carriers, vessels used for their carriage are specifically designed for such purposes. For the purposes of this text, however, bulk cargo can be seen as any commodity or product which is transported in large quantities or consignments in order to reduce the unit cost of such transport and maximise the efficiency of such carriage.

The maritime bulk commodity trade may be categorised as follows:

Liquid bulks	Six major bulks	Minor bulks
Crude oil/hydrocarbons Oil/petroleum products LPG (liquefied petroleum gas) LNG (liquefied natural gas) Chemicals	Iron ore Coking coal Thermal coal Grain Bauxite and alumina Phosphate rock	Steel products Forest products Cement Fertilisers Manganese Sugar Soya meal Scrap Coke Pig iron Rice

The above list may not be fully comprehensive, but it illustrates the commodities which are most commonly traded and transported in bulk carriers.

The physical character and nature of each commodity determines the type and size of vessel used for its transportation, the type of cargo handling equipment required for loading and unloading of the vessel, and thus the overall structure of the sea transport system for bulk transportation. With regard to transportation and handling characteristics, the commodities shipped by sea are hugely diverse, but in general can be categorised into five main groups:

- liquid bulk cargoes stored in tanks, handled by pumping mechanisms and transported in tankers;
- homogeneous bulk cargoes covering a wide range of commodities with a granular or lumpy composition, such as coal or iron ore, which can be handled with automated equipment such as grabs or conveyors, and are included in the five major bulks category;
- unit load cargoes involving items which must be handled separately, such as forest products such as timber, steel products, rolls of paper, bags or sacks of fertilizer or foodstuffs such as tea leaves or coffee beans, etc. (although such items may also be palletised);
- wheeled cargo requires special ships with access ramps and multiple deck structures, such as car carriers belonging to companies such as EUKOR or HUAL (Hoegh-Ugland);
- refrigerated cargoes are a special case because of the need for chilling or refrigerated transport, often in specialised reefer (refrigerated) ships or containers. These trades cover commodities such as meat, fish, bananas and other fruits.

Special terminal facilities with deep water capacity designed to accommodate bulk carriers with extreme draught (such as the *Berge Stahl*, owned by the

Norwegian company Bergesen) and capable of handling the various bulk commodities efficiently play an essential part in the seaborne bulk transport sector. No single terminal can handle all types of bulk cargoes efficiently, because of the depth of water coupled with the cargo handling facilities required shore-based storage facilities and the through transport methods required vary from one cargo type to another. In this respect, modern ports such as Rotterdam Europort have developed into a collection of specialist terminals, often so large that they extend for several miles inland, along the waterway linking them with the sea.

2.1 Liquid Bulk Cargoes

Liquid bulk cargoes fall into three main groups, namely crude oil and products, liquefied gases (LNG and LPG), and vegetable oils and liquid chemicals such as ammonia and acids. Together, these commodities account for half of world maritime trade, with crude oil and oil products accounting for most of the volume.

Crude oil and oil products require different types of handling terminals. Given that the carriage of crude oil and petroleum uses very large tankers (VLCCs), loading and discharge terminals are generally located in deep water terminal locations with drafts up to 22 metres, such as Milford Haven, Wales, and Bantry Bay, Ireland. Often, these requirements can only be satisfied by offshore terminals with strong fendering systems designed to absorb the berthing impact large tankers with their huge deadweights.

The typical oil terminal comprises storage tanks on land linked by pipeline to the piers and jetties where the tankers are berthed. These storage tanks must have sufficient capacity to service vessels using the port. Cargo is loaded by pumping oil from the storage tanks to the ship using the terminal's own pumping capacity. Discharge, however, relies on the vessel's pumps. Large tankers generally have four cargo pumps, located in a pump room between the engine room and the cargo tanks, so as to facilitate the use of power from the engine room facilities.

Products terminals, however, are generally smaller in size and area, and can often be located within the port complex, although at a substantial distance from other activities owing to the hazardous nature of the products they handle and store. Handling and loading/unloading techniques are mainly similar to those for crude oil, but they must be capable of dealing with many small amounts of different product. These include "black" or heavy oils such as furnace, fuel oils and heavy diesel oils, and refined "white" lighter oils such as kerosene, aviation spirits, petrol/gasoline, gas oil and MTBE (a liquid petroleum feedstock used in the agricultural sector). In many cases, these terminals often have oil refineries located close to them, where the crude oil is refined into its various products after being discharged from a crude carrier. This arrangement is to ensure that logistics and safety considerations are kept within a manageable framework, as well as exerting a greater degree of control over the handling of such products.

Since crude oil is still the largest maritime commodity trade, a large and sophisticated industry has emerged specialising in the transportation of crude oil by sea. Crude oil is generally transported from the oilfield to the coast by pipeline, linking in to large collection terminal areas with storage tanks and capable of holding huge quantities of crude petroleum. The oil is then loaded into tankers, mainly VLCCs (Very Large Crude Carriers) and shipped to its destination, where it is off-loaded into another bulk terminal. Such vessels require a dedicated port infrastructure, and most of the terminals used in this sector are often located in remote locations. The very size of the maritime leviathans used in such transport places restrictions on their use of key shipping lanes such as the Straits of Dover, the Malacca Straits and the Suez Canal. The Straits of Dover and Malacca have a draught of 23–25 metres and 18 metres respectively, which limits the size of vessel that is capable of navigating these straits.

The liquefied gas trade is more specific and specialised. The hazardous nature of Liquefied Natural Gas (LNG), such as methane, and its very low temperatures mean that special facilities for the liquefaction, storage, refrigeration, loading, unloading and regasification of LNG are required at the terminal. These facilities are isolated from the rest of the port. However, depending upon the distance from the gas production area, not all of these processes may be undertaken at the terminal itself. Specialised commercial transport of these products started in 1964 between Algeria and Canvey Island in Essex, UK, with two vessels, the *Methane Princess* and *Methane Progress*, followed shortly afterwards by the export of LNG from Brunei to Japan, and then a number of other projects to export natural gas from gas fields in Algeria, Indonesia, Abu Dhabi and Malaysia. With the discovery of increasing numbers of gas fields throughout the world, this trade has increased enormously. Liquefied Petroleum Gas (LPG) is mainly produced from oilfields, and is recognisable by the fact that in many cases it is "flared off"—hence the large flames emerging form oil refineries and offshore oil production platforms. Like LNG, LPG must be liquefied for maritime transportation, either by cooling it to a temperature of approximately –50 degrees Celsius, or by subjecting it to 10–12 bar pressure. Like LNG, LPG transport by sea requires a substantial investment in liquefaction and cargo handling facilities as well as the construction of specialist tonnage of vessels.

2.2 Handling of Homogeneous Bulk Cargoes

Homogeneous dry bulks such as iron ore and coal are handled very efficiently using single purpose terminals. The commodity arrives at the port in rail trucks or hopper wagons, whose doors are then opened to allow the contents to drop into hoppers beneath the track. The ore then moves to the stockpile by conveyor, where it is collected and then made ready for loading aboard the vessel. The stockpile thus acts as a storage area capable of handling sufficient of the commodity to ensure that it has sufficient ore to load aboard the vessel when it arrives. The essence of the exercise is to ensure that the vessel is kept waiting in laytime no longer than is necessary, to maximise efficiency in terms of minimalisation of loading time. To ensure the accuracy of shipping documentation, the commodity is weighed while on the conveyor system using an automatic weighing machine. Sampling may also be undertaken to satisfy the purchaser that the material is in accordance with specifications.

At the other end of the voyage, the ore is unloaded with a grab unloader which lifts material from the vessel's hold and discharges it into a hopper at the quay edge, from which it is fed on to a belt conveyor. The grab unloader is generally used for commodities such as iron ore, coal, bauxite, alumina and phosphate rock. Other commodities which can be handled by smaller mobile grabbing machines include raw sugar, bulk fertilisers, petroleum coke and various forms of beans and nut kernels. Pneumatic systems, such as vacuum or suction pressure types, are suitable for handling bulk cargo of low specific gravity and viscosity, such as grains, powders such as cement and powdered coal.

2.3 The Hunterston Bulk Terminal

A good example of a bulk handing terminal is that of Clydeport Hunterston, located next to Fairlie, on the North Ayrshire coast of the Firth of Clyde in South-Western Scotland, on a deep-water channel. Hunterston has one of the deepest sea entrance channels in Northern Europe, giving it the capability of accommodating the largest Cape Size bulk carrier vessels afloat. The terminal claims to have the fastest discharging rates in the UK, ensuring the efficient and cost-effective movement of bulk materials. It is the UK's foremost facility for coal imports and is ideally located for the UK, Irish and European markets. The hub, which operates on a 24/7 basis, offers ship-to-ship transfer, road and rail links.

The terminal comprises:

- unloading/loading deep water berths;
- coal storage area for 1.3 million tonnes;
- overflow area;
- forward-loading area;
- coal stock-holding area for on-site merchants.

There are two main berths, namely the outer berth, measuring 443 metres, and the inner berth, measuring 300 metres. The outer berth has a draft of 23 metres, and can handle vessels of 350,000 dwt, while the inner berth has a draft of 19.8 metres, and can handle vessels of 95,000 dwt. The Hunterston deep-water channel has a depth of 26 metres, with under-keel clearance of 2 metres, and a tidal range of 3 metres.

Unloading cranage comprises two 1,400 tph (tonnes per hour) cranes. The out-loader outreach is 50 metres, with a maximum air draft of 49.28 metres. Loading carnage comprises one 2,000 tph crane, mainly used for loading coal, with a loader outreach of 31.5 metres. All cranes can be operated simultaneously on loading and unloading activities. Storage area at the terminal totals 200 hectares.

Figure 3.1: Bulk carrier at Port of Blyth

2.4 Bulk Cargoes

The dry bulk cargoes described in this section fall into the category of the five major dry bulks, namely:

- iron ore;
- coal;
- grain;
- bauxite and alumina;
- phosphate rock.

Iron ore, by far the greatest of the dry bulk trades, grew rapidly until the mid-1970s, when its growth became slower, to the extent that many of the bulk carriers designed and built for this trade were laid up for some time in the late 1970s, before being sold off. Coal followed a similar pattern until the same period, but continued to grow at a greater rate, doubling between 1975 and 1985, and increasing by 50% between 1985 and 1995. The trade in grain grew steadily until 1985 and then stagnated, although it fluctuated from year to year from then on. Trade in bauxite grew rapidly during the 1960s, when demand for aluminium products was high, but then stagnated during the 1970s. In the 1980s, it revived, increasing by 25% between 1985 and 1995. The exception was phosphate rock, which showed no substantial growth over the 30-year period between the 1960s and the 1990s. It grew slightly, and then it declined. However, the combination of all these trades has proven of significant importance to the bulk shipping industry.

Iron ore is the essential ingredient and raw material for the steel industry, whose rapid expansion in the 1960s fuelled the boom on the construction of bulk carriers in the same period. The Japanese and European steel companies were prepared to offer long-term charters to meet the demand and requirements for raw materials to supply the burgeoning steel industry, especially considering that the source of such materials was located, in many cases, on the other side of the world from such industries, in countries such as Canada, Brazil and South Africa. However, during the 1970s, recession loomed and the steel industry saturated and then somewhat declined, mainly as the output of the steel users had reached a plateau. With the decline in traffic, so the requirement for the large bulk carriers also decreased. However, with the progression of time, the use of steel has reached a reasonably constant level, with the result that there is a regular traffic in the transport of iron ore from the countries where the raw material is mined, such as Brazil, Canada, South Africa and Australia, to the countries producing steel products, such as the European Union, Japan, South Korea and China. The demand for larger numbers of bulk carriers has, however, decreased, with the average tonnage of the vessels being used at present for the carriage of these materials having risen over recent years, the largest bulk carrier in the world being the *Berge Stahl* at over 364,000 tonnes. This rise in tonnage has been gradual, with the first bulk iron ore carrier vessel displacing over 300,000 tonnes, the *Bergeland*, being delivered to her owners Bergesen in 1991.

Coal is the next largest of the dry bulk trades behind iron ore, but is more complex than that of iron ore, as there are two distinct coal markets. One is as a raw material for steel-making, and the second is as a fuel for the power-generating industry, but is carriage by sea is basically the same as that for iron ore. However, the bulk carriers used for the carriage of coal are generally smaller than those used for the carriage of iron ore, mainly because the volumes of coal used are smaller than those of iron ore, and also because in an age of climate awareness, the use of fossil fuels is being more closely monitored and controlled. The other prevalent factor in the carriage of coal is the fact that the carriage of coal has a higher risk than that of iron ore, given its propensity to suffer spontaneous combustion in very large units, thus posing a greater threat to the vessel and crew.

Although grain is grouped with iron ore and coal as one of the five major dry bulks, it is fundamentally a different business in shipping terms. Whereas iron ore and coal form part of the industrial sector, grain is a commodity which belongs to the agricultural sector, seasonal in its trade and irregular in both volume and route. It is consequently difficult to control, plan and optimise grain shipments, and the trade depends heavily upon general-purpose cargo vessel tonnage drawn from the charter market. Although much grain is intended to supply basic needs to meet harvest shortfalls, most of the volume of grain transport is intended to supply animal feeds in industrial societies where meat production requires large quantities of animal feeds.

The shipping process for grain is little different from that for iron ore, in the sense that large quantities of grain are transported from the farmlands of the interior to the port by rail hopper wagon, where the consignment is offloaded on to a conveyor system. It is then moved into an elevator, from where it is transferred into a ship. The same process happens in reverse at the port of arrival. The grain is offloaded from the vessel into an elevator, which then transfers it by conveyor to waiting transport, either by road or by rail. However, because the grain market is less regular and controlled than the iron ore market, shippers rely heavily on the spot market, using the vessels which are available at the time. Because of the lack of predictability in the market and its constant fluctuations, transport planning is both difficult and complex, with the charter of any vessel for such transport depending upon the freight and charter rate at the time of negotiation.

The maritime markets for the transport of bauxite and phosphate are much smaller than the other dry bulk trades, accounting for less than 10% of the total trade in dry bulks. Bauxite is the raw material used to make aluminium, while alumina is the semi-refined product. Bauxite becomes alumina, which in turn becomes aluminium. Whereas the production of aluminium optimises the shipping operation by using vessels of Panamax size or above, the alumina trade uses vessels of a smaller size, since alumina has a high value, and needs to be stored under cover. Furthermore, the quantities of material required by an alumina smelter are too small to warrant large bulk deliveries. Phosphate, on the other hand, is derived from phosphate rock, and is used in bulk as a raw material for fertiliser. It can be processed in small plants, and therefore requires smaller vessels for its transport, with little need for large carriers.

The minor bulk trades, which include steel products, forest products, meat, fruits, vegetables and automotive products, do not require the use of large vessels, except in the case of the car-carrying business, where there is a niche market for maritime car carriers, operated by companies such as Hoegh-Ugland (HUAL) and EUKOR. Although the automotive market is specialist, it still accounts for a sizeable section of the bulk trade, given the large volumes of vehicles shipped form the Far East to Europe and the Americas, as well as from the European car plants to other worldwide destinations. Cars are high volume, low density, high value items, and are moved in large numbers out of their production plants in Western Europe and the Far East to central distribution points, where they are stored for a short time prior to being shipped overseas in purpose-built vehicle carriers, designed to carry several thousands of vehicles on any voyage. The vehicles are driven aboard vessel by way of special ramps located at the stern of the vessel, and are then positioned on one of several decks on the vessel. Once the vessel is full, the ramps are raised, and it departs for its destination.

Forest products, such as timber or paper, can be shipped either in loose form in bulk or in containers. However, due to the difference in density between various kinds of timber, the handling of such products varies according to their type, as more room may be required in the stowage process to allow for air space within the vessel's cargo hold, especially depending upon whether the timber is in log or bundle form, or is sawn to length. Much of the sector originates in Scandinavia, Russia and North America, and is destined for the other markets around Europe. Although general-purpose cargo ships can be used for this trade, it has been found that in some cases there is a requirement for purpose-built vessels designed for the carriage of timber. A timber-carrying vessel, the *Ice Prince*, foundered off Portland Bill in the Channel in January 2008 after her cargo shifted in a storm. The vessel subsequently sank, and the cargo of loose sawn timber was washed up on the coast of Southern England shortly afterwards.

Other trades, such as cement and fertilisers, can be undertaken in loose bulk, containerised or bagged form. The cement trade is, like various other maritime trades, volatile, and vessels are generally chartered on an *ad hoc* basis, often to carry cement to major construction projects around the world. Fertilisers are usually in powder or granular form, and can be carried loose or bagged on general cargo vessels. They are relatively easy to handle, but normally require undercover storage, in order to keep them dry.

The sugar trade comprises three elements, namely raw sugar, which is shipped loosely in bulk, refined sugar, which is shipped in bags, and molasses, which is viscous and is shipped in tankers. Most of the sugar carried by sea originates in the Caribbean, Central and South America, with the Philippines and Australia also accounting for a smaller quantity of sugar exports. Tropical fruits, such as bananas, and meat require transport in refrigerated (reefer) vessels, either in bulk form or in refrigerated (reefer) containers. Again, the trade is specific, especially in the banana sector, with specific shipping lines, such as Star Reefers and Chiquita, specialising in the traffic of such commodities.

Food commodities transported by sea are perishable, and require transportation at carefully-regulated temperatures. Refrigerated cargoes can be divided into three groups, namely:

- *Frozen cargo.* Certain products such as meat and fish need to be fully frozen, and transported at temperatures of up to −26 degrees C;
- *Chilled cargo.* Dairy products, such as milk, butter and cheese, and other perishables are transported at low temperatures, although above freezing point, in order to prevent decomposition;
- *Controlled temperatures.* Fruit transported by sea is generally picked in a semi-ripe condition, and allowed to finish ripening at sea at a carefully-

controlled temperature. Bananas, for example, require precisely 13 degrees C.

In all the above cases, it is vital that temperatures are maintained consistently throughout the ship in order to prevent deterioration of the cargoes. Even quite small deviations or fluctuations in temperature can be disastrous, especially for tropical fruit. It has been known that, in the case of malfunction of chilling equipment in some reefer containers, the captain of the vessel has switched the system to freeze in order to guarantee a safe arrival of the product at the port of destination, although the freezing of some fruits is not always to be recommended. In all these cases, however, a reliable transportation system is required, from harvesting of the product through loading aboard vessel to storage and distribution. Even with the containerisation of such traffic, the degree of automation in the process varies significantly. In some cases, manual labour is still used to carry consignments aboard vessel. In others, conveyors are used to load the consignment aboard. In other cases, the vessel uses its own derricks to load consignments, including containers, on board, while in more advanced instances, dockside equipment is used to load reefer containers aboard vessel. To this extent, palletisation has been introduced on an extensive basis in the reefer trades to render the transportation of refrigerated cargo more efficient. Reefer containers are fully insulated, and many have their own refrigeration plants which can be plugged into an electric socket on the ship, while others rely on receiving cold air from a central shipboard system in reefer container ships. The advantage of reefer containers is that the temperature inside the container can be more closely and accurately regulated than is possible in the hold of a conventional refrigerated ship. In addition, reefer containers can be used more efficiently to facilitate the transportation of refrigerated cargo through ports which have no refrigerated storage capacity.

Bulk cargoes are generally carried as unit loads, and are thus subject to prices for the full load, generally quantified as the cost per ton or metric tonne, and defined as "freight". The revenue gained from freight must therefore include all the elements associated with operating the vessel, including laytime for loading and unloading purposes. The costs of operating the vessel would include all the charges associated with the following activities:

- number of days at sea;
- bunkering (fuel);
- harbour and light dues;
- berthing charges;
- crew wages;
- stores;
- victualling;
- laytime for loading/unloading.

The revenue is a function of the cargo carrying capacity, and depends upon the vessel's cubic capacity and stowage factor of the cargo being carried, depending upon its density, volume and weight, as well as the draft of the vessel. Thus, the freight revenue is governed by the following factors:

- deadweight;
- cargo intake;
- freight rate;
- bunker adjustment factor (BAF);
- currency adjustment factor (CAF).

The surplus, or profit, is therefore calculated by the total freight revenue less all expenses.

Bulk freight is governed by the value of the commodity concerned. Thus, the freight rate for iron ore will differ from that for coal, and equally from that for grain, and so on. For evident reasons, it is impossible to say that the revenue gained for shipping one commodity relates to that for shipping another commodity, as several factors intervene, including the freight rate, the size of the vessel, the vessel operating costs, and the bunkering costs. Given that bulk freight is governed by specific INCOTERM sales, namely FOB, CFR and CIF, the latter two being the delivered cost at the port of discharge, then the cost of shipment of the commodity can be determined as per that particular shipment. In the case of FOB (*Free on Board*), the buyer pays all costs associated with the shipment, and this term is included in the charter party agreement. Where the terms are CFR (*Cost and Freight*) or CIF (*Cost Insurance Freight*), then the seller is responsible for the shipment and will also be responsible for the charter party agreement. IN many cases, however, the buyer is contracting with the seller to purchase the commodity in question, and the charterparty contract is negotiated according to which party is prepared to charter the vessel for the carriage of that commodity, as well as arranging the freight. In reality, an FOB price plus freight should equal the quoted CIF price. However, depending upon how the freight is negotiated, freight costs may differ depending upon which party arranges the shipment. For a voyage charter, the freight is based on the charter as a single entity, whereas in the case of a time charter, the freight is based on the anticipation by the ship owner of how much the vessel will earn on a daily basis, thus enabling the vessel owner to measure how he is performing against his running and amortisation costs. This will take into account the age and operating efficiency of the vessel concerned, and works out at an average rate for the vessel being used.

Whoever controls the freight and shipping details also controls the practical issues concerning the shipment such as the quantity shipped, the exact dates of shipment and the dates of delivery at the port of discharge. It is the responsibility of the party arranging such details to ensure that the arrival of the vessel at the port of discharge is not affected by port congestion and occupancy of the berth in question by other vessels. Failure to take these aspects into account can result in huge demurrage or laytime costs which will inevitable be the responsibility of the party arranging the shipment. The only other extra responsibility for either party is the issue of cargo insurance. Where a CIF contract exists, the responsibility for insurance lies with the seller, who pays the insurance premium and passes the insurance policy to the buyer at the time of loading of the consignment aboard vessel. However, in the case of CFR or FOB contracts, it is the buyer who assumes responsibility for the insurance of the cargo. Insurance premiums depend upon the value of the cargo, and based on the prevailing commodity market, it is essential that both buyer and seller ensure that the best possible deal is struck, since the cost of the insurance premium depends upon the value of the cargo at the time of sale.

Whereas for a single bulk voyage charter, the charterer pays for the use of the vessel, and the shipment is paid for on a single-journey basis, with a voyage charter, the charterer pays for the continual use of the vessel throughout the period of the charter, regardless of whether the vessel is fully-laden or operating in ballast (i.e. empty). This is particularly the case where a bulk carrier carries full bulk loads in one direction, and returns empty in the other direction to reload once it reaches its destination, as in the case of bulk iron ore shipments between Brazil and Europe. Assuming that the vessel concerned is operating according to a time charter arrangement, the freight rate for such shipments must include not only the cost for the vessel while it is sailing fully loaded between Brazil and Europe, but must also take into account the return voyages to Brazil made under ballast, as these still incur costs associated with operating the vessel.

Bulk shipping is by far the main form of shipping worldwide, basically because of the nature of the commodities shipped. However, the market in bulk commodities is volatile, and fluctuates according to global supply and demand, hence the *ad hoc* nature of the bulk charter business. In recent times, the markets dropped to the extent that many bulk carriers were laid up for significant periods of time, whereas at other periods, the need for larger bulk carrier vessels has prevailed to the extent that leviathan vessels such as the *Berge Stahl* and *Bergeland* are constantly deployed in the carriage or iron ore between specific destinations on a regular time charter basis. Similarly, the smaller bulk trades of the perishable foodstuffs sector also maintain significant levels of traffic, owing to the constant demands of the large-scale retail food sector for such commodities.

Even despite the size of the bulk market worldwide, it is dependent upon and hugely influenced by the economic forces of supply and demand in the commodity market, hence its relative volatility, especially in the trade in the five major dry bulks. Consequently, there are no fixed schedules for bulk carrier sailings, other than for the more constant bulk markets such as foodstuffs. Much, if not the vast majority, of the bulk trade is based on *ad hoc* charters, especially in the dry bulk sector. If commodity prices rise, so demand for bulk material shipments falls, especially in the price-sensitive dry bulk commodity sectors, where price and demand are elastic, and hence the demand for shipments of dry bulk materials diminishes. However, if commodity prices fall, demand for bulk shipments rises, thus increasing the dry bulk trade. In cases where regional commodity markets increase in size, especially in the case of the increased availability and supply of raw materials such as iron ore, demand for raw material commodities from that region will also increase, thus creating extra requirements for bulk shipments from that region to satisfy demand for that raw material elsewhere in the world.

The exception is the oil market. Increasing demand for oil throughout the world has forced the price per barrel of petroleum to rise significantly, yet the increasing worldwide demand for oil has also led to increasing demands on worldwide bulk shipments of petroleum, thus requiring greater levels of tonnage in the tanker sector. The constant demand for oil means that the world's tanker fleets are constantly in demand.

The bulk trade sector is also extremely sensitive and vulnerable to recession. In times of economic growth, the bulk shipping market prospers. In times of economic recession, the bulk shipping market contracts, with the result that many bulk carriers are laid up, as exemplified by the recessions brought about by the oil crises of the 1970s, resulting in many bulk carriers being rendered surplus to requirements, and laid up or sold off in the late 1970s. An example of this is the Seabridge consortium, which included, *inter alia*, the shipping companies Furness Withy and Bibby Line. In the late 1960s and early 1970s, several large bulk carriers were built for the consortium, each with names ending in . . . *Bridge*, e.g. *Canadian Bridge*, *Tyne Bridge*, *Westminster Bridge* and *Liverpool Bridge*. Prior to the Yom Kippur War of 1973 and the consequent oil price shocks, oil was cheap and these vessels were constantly in demand for the bulk shipment of iron ore from the rich fields of Canada, bound for the Far East and Europe. With the sudden rise in oil prices later in the 1970s, the global economy suffered a significant downturn, and the cost of running these vessels spiralled. The result was that the charter contracts with the consortium ended abruptly, and several vessels were either sold to other owners or were mothballed. Although some were to be used for some years more, other OBO (Oil/Bulk/Ore) carriers, such as the 91,000 grt *Liverpool Bridge/Derbyshire*, which was brought back into Bibby Line operation in 1979, were not to enjoy prolonged future use. The *Derbyshire*, shortly after its incorporation in the Bibby Line fleet in 1979, disappeared off the Japanese island of Okinawa during a typhoon in the Pacific Ocean in September 1980. There were no survivors. Two other carriers, the *Berge Istra* and *Berge Vanga*, owned by the Norwegian shipping company Bergesen, disappeared in mysterious circumstances en route between Brazil and Japan in December 1975 and November 1979 respectively, and in the light of these tragedies and other prevailing factors, the decision was later taken not to build any more carriers of this type, concentrating purely on dedicated bulk iron ore carriers instead.

Despite these setbacks, the size of the iron ore bulk carrier has increased, owing to the economics of the bulk carriage of iron ore, to the point that the largest bulk carrier of iron ore in the world, the *Berge Stahl*, owned by Bergesen, the same company which originally owned the *Berge Instra* and *Berge Vanga*, tops the list of large vessels at 364,000 grt. Such is the market for iron ore, that she is constantly kept busy, plying the route between Ponta da Madeira in North-Eastern Brazil and the port of Europoort, Rotterdam some 13 times per year.

CHAPTER 4

ORGANISATIONS AND PROCESSES

1 MARITIME ORGANISATIONS

The maritime carriage of cargoes is governed not only by a set of laws and regulations, but is also overseen and monitored by several international maritime organisations, although none of the organisations detailed in this section are directly responsible for the global administration of marine cargo management. Each organisation touches upon the issue as part of its overall remit, but does not concentrate on the subject as its main function.

The organisations concerned in various ways with marine management are as follows:

- International Maritime Organisation (IMO);
- Comité Maritime International;
- United Nationals Commission on International Trade Law (UNCITRAL);
- The Baltic Exchange.

Both the IMO and UNCITRAL are part of the United Nations structure, whereas the CMI and the Baltic Exchange are separate organisations.

1.1 The International Maritime Organisation (IMO)

The IMO is based in London, and oversees all aspects of maritime activity, ranging from the management, security and safety of vessels to marine pollution, the marine environment and maritime cargo security. It is recognised that the ownership and management chain surrounding any vessel, its movements and what it carries can embrace many countries, considering that most vessels spend their economic life moving between different countries with many different national jurisdictions and maritime regimes, often far from their country of registry. Indeed, the nationality and ownership of the vessels may differ radically, with the vessel being registered in a location completely different from the headquarters of the organisation that owns it. Equally, the cargo it carries may originate in so many countries, it is almost impossible to apply a specific regime to that cargo once it is being carried on the high seas. There is therefore the need for a regime and structure of international standards to regulate shipping, which can be adopted and accepted by all the world's maritime countries. The first maritime treaties date back to the 19th century, including the introduction of the universally-accepted load line (The "Plimsoll Line", invented by Samuel Plimsoll). Later, the disaster of the

Titanic in 1912 gave rise to the first international safety of life at sea convention—later consolidated as the SOLAS (Safety of Life at Sea) Convention, which is still the most important international Treaty addressing maritime safety.

The Convention establishing the International Maritime Organisation (IMO) was adopted in 1948, and entered into force in 1958. The IMO as an organisation met for the first time in 1959. Its main task has been to develop and maintain a comprehensive regulatory framework for shipping. Its present remit includes the safety of vessels, environmental concerns, legal matters, technical co-operation, maritime security and the efficiency of shipping. It is based in London and comprises 167 Member States and three Associate Members. It is made up of an Assembly and a Council, comprising 32 member states elected by the Assembly, which acts as the governing body. There are also several specialised committees and sub-committees, as follows:

- Maritime Safety Committee (safety at sea);
- Marine Environment Protection Committee (marine pollution);
- Technical Co-operation Committee (implementation of technical measures);
- Legal Committee (Legal matters within the scope of the organisation);
- Facilitation Committee (Reducing the formalities and simplifying the documentation associated with the flow of international maritime traffic, especially concerning vessels entering or leaving ports and terminals).

These committees are the focus of the technical work to review and update existing legislation or to develop and adopt new maritime-based regulations, with meetings attended by maritime experts from Member Governments, together with those from interested inter-governmental and non-governmental organisations. The result is a comprehensive body of international conventions, supported by a large number of recommendations governing and concerning every aspect of shipping. There are measures aimed at the prevention of accidents, including standards for vessel design, construction, equipment, operation and manning. Key Treaties include SOLAS (Safety of Lives at Sea), first agreed in 1960, which was the most important of all the treaties dealing with maritime safety. The SOLAS was further enhanced and reviewed in 1974, and it is this version which provides the basis for all international maritime safety standards used today, the latest standards including the removal of all combustible substances and materials from the interiors of commercial vessels as part of the SOLAS 2010 regulations. The MARPOL (Marine Pollution) Convention for the prevention of pollution by ships was agreed later, following the disastrous wreck of the *Torrey Canyon* tanker off the Isles of Scilly in 1967 and the subsequent oil pollution of the nearby coastlines as a result of the spillage from the wreck, estimated at 120,000 tonnes of crude oil. The result was the International Convention for the Prevention of Pollution from Ships, in 1973, as modified by the later Protocol of 1978 relating thereto, and referred to as MARPOL 73/78. This Convention covers not only oil spillage and pollution, but also pollution by chemicals, goods in packaged form, sewage, garbage and general waste and air pollution, including that caused by emissions from the engines of marine vessels. This was followed by the STCW Convention on standards of training for seafarers.

There are also measures concerning distress and safety communications, one notable result of which was the establishment of the Global Maritime Distress and Safety System (GMDSS), which was adopted in 1988. This was phased in from 1992 and became fully operational in 1999. The International Convention on Search and Rescue (SAR) was initiated in the 1970s. This eventually established the International Mobile Satellite Organisation (IMSO), which has greatly enhanced the provision of radio and other messages to ships. There is also the International Convention on Oil Pollution Preparedness, Response and Co-operation. Further measures include the establishment of Compensation and Liability Regimes, including the International Convention on Civil Liability for Oil Pollution Damage, the Convention establishing the International Fund for Compensation for Oil Pollution Damage, and the Athens Convention covering liability and compensation for passengers at sea. Two treaties were adopted in 1969 and 1971, enabling the victims of oil pollution to obtain compensation much more easily and quickly than had hitherto been possible. Both treaties were amended in 1992 and again in 2000, to increase the limits of compensation payable to the victims of pollution. A number of other legal conventions have been developed since then, most of which concern liability and compensation issues.

Inspection and monitoring of compliance with all the relevant Conventions and Regulations are the responsibility of all the Member States of the IMO, but the adoption of a Voluntary IMO Member State Audit Scheme is expected to play a key role in enhancing the implementation of IMO Standards. The International Maritime Organisation also has an extensive technical co-operation programme, which identifies needs among members whose resources are more limited, and matches them to assistance, such as education and training. The IMO has also founded three advanced level Maritime Educational Institutes in Malmö in Sweden (The World Maritime University—WMU), Malta, and Trieste, Italy.

1.2 The Comité Maritime International (CMI)

The Comité Maritime International (CMI), formally established in 1897, is the oldest international organisation in the worldwide maritime field. Its foundation followed that of the International Law Association (ILA) by several years, and indeed the CMI was seen as being a descendant of the ILA. However, the CMI was the first international organisation to be concerned exclusively with maritime law and related commercial practices. Its origins date back further than 1897, and stem from the efforts of a group led by Belgian commercial and political people who came together in the early 1880s to discuss and to put before the newly-founded ILA a proposal to codify the whole body of maritime international law. It had been acknowledged and accepted for some time that the courts of admiralty and maritime law were courts of international law, and in the 1860s the first international codification of the principles of General Average (the basic principle of marine insurance) was drawn up in London. This culminated in the ILA conference of 1890, which adopted the first *York/Antwerp Rules* relating to damage caused to both vessels and cargo and the subsequent remedies and means of compensation for such damage. These Rules have been subsequently amended and reviewed on many occasions, with the most recent amendments being in 1994.

Following two failed diplomatic international conferences in Antwerp and Brussels in the 1880s concerning attempts to internationally unify the various codifications of maritime law, the CMI was formally organised as a direct result of these two conferences. The ILA decided not to continue with such codification, and it was eventually agreed by the ILA that those interested in pursuing such a goal should form a separate body whose purpose would be to continue with this task. The agreement with the ILA was announced in a circular letter from the Comité Maritime International dated 2 July 1896. From this it may be deduced that the embryonic CMI already existed in an initial form, however limited, prior to its formal establishment in 1897. The letter conveyed the decision that the CMI would promote the establishment of national associations of maritime law, and would ensure a structured relationship between these associations. It also stated that each national association should be composed of lawyers, mercantile and insurance interests, and that its goal should ultimately be the unification and codification of international maritime law.

The CMI was established in Antwerp, Belgium, by several eminent Belgian figures, most of whom were involved in the maritime sector from a legal and insurance aspect, and these were joined by other figures from the Belgian Government, the judiciary and legal profession, shipowners, average adjusters, and insurance and commercial figures, all of whom signed a second circular letter in August 1896. This letter suggested that a "Belgian Association for the Unification of Maritime Law" should be formed. The same people who were to form the Association were also to form the first Bureau of the CMI.

The Belgian initiative was soon followed by efforts from other countries. The CMI's founders were joined by people from other countries who were actively working to organise national maritime law associations, and they all convened in Brussels in June 1897 to formally establish the CMI as the parent international organisation to continue the effort to unify the world's maritime laws and to adopt a constitution. Representatives of eight nations attended the meeting, The first international conference of the CMI led directly to the formation of several new National Member Associations (NMAs).

The original failed conferences of the 1880s also laid the foundation for the partnership between the Belgian Government and the Comité that resulted in the series of "Brussels Diplomatic Conferences on Maritime Law". These conferences adopted the many conventions and protocols drafted by the CMI over more than 80 years, and were held between 1910 (Collision and Salvage) and 1979 (Hague-Visby/SDR). The CMI Liverpool Conference of 1905 adopted a resolution requesting the Belgian Government to convene an international conference to examine the Comité's draft conventions on collision and salvage, and so the first Conférence Diplomatique de Droit Maritime (Diplomatic Conference on Maritime Law) took place in 1910. It was primarily concerned with issues of collision and salvage.

The Constitution was eventually drawn up, setting up the number of both Titular Members (nine per country) and delegates of NMAs (six per NMA). It also established a "Bureau Permanent" as the interim governing body of the CMI to function between Conferences. Conferences were to be held once a year, but they were also to fulfil the role of a general assembly, so were not solely limited to the debate and adoption of drafts and resolutions. Between 1899 and 1955, the number of Titular members increased to 10 per country and in 1955, the Madrid Conference adopted the constitution which allowed for one or more Vice-Presidents, one or more Secretaries-General and Secretaries and a Secretary for Administration, as well as the President, Treasurer and one delegate from each NMA. An Administrative Council was added, and was given most of the functions originally assigned to the Bureau Permanent. To date, the number of International Conferences has declined, only convening every three to four years. Because the administrative structure of the CMI eventually became too unwieldy and unmanageable, the 1972 Antwerp Conference was devoted to reforming the constitutional structure of the Comité, and the Administrative Council and Bureau Permanent were replaced by an Executive Council composed of the CMI Officers and six representatives elected by the Assembly. The International Conference was itself replaced by an annual General Assembly of the NMAs. A further Constitution was adopted at the 1992 Genoa Assembly and effectively completed the restructuring of the CMI, as well as creating two new categories of membership and clarifying a third, namely the category of Consultative Membership, which brings the CMI into closer working relationships with other international organisations such as the United Nations and the IMO. However, certain roles of the CMI have been effectively removed from the organisation's function and transferred to other bodies. With the formation of the Legal Committee of the International Maritime Organisation (IMO) in 1968 following the *Torrey Canyon* disaster and resulting pollution, the IMO began to take over the role of organising diplomatic conferences in the field of maritime law from the Government of Belgium. However, this did not bring the preparatory role of the CMI to an end, although it may not be appreciated how much the work has been carried out by the International sub-committees and subsequent conferences of the Comité in order to compose the initial drafting of every convention considered by the IMO Legal Committee except the 1969 Intervention Committee and 1973 Protocol and the 1996 HNS Convention.

In addition to its continuing work on maritime conventions, the CMI is involved in the formation and maintenance of codes of maritime and related commercial practice. In 1990 the CMI adopted uniform rules for SeaWaybills, and for most of its existence the Comité has been custodian of the York/Antwerp Rules for the adjustment of General Average, which were revised by the CMI at its 35th International Conference in Sydney in 1994. The Comité was also responsible for much of the law relating to the carriage of goods at sea, including the updated laws contained in the Hague-Visby Rules of 1968, which, in the case of the UK, became part of the Law contained in the Carriage of Goods by Sea Act (COGSA) of 1971. The Comité is presently working with UNCITRAL (United Nations Committee on International Trade Law) on standards for Electronic Document/Data Interchange (EDI) which covers the Electronic Bill of Lading. There is also the possibility of the CMI co-ordinating the work of a number of non-governmental international organisations in a study for UNCITRAL of the issues involved in the structuring of a comprehensive convention on maritime transport which could have a scope far beyond that of any of the past conventions. The 1972 Constitution declared the object of the Comité to be the unification of maritime and commercial law, maritime customs, usages and practices. The 1992 Constitution broadened the scope of activity of the Comité to cover maritime law in all its aspects, including the CMI's work carried out on the legal status of offshore mobile craft involved in oil exploration and production beneath the high seas.

1.3 United Nations Commission on International Trade Law (UNCITRAL)

The UN Commission on International Trade Law (UNCITRAL) was established by the UN General Assembly in 1966. In establishing the Commission, the General Assembly recognised that disparities in national laws governing international trade created obstacles to the flow of trade, and it regarded the Commission as a vehicle by which the United Nations could play a more active role in reducing or removing these obstacles. Although not strictly an international maritime organisation, it has nevertheless worked closely with other organisations such as the IMO and the CMI in establishing conventions which have greatly enhanced the maritime means by which freight may move around the globe.

The UN General Assembly gave the Commissions the general mandate to further the progressive harmonisation and unification of the law of international trade. The Commission has since come to be the core legal body of the United Nations system in the scope and field of international trade law.

The Commission is composed of 60 Member States elected by the UN General Assembly. Membership is structured so as to be representative of the world's various geographic regions and its principal economic and legal systems. Members of the Commission are elected for terms of six years, the terms of half the members expiring every three years. The Commission carries out its work at annual sessions, held in alternate years at UN Headquarters in New York and at the Vienna International Centre at Vienna, Austria. Each Working Group of the Commission typically holds one or two sessions per year, depending upon the subject matter to be covered. These sessions also alternate between New York and Vienna. In addition to Member States, all States that are not members of the Commission, as well as interested international organisations, are invited to attend sessions of the Commission and its working groups as observers. Observers are permitted to participate in discussions at sessions of the Commission and its working groups to the same extent as members.

The Commission has established six Working Groups to perform the substantive preparatory work on topics within the Commission's programme of work. Each of the working groups is composed of all Member States of the Commission. The six Working Groups and their current topics of activity are as follows:

- Working Group I—Procurement.
- Working Group II—International arbitration and conciliation.
- Working Group III—Transport law.
- Working Group IV—Electronic commerce.
- Working Group V—Insolvency law.
- Working Group VI—Security interests.

The International Transport of Goods has been a major part of the Commission's activities for some time. In 1978, the UN Convention on the Carriage of Goods by Sea—the "Hamburg Rules", was initiated, and this had far-reaching effects on how the maritime carriage of goods was to be undertaken, over and above existing legislation, both nationally and internationally. The Convention, passed in March 1978, established a uniform legal regime governing the rights and obligations of shippers, carriers and consignees under a contract of carriage of goods by sea. It was prepared at the request of developing countries and its adoption has been endorsed by such intergovernmental organisations as UNCTAD, the Asian-African Legal Consultative Committee and the Organisation of American States (OAS). The Convention entered into force on 1 November 1992, supplementing the Hague-Visby Rules, which were passed in 1968 with the Brussels Protocol, and became part of international and national legislation.

1.4 The Baltic Exchange

The Baltic Exchange is the only international shipping exchange in the world, and also contributes in a significant way to the economy of the UK. It is based in London, and is a membership-based organisation at the heart of the global maritime marketplace. The Baltic Exchange derived its name from the fact that at its origins, merchants and shipowners met in London at various coffee houses to do business and the cargoes which they traded came from the American colonies and the countries on the Baltic Seaboard. A coffee house where such business took place, the "Virginia & Maryland", became known from 1744 as the "Virginia & Baltic" because of this business. The proprietors of the coffee house provided newspapers and commercial information for their customers as well as refreshments, and cargoes were traded there by auction. In 1810, it acquired larger premises at the Antwerp Tavern in Threadneedle Street in the heart of the City of London, which was renamed the Baltic. A Committee was set up in 1823 to control the organisation's affairs, and membership of the organisation increased. In 1903 the organisation moved to St Mary Axe in the City, and, apart from moving from one building to another between then and the present, it has remained in the same street ever since. It moved to a new building at 38 St Mary Axe in 1995.

Today, the Baltic Exchange provides independent daily shipping market information, maintains professional shipbroking standards and resolves maritime disputes. Its members are equally at the heart of world trade, arranging for the ocean transportation of industrial bulk commodities from producer to end-user. The bulk freight market relies on the co-operation of shipbrokers, shipowners and charterers to ensure the free flow of maritime-based trade. It deals with freight rates for dry cargo market shipments and monitors the rise in fall of these rates on the world market.

The Exchange provides a unique professional market for cargo interests, ship owners, shipbrokers, port operators, agents and all parties involved in the sector of international freight transport by maritime means. As its name suggests, overall it is a marketplace which is self-regulated with strict business ethics and practices. It deals with cargoes for ships, ships for cargoes, buying and selling ships, chartering of vessels, commodities and, outside the maritime scope, aircraft chartering. Much of the world's shipbroking—the buying, selling and management of ships—is focused on the Baltic Exchange. It is famous throughout the world, and its shipbroking services are fully integrated into the maritime, insurance and financial markets of the City of London. Although most of its members are based in the London area, increasing numbers are joining the Exchange from overseas, enjoying a new category of membership for overseas-based brokers.

The brokers involved with the Exchange deal in a variety of commodities, including foodstuffs and other dry raw material commodities such as grain, sugar, fertilizers, coal, iron ore, cement, timber and steel. The Exchange also deals with wet commodities, in particular crude petroleum, which in reality could be sold from one trader to another several times while it is being carried form the Middle East to its destination in Europe. Throughout all this, the final buyer will need to know the freight cost of the ocean transport, since he was not party to such freight agreements at the time of their negotiation. Although the value of the cargo may change several times throughout the voyage owing to the trading of the commodity on the Exchange, the freight cost relating to the maritime voyage remains fixed, as it was negotiated prior to the cargo being loaded aboard vessel. In reality, the INCOTERM originally agreed for such a shipment becomes superfluous, as the party arranging the voyage and the freight may already have relinquished responsibility several transactions ago prior to the consignment arriving at its destination. Up to two-thirds of all tanker broking is undertaken through the London market, except for those cargoes shipped in tankers belonging to the major oil companies such as Shell and BP. However, the number of tankers owned directly by the oil companies is decreasing, as these companies are opting out of vessel ownership and prefer to charter in vessels as the need arises, owing to the constant fluctuation in the petroleum market.

As well as trading in cargoes, and representing ship owners, brokers also buy and sell ships. The London-based brokers handle most of the world's purchase and sale deals on vessels, from new builds to the second- or third-hand market. The broker needs to arrange an acceptable price for a new build, as well as its delivery to the fleet upon completion. The broker also arranged the onward sale of the vessel to new owners during its life, and at the end of the vessel's life, the broker takes charge of the sale of the vessel to the shipbreakers and also its final voyage to the scrapyard, which is often on a beach in some far-off location. To this extent, the work of the shipbroker is a varied affair, dealing with the trading of vessels and cargoes, as well as representing the shipowners and vessel charterers at various ports.

The BIFFEX The Baltic Exchange Financial Futures Exchange Index is located at the Baltic Exchange. The Exchange calculates the Baltic Freight Index (BFI) on a daily basis from a panel of its brokers, and displays the rapidly-changing cost of transporting the world's major dry commodities by sea, usually by bulk, which thus can be represented in the cost per tonne of each commodity.

2 THE INTERNATIONAL COMMERCIAL TERMS OF DELIVERY (INCOTERMS)

The term "INCOTERMS" refers to the rights, responsibilities and risks associated with the international movement of cargoes, and which party, either seller or buyer, bears those risks and responsibilities. In short, it covers the issue of "who pays the ferryman". INCOTERM is an acronym, meaning the International Commercial Terms of Delivery. There are 13 Terms in all, although some are abbreviated to a simplified form depending on how the

~~consignment is to be arranged~~. Over the past several decades, several INCO-
TERMS have been changed depending upon their relevance, although those
which have been removed, such as "Franco Domicile" are still understood by
many who have worked in the international trade field for some years. The
most recent review of the INCOTERMS was in 2000.

The 13 Terms are arranged as follows:

- EXW (Ex Works);
- FCA (Free Carrier);
- FAS (Free Alongside Ship);
- FOB (Free on Board);
- C&F/CFR (Cost and Freight);
- CPT (Carriage Paid To . . .);
- CIF (Cost Insurance Freight);
- CIP (Carriage and Insurance Paid . . .);
- DES (Delivered Ex Ship);
- DEQ (Delivered Ex Quay);
- DAF (Delivered at Frontier);
- DDU (Delivered Duty Unpaid);
- DDP (Delivered Duty Paid).

Not sea, road! (handwritten note)

The two abbreviated Terms are:

- Freight Collect;
- Freight Prepaid.

Some of the above INCOTERMS are not used for sea freight, and these
(namely DAF and DDP, which are primarily used for road freight) will be
omitted for the purpose of this book. Certain other terms, such as FCA, CPT,
CIP and DDU, can also be used for air freight, as they cover a multi-modal
form of transportation. One Term, EXW, is not necessarily an International
Term of Delivery, as it simply allows for the collection of the goods from the
seller's premises by the buyer, regardless of where the buyer is located. The
main terms, however, for sea freight alone are:

- FAS;
- FOB;
- C&F;
- CIF;
- DES;
- DEQ.

2.1 EXW (Ex Works)

The only responsibility of the seller is to make the consignment ready for
shipment at their premises (the "factory gate") and to notify the buyer that the
consignment is ready for collection. It is the responsibility of the buyer to

arrange and pay for all transport for the consignment to the ultimate destination and the buyer's premises, as well as to shoulder all risks associated with the transport of that consignment. The buyer arranges all documentation for the shipment, as well as all export and import customs clearance in the case where the consignment passes through customs control en route to its final destination. The seller bears no risks or responsibilities connected with the shipment, other than making the consignment ready for collection by the buyer's representative, although in reality they are deemed to be the exporter of record by their national customs authority, and thus require some form of proof of shipment, such as a certificate of shipment provided by the freight forwarder of the carrier, and a copy of the appropriate customs export declaration at the point of export for customs purposes. It is also the express duty of the seller to inform the buyer of the exact nature of the cargo to ensure that the correct shipping documentation is raised, especially where the cargo is of a hazardous or dangerous nature.

2.2 FCA (Free Carrier)

The term FCA has two distinct meanings, and these are explained as follows.

Firstly, whereas under the EXW term, the seller simply notifies the buyer that the consignment is ready for shipment and does not even bear responsibility for loading the vehicle at the point of despatch, under the FCA term, the seller has the responsibility of loading the vehicle and obtaining a despatch document, as well as a customs export declaration.

Secondly, where a consolidation is involved and the consignment is to be grouped or consolidated with several other loads at a central point, the seller is responsible for the carriage of the consignment to that point and ensuring that it is loaded aboard the container. In general, the buyer pays for and arranges the actual loading of the container by the consolidating agent. The consolidating agent arranges both the consolidation, or Master Bill of Lading for the container, plus the individual House Bills of Lading for each consignment loaded aboard the container. The buyer arranges the consolidation and the full international journey of the container or their consignment within that container right up to their premises, assuming that there will be a deconsolidation or break-bulk operation conducted at a point close to their premises.

2.3 FAS (Free Alongside Ship)

This terms is very much of a maritime nature, and concerns the passing of risk and responsibility from the seller to the buyer at the quayside where the consignment is to be loaded aboard vessel. The buyer takes complete control from there on, and therefore has responsibility for loading the consignment off the quayside and on board the vessel, thus also accepting liability for all port

handling and loading charges. In this respect, FAS is also usable in conjunction with the "net form" of voyage charter of a vessel, where the charterer
takes charge of all loading activities and responsibilities for the cargo when
loading the vessel. FAS, however, is not normally used with container shipments, as the arrangement to load the container will have taken place at some
point inland from the port of loading.

2.4 FOB (Free On Board)

The term "free on board" has a variety of applications, although its actual
meaning is fairly simple. It implies that the responsibility for the carriage of the
consignment transfers from seller to buyer the moment the container or cargo
passes over the ship's rail at the point of loading. Although it does apply to
container transport, it has always applied to more general cargo, given the
means by which the cargo is lifted from the quayside and is lowered into the
hold of the vessel. There is a legal implication to the term under the conditions
of an FOB contract. The term is used with the "gross form" of voyage charter,
where the shipper relies on the owner of the vessel to ensure that the cargo is
correctly loaded aboard vessel. In the same way, the shipper is reliant upon the
port authority to ensure that the cargo is correctly lifted from the quayside and
on to the vessel. Should the consignment fall from the crane, two possibilities
arise:

- The cargo lands on the quayside and is damaged. The seller is responsible for the damage and must either replace the consignment or reim-
  burse the buyer;
- The cargo falls from the crane and lands on the vessel, damaging the
  vessel as well as being damaged itself. The buyer is responsible for all
  damage, including that to the vessel, and must pay the appropriate
  amount of money as well as incurring costs for a replacement
  consignment.

Under the terms of a strict FOB contract, the buyer can reject a consignment
at the point of loading if they feel that the contract has not been properly
fulfilled, in operational or documentary terms. This is partly because at the
time of loading, a Bill of Lading has not yet been issued and thus the buyer is
not fully responsible for the shipment until the vessel has been properly loaded
with the consignment. Once this has been undertaken, the buyer becomes
responsible for the issuing of the Bills of Lading and thus the contract of
carriage with the carrier. The seller, however, is responsible for customs
clearance and the raising of the Customs Export Declaration, which will in any
case be lodged with, and acknowledged by, the customs authority prior to the
consignment being loaded at port.

The other use of the FOB term is in generating export statistics. The FOB
term signifies an export in terms of its value, and thus contributes to the

overall data compiled by the government in support of its annual trade balance.

2.5 C&F/CFR (Cost and Freight)

Whereas the FOB term refers to the passage of risk and responsibility for the cargo consignment from seller to buyer at the time of loading, C&F/CFR implies that the seller arranges the shipment up to the point of unloading at a named overseas port. The seller arranges the international shipment by sea and pays for the freight, as well as the cost of port handling charges at the port of loading. However, the risk and responsibility for the consignment passes from seller to buyer when the consignment is being loaded over the ship's rail on board the vessel. The buyer is responsible for insuring the consignment, as well as the carriage of the consignment from the point of loading. The seller also arranges for the issuing of all Bills of Lading, and their transfer to the buyer, as well as all customs clearance at the point of export.

2.6 CPT (Carriage Paid To . . .)

Every INCOTERM is accompanied by a named place or port. In maritime terms, the term CPT refers to the carriage of the consignment to an inland destination, usually by multimodal or intermodal transport. In this respect the term is the reverse of FCA, and implies that the consignment will be consolidated at an inland point along with other consignments into a container, transported to the port, loaded aboard vessel, shipped to an overseas port, then unloaded and transported to an inland destination, where it will be deconsolidated at the named inland destination. The seller arranges this total shipment, and passes all responsibility and risk for it other than the insurance of the consignment to the buyer at the point of loading as with the term CFR. The shipping documents raised for the consignment can be either through Bills of Lading, Container Bills of Lading or Combined Transport Bills of Lading, detailing, where appropriate, all means of transport up to the point of deconsolidation and unloading from the container, and clearance through customs.

2.7 CIF (Cost Insurance Freight)

The term CIF is one of the most common terms in the process of International Trade. Like C&F, it implies that the seller arranges the international carriage of the consignment to a named port of destination but passes the risk and responsibility for the carriage of the consignment at the point of loading aboard vessel, literally at the time the consignment passes over the ship's rail. As with the C&F term, whereas the seller is responsible for the loading of the vessel at the port of despatch, the buyer is responsible for the unloading of the vessel at the port of destination. However, the main difference between C&F

and CIF lies in the application of insurance. With C&F (CFR), the buyer is responsible for the arrangement of insurance of the cargo. With CIF, the seller arranges the insurance for the cargo and transfers the insurance policy to the buyer at the point of loading over the ship's rail, in the same manner as the transfer of risk from seller to buyer in an FOB contract, and equally under CFR Terms.

The buyer then assumes responsibility for the insurance of the cargo the moment it passes over the ship's rail. However, although the buyer may have the right of claiming indemnity for the cargo in the event of loss or damage while the cargo is in the charge of the carrier, they cannot actually claim the cargo at the point of arrival until they have received a copy of the Bill of Lading, assuming that the Bill of Lading is of the negotiable form.

Under a CIF contract, the buyer must have paid for the consignment in order to receive the Bills of Lading from their bank. The bills are sent to the buyer's Bank by the exporter under the payment terms "cash against documents", and a Bill of Exchange is sent along with the invoice to the buyer. The buyer is obliged to pay or make suitable credit term arrangements with the seller through the buyer's bank in order to facilitate the transfer of the Bills of Lading by the bank to the buyer. Once this transaction has been achieved, the buyer may then present the Bills of Lading to the shipping agent for the transfer of the consignment. The shipping agent, or the shipping line, will only release the consignment to the buyer once the buyer has presented the agent with the Bill of Lading. In this respect, the carrier is responsible for the carriage of the consignment up to the point where the consignment is released and handed over to the buyer or the buyer's representative in the form of the import freight agent or customs clearance broker. Owing to the terms of payment involved in this form of contract, the ownership or title of the consignment can pass from seller to buyer while the consignment is being carried on the high seas. The carrier must be notified of this arrangement, as they will only release the consignment at the point of arrival at the port of destination to the legal owner of the consignment. Under the terms of a charter party, the charterer of the vessel may also be the owner of the cargo, in which case the charterer must also be the holder of the Bills of Lading. Where ownership of the consignment passes from the charterer to the buyer under a CIF contract, this point of transfer must be notified to all parties concerned with the transaction, especially where responsibility for unloading the vessel is concerned.

2.8 CIP (Carriage and Insurance Paid . . .)

The term CIP operates in a similar manner to the term CIF, except that the contract of carriage is less strict under CIP conditions. CIP is an intermodal term, implying that the responsibility and risk associated with the carriage of the consignment passes from seller to buyer at the point of loading of the consignment. Unlike CPT, the seller arranges the insurance of the consignment, and passes the insurance policy to the buyer prior to the arrival of the consignment at its destination. As with the term CPT, through Bills of Lading may be issued, as these refer to the entire intermodal or multimodal journey, inclusive of all modes of transport up to its destination. In general, the CIP Term is used predominantly with container transport, in the grounds that the container will be transported from the port of arrival to an inland destination for unloading and deconsolidating.

2.9 DES (Delivered Ex Ship)

The term CIF implies that the buyer is responsible for the unloading of the vessel at the port of arrival. Under the term DES, the buyer is responsible for the unloading of the vessel, and the subsequent release of the consignment to the buyer. This term can be used with the "gross form" of voyage charter, where the shipowner is responsible for the loading and unloading of the vessel, and passes all charges for these activities to the buyer or charterer at the point of unloading of the consignment. Under a slot charter, the charter is completed when the consignment is unloaded off the vessel, implicitly under either CFR, CIF or DES terms.

2.10 DEQ (Delivered Ex Quay)

The difference between the terms DES and DEQ is quite subtle. Whereas under the term DES, the responsibility and risk for the consignment passes from seller to buyer *before* the consignment has been unloaded from the vessel, under the term DEQ that responsibility and risk passes once the consignment has been unloaded from the vessel, and, in some cases, transferred into a warehouse either adjacent to the quay or close by, such as in a free zone or in a remote transit shed. In this respect, the term DEQ can be used alongside CPT or CIP, and is the exact opposite of the term FCA. However, the term DEQ is more often used for the purposes of the carriage of bulk consignments, where the cargo is to be unloaded from the vessel and into a storage area close to the quayside prior to being cleared through customs and delivered to the buyer.

2.11 Freight Collect and Freight Prepaid

In this era of integrated container transport from seller to buyer, the use of INCOTERMS has become a somewhat convoluted affair. There is no need for the use of some of the traditional INCOTERMS, as the responsibility and risk for the consignment do not always pass from seller to buyer at these points. The container is loaded inland, and is unloaded at an inland destination away from the port. Although the terms FCA and CIP exist for this kind of operation, there are two terms which are more commonly and widely used for this purpose. They are "freight collect" and "freight prepaid".

Freight collect is the term used where the buyer pays for the freight and arranges the shipment from the point of loading the container to the point of unloading.

Freight prepaid is the term used where the seller pays for the freight and arranges the shipment from the point of loading the container to the point of unloading, and passes the cost on to the buyer. Insurance may be arranged by either party.

Either term must be stated on the Bills of Lading, as it must be made completely clear which party is arranging and paying for the shipment, under the terms of the Bill of Lading. It then becomes clear which party has contracted with the carrier for the carriage of the consignment.

3 THE SHIPPING ORGANISATION AND SHIPPING PROCESS

The shipping organisation demands an understanding of the various parties involved in the process, but it is primarily an understanding of the role and function of each individual party involved. There is often the mistaken view taken in the international trade sector that the exporter or importer need do no more than make the consignment ready to be picked up (the exporter's view) and that the freight forwarder will do the rest (the view of both the importer and exporter). Both attitudes are erroneous, in that although the Ex works INCOTERM allows the exporter to simply make the consignment ready for shipment at the factory gate, the national authority requires the exporter to keep documentary proof that the shipment was made and that it has left the country. The exporter is also expected to make the export declaration to the customs authority, a procedure nearly always left to the freight forwarder, and often resulting in no evidence of the export declaration ever being sent to the exporter by the agent. The exporter and importer also expect that the freight forwarder arranges the shipment by sea, and that the freight charges reflect this. What they least imagine is the detail of just how the consignment is transported across the ocean waves, especially as much of the cost of transporting the freight is absorbed within the freight pricing structure.

The previous section concerning the INCOTERMS dealt with all the terms used in the transportation of ocean freight worldwide, and the various risks and responsibilities associated with such transportation as far as both seller and buyer are concerned. Both parties will use the services of a freight agent, but the responsibilities and activities of the freight agent with reference to the party employing them vary depending upon which INCOTERM is used. In each case, however, there has to be the use of a freight agent at both export and import organisational stages in the shipping process.

There are several agencies involved in the shipping process, and these are:

- Freight forwarder;

- Liner/port/shipping agent;
- NVOCC/Container operator;
- Shipping line (where different from the liner agent);
- Vessel charterer;
- Customs broker (where different from the freight forwarder).

These agents have different roles to play in the shipping process, but are equally important in the chain of activities.

3.1 The Freight Forwarder

The freight forwarder is the agency dealing directly with the exporter or importer (the shipper), and responsible for arranging the shipment on the shipper's behalf. The forwarder is responsible for acting on the instructions of the shipper to move the consignment from one place to another. Therefore, the forwarder will contact the shipping line, NVOCC or liner agent on behalf of the shipper to arrange transport on a vessel, usually by using a container. Where an NVOCC (Non-Vessel-Owning Common Carrier) deals with the hiring out of containers on behalf of the shipping line, the forwarder will deal with that agency. The forwarder books a container, and ensures that the container is sent to the seller's premises or a suitable consolidation point for loading. Once the container is loaded, arrangements are made by the forwarder and the shipping agent to transport the container, usually by road, to the port for loading aboard vessel. It is usually the responsibility of the forwarder to complete the export declaration for submission to the national customs authority. Once the consignment has been declared to customs and has been loaded aboard vessel, the forwarder obtains copies of the Bill of Lading and sends them to the shipper (i.e. the party arranging the shipment according to the relevant INCOTERMS).

Often, the freight forwarder uses their own premises to consolidate and deconsolidate cargoes. The nature of the forwarding business is such that the forwarder may provide a fully-integrated service to the shipper, arranging container and trailer transport, filling (stuffing) the container or trailer and ensuring that it is moved to the port of loading, as well as conversely arranging the movement of the container or trailer to a suitable inland premises for unloading (unstuffing) and customs clearance, and thence delivery to the customer.

Correspondingly, the freight forwarder at the point of import is responsible for submitting the copies of the Bill of Lading to the port agent representing the shipping line, ensuring that the cargo is correctly declared through customs and delivered to the importer, as well as submitting the relevant customs documentation (i.e. import declarations) to the importer. Thus, the freight forwarder plays a pivotal role in the management of the shipping process and operation.

3.2 The Liner Agent

The liner agent plays an equally important role in the shipping process. Many shipowning companies, or shipping lines, do not have offices in all the ports their vessels serve. Where charter parties are involved, they will have devolved the responsibility for operating the vessel to the charterer, and do not necessarily become involved in port operations at the vessel's port of departure or destination. It is normal for the shipping line to employ the services of a liner agent, who acts on behalf of the shipping line as their port agent for all the ports where the vessels concerned will serve. It is the responsibility of the liner agent to represent the shipping line or vessel charterer in all aspects of dealing with the vessel and its crew when it berths at the port, and to ensure that all associated activities are carried out in relation to the vessel and its crew to the satisfaction of the shipowner, as well as the Port Authority. In this respect, the liner agent not only represents the shipping line itself, but also acts as the main point of contact with relation to communication with the Port Authority concerning the vessels it represents. It pays all charges associated with the vessel and its cargo while the vessel is in port and duly passes these charges on to the freight forwarder (freight handling, loading and unloading) and the shipping line (vessel and crew costs).

The contract between the shipping line and the liner agency provides for a general agency with the following responsibilities:

- The selection of stevedoring and terminal operators as well as the necessary supporting services such as security guards and cargo checkers.
- Serving as the traffic department, seeking shippers of cargo and dealing with consignees of incoming cargo.
- The issuing of Bills of Lading, as required.
- The provision of adequate communication services to reflect the booking of outbound cargo and the receipt of inbound cargo.
- The reporting of local conditions (including competition) that may affect the profitable and efficient operation of the ships.
- Supervision of the operation of the cargo terminal.
- Submitting disbursement accounts for every call of every vessel at the general agent's ports.
- Attending conferences dealing with the procurement of cargo, regulation of vessel operation, and other matters affecting the efficiency of the ships.

If the general agency agreement extends to operations in smaller ports elsewhere, known as out-ports, the demands placed upon the local representative agent may be reduced to arranging the arrival of the vessel, berthing, cargo handling, and sailing of the ship. Equally, it is not unusual for an agency to contract to service two or more ports, indeed to the point of being an exclusive agent acting on behalf of one or more shipping lines in a specific country, and therefore having offices in several ports in that country (e.g. Denholm Agency, which acts as agent for a variety of shipping lines in the UK, and has offices throughout the UK in several ports, including Glasgow, Grangemouth, Rosyth, Tyne and Liverpool).

The port or liner agent is responsible for ensuring not only that the vessel and the cargo are correctly managed while in port, but also that all documentation pertaining to such activities is correctly arranged and submitted. The agent will therefore arrange for the issuing of all Bills of Lading and cargo manifests, to ensure that the cargo is correctly loaded and stowed aboard vessel. In this respect, the agent communicates with the port authority to ensure that all loading and unloading has been carried out correctly and that the cargo is correctly stowed aboard vessel, especially where hazardous or dangerous cargoes are concerned. Once the cargo has been loaded aboard vessel, the agent ensures that all documentation is in order and that the vessel is cleared to sail. The agent will generally pick up all charges in relation to the loading and handling of the cargo and will pass these charges on to the party responsible, usually the cargo owner or shipper.

3.3 The NVOCC

The Non-Vessel Operating Common Carrier (NVOCC) or Non-Vessel Operating Carrier (NVOC) is a vital part of multi-modalism, where the cargo is carried internationally by more than one form of transport. The principle of multi-modalism is that a cargo is loaded aboard a container at an inland point, and is then moved by road or rail to a port of loading. The container is then transported by vessel across the sea to another port of destination, where it is unloaded from the vessel on to another road vehicle or rail wagon, and is transported inland to its final destination. This form of transport is designed as a fully integrated package, and allows for simplified movement techniques with the minimum of documentation and clearance formalities. Indeed, the INCOTERMS used for such transport movement have also been rationalised, with only a few INCOTERMS applying to such transport. Bills of Lading are arranged for the multimodal movement, and are generally in the form of Through Bills of Lading. In many cases, the container method used for such shipments is that of consolidation, with containers being consolidated at a central inland point as LCLs (less-than-full container loads), and then transported overseas to another inland destination, where the container load is deconsolidated and the individual cargoes are delivered to their respective customers. However, FCLs (full container loads) are also transported using this form of methodology, as the container load may be shipped by one specific shipper to another as a full load.

In such situations, carriers of the NVOCC or NVOC type will issue Bills of Lading on behalf of the shipping line for the carriage of goods on vessels which they neither own nor operate, but simply represent. The carrier is usually a freight forwarder issuing a "House" Bill of Lading for a container or trailer movement, or, in the case of intra-European shipments, a CMR consignment note. In the case of deep-sea container movements, the shipping line or their appointed agent will issue a "Master" Bill of Lading covering the container itself, covering the slot charter for the container on board the vessel. The Master Bill of Lading is derived from the information sent by the NVOCC to the shipping agent in advance of the shipment which forms the basis for the cargo manifest, the overall document detailing all containers to be loaded aboard vessel. Once the container has been loaded aboard vessel, the Master Bill of Lading is issued, and this must reconcile against the House Bills covering all the cargoes in that particular container. The NVOC or NVOCC is also responsible for arranging and submitting the individual Export Customs Declarations for all the cargoes loaded inside the container, as these must be pre-lodged on the electronic customs system prior to the cargo being despatched to the port of loading. Once the container has been loaded and each individual declaration submitted, a master export declaration covering the entire container load can then be submitted, for the purpose of loading the container aboard vessel.

The NVOCC or NVOC allows shipping companies to concentrate on ship management and the freight forwarder to use his own expertise and specialist knowledge in marketing and cargo consolidation/groupage. However, the principle of multi-modalism requires a good infrastructure to enable it to operate efficiently and effectively, thus it involves a dedicated service using NVOCC or NVOC arrangements.

There are various reasons why shippers favour multi-modalism:

- the service is reliable, frequent and competitively priced;
- goods arrive within a scheduled programme involving various transport modes and carriers operating in different countries;
- in many companies it features as a global network either as a supply or a retail chain;
- many companies operate a "just-in-time" strategy, requiring dedicated and integrated schedules for the delivery of their products within the shipper's warehouse and distribution arrangements;
- the service is tailor-made to the trade or commodities it serves involving purpose-built equipment, providing adequate protection to the goods and arrival at the buyer's premises in excellent condition;
- it has a high profile in the transportation and logistics sector;
- the documentation requirements are minimal with the Combined Transport Bill of Lading involving one through freight rate and a common code of conditions;
- multi-modalism involves quick transit times, thus speeding up the logistics process;
- there is a high level of facilities provided for such activities at the terminal warehouse, including state-of-the-art warehousing and storage systems inside purpose-built facilities.

The NVOCC is thus in a position to offer a wide range of activities and services to the trader, and thus cater for the ever-changing needs and requirements associated with the present demands of international trade. Their professionalism is an evident requirement, as there is a need to maintain a relationship not only with the trader but also with the shipping lines and liner agents on a constant basis, in order to facilitate a smooth and efficient freight flow system. As more trade is undertaken by container means, so the increasing need exists for the NVOCC to facilitate such freight movements across the globe, especially as ports become increasingly congested and the need exists to deal with container movements and loading/unloading facilities inland, far removed from the port itself.

3.4 Shipping Lines and Liner Trades

The shipping line operates the vessels carrying the goods, or charters the vessels to another company undertaking to operate a carriage service. It carries the cargoes, but leaves the arrangements for the booking of cargo aboard vessel to the agents, as well as all loading and unloading activities. In this respect, the shipping line becomes responsible solely for the management, maintenance and operation of the vessel, as well as the employment of its crew. In many cases, however, it may devolve the management of the vessel to separate independent vessel management companies, who take charge of the day-to-day management of the ship owner's vessels and charge a fixed fee for this service. In summary, the ship owner may own the vessel but may not necessarily manage it. The ship owner simply enjoys the profit gained from the vessel's operation, but leaves the administration and management of the vessel to other outside parties. Furthermore, ship owners have chosen to devolve the actual ownership and registration of vessels to overseas companies for tax reasons, to avoid heavy tax burdens for operations conducted from their own country. In many cases, the actual shipowner is a bank, or a collection of wealthy individuals who pool some of their financial resources with others to take a share in a vessel or several vessels. They in turn allow the vessel to be operated by a shipping line, which operates and manages the vessel on a management basis.

Historically, the shipping line used to be a company which was simply involved in the maritime carriage of cargoes from one international seaport to another. It had little involvement with the inland movement of cargoes, as these would be arranged and managed by inland haulage companies separate from the shipping line, especially in the days before containers appeared on the scene and general cargo was the norm. Since containerisation, the role of the shipping line has radically changed, with most major shipping lines offering a variety of service, from maritime carriage to inland haulage, freight forwarding, agency and storage. In today's fast-moving logistics sector, the shipping line has become the instrument of the integrated movement of goods from one place to another, dealing with every aspect of freight movements. Whereas at one time, the shipping line would offer freight rates from one port to another using traditional INCOTERMS such as FOB or CIF, the present-day shipping line will offer freight rates for the entire door-to-door journey, along with all associated services.

Another change of role for the shipping line is that of the maritime service offered. The historical role of many shipping lines was that of tramp operations, where vessels steamed from port to port picking up business as it arose, and without a fixed schedule of services. Sailings were based on demand for cargo carrying services, and in many cases, a vessel would not sail until its cargo-carrying capacity was filled. As demand for trade on certain routes increased, so the need arose for more guaranteed services on the routes concerned, and scheduled steamship services were duly introduced. The introduction of what became known as the "liner" service in the late 19th century changed this method of operation by offering fixed services and schedules along with specific vessels operating on specific routes. Bookings for cargo space on board vessel are made in advance although there is no guarantee that the vessel will sail filled to capacity, as the vessel will sail according to its fixed schedule. Indeed, owing to significant trade imbalances throughout the world, many sailings are made on the basis of the relocation of empty containers, rather than pure revenue-earning services, especially on those between Europe and the Far East. Present-day liner services operate around the containerised market, with specific shipping lines offering specified scheduled services on most routes.

The liner company must charge an economical price that covers all its costs, as if this is not achieved, then the shipping company would sooner or later go out of business. Costs may be fixed or variable, depending upon the frequency of service and the capacity of the vessel. The cost of running a vessel may be fixed, as there is a defined cost per day for running a vessel. Freight costs may be variable, in that these are not incurred if there is no cargo. In the case of the double voyage (i.e. an outbound and return voyage) and where there is a severe trade imbalance, then the shipping line must ensure that the cost it charges for whichever sailing earns significant revenue also accounts for, and compensates for, the sailing where little revenue is earned. Hence the imbalance in freight rates between sailings from the Far East to Europe and vice versa.

Demand for liner services depends upon a variety of factors, which can be categorised as follows:

- *Freight cost.* The charge for transporting the container from origin to destination, including additional costs such as terminal handling charges, customs clearance and storage.
- *Frequency of sailings.* Maritime transport is one stage in the overall production process and the international supply chain. Frequent sailings offer the manufacturer or producer the opportunity to service one-

off orders rapidly and enable the producer to reduce the level of stocks held at each end of the transport operation.

- *Transit time door-to-door.* On long voyages, especially in the case of high-value products, the speed of transit may be a major consideration owing to the cost of inventory, as well as the need to include lead times for delivery of the consignment.
- *Reliability of timekeeping.* On deep-sea routes, the liner service is the supplier's only direct link to the export market and is customers. Most shippers are likely to value the reliability of the service. In this respect, adherence to fixed schedules and punctual pick-up and delivery times are very important.
- *Reliability of administration.* Shippers value prompt and accurate administration. The ability to provide timely and accurate quotations, accurate documentation, including Bills of Lading and manifests, prompt notices of arrival, accurate invoices, and the resolution of problems when they arise, all play a significant role in the customer's evaluation of the liner company's performance.
- *Professionalism.* Shippers need to know they can rely on the services of the liner company. The knowledge of the contact at the liner company about the business is a vital aspect of the business, in order to raise the confidence of the shipper that the cargo will be handled and shipped correctly, efficiently and punctually. Professional knowledge of the business means that there is less likelihood of major problems arising, especially through the competence of the liner company and its employees to carry out all relevant tasks and resolve potential problems effectively and in a satisfactory fashion.
- *Space availability.* The ability of the service to accept cargo, even at short notice, may be valued by businesses that are not able to plan their transport requirements far in advance.

Most shippers will look for a combination of these factors, although it would appear that there is no clear pattern of preferences which applies to all shippers. Different shippers often require different results.

3.5 Liner Conferences

In many cases, shipping lines operate independently of each other, plying the ocean waves in competition with other shipping lines. However, in many cases, shipping lines pool their resources on several routes, a process known as "conferences". These conferences agree the following issues:

- the pooling of maritime resources, including vessels and agents;
- common pricing and tariff arrangements, also known as price-fixing;
- stability of freight rates, guaranteeing forward contracts for carriage;
- conference terms;
- conditions of carriage;

- the number and types of vessel each member will contribute;
- timetables for sailings;
- greater frequency of sailings, with more guarantees for the arranging of container transport on the vessels concerned;
- the pooling of revenues earned for such services;
- guaranteed sailing schedules;
- equality of treatment;
- economies of service.

Many shipping routes around the world, especially those from the Far East westbound and eastbound, are operated by several shipping lines, especially with regard to the movement of containers. Because of the number of shipping lines on these routes, especially between the Far East and Europe, an arrangement arose some time ago to pool shipping resources, as well as fixing freight rates throughout the group of companies operating the routes. This arrangement is known as a conference, referred to as a "liner conference", "freight conference" or "shipping conference" and involves several shipping lines on the same route. In principle, all the lines concerned offer a joint service, although there may be variations in the ports served as part of the routes between the Far East and Europe.

A conference secretariat is organised and often run by one of the members, which co-ordinates activities for and on behalf of the whole conference. Each member shipping line may still make its own cargo bookings for its own vessels, or it may pool the business in the form of a slot charter arrangement, so that a container from one shipping line may be carried on a vessel of either that shipping line or another line within the conference arrangement, depending upon:

- when the container arrives at the port of loading;
- when the container is required at its destination;
- which vessel is sailing first;
- available space aboard vessel.

Pool accounts for the conference are produced annually and income and expenditure is apportioned out between the members in accordance with their level of contribution to the service. As business fluctuates, members may contribute more vessels to the service or withdraw vessels from a particular pool. If business declines sharply, members may withdraw their vessels completely from the service, but may remain members of the conference and contribute freight to the pool, thus continuing to share in the profits.

The conference system originated in the mid-1870s, when it was found that competition between shipping lines on the high seas was forcing tariffs down to such levels that companies simply could not cover their costs. As competition got stiffer, so freight rates fell. As more vessels were built, so capacity increased to the point that there was excess capacity. Trade was also seasonal, especially in agricultural products, so that for much of the year the vessels were only partially full. Coupled with this, there was also an imbalance between eastbound and westbound trade, with demand for shipping space from China to the UK greatly exceeding that of space from the UK to China, a situation which is equally prevalent in the present day. Eastbound, there was therefore more shipping space than cargo. In today's market, the same situation exists concerning the shipment of containers, with empty containers being relocated to the Far East from Europe. It was found in the 1870s, that because of such imbalances in trade and the fact that several shipping lines were regularly engaged in the same shipping trade, that they would be in a much better position if they formed a cartel to fix rates to maintain viable business levels. The lack of government control over ocean freight rates, despite the attempts by the GATS (General Agreement on Trade in Services) to liberalise world shipping markets, meant that the liner conferences had a free rein in setting their own tariffs without any external interference.

The first conference was formed in 1875 by the lines trading between the UK and Calcutta. Because of the fixed rates applying to this service, some merchants threatened not to use the conference and to use vessels outside the conference that would offer lower rates. In 1877, a reduction in freight rates was made to merchants who shipped exclusively with the conference for a period of six months. However, the rebate was not paid until a further six months had elapsed, during which time the rebate was withheld if the merchant used a vessel owned by a shipping line which was not a member of the conference. This effectively meant that shippers who were tempted by lower prices of non-conference lines stood to lose a substantial sum of money from the conference lines if they accepted the non-conference prices.

Over the next hundred years, further networks of shipping agreements emerged, covering freight rates, the number of sailings, ports served, the goods carried, and the sharing of freight revenues (i.e. the pooling arrangements of the lines and vessels). Two forms of conference type emerged: the *closed conference* and the *open conference*. The *closed* conference controls membership, shares cargo and uses price discrimination to encourage the major shippers to ship exclusively with the conference lines, by way of the use of a lower "contract" rate given to loyal shippers, with a higher rate for shippers who sometimes use outside operators (i.e. non-conference lines). *Open* conferences allow any company to join provided they comply with the freight rate agreements. Members are thus guaranteed the prices set by the conference, but, since there is no control on the number of vessels in service, open conferences are more vulnerable to over-tonnaging on the basis of there being an over-capacity of vessels in service on the same routes. And as the size of vessels increases in terms of both gross tonnage and TEU container capacity, then over-capacity becomes a major issue, especially where the relocation of empty containers is concerned. So important did the conference system become, that in the early 1970s there were over 360 conferences worldwide, with membership ranging from two to 40 shipping lines in some conferences.

There are, however, disadvantages with conference arrangements. The shipper is tied to using such conferences for trade between certain parts of the world, and cannot use other forms of carriage such as tramp or *ad hoc* services which operate according to demand or need. Furthermore, with conference services, the freight rates are fixed and discounts for larger frequency use are not available. In this respect, conference operators are able to raise or lower freight rates at will, as well as imposing BAF (bunker adjustment factor) or CAF (currency adjustment factor) surcharges as they choose. With the fluctuation in oil prices, such charges become more prevalent, and can add significant amounts of money to existing freight rates. The UNCTAD (United Nations Conference on Trade and Development) concluded a Liner Conference Code in April 1974, which effectively limited the power and extent of liner conferences, allowing the developing nations to maintain their own liner fleets and thus have a more economical share in the world maritime market. This entered into force in October 1983. However, the conference system still exists, and is very much prevalent on the North Atlantic and Far East trade routes, although the main beneficiaries of this system are the European shipping lines dominated by the Maersk Line, Hapag-Lloyd, CMA-CGM and Mediterranean Shipping Company (MSC), along with other notable carriers such as OOCL and NYK. In the main, the Far East-based shipping lines such as Mitsui-OSK (MOL), Nippon Yusen Kaisha (NYK), the "K" Line and Evergreen have not ventured into conference arrangements, preferring to operate independently of each other as they know that the market is large enough and buoyant enough to sustain all their operations. Despite the efforts of the UNCTAD, the conference system is alive and well and operating on a large scale throughout the world.

Conferences are seen by many as cartels, seeking to control the shipping market by collective oligopoly, an economic factor seen by many authorities, including the European Union, as anti-competitive. The Far East Freight Conference (FEFC) was challenged by legal means in 1887 by the Mogul Line, when the latter sought an injunction to stop the FEFC from refusing rebates to shippers using Mogul Line vessels. Mogul Line had itself applied for membership of the FEFC, but was refused because it did not bear a full share of running regular services at off-peak periods. However, following a protracted war between the Mogul Line and the FEFC, the injunction was refused, thus confirming the legality of the conference. By the 1950s, the conference system had reached its zenith, and the dominance of the conferences over the liner shipping market was illustrated by the UNCTAD Code of Conduct for Liner Conferences which was initiated at the first UNCTAD conference in Geneva, Switzerland, in 1964. The issue concerned the emergence of the developing countries, many of which had gained their independence in the previous decade, and which sought to establish their own national shipping lines to boost their fledgling economies. However, the establishment of these new shipping lines was not supported by the dominant liner conferences, and in any case, the emerging nations lacked the power and experience in the maritime field and the liner shipping business to further their cause. This led to political action by the so-called "Group of 77", a pressure group of 77 developing countries within the UNCTAD framework, which resulted in the UNCTAD Code which aimed to give each country the right to participate in the liner conferences servicing its trade.

The UNCTAD Code covers three main areas of liner shipping:

- The provision of the right to automatic conference membership for the national shipping lines of the countries served by the conference.
- A cargo-sharing formula which gives national shipping lines equal rights to participate in the volume of traffic generated by their mutual trade with third parties carrying the residual or remainder of cargo from their ports.
- Shipping conferences are required to consult shippers over freight rates, and national lines have the right of consent on all major conference decisions affecting the countries serviced.

The Code had its drawbacks. It took 20 years to develop, and was only ratified and fully implemented in 1983, although it was never ratified by the United States. By this time, the liner business had changed significantly, with some shipping lines merging and the complete disappearance of others. Further challenges emerged to the liner conference system, especially from the United States, which placed severe limitations on conference activities through the US Merchant Shipping Act (1984), and the European Union, which in 1986 implemented EC Regulation 4056 through the auspices of the European Commission Competition Directorate, which excluded liner conferences from European anti-trust law. By this time, the conference system had become seriously weakened, mainly as a result of legislation enacted by several governments worldwide and also because of a general view that the conference system was protectionist and sought to stifle competition. Worldwide regulatory authorities have long disapproved of the price-fixing arrangements of the liner conferences, although they have never been able to provide a practical alternative. Other regional agreements have emerged over several years, including the Trans-Pacific Discussion Agreement (TPDA) and the Trans-Atlantic Agreement (TAA), formed in 1992, which subsequently became a conference in its own right, the Trans-Atlantic Conference Agreement (TACA), in 1994, comprising Maersk Line, Atlantic Container Lines (ACL), Mediterranean Shipping Company (MSC), Nippon Yusen Kaisha (NYK) Line and Orient Overseas Container Line (OOCL). Others, such as Canada Maritime (now absorbed into Hapag-Lloyd) and COSCO, a recent arrival on the container run between the Port of Liverpool and the US, were not included. The Far East Freight Conference (FEFC), which is due to be abolished in October 2008, is much larger, comprising the following shipping lines:

- ANL Container Lines Pty Ltd;
- APL Co Pte Ltd (Singapore-based, part of Neptune Orient Lines);
- CMA CGM;
- CSAV Norasia;
- Egyptian National Shipping Company;
- Hapag-Lloyd AG;
- Hyundai Merchant Marine Company;
- Kawasaki Kisen Kaisha ("K" Line);
- Maersk Line;
- MISC Berhad;
- Mitsui OSK Lines (MOL);
- Mediterranean Shipping Company SA (MSC);
- Nippon Yusen Kaisha (NYK);
- Orient Overseas Container Line (OOCL);
- Safmarine;
- Yang Ming Marine Transport Corporation.

Others, such as Evergreen Line and COSCO, are not included in the conference.

Even considering its supposed weakness, 60% of the liner capacity on the major maritime routes belonged to some form of conference system by the 1990s, although the present-day open conference groups are somewhat different form the tightly-controlled closed conferences of the 1950s. However, the European Union has sought to limit the power of even these conferences, and has implemented legislation to outlaw the conference system in Europe by October 2008, replacing it with the European Liner Affairs Association (ELAA), which will operate under anti-cartel guidelines dictated by Brussels as from 2008. Whether the conference system survives elsewhere in the world depends upon the initiative of other national governments to implement the same anti-cartel legislation as the European Union. Although the principle of anti-cartel initiatives is to be applauded, there are drawbacks to the demise of the conference system. A fully competitive system allows for a pricing and freight rate free-for-all, with a return to the days prior to conference agreements when freight rates hit rock bottom. In a system of equal competition amongst all the shipping lines, if one line reduces its freight rates, then all the others have to follow suit, as failure to do so would result in the zero-sum game as defined by the principle of the game theory. A gain for one shipping line through reduced rates and hence increased business would result in loss for all the others, thus resulting in the formula $(+1, -1) = 0$. However, if all the shipping lines also reduce their rates, the shipping market could risk sliding towards a loss, with little profit being realised by any of the shipping lines as a result of the consequent succession in freight rate reductions. Sooner or later, profit reduction would force some of the smaller and less profitable shipping lines off the major routes and even out of business, or could force them into alliances and mergers, which would inevitably reduce the number of different shipping lines operating worldwide container liner services.

The conference system has also revealed the extent of the imbalance in freight traffic between the Far East and Europe/UK, and, to a certain extent, reveals the problems faced by the shipping lines once the conference system is abolished, especially concerning the economic imbalance of traffic movements.

The following tables shows the quantity of TEUs carried in each direction over the past six years:

Table 1: Europe–Far East container movements

Europe–Far East

	2002	2003	2004	2005	2006	2007
Westbound	2858493	3405620	3930914	4135473	5049837	6190655
Eastbound	1921565	2043168	2335380	2418178	2590463	2835320

Note that from 2005 onwards, westbound TEU traffic was double that of eastbound traffic.

Table 2: UK–Far East container movements

UK–Far East

	2003	2004	2005	2006	2007
Westbound	914241	1017098	1031868	1211359	1426755
Eastbound	282973	316607	377664	426947	497203

Source: Far East Freight Conference: www.fefclondon.com

Note that, in this case, westbound traffic to the UK is three times that of eastbound traffic to the Far East, thus showing a pronounced divergence in import/export figures. To this extent, there is a lesser imbalance concerning trade between the Far East and Europe than there is between the Far East and the UK.

A further drawback of the removal of the conference system is a risk of over-capacity, with the dominant shipping lines gaining the business from less-powerful lines, thus leading to the dominance of the largest shipping companies, as well as generating over-capacity on some routes. As the tonnage and container capacity of container vessels increases, the lines operating such vessels will seek more business to maintain the viability of such vessels, thus forcing the smaller vessels (and consequently their operators) off some routes.

The inevitability of such a policy is to eventually reduce the number of shipping lines operating on the major routes around the world.

3.6 The Customs Broker

In several countries throughout the world, the freight forwarder may have responsibility for the movement of the cargo, but does not necessarily have the power and authorisation to clear consignments through customs at the point of export or import. The national regime of such countries requires that all customs clearance be carried out by a licensed customs broker, who has taken the necessary examinations and gained the appropriate qualifications to be approved, authorised and licensed as a customs broker.

The customs broker is responsible for the submission of all import and export customs declarations to the National Customs Authority, and to take responsibility for the accuracy and content of those declarations on behalf of the importer or exporter. However, they are not usually the importer or exporter of record (i.e. the trader registered with the customs authority for import or export purposes) and thus still rely on the importer or exporter for the information necessary to correctly clear the consignment through customs controls. In the United States, Canada and Mexico, this regime is especially prevalent, as the customs authorities of each country require the services of qualified and authorised customs brokers for the clearance of all incoming and outgoing consignments through customs controls. The customs broker provides their services for both the importer or exporter and the freight forwarder, although in many cases the freight forwarder is also qualified as a licensed customs broker for the purposes of both import and export clearances through customs. The major international freight forwarding companies are also licensed customs brokers given the range of services they provide, and are also legally empowered to represent the importer or exporter when handling and arranging the shipment of their cargoes.

3.7 The Shipping Process

There is a generally-accepted sequence to the process, in terms of events associated with the shipment of the consignment. These are:

- the exporter notifies the freight forwarder of the consignment to be shipped;
- the freight agent contact the shipping line or shipping agent to book a container and a slot on board vessel;
- the freight agent arranges loading of the container and shipping documentation;
- the freight agent arranges the transport of the container to the port;
- the shipping agent receives the container at the port and arranges the loading of the container aboard vessel through the Port Authority;
- the shipping line transports the container to its port of destination;

- the shipping agent arranges the unloading of the container through the Port Authority at destination and contacts the freight agent/customs broker at the port of destination;
- the freight agent requests clearance instructions from the importer;
- the container is unloaded and documents are submitted for import clearance through customs by the clearing agent or customs broker;
- the consignment is delivered to the importer.

This process is standard for most shipments. Where consolidation and deconsolidation is concerned, other parties such as NVOCCs are involved, as the consignment will be consolidated and deconsolidated at a specific premises distant from the exporter and importer, as well as being cleared through customs for both import and export at such a premises for ease of convenience and practicality. Once the consignment has been cleared, arrangements can be made with the importer for the delivery of the consignment to the importer's premises.

4 ROLL-ON ROLL-OFF (RO-RO) SHIPMENTS

The Ro-Ro system of marine cargo management operates on a very different basis from deep sea operations by nature of its existence and function. There are several reasons for this difference, mainly because of the nature of Ro-Ro movements, the means of cargo transport aboard the vessel, and also because of the duration of the voyages involved. The Ro-Ro vehicle ferry system is also more simplified than deep sea movements, and requires less operating procedures and detailed transport documentation as a result.

Deep-sea shipments involve the carriage of either bulk cargoes or containerised cargoes. These shipments refer to the use of specific vessels, and require the arrangement of the shipment well in advance of the voyage. There may be a need for specific loading requirements, or the hiring of containers for the transport of the consignments in question. As a result, specific documentation is also required, mainly referring to the issuing of Bills of Lading for each consignment.

Ro-Ro vessels are somewhat like large, floating multi-storey trailer and car parks. They have large doors at their sterns or on their sides, or in some cases, both, to facilitate the simultaneous loading and unloading of both cars and commercial vehicles. Ramps are stretched from the shore to the vessel, and cargo is moved on and off the ship in trailers, using either their own tractors (accompanied) or tractors operated by the port authority (unaccompanied). Their purpose is to carry cars on one or two decks, and trailers on the other vehicle decks. The decks are arranged within the vessel in such a way that the vehicles enter at the stern, drive to the bow and swing round to face the stern again. There are no bow doors or moveable bow visors on the newer vessels, owing to certain disasters involving two ferries in particular, the Townsend

Thoresen vessel *Herald of Free Enterprise* out of Zeebrugge in 1987, and the Estline vessel *Estonia* out of Tallinn in 1994, both tragedies occurring because of the sudden ingress of water through the opened bow doors. Both sinkings resulted in a the tragic loss of a large number of lives, and safety measures were taken by the authorities to ensure that from then on, all ferries would be built with solid bows and only stern-accessed ramps and doors.

The size of Ro-Ro ferries has steadily grown over the decades, with the original cross-channel car ferries weighing little more than 2,500 tons, to the present leviathans of the Channel crossings weighing some 35,000 grt. The progressive scale of Ro-Ro vessel size has increased over some four decades. The original ferries on the North Sea route between Hull and Rotterdam, the *Norwind* and *Norwave*, both operated by North Sea Ferries, weighed 4,000 tons apiece. In 1974, they were succeeded by two larger ferries, pioneers in their size, the *Norland* and *Norstar*, each weighing 12,000 tons, and at the time the largest ferries of their kind. In turn, they were succeeded in 1987 by two much larger ferries, the *Norsea* and *Norsun*, both weighing over 31,000 tons, and at the time of introduction the largest ferries on any of the European waters, thus making the company North Sea Ferries a pioneer in ferry operations over several decades. In 1987, the *Norland* and *Norstar* were both lengthened for entry into service on the Hull-Zeebrugge route, increasing their overall tonnage to some 26,000 grt per vessel. There are much larger Ro-Ro vehicle ferries operating elsewhere, both on the North Sea and Scandinavian routes, with the largest ferries operating on the P&O Ferries North Sea route between Hull and Rotterdam, *Pride of Hull* and *Pride of Rotterdam*, each weighing some 60,000 grt, again the largest ferries afloat at the time of their construction in 2001, and two larger Ro-Ro vehicle ferries, *Color Fantasy* and *Color Magic*, built shortly afterwards, and operating for Color Line between Oslo (Norway) and Kiel (Germany), each weighing 74,000 grt. These vessels are even larger than many cruise liners, never mind their Ro-Ro counterparts elsewhere.

Where Ro-Ro movements are involved, such shipping requirements are not necessary. The nature of a Ro-Ro (Roll-On, Roll-Off) movement infers the loading of road trailers aboard vessel by the process of driving these trailers aboard vessel at the port of departure, and driving them off at the port of arrival. In this respect, the Ro-Ro system is often referred to as a moveable extension of the road, given that the actual trailer movement is an integrated movement from the seller's premises to that of the buyer, using any road or maritime infrastructure in between. The ferry acts as a moveable element within that road movement, and carries the trailer from one road network to another. The process of shipping documentation associated with Ro-Ro transport reflects this form of operation, with an International Consignment Note (CMR) issued for the entire journey from the seller's premises to the buyer's premises inclusive of both the road journey and the ferry crossing, rather than for the specific marine sector of the journey. Although the name of the vessel and the ferry company may often be stated on the CMR, this is not always the case, as the cargo booking aboard vessel may only be made at the last minute before the vehicle arrives at the port, or even when the vehicle actually arrives at the port of departure, especially in the case of the cross-channel voyages between Dover and Calais. For longer ferry voyages, it is essential to book a space aboard vessel in advance, to ensure that space is available in the next voyage, and that the ferry company has time to process all the information concerning the trailer and its cargo for the purposes of the trailer manifest. This is also the case where only one ferry service operates daily, as to miss one voyage would result in the trailer being delayed for a further 24 hours until the next sailing.

However, as far as the ferry company is concerned, the process still demands a definitive audit trail concerning the cargoes carried aboard vessel. The shipper and the road haulage operator are still required to submit all relevant information to the ferry operator in order to fulfil all aspects of the safety requirements relating to the carriage of goods by sea, and this requires the completion of a full cargo manifest by the ferry operator containing details of all trailers loaded aboard vessel and their contents. This information must therefore be contained in the consignment note issued by the road carrier, and must convey exact details of each shipment, especially where the carriage of hazardous or dangerous goods is involved. Such conditions are contained in the CMR Convention of 1956, which states in Article 2 that the carriage of goods by trailer is still covered by the provisions of the carriage of goods by sea as defined in the Carriage of Goods by Sea Act 1971, and thus places the same responsibilities of carriage on the marine carrier as would apply to a carrier of other forms of cargo by maritime means.

In this respect, last-minute bookings of cargoes are not always recommended, as there may be little time to ensure that all relevant information concerning the trailers aboard vessel can be conveyed to the vessel's master. It is therefore the duty of both the shipper and the road carrier to ensure that the journey is planned in advance wherever possible, and that all relevant information is conveyed to the ferry operator in sufficient time to ensure that such information can be included in the vessel's cargo manifest. The ISPS and IMDG requirements set out by the International Maritime Organisation (IMO) stipulate that all possible measures are to be taken to ensure that all necessary information pertaining to the cargo is correctly conveyed to the ferry operator in the same way that such information would be conveyed in advance to a deep sea shipping line, in order to ensure that suitable arrangements are made by the ferry operator for the carriage of such cargoes in accordance with the IMO regulations on such carriage by maritime means.

However, it is often the case that the shipper may not know which ferry operator is being used for the carriage of a specific shipment, or even the name of the vessel used, where more than one vessel operates the route, as in the case of the Dover-Calais route, which is operated by two companies, P&O

Ferries and SeaFrance. Throughout the day, there are many cross-Channel sailings, operated by five P&O vessels and three SeaFrance vessels, along with several more between Dover and Dunkerque, operated by Ro-Ro vessels of Norfolk Line, part of the Maersk Group. In many cases, the truck driver arrives at the port of either Dover or Calais, and books the vehicle on to the next available ferry, paying in the region of £100 for the crossing. This information is often only known by only the road carrier and the ferry operator, and is not divulged to the shipper. Such practices are not always to be recommended, as the shipper may be obliged to produce evidence of shipment for either customs and VAT purposes or because of insurance purposes.

Figure 4.1: Superfast ferry

Because of the nature of international shipments, it is essential that the shipper retains details of the means and date of the shipment for compliance purposes, even where the shipment is being arranged under Ex Works (EXW) conditions by the buyer. It is often the case that the buyer arranges all aspects of the shipment, including trailer consolidations, and does not send details of the international movement to the seller. Under data protection laws, neither the ferry operator nor the road carrier may be obliged to furnish the seller with such details, although under customs regulations and law, the seller is obliged to hold sufficient evidence as to prove that the shipment was made. Under such circumstances, a certificate of shipment may be issued by the carrier to show evidence that the consignment was shipped out of the exporter's country by a specific means. However, the buyer is still obliged to ensure that the correct information pertaining to all consignments involved in the shipment by trailer are conveyed to the ferry operator for regulatory and security reasons. In this way, the ferry operator is also obliged to issue the correct documentation relating to the Ro-Ro voyage and all costs associated therewith to the road carrier, for inclusion in their records as well as those of the ferry operator. The consignment note acts as both a receipt for the consignment as well as evidence of the contract of carriage, and under maritime law, this contract for a Ro-Ro voyage is as important as a contract of carriage aboard a deep-sea vessel. To this extent, because a marine voyage is involved in a Ro-Ro movement, there is a definitive and legal need for proof of carriage aboard a marine vessel in accordance with the Carriage of Goods by Sea Acts.

Ro-Ro carriage may be convenient, but it is no different from other forms of maritime carriage, in the sense that a clear audit trail is required for every cargo shipment carried by Ro-Ro means. Although the documentation may differ from deep-sea carriage, and the methods of carriage are more simple in their operation and practice, there is still a specific form of procedure required for Ro-Ro movements, and it is vital that this is understood by both the carrier and the agent. The Ro-Ro form of transport may be seen as a maritime extension of the road system, but it still obeys maritime rules and regulations, and is thus subject to the same overall maritime laws and regulations as other forms of maritime transport, especially as laid down by the rules and regulations contained in the 1974 SOLAS Convention implemented by the IMO. In this way, a strict set of documentation and procedures applies to Ro-Ro cargo management, with the need for evidence of both cargo manifests and other specific cargo documentation for all ferry sailings. These conditions are set out by the 1956 CMR Convention, and apply to all ferry services, both national and international. SOLAS rules apply to all commercial vessels, and Ro-Ro services are no exception. The master of a Ro-Ro vessel has the right to refuse to allow the loading of any cargo he has any doubt about, and can delay the loading of such shipments until he has more detailed information about the consignment in the trailer. Even road trailer cargoes carried on domestic ferry services such as those in Scottish waters between the Scottish mainland and the islands to the west and the north of Scotland are subject to the same rules as those carried on international ferry routes, and it is vital that the correct procedures are carried out with relation to such shipments. Given the ease with which road transport cargoes may be carried aboard such vessels, it is essential that the correct procedures are undertaken and the correct documentation is raised with regard to the carriage of road trailers aboard vessel.

Ro-Ro movements have significantly increased over several years, with the primary routes being those across the Channel between the UK and the continent. However, the Ro-Ro sector has always been seen as an abbreviated form of maritime transport, given the view that the vehicle ferry is little more than an extension of the road. The essence of the management of cargo using Ro-Ro facilities is that a proper audit trail is maintained by the shipper, the haulage company and the maritime carrier, as without such a trail, unnecessary breakdowns in communication occur and the safety and security of cargoes carried by such means can be compromised.

5 FREIGHT DOCUMENTATION

There is a standard regime for sea freight documentation, depending upon the documentary requirement by the shipper. For each form of maritime transport, there is a specific transport document, and it has different levels of significance depending upon the mode of maritime transport. If the shipment is of a deep-sea nature, then the documentation required will be either a Bill of Lading or a sea waybill. If the shipment is of a short-sea nature, then the documentation may be a Bill of Lading (if a container feeder vessel is used), a sea waybill or a CMR consignment note (if the consignment is loaded in a trailer for Ro-Ro ferry purposes). The main difference between the CMR consignment note and the Bill of Lading or sea waybill is that the consignment note covers the whole freight movement using the road trailer, and does not refer specifically to a ferry journey as part of that movement. However, all shipping documents refer to the vessel cargo manifest, which is the document showing all cargoes loaded aboard vessel, and which gives summary details of each cargo. In turn, a copy of the cargo manifest is always presented to the vessel's Master prior to the vessel's departure, and a mate's receipt is signed and handed back to the ship's agent prior to the vessel leaving port, as proof of receipt of the cargo aboard vessel.

5.1 The Bill of Lading

A Bill of Lading (often referred to by its full title, namely an Ocean or Marine Bill of Lading) is a receipt for goods shipped on board a vessel, signed by the person (or their representative, the agent) who contracts to carry them, and stating the conditions in which the goods were delivered to (and received by) the ship. It is not the actual contract, which is inferred from the action of the shipper or shipowner in delivering or receiving the cargo, but forms adequate evidence of the terms of the contract. It is also a document of title (ownership) to the goods which is the subject of the contract between the seller (exporter) and the buyer (importer). Furthermore, it may be seen as a proof of loading aboard vessel in its "shipped on board" format, and is therefore seen as proof of shipment of the consignment. It is therefore the most important commercial document in the process of international trade, and is used to control the delivery of goods transported by sea. It therefore has three primary functions:

- Document of title (ownership);
- Evidence of the contract of carriage;
- Receipt for the goods.

The history of the Bill of Lading dates back to an era where the master of the vessel actually purchased goods for resale overseas and carried them to their destination, where he sold them at a profit. During this time, the goods remained in the possession and thus ownership of the master of the vessel. As the size of vessels increased, so it became common for other parties to invest in these ventures, the master still purchasing the goods for his own account with the money invested which he would then sell at a profit elsewhere, this profit being divided among the investors. On this basis, such investment became the basis for insurance of cargo on the high seas. As international trade developed, so the vessel's master no longer purchased the commodities in his own right but carried goods on behalf of third parties (the owners of the goods, namely exporters (sellers) or importers (buyers)). The master received freight charges as payment for his services of carriage. As time progressed and vessel size increased further, the master became the servant of the shipowner, who became the carrier and thus the shipowner received the payment for carriage of the goods concerned. These developments meant that a secure method of identifying the rightful owner of the goods became essential (who was entitled to claim and receive the goods at the point of destination). Considering that communication between the point of loading and the point of unloading was to all effects non-existent, a foolproof system of identification was required. The answer was a document that would identify the seller (the original owner of the goods), giving the buyer (the new owner of the goods assuming his payment for the goods in question) the right to claim the goods at the point of destination (the port of unloading of the cargo) and also acting as proof of carriage so that freight (the cost of maritime carriage) could be charged. This document of affreightment was the forerunner of the Bill of Lading that is used today. There is historical evidence of the use of these documents as far back as the 16th century, and legal disputes relating to the use of these documents can be found in the 18th century, with an important principle, that of "negotiability" (a legally-recognised transfer) being established in law as far back as 1794. These disputes resulted in the Bills of Lading Act (1855), which was eventually repealed and replaced by the Carriage of Goods by Sea Act (1992), embodied in the Hague-Visby Rules (1992).

The Ocean (Marine) Bill of Lading contains or provides evidence of the contract of carriage between the carrier and the shipper, under which both the carrier and the shipper promise that the goods will be carried from the port of loading by maritime vessel and safely delivered at the port of discharge. During the voyage, the ownership of the goods will normally be transferred from the original seller to the ultimate buyer (deemed to be the receiver of the consignment) who will take delivery of the goods from the ship. Effectively, the Bill of Lading in its legal format places the responsibility for looking after the goods while in transit firmly in the hands of the carrier, who then becomes liable for the consignment in the event of loss or damage while the goods are in transit on the high seas. This responsibility is detailed the Carriage of Goods by Sea Acts in force in national legislation. The Bill of Lading is in reality only raised once the vessel has sailed, given that it is a document which proves that the consignment has been loaded aboard vessel, and is on its way to the port of destination. It is raised essentially from the cargo manifest, which is prepared in advance of the vessel being loaded, and details all cargoes to be loaded aboard vessel.

The main points incorporated in a Bill of Lading are listed as follows:

- the name of the carrier, agent or NVOCC;
- the name of the shipper (usually the exporter);
- the name of the carrying vessel;
- a full description of the cargo (provided it is not bulk cargo) including any shipping marks, individual package numbers in the consignment, contents, cubic measurement and gross weight;
- the marks and numbers identifying the goods;
- port of loading/shipment;
- port of unloading/discharge;
- full details of freight charges, when and where payable, whether freight prepaid or payable at destination (freight collect);
- name of consignee or, if the shipper prefers to withhold the consignee's name, the shipper's order (To the order of . . .);
- the terms of the contract of carriage;
- the date the goods were received for shipment and/or loaded aboard the vessel;
- the name and address of the notified party (the person to be notified on arrival of the shipment, usually the buyer);
- the number of Bills of Lading signed on behalf of the vessel's master or his agent, acknowledging receipt of the goods;
- the signature of the vessel's master or his agent and the date of signature.

There is also the clause stating that the consignment was "received in apparent good order and condition" by the carrier, which absolves the carrier from any liability in the case of the consignment arriving at the quayside already damaged. If damage has occurred to the consignment up to the point of receipt by the carrier, this clause is struck through, and the Bill becomes a "Claused" Bill of Lading, requiring the seller to assume responsibility for any damage to the consignment.

There are several types and forms of Bills of Lading, and these are as follows.

The shipped on board Bill of Lading

Under the Carriage of Goods by Sea Act 1971 (Hague-Visby Rules), the shipper can demand that the shipowner supplies Bills of Lading proving that the goods have actually been shipped, in other words, that they have been loaded aboard vessel and that the vessel has sailed from the port of departure.

This set of conditions is always required by a bank, especially where a letter of credit or cash against documents payment terms are used between seller and buyer. For these reasons, most Bill of Lading forms are already printed as shipped on board bills and commence with the words "Shipped in apparent good order and condition". It confirms that the goods are actually on board vessel.

The received Bill of Lading

This document is used where the words "shipped" or "shipped on board" do not appear on the Bill of Lading. The term simply confirms that the goods have been handed over to the shipowner or operator and are in their care. The cargo may be in the dock, warehouse or transit shed of the shipping line, or even inland at an inland clearance depot (ICD). This Bill, however, does not have the same meaning or importance as a "shipped on board" Bill, and the buyer, under a CIF or CFR contract, is not legally obliged to accept such a Bill for ultimate financial settlement through a bank unless provision has been made for this in the contract of sale. In general, forwarding agents will avoid handling "received bills" for their customers unless special circumstances require.

Through Bills of Lading

In many cases, it is necessary to use the services of two or more carriers to ship the goods to their final destination. The on-carriage may be either by a second vessel or by a different form of transport, e.g. the trans-shipment of a cargo such as a container of Scotch whisky from the Port of Grangemouth to Hong Kong via the Port of Rotterdam, or the use of rail freight to ship a containerised consignment from Liverpool via the Port of Montréal to Chicago. In the first example, a container feeder vessel ships the consignment to the Port of Rotterdam, and then the consignment is trans-shipped on to a larger deep-sea container vessel to the Port of Hong Kong. In the second example, the container vessel sails from Liverpool to the Port of Montréal, and then the consignment is trans-shipped on to a waiting container train for onward shipment to Chicago. In such cases, it would be very complicated and more expensive if the shipper had to arrange on-carriage themselves by employing an agent at the point of trans-shipment. Shipping companies, therefore, issue Bills of Lading which cover the whole transit, and the shipper deals only with the first carrier. In the case of the trans-shipment, the shipping agent will arrange the whole set of voyages, as well as the unloading and loading at the port of trans-shipment, and special Bills of Lading need to be prepared for such through-consigned cargo. This type of Bill enables a through rate to be quoted, and is growing in popularity, as well as necessity in many cases, with the development of containerisation. As hub-and-spoke container ship networks expand, especially with relation to European Ports, the trend is for more trans-shipment operations, with the large container vessels only visiting a few select ports which are capable of handling large-scale container operations, and then trans-shipping many of the containers on to smaller feeder vessels for onward shipment to other regional European Ports.

Groupage (Master) and house Bills of Lading

Another sector of the container business which is experiencing significant growth is the principle whereby consignments from individual consignors destined for several consignees located in the same country or region are forwarded as one single consolidated consignment in a single container load, classed as an LCL (Less-than-full container load). Each consignment is not large enough to completely fill the container, so it is grouped or consolidated with several other consignments at an inland depot, and is shipped as a container load to the port and on to the waiting vessel.

At the point of consolidation, the shipping line issues a Groupage Bill of Lading to the Forwarder or NVOCC. This is the Ocean Bill of Lading, and it shows a number of consignments of groupage of a certain weight and cubic measurement in a cargo manifest format, often supported by a load list. The forwarder then issues subsequent cross-referencing to the Ocean Bill of Lading (the Master Bill) through the house Bills of Lading, each Bill referring to the separate consignments within the groupage or consolidation. The house Bill is simply a receipt for the cargo and does not have the same status as the Ocean Bill of Lading (the Master Bill) issued by the shipping line. The advantages of grouping or consolidation include the following:

- Less packing;
- Lower insurance premiums;
- Quicker transits;
- Less risk of damage and pilferage;
- Lower rates when compared with such cargo being despatched as an individual parcel or consignment.

Trans-shipment Bill of Lading

In some respects, the Trans-shipment Bill of Lading is very similar to the Through Bill of Lading, but more often is issued by shipping companies when there is no direct service between two ports, but when the shipowner is prepared to trans-ship the cargo at an intermediate port at their expense. In the example used of the shipment of Scotch whisky out of the Port of Grangemouth to Hong Kong, a trans-shipment Bill of Lading could be used rather than a Through Bill of Lading, since there is no direct container vessel service between Grangemouth and Hong Kong. There is a need to trans-ship the container via a third port, such as Felixstowe or Rotterdam.

Combined transport Bill of Lading

With the development of combined transport operations such as sea and rail or sea and road, an increasing volume of both liner cargo trade and bulk cargo shipments will be carried involving the Bill of Lading being issued in association with a selected charter party. Details can be found in Notice 298 of the ICC/UNCTAD Rules pertaining to Combined Transport.

Negotiable FIATA combined transport Bill

This form of Bill of Lading is becoming increasingly common in international trade, and is a FIATA Bill of Lading (FBL), used as a combined transport document with negotiable status, in that it can be used as a document of title (ownership) and hence as collateral between seller and buyer for payment purposes. It has been developed by the International Federation of Forwarding Agents Associations (FIATA), and is acceptable under the ICC Rules Uniform Customs and Practice for Documentary Credits. The FIATA Bill of Lading should be stipulated in letters of credit where the forwarders' contract groupage service is to be utilised and a house Bill of Lading (which is normally non-negotiable) is to be issued. FIATA states that a forwarder issuing a FIATA Bill of Lading must comply with the following:

- the goods are in apparent good order and condition;
- the forwarder has received the consignment and has sole right of disposal;
- the details set out on the face of the FBL correspond exactly with the instructions the forwarder has received;
- the insurance details have been clarified—the FBL contains a specific delete option box which must be completed;
- the FBL clearly indicates whether one or more originals of the Bill have been issued.

The FIATA FBL terms create more shipper obligations in the areas of packing, general average, payment of charges and description of goods. Additional rights are also conferred on the forwarder in the areas of lien (right of ownership), routing of cargo and storage handling and transport of consignments.

FIATA multi-modal transport Bill of Lading

The FIATA Multi-Modal Transport Bill of Lading (MTBL) is recognised worldwide as a negotiable shipping document of title in line with the International Chamber of Commerce (ICC) Uniform Rules for such documents.

Container Bills of Lading

Containers are now the standard form of transport for most general cargoes, and as a result container Bills of Lading are commonly in use. They cover the goods from port to port or from inland point of departure to inland point of destination, usually an inland clearance depot or container base.

There are also various types of status of any Bill of Lading, and these are detailed as follows.

Negotiable Bills of Lading

If the words "or his or their assigns" are contained in the Bill of Lading, it is negotiable, along with the term "Negotiable Bill of Lading" at the top of the Bill. There are, however, variations in this terminology, for example, the word "bearer" may be inserted, or another party may be stated in the preamble to this phrase. Bills of Lading may be negotiable by endorsement or by transfer. If they are negotiable, the Bills are used as collateral by the seller to secure payment from the Buyer, especially where the "cash against documents" payment term is used. Each Bill must be individually signed by a representative of the agent or the shipping line, and then presented to the party exercising lien (right of ownership) over the goods.

Non-negotiable Bills of Lading

When the words "or his or their assigns" are deleted from the Bill of Lading, or the words "non-negotiable Bill of Lading" appear at the top of the Bill, the Bill of Lading is regarded as non-negotiable. The effect of this deletion is that the consignee (or other named party) cannot transfer the property or goods by transfer of the Bills to the buyer.

Clean Bills of Lading

Each Bill of Lading states the expression "received in apparent good order and condition", which refers to the cargo received by the shipping line. If this statement is not modified by the shipowner or vessel operator, the Bill of Lading is considered as "clean" or "unclaused". By issuing clean Bills of Lading, the shipowner or vessel operator admits their full liability of the cargo described in the Bill under the law and their contract with the shipper, while the cargo is in their care.

Claused Bills of Lading

If the shipowner or vessel operator does not agree with any of the statements made in the Bill of Lading, or knows that a cargo has been damaged prior to them receiving it at the port of loading, they will add a clause to this effect, or will strike out the "received in apparent good order and condition" clause on the Bill, thereby causing the Bill of Lading to be termed as "unclean", "foul" or "claused". There are many recurring types of such clauses including the following:

- inadequate packaging;
- unprotected machinery;
- second-hand cases;
- wet or stained cartons (especially in the case of alcoholic goods);
- damaged crates;
- cartons missing.

The clause "shipped on deck at owner's risk" may thus be considered to render a Bill claused under this heading. Such Bills would normally lead to the buyer seeking some form of compensation or replacement of goods from the seller, and can in some cases lead to total rejection of the consignment by the buyer.

The Bill of Lading is a complex document, and must be fully understood if it is to be used correctly. It is, after all, a legal document, in that it acts as evidence of the contract of carriage between the shipper and the shipowner or vessel operator. It also acts as a document of title (ownership of the goods), and therefore is seen as the means of collateral by which the seller may secure payment at some point in time for the goods being sold to the buyer, prior to the goods being delivered off the vessel at the port of destination. If the delivery of the goods from the ship at that point occurs before the Bills are submitted to the consignee, then the Bill of Lading is considered to be stale, and thus invalid. A cargo cannot normally be delivered by the ship owner to the importer or receiver of the consignment without the valid Bill of Lading, and the late arrival of this all-important document may have undesirable consequences such as demurrage costs or warehouse rent at the port.

5.2 The Sea Waybill

The sea waybill is also a maritime transport document, but unlike a Bill of Lading, it is not a negotiable document, and therefore does not have the status of a document of title. It is, however, still seen as evidence of a contract of carriage between the ship owner or vessel operator and the shipper, and is also a document of receipt for the goods by the shipping line. It is more often used for short-sea shipments, as the time taken to transport such consignments is in the nature of some 24 hours, especially in the case of shipments through European waters, and there is no time to consider the use of the Bill of Lading as a negotiable instrument between seller and buyer. The sea waybill is also used where there is no specific need for the evidence of transfer of title from seller to buyer on the grounds of different means of payment terms between the two parties, and this means that the legalities of a Bill of Lading are not required.

5.3 The CMR Consignment Note

The CMR (Consigne de Marchandise Routière) consignment note is a transport document, but without the same legality as a Bill of Lading. In some ways, its function is similar to that of a sea waybill, except that it covers a road transport journey, usually with an element of sea transport integrated within it, namely a short sea Ro-Ro ferry crossing. The CMR consignment note is issued by the road haulage company for the consignment within a trailer load, is transferred to the shipper through the freight forwarder and includes any arrangements to ship the goods by Ro-Ro ferry where appropriate, especially where the consignment is travelling form the UK to a continental destination. The consignment note can cover not only the consignment itself, but also the entire trailer load where required.

In general, the maritime element of the journey is not specified on the consignment note, as in many ways the Ro-Ro ferry is only considered an extension of the roadway, but in reality a distinct booking must be made by the haulier with the ferry operator for the loading of the trailer on board the vessel, which is then seen as a maritime contract of carriage in its own right. However, there is a box on the CMR detailing any successive carriers, and the name of the ferry company could be inserted in this space on the note.

Even if the shipper is not aware of the short sea Ro-Ro ferry route taken by the trailer, the haulier is aware of it, as not only is the responsibility of the ferry crossing on the shoulders of the haulage company, but also the cost of the journey must be taken into account by the haulage company and included in the freight invoice to the shipper, even where the ferry crossing is booked and paid for at the last minute, often by the driver of the vehicle himself. However, because of the nature of road haulage and the expediency of using the least-cost means of shipment, the haulage contractor may not decide until the last minute which ferry crossing the trailer is to take. Therefore, it is not always expedient to book a ferry crossing well in advance, as the choice of ferry service may only be made while the trailer is on the move. This does not mean that the trailer is always accompanied by the driver; in many cases, the tractor is removed from the trailer prior to loading aboard vessel and the trailer is moved onto the ferry by a separate tug, which leaves the trailer on board and drives off the ferry prior to its departure. The trailer is carried in an unaccompanied state to the port of destination, where it is driven off the vessel by another tug and is collected by a waiting driver in his own tractor unit ready for onward transport to its final destination. As long as the correct documentation refers to the trailer load, then the carriage may be undertaken without issue.

Ferry companies are in stiff competition with each other and it is the cost, expediency and convenience factors which will ultimately influence the trailer operator as to which ferry service will be used for a particular journey, which is why, in many cases, the details of the ferry company and the specific sea crossing may not be included in the consignment note when it is raised and issued to the shipper. It is often the case that on a journey from one country to another, the road haulage operator may only decide at the last minute which ferry service is to be used across the Channel or North Sea, as there may be little time to arrange the crossing once the trailer is on the move from its point of loading. For convenience purposes, many haulage companies elect to take the shortest crossing of the Channel, namely Dover-Calais, which lasts only 1.5 hours. Even considering the cost of road diesel fuel, many road transport operators based in the north prefer to drive south to the Channel coast and use the shortest cross-channel route, rather than pay greater amounts of money to use the overnight sailings from the Tyne, Tees or Hull.

However, the 1956 CMR Convention requires the details of the ferry crossing to be included in the CMR note, as this determines the identification of the ferry company involved in the marine part of the journey, and thus places the ultimate responsibilities for the marine part of the carriage of the consignment on the shoulders of the ferry company. There is still the duty of care on the part of the trailer operator to inform the ferry company of the nature of the consignments inside the trailer, for the purposes of maritime regulations as dictated by the laws of Carriage of Goods by Sea, so that a cargo manifest may be issued and presented to the master of the ferry prior to its departure. If the master is not satisfied with the contents of the cargo manifest, or more specifically the contents of a trailer in particular, he may elect to refuse to allow the trailer on board the vessel, although this occurrence is not common.

Only where a case of damage or loss occurs to a trailer or consignment while the trailer is on board a ferry will any account of the sea voyage be taken, as in the aftermath of the disaster befalling the ferry *Herald of Free Enterprise* off the Belgian Coast in the late 1980s, when the ferry capsised shortly after departure from the Port of Zeebrugge, and all the cargoes and trailers on board were lost. Under such circumstances, the CMR consignment note can be used by a shipper to determine which ferry crossing was taken, so that action can be taken against the ferry company to secure compensation for any such loss or damage under the terms and appropriate Articles of the 1956 CMR Convention concerning the Carriage of Goods by Road, detailed earlier. It is thus important for the CMR document to contain full details of the ferry crossing as part of the overall trailer movement, including the date of sailing, the ferry company used and the name of the vessel, as without such information, the sea carrier concerned could not necessarily be made liable for any damage caused to a consignment while aboard the vessel.

5.4 The Cargo Manifest

The cargo manifest is often overlooked as a freight document, in that it is not normally issued to either seller or buyer, but it nevertheless plays a vital role in the process of the movement of goods by sea. The cargo manifest is the first main document to be produced by the agent for all shipments being loaded aboard the vessel. It is based on the load list submitted for the contents of every container, or even a list of all cargoes being loaded aboard a general cargo vessel, and details those cargoes to be loaded aboard the vessel. In the case of a container vessel, it details all the containers to be loaded aboard the vessel and the contents of each container. It is from this information that the Bill of Lading can be derived, although on many occasions, the Export Cargo Shipping Instructions (ECSI) will perform the same function.

There are several copies of the cargo manifest, and these are kept by the following parties:

- the vessel;
- the shipping line;
- the shipping agent at the port of departure;
- the shipping agent at the port of arrival;
- export customs;
- import customs.

It is vital that a copy of the cargo manifest is kept on board the vessel, as this performs three distinct functions;

- It notifies the Master of the vessel of all cargoes aboard vessel;
- It acts as the Master's receipt for such cargoes;
- It acts as a legal function verifying that the Master of the vessel is fully aware of the cargoes he is carrying.

Under the Carriage of Goods by Sea Acts, the Master of the vessel is fully responsible as the carrier's representative for all cargoes carried aboard vessel, and therefore must be fully aware of all the cargoes carried by that vessel, especially in the case of accidents or emergencies, should action be required to limit damage or problems which might endanger and prejudice the safety of the vessel and its crew. In this respect, the cargo manifest is also specified as an IMO FAL Document (FAL Form 2), one of the main maritime documents as specified by the International Maritime Organisation (IMO). The FAL Form 2 is the IMO Cargo Declaration and nowadays it is transmitted and stored by electronic means, especially in its function as a Customs Cargo Report (CUSCAR). The electronic CUSCAR message can be used as:

- arrival declaration;
- departure declaration.

It enables the customs authority to check the details of the vessel's cargo in advance of the arrival of the vessel at port, and also enables the customs authority to select containers and cargoes for examination, where deemed appropriate. However, the cargo manifest is not sent to the shipper, on the grounds that it is not seen as evidence of the contract of carriage between the shipper and the carrier. The documents sent to the shipper (the Bills of Lading, reflect solely the subject of the contract—the individual cargo which is the interest of the shipper).

Whereas the IMO FAL Form 2 is an overall cargo declaration (now covered by the CUSCAR regime) as well as being a summary of all cargoes carried aboard a vessel, the marine Bill of Lading is an individual declaration and a documentary description of a specific cargo consignment, usually in a container, and also represents a specific cargo detailed in the cargo manifest. A specimen representative example of the IMO FAL Form 2, along with its electronic replacement, is shown in the Appendices following the text. An example of an ocean (marine) Bill of Lading is shown in Appendix 1.

There is a clause at the bottom right of the Bill, stating that the Goods are "*Received by the Carrier from Shipper in apparent good order and condition [unless otherwise noted herein]*" (i.e. that the carrier bears no responsibility for loss or damage to the consignment prior to receiving it at the appointed place). The Bill of Lading is issued following the departure of the vessel from the port of loading, thus proving, especially in the case of a shipped on board Bill of Lading, that the consignment was confirmed as having been loaded aboard vessel. This confirmation is supported by the evidence of an export declaration to customs, followed by a series of electronic messages confirming not only loading of the consignment aboard vessel but also the clearance of the vessel by customs and its subsequent departure. The cargo manifest in either its manual or electronic format, is produced by the port agents prior to the loading of the vessel. In the case of the US-led CT-PAT initiative, this is a legal requirement for all consignments to be exported to the United States since 2002, for the purposes of the presentation of the cargo manifest to US customs officials at the port of loading at least 24 hours prior to the vessel being loaded. Thus, for export purposes, a comprehensive reporting system exists, assuming that all consignments within a container are correctly detailed on a Bill of Lading, although anomalies pertaining to this accuracy of information are detailed in the following section. In the case of an FCL, this may be so, whereas in the case of an LCL groupage load, there is every possibility that only a generic description is given on the master Bill of Lading, which will also refer to and be referred to by the FAL 2 cargo manifest.

A further issue concerning the information supplied on a cargo manifest concerns the mixture of non-EU and EU consignments carried on various vessels. The EU Authorities have decreed that the issuers of the cargo manifest may voluntarily include details of EU-originating cargoes alongside details of non-EU cargoes on vessels which are moving between two or more EU Member States. Although this can include deep-sea container vessels, it is more likely to refer to short-sea container vessel services where the vessel may be part of a feeder service to link in with a deep-sea container service, or may simply be operating on a service between various EU ports independently of any feeder service. Such services also include authorised regular operators, who operate Ro-Ro Ferries in areas such as the North Sea and the Baltic Sea. Although the information they provide is more abbreviated and does not require the same detailed information as that supplied by deep-sea operators or charter services on the grounds of the frequency and regularity of their sailings, there is still the need for a manifest covering all trailer and container loads aboard vessel for each sailing, as the vessel may carry both EU-originating cargoes, or at least those cargoes deemed to be in EU duty-paid free circulation, as well as non-EU cargoes not in free circulation (i.e. those cargoes under Community transit status, on which import duty still has to be paid, or cargoes transiting the European Community territory en route for a non-EU destination). The EU-originating cargoes should be covered by a T2L document. This gives the consignments under this document EU treatment by the customs authority when they are unloaded at the EU port of destination.

These cases can be represented by the following matrix categorisation:

Table 3: The Community Transit (CT) matrix

EU-Originating consignments Duty Paid (T2L)	*Non-EU Consignments (Free Cir)* Duty Paid (T2L)*
Non-EU Consignments Duty to be paid on arrival at port	*Non-EU Consignments* Community transit—Leaving EU (T1)

* In reality, the non-originating consignment will be loaded aboard vessel at a port within the EU under Community Transit status, using a T1 document. Import duty and VAT will be paid at the point of declaration at the port of destination in the final country of destination.

A Bill of Lading has more distinct functions than does a cargo manifest. Whereas a manifest gives overall details of a set of cargoes, which can then be summarily scrutinised by the customs authority for the purpose of examination of a specific cargo or the container in which it is located at the port, a Bill of Lading will be used for the purpose of an import customs declaration, and may be scrutinised by a landing officer of the customs authority for details with relation to the assessment of import duties and taxes, which cannot be undertaken with a cargo manifest. Furthermore, the Bill of Lading has three distinct functions which do not relate to a cargo manifest. These are:

- document of title (ownership of the consignment);
- evidence of contract of carriage;
- receipt by the carrier for the consignment.

In these respects, the Bill of Lading is a legal document and can be used as collateral in the contract of sale, as well as proof of responsibility for the carriage of the shipment. In this respect, it may be used as legal evidence where a cargo manifest cannot. In cases where a Non-Vessel-Owning Common Carrier (NVOCC) (i.e. a shipping company which owns or leases containers but does not operate its own maritime vessels) issues Bills of Lading, the Bill will represent a slot charter (i.e. a transaction where the NVOCC has chartered space aboard a vessel owned by another shipping line for the purposes of shipping several containers to an overseas destination). In this case, there will not only be a Bill of Lading issued by the NVOCC, but also a further Bill of Lading issued by the carrier with respect to the containers owned by the NVOCC which will be passed from the carrier to the NVOCC. It should then be possible to trace every container carried by a container vessel with respect to the owners of the containers and hence the consignments loaded aboard each container. In reality, containers aboard vessel may be owned by various different NVOCC owners, as well as containing varying degrees of information pertaining to their respective loads. Given the increasing size of container vessels along with their capacity to carry larger numbers of containers (>8,000 TEUs), the relative facility to trace each container is becoming more complex and increasingly less straightforward, especially when it is admitted that the sheer quantity and volume of information held on a cargo manifest relating to such vessels is resulting in the manifest becoming more unmanageable, even in its CUSCAR electronic format. Imagine, therefore, that for every container loaded aboard such a vessel, there are even more Bills of Lading to raise, which infers more time being spent in raising such documents. Hence the increasing burden of work placed upon the companies, especially shipping agencies, issuing both Bills of Lading and cargo manifests every time a container vessel sails, and equally the risk of inadequate information being input to complete both a Bill of Lading and a cargo manifest, resulting in a failure on the part of the vessel's master to be fully aware of the consignments aboard vessel, let alone the risk of failure to fully report these cargoes to the port of arrival.

5.5 The T2L Document

The T2L is an EU Community status document used to transport consignments in EU free circulation by sea between two points within the EU under the following circumstances:

- by a non-EU flagged vessel;
- by a vessel which may not have started its journey from a non-EU port;
- by a vessel which may end its journey at a non-EU port;
- by a vessel carrying non-EU cargoes.

The document is usually raised by the shipping line or its agent representative, as this document is used for the purposes of landing and clearance once the cargo is landed at the port of arrival. The T2L is based on the details of the cargo provided by the shipper or their freight agent, and must be completed and issued prior to the cargo being loaded aboard vessel at the port of departure. It can be sent straight to the agents at the port of arrival, or it can accompany the manifest for the cargo on board vessel. The T2L can be replaced by a commercial invoice or shipping document, or a shipping company's cargo manifest. An invoice or transport document used as a Community status declaration must relate only to EU Community goods (i.e. goods in EU free circulation) and must contain the following information:

- the quantity, type of goods, marks and reference numbers of the packages;
- the full name and address of the consignor or the person concerned where this is not the consignor;
- the description of the goods;
- the gross mass in kilograms;
- container numbers, where appropriate;
- the symbol "T2L" or "T2LF", as appropriate;
- the declarant's signature.

A shipping company's manifest used as Community status declaration must include the following information:

- the name and full address of the shipping company;
- the name of the vessel;
- the place/port and date of loading of the cargo;
- the place/port of unloading of the cargo.

For each consignment, further information must be inserted, namely:

- a reference to the Bill of Lading or other commercial document;
- the number, description, marks or reference numbers of the packages;
- the normal trade description of the goods, including sufficient detail to permit their identification;
- the gross mass, in kilogrammes;
- the container identification number, if appropriate;
- the following entries for status of the goods, as appropriate:
  - the letter "C" (equivalent to T2L) for Community status goods;
  - The letter "F" (equivalent to T2LF) for Community status goods, consigned to or from a part of the Community customs territory where normal Community fiscal rules do not apply;
  - The letter "N" for all other goods.

The T2L is then submitted to customs by the shipping agent, so that the goods are to be cleared without the need for a full customs import entry, and are thus subject to normal intra-Community movement rules and regulations.

CHAPTER 5

LEGAL, FINANCIAL AND INSURANCE ISSUES

1 MARITIME CARGO LEGISLATION AND CARRIAGE CONTRACTS

There is a strict set of laws concerning the maritime carriage of goods, and these laws have been updated over the years on a regular basis, in accordance with the changes in shipping trends and the use of container transport. There are three main areas of law worth covering, some of which refer to UK legislation and others which concern international rules concerning the maritime transport of cargo. These are

- The Carriage of Goods at Sea Acts 1971 & 1992 (UK);
- The Hamburg Rules (International);
- The CMI/UNCITRAL project.

1.1 The Carriage of Goods at Sea Acts 1971 and 1992

The Carriage of Goods at Sea Acts were passed to define more closely the laws concerning the maritime transport of cargo from a UK perspective and incorporate the international laws passed concerning all maritime trading nations.

Contracts pertaining to the carriage of goods by sea are concerned with the legal relationship between the carrier and any person who is legally interested in the ship and the cargo aboard it. The emphasis of the law may be divided into two main areas: charterparties and contracts of affreightment represented by a Marine Bill of Lading. As far as charterparties are concerned, the concentration is on the rules of the common law governing the duties and undertakings of the carrier. These principles apply insofar as they have not been modified by contract.

The issue of charterparties was covered in a previous section, but the second area, namely that of Bills of Lading, is much wider and covers contracts of carriage governed by the Hague-Visby Rules (as incorporated in the *Carriage of Goods by Sea Act 1971 [COGSA]*). This is frequently the case with shippers of a small quantity of cargo who would naturally find chartering an entire vessel quite unsound and a non-viable business practice. Once the cargo has been loaded aboard vessel, the Bill of Lading as issued will act as a *prima facie* evidence of the contract of carriage. In view of the disparity in bargaining positions between the carrier and the shipper, the Hague-Visby Rules make

115

special provisions protecting the shipper from being exploited by the carrier. It is therefore impossible for either party to contract out of the Rules, unless it is to maske the terms more onerous or burdensome for the carrier. The duties, responsibilities and obligations laid down in the Rules are of great importance.

The Rules apply to all contracts of carriage of goods covered by a Bill of Lading or any other similar document of title (ownership) that relates to the carriage of goods by sea where the port of shipment is a port within the UK. Where the Bill of Lading relates to carriage between ports in two different States and it is issued in or the carriage is from a Contracting State, then the Rules will also apply. A third possibility is where the Bill of Lading contains the Rules themselves or incorporates the legislation of any State that gives effect to them.

The Rules impose the following duties on the carrier:

- the duty to make the ship seaworthy before and at the beginning of the voyage using due diligence;
- the duty to properly and carefully load, handle, stow, carry, keep, care for and discharge the goods;
- the duty to issue to the shipper on demand a Bill of Lading showing, *inter alia*, identification marks of the goods, the quantity or weight of the goods and the apparent order and condition of the goods;
- the duty not to deviate from the route agreed unless it is to save life or property at sea or other reasonable cause.

The second duty is, however, subject to the governance of certain exceptions. These include act, neglect or default of the vessel's master or other servants or employees of the carrier in the navigation or in the management of the ship, fire-caused damage, perils of the sea, *force majeure*, hostilities, latent or inherent defects or other elements seen as being prejudicial to the safety of the ship, its crew and its cargo (Article IV).

The *Carriage of Goods by Sea Act 1992* came into force on 16 September the same year and governs all contracts of carriage concluded on or after that date, as well as amending certain elements of the COGSA 1971. Unlike its predecessor, the Bills of Lading Act of 1855, which applied only to Bills of Lading, the provisions of the 1992 Act also cover sea waybills and ship's delivery orders. In the case of Bills of Lading, it is immaterial whether the document is a Shipped on Board or Received for Shipment Bill, although the former is the normal document issued by a shipping line in that it carries more weight as evidence that the cargo has been loaded on board the vessel, especially as it is only issued by the carrier once the vessel has sailed. The Secretary of State (for Transport) is also empowered to draft regulations extending the provisions of the Act to cover any electronic transmission of information which might in the future replace written or printed documentation.

The 1992 legislation covers two main departures from previous law:

- the title to sue is no longer linked to property in the goods (i.e. it is not restricted to the actual owner of the goods at the time of any accident or loss);
- the transfer of rights under a contract of carriage is effected independently of any transfer of liabilities.

The present law as defined by the 1992 Act can be stated as follows:

- Title to sue is now vested in the lawful holder of a Bill of Lading, the consignee identified in a sea waybill or the person entitled to delivery under a ship's delivery order, irrespective of whether or not they are owners of the goods covered by the document;
- The "lawful holder" of a Bill of Lading is defined as a person in possession of the Bill of Lading in good faith.

This person or party may be either:

- identified on the Bill as consignee; or
- an indorsee of the Bill; or
- a person who would have fallen within the above two categories if he had come into possession of the Bill before it ceased to be a document of title.

In short, any lawsuit is not restricted to the party holding the Bill of Lading as the owner of the consignment. Even if the consignee does not own the goods, especially under the terms of payment where payment is due at a future date as defined by credit terms or those of a Bill of Exchange, the holder of the goods under such terms may sue for loss or damage sustained during transit. The final provision as detailed above covers such a situation (i.e. where the goods are delivered to the buyer against a bank guarantee before the Bill comes into the possession of the consignee or an endorsee). Such arrangements concern sea waybills as much as they do marine Bills of Lading, especially where the Bill of Lading is non-negotiable and is thus not necessarily seen as a document of title or ownership.

The transfer of the right to sue under section 2(1) of the Act, from one lawful holder of a Bill of Lading to another, will cancel out the contractual rights of the shipper or of any intermediate holder of the Bill of Lading. This result will follow even if the shipper retains the property in the goods (i.e. ownership of the consignment) after such endorsement and he will not regain title to sue even though he regains possession of the relevant documents unless they have been re-endorsed back to him.

Since title to sue is divorced from ownership of the goods, a person with rights of lawsuit under section 2(1) of the Act may not have suffered personal loss or damage resulting from the carrier's breach of contract. In such an event, he is entitled to exercise rights of lawsuit for the benefit of the party who has actually suffered the loss, and will then hold any damages recovered from the carrier for the account of such person. This stated, although the holder of the Bill can sue on behalf of the other party, he is not placed under any obligation to do so by the 1992 Act.

Under section 3 of the 1992 Act, liabilities will only attach to persons or parties in whom rights of lawsuit are vested when they either:

- take or demand delivery of the goods; or
- make a claim under the contract of carriage; or
- took or demanded delivery of the goods before rights of lawsuit vested in them under section 2(1) of the 1992 Act.

The final provision covers the situation where the recipients (i.e. the intended buyers) took delivery of the goods against a bank indemnity before they became "lawful holders" of the relevant Bills of Lading within the meaning of the Act.

Finally, the 1992 Act provides that such a transfer of liabilities is without prejudice to the existing liabilities of the original party to the contract. Intermediate holders of the Bill of Lading will no longer incur liability under the contract of carriage once they have transferred title to sue to a subsequent holder of the Bill.

The provisions outlined above apply equally to the consignee identified in a sea waybill or the person entitled to delivery under a ship's delivery order. The former is entitled to sue on the contract evidenced by the sea waybill, and the latter to enforce the terms of the undertaking contained in the delivery order, but only with relation to the goods specifically covered by that order. Both will incur liability only when they seek to enforce the respective contractual undertakings. Sea waybills are by nature non-negotiable, as they no not have the provision of being a document of title (ownership), but they often contain provision for an alternative consignee to be nominated by the shipper. In such a case, title to sue will be transferred on the shipper instructing the carrier to deliver to a person other than the consignee named in the sea waybill.

1.2 The Hamburg Rules

The Hamburg Rules resulted from the need to consolidate and re-appraise the liability of carriers in the wake of modifications to the Hague Rules effected by the Brussels Protocol of 1968. These modifications did not gain universal approval throughout the world and were regarded by many cargo-owning companies merely as a temporary expedient and there was a growing demand for a re-appraisal of carrier liability. Such re-appraisal was designed to produce a comprehensive code covering all aspects of the contract of carriage. This initiative culminated in the drafting of a new Convention which was adopted in March 1978 at an international conference in Hamburg sponsored by the United Nations. The Convention, known as the "Hamburg Rules", became effective on 1 November 1992 on the expiration of one year from the date of deposit of the twentieth instrument of ratification, acceptance and approval or accession (Article 30(1)).

Instead of simply amending the Hague Rules, the Hamburg Rules adopted a new approach to cargo liability. Under these Rules, the carrier is held responsible for the loss of, or damage to, goods whilst in their care, unless they can prove that all reasonable measures to avoid damage or loss were taken. Carrier liability is extended to reflect the different categories of cargo now carried, new technology and loading methods, and other practical problems incurred by shippers such as losses incurred through delays in delivery.

Although 29 states adhered to the Convention as at 2004, no major maritime nation has ratified it to date, reflecting a general view that the Hamburg Rules have over-compensated in their effort to redress a perceived imbalance in the Hague Rules in favour of shipowners. To this extent, the Hamburg Rules cover less than 5% of total world maritime trade.

The Hamburg Rules apply to contracts of carriage by sea which are defined as "any contract whereby the carrier undertakes against payment of freight to carry goods by sea from one port to another". Where the contract takes into account some form of multimodal carriage (i.e. carriage involving more than another form of transport as well as maritime transport, the application of the Rules will be restricted to the sea leg of the journey). This approach differs significantly from that of either the Hague or Hague/Visby Rules which concentrate on "contracts of carriage covered by a Bill of Lading or any similar document of title". As far as the Hamburg Rules are concerned, it is immaterial whether a Bill of Lading or a non-negotiable receipt is issued and the definition of "Bill of Lading" in Article 1.7 is worded accordingly. However, the Hamburg Convention follows its predecessors in that its provisions are not applicable to charterparties or to Bills of Lading issued in accordance with them unless such a Bill "governs the relation between the carrier and the holder" (i.e. that it has been issued or negotiated to a party other than the charterer).

The application of the provisions of the Hamburg Convention is restricted to contracts of carriage by sea between ports in two different states, in that it does not apply to coastal trade between two ports of the same country (e.g. Grangemouth (Scotland) and Felixstowe (England)). The Hamburg Rules govern both inward and outward Bills of Lading, which is an important factor which must be taken into account by shipowners who trade with countries in which the Convention is effective. Provision is also made for the parties involved expressly to incorporate the Rules into the Bill of Lading or other document showing evidence of the contract.

The Hamburg Rules have adopted the argument that carrier liability should be based exclusively on fault and that a carrier should be responsible without exception for all loss of, and damage to, cargo in their care that results from their own fault or the fault of their servants or agents, unless they can prove that the carrier, their servants or employees or agents took all measures that could reasonably be required to avoid any detrimental occurrence or its consequences.

There are three recent occurrences where the Hamburg Rules must be questioned, namely the incidents involving the container vessels *CMA CGM Verdi*, *MSC Napoli* and *Hyundai Fortune*. All three cases involves the loss of cargo, although only two involve loss of cargo during storm conditions, although in the case of the *CMA CGM Verdi*, containers were actually washed overboard during a storm in the Bay of Biscay. The other incident, involving the *Hyundai Fortune*, involves an explosion in a container and subsequent fire aboard vessel.

The *CMA CGM Verdi*, owned by the French Line CMA CGM, was on an inbound voyage from the Far East into Europe in February 2006 when it encountered a violent storm in the Bay of Biscay. As a result of the rolling of the vessel, some 80 containers were washed overboard and many others were damaged while still locked on board the vessel's deck. The vessel docked at Southampton and an assessment was made of the damage, with the result that several claims were made against the carrier. Assuming that the carrier argued against liability, the argument would be that the incident occurred as a result of *force majeure* and not as a result of any negligence or fault on the part of the carrier. Insurance claims would be made against the carrier, and these could be resolved under the principle of General Average, where the pooled insurance premiums paid against all cargoes on board the vessel could be used to indemnify the parties which suffered loss as a result of the incident. The carrier's liability under the Law of Carriage of Goods at Sea, including the Hamburg Rules, would, however, be much more limited. However, the overall insurance claims resulting from the incident will impact upon many underwriters around the world given the damage sustained by the containers involved, and these claims may not necessarily be covered under the principle of General Average.

The case of the *MSC Napoli* is less clear-cut. The vessel, operated by the Mediterranean Shipping Company (MSC), was outbound from Europe bound for South Africa and beyond when she encountered difficulties in the Western part of the Channel in January 2007, during a storm. The hull of the vessel cracked and started taking on water, and the decision was made to beach the vessel in shallow water off Branscombe Beach, South-East Devon, close to Lyme Bay, rather than to attempt to tow the vessel to nearby Portland Harbour, for risk of damaging the vessel further and risk her capsizing. Once all containers were removed, the ship was partially broken up for the purpose of removal from the area. It transpired that the vessel had previously been involved in a grounding on a reef close to Singapore, and that her hull had been damaged in the process. She was subsequently repaired, and her hull was apparently strengthened. However, it would appear that the storm in the Channel in early 2007 may have caused further problems below the waterline, and this may have led to the calamity which she has now suffered. Although *force majeure* may have been a contributory factor, there is a question as to whether the ship should have been allowed to re-enter commercial service following her mishap off Singapore, and whether more serious long-term problems could have been precipitated as a result of her re-entry into service. Although the insurers were content enough to allow underwriters to shoulder the risk of maintaining cover on the vessel, it must now be questioned whether this was overall a prudent decision under the conditions and provisions of the Hamburg Rules, especially given the loss of many of her containers stowed above deck, and which were washed ashore on Branscombe Beach itself. There is therefore the question of whether some fault could be attributed to the owners of the vessel in allowing her to maintain commercial operations. The case is by no means settled yet, and is set to rumble on for some time to come.

The third case is that of the *Hyundai Fortune*, a container vessel belonging to Hyundai Marine which was on its way from the Far East to the Middle East and Europe in March 2006, when a serious explosion and fire ripped through the after-part of the ship off the Yemeni coast, close to the entrance to the Red Sea. The explosion is deemed to have occurred below deck in the area close to the engine room, damaging both the vessel's hull and the cargoes stowed on that part of the vessel. The fire spread to several containers, some of which contained dangerous goods in the form of fireworks destined for the European markets. Although the cause of the accident cannot be directly attributed to the cargo itself, which, in the case of the fireworks would undoubtedly have contributed to the inferno once it had spread to the containers involved, there is an inference that the dangerous cargo played a significant part in the fire. The hull was seriously damaged by the force of the explosion and there is every possibility that the only destination for the vessel is the breaker's yard. However, the stowage location of the containers holding the fireworks must be questioned, as experts have criticised their location on the vessel, claiming that the loaders and handling agents at the ports of loading should have recognised that no containers loaded with dangerous cargoes should ever be stowed close to or above the area of the vessel containing the engine room and the accommodation quarters, namely towards the stern of the vessel, which is where the containers holding the dangerous cargoes were located. It is considered that the greatest risk of problems occurs in this part of the vessel, where machinery and human activity take place, and that no dangerous cargoes should ever be stowed close by. In this case, it could be argued under the provisions of the Hamburg Rules (which were not ratified by the countries where the above respective shipping lines are based) that the shipowners were at fault for allowing such cargoes to be stowed in the location where they were and that equally their agents could be rendered at fault for having allowed such stowage, assuming that they were in full knowledge of the contents of the containers concerned. Indeed, certain insurers based in London have expressed concern that with certain shipping lines refusing to handle potentially unstable cargoes, shippers may be deliberately not declaring the contents of many containers, thus putting vessels and the lives of crews in danger (Hazcheck

Systems, www.hazcheck.com). Not only would such actions contravene the provisions of the Hamburg Rules with reference to the carrier's liability, but they would also contravene the conditions of the UN's SOLAS (Safety of Lives at Sea) Convention.

The application of the Hamburg Rules to such incidents varies. The purpose of the Rules was to remove the inconsistencies associated with the Hague and Hague/Visby Rules. Under the latter, the obligation of the carrier to provide a seaworthy ship was limited to a duty to exercise "due diligence", while he was required to look "properly and carefully" after the cargo throughout the carriage. Under the Hamburg Rules, the carrier's duty and responsibility to provide a seaworthy ship is to be assessed and judged on the same basis as his duty and responsibility towards the cargo and both sets of obligations are to apply and operate throughout the period of carriage. The only issue remaining to be resolved is the interpretation to be placed by the national courts on the carrier's duty to take "all measures that could reasonably be required to avoid the occurrence and its consequences". This issue alone brings into question the duty exercised by the carrier in the cases of both the *MSC Napoli* and the *Hyundai Fortune*, especially in the case of the latter. Given the fact that in each of the three cases mentioned, the cargo to be lost was stowed above deck, this is covered in Article 9 of the Convention, where deck cargo is treated as normal cargo and is thus subject to the Rules, where it is shipped "in an accordance with an agreement with the shipper, or with the usage of the particular trade or is required by statutory rules or regulations". Cargo shipped on deck by agreement with the shipper must be recorded on the Bill of Lading, otherwise the carrier will have the burden of proving its existence. In the case where the cargo is mis-declared, such burden of proof may shift to the shipper, who was seeking to mislead the carrier concerning the stowage of the cargo. Should the cargo be shipped on deck without consent or authority, this would no longer constitute a fundamental breach of contract, but the carrier's liability for loss, damage or delay in delivery would be restricted to that "resulting solely from the carriage on deck".

The Convention obliges the carrier to issue a Bill of Lading once the goods have been taken into his charge, and the Bill of Lading requires the stating of the general nature of the goods, all necessary marks and numbers required for the identification of the goods, an express statement, where applicable, relating to the dangerous character of the goods (e.g. the fireworks contained in the containers on board the *Hyundai Fortune*), the number of packages or pieces and the weight of the goods or their quantity otherwise expressed, all such particulars as furnished by the shipper (Article 14). The carrier is also required to acknowledge the apparent condition of the goods, as expressed by the specific clause contained on the Bill of Lading. Once the goods have been loaded aboard vessel, the shipper is also entitled to demand a "Shipped on Board" Bill of Lading which must state that the goods are on board a named ship or ships together with the date of loading (Article 15.2). In return, the shipper is required to indemnify the carrier against any loss resulting from inaccuracies in the particulars supplied by him.

The Hamburg Rules introduce three new requirements for the shipment of dangerous goods. These are:

- the shipper must mark or label the goods in such a way as to indicate that they are dangerous;
- the shipper must inform the carrier of the dangerous character of the goods and of any necessary precautions to be taken; and
- the Bill of Lading must include an express statement that the goods are dangerous.

Otherwise, the sanctions for failure to comply with these requirements are more or less identical with those provided in the Hague and Hague/Visby Rules. If the seller fails to disclose the dangerous nature of the goods, and the carrier is not otherwise aware of this nature, not only will the shipper be liable for any loss resulting from their shipment, but the carrier is empowered at any time to unload, destroy or render the cargo innocuous, "as the circumstances may require" without payment of compensation (Article 13.2). Even if he has consented to their shipment, the carrier may take similar action should the cargo become an actual danger to life or property during the voyage (Article 13.4). In the case of containers locked into place on deck, this course of action is less practical, given the absence of enough crew members capable of unlocking the screw-locks holding the containers in position. And in the case of an inferno aboard vessel, as with the *Hyundai Fortune* incident, this course of action would be impossible in any case. Furthermore, where the nature of the cargo was not fully divulged to the carrier and the insurers, the insurance policy covering such a consignment could be rendered invalid under the principle of duty of disclosure of *uberrimae fidei* (in utmost good faith), as well as possibly giving rise to legal action on the basis of the vessel, its crew and its cargo being unnecessarily prejudiced by a failure on the part of the shipper to correctly or fully disclose the true nature of the cargo being carried on board the vessel.

1.3 The CMI/UNCITRAL Project

At the request of UNCITRAL, the Comité Maritime International (CMI) prepared a "Draft Instrument on Transport Law" which it submitted to the UNCITRAL Secretariat in December 2001, which was subsequently addressed by a UNCITRAL Working Group in 2003–4. This project was designed to follow on from the UN Convention of 1980 concerning the International Intermodal Transport of Goods, a subject covered in Chapter 2. The purpose of the project is to gain a full international agreement on a new updated liability regime for the carriage of goods by maritime means and which is capable of meeting the requirements of present-day commerce while promoting and facilitating as great a degree of uniformity as possible. Although a final draft has yet to appear, the proposed convention deals far more with door-to-door shipments rather than port-to-port movements, especially given the trend in present-day container movements which are conducted more on the basis of an integrated transport multimodal movement, rather than a transaction which simply infers loading the container on board vessel at the port of departure and unloading it at the port of arrival, independently of any other associated form of transport at each end of the journey. The main condition is that some part of the integrated multimodal movement involves an international cross-border sea leg. Another departure from the Hamburg Rules is as follows. In the case of the Hamburg Rules, the carrier will only be considered liable where the fault for loss or damage to the cargo lies in the hands of the carrier or his agents. In the case of the new convention, if the claimant can establish that the loss, damage or delay occurred during the carrier's period of responsibility, the carrier will be liable unless it can prove that neither it nor any other "performing party", such as a handling agent or the loading personnel employed by the authority of the port of loading or unloading, caused or contributed to the loss, damage or delay and that such damage, loss or delay resulted from events outside their control. At the time of writing, a final draft has yet to emerge, as many of the issues being discussed by the UNCITRAL Working Group are somewhat controversial and do not meet with full agreement from all the Member States concerned in the project, especially the major trading nations. These may require extensive re-drafting before any final version of the convention is agreed.

1.4 The Convention relating to Contracts for International Carriage of Goods by Road 1956 (CMR)

In itself, the 1956 CMR Convention covers road transport, but it impinges upon the carriage of goods by sea insofar as it also covers sea journeys where road trailers are carried aboard a ferry in national or international waters. It thus covers all cross-channel and short sea journeys, especially between the UK and the continent. Article 1 makes the Convention applicable to the whole of the carriage, if the vehicle containing the consignment is carried by sea for part of the journey and the consignment is not unloaded from the vehicle. However, if any loss, damage or delay is caused by an event during sea transport on board a vehicle ferry and the carrier by road is also the carrier by sea, the carrier's liability is to be determined as if the contract was for the carriage of goods by sea (Articles 2 and 10(2)). According to Article 31(1), jurisdiction is allocated to a court of a Contracting State that has been designated by agreement of the parties to a contract of carriage under the CMR terms and evidenced by a CMR consignment note. This jurisdiction can also extend to the country where the contract of carriage was made, or where the defendant party resides or has their principal place of business, especially where a ferry company may be based in, say, Greece, but operates throughout Europe, including the Baltic Sea and the North Sea. Jurisdiction may also extend to the country where the ultimate delivery of the consignment affected was to be made, given the integrated nature of the journey. In the above respects, the CMR Convention has similar characteristics to the Law of Carriage of Goods by Sea and places the same responsibilities on a ferry operator as the Law of Carriage of Goods by Sea places on a shipping line as a carrier.

1.5 Marine Cargo Contracts

Much of the business of marine cargo management revolves around the basic principle of the contract arranged between seller and buyer and to what extent this also affects the carrier. The documentation used in the carriage of goods is addressed in Chapter 4, section 5, especially the functions of a Bill of Lading, which is a legal document of title, as well as being documentary evidence of a contract of carriage between the shipper and the carrier. As well as the contract of carriage concerning the carrier, there is also a contract arranged between the seller and the buyer, depending at what point both the responsibility and risk for the maritime venture change between the two. The contracts concerned depend upon the use of the INCOTERMS FOB and CIF and differ depending upon which INCOTERM is used, although the term EXW can also be used in contractual terms.

An EXW contract

Under an EXW contract, it is the duty of the buyer to take delivery of the goods at the works, literally the Factory Gate of the seller's premises, or the door of the factory used for goods despatches. The property and risk usually pass when the buyer takes delivery of the goods (i.e. at the factory gate of the seller). These sales are almost always of unascertained goods, the appropriation or transfer taking place when the goods are selected or handed over at the works. The buyer is thus responsible contractually for all aspects of the shipment, including the loading of the goods vehicle or container, the arrangement of all transport, and all risks.

With so many more shipments being arranged on a door-to-door basis, the FCA contract becomes increasingly used. The term FCA (Free Carrier) implies that the seller has the obligation of ensuring that the goods are delivered to the place of loading and ensuring that the goods are loaded aboard the vehicle or container. Similarly, where the term FCA starts at the seller's premises, then the seller has the obligation of ensuring that the goods are loaded correctly aboard the vehicle or container, as well as ensuring that for the purposes of documentation, all the information pertaining to the load is correct. In this respect, FCA differs legally form EXW, as in an EXW contract, the seller is only legally responsible for ensuring that the goods are made sufficiently ready for despatch and collection by the buyer's arranged means of transport.

An FOB contract

An FOB contract is made when the seller passes the responsibility and risk for the shipment to the Buyer at the point of loading the cargo over the ship's rail. Under such a contract, the seller must put the consignment *free on board* a vessel for despatch to the buyer at the point of loading. The buyer is responsible for selecting the port of shipment and the date of shipment of the goods concerned. Where the contract allows for a range of ports from which the goods are to be shipped (e.g. a UK port), it is the buyer's right and duty to select one of them, usually the most suitable and proximate to the seller, and to give the seller sufficient notice of his selection (see also *David T Boyd & Co Ltd v Louis Louca* [1973] 1 Lloyd's Rep 209). The seller pays all charges incurred prior to the goods being loaded aboard vessel, but the buyer is responsible for the payment of freight and insurance relating to the whole international journey, right up to the point of discharge at the buyer's premises. Once the goods have been loaded over the ship's rail, they are normally at the buyer's risk.

It is the responsibility of the buyer to insure the goods and is therefore his risk if the goods are lost, damaged, delayed or uninsured en route (*Frebold v Circle Products Ltd* [1970] 1 Lloyd's Rep 499). The seller may, under a particular contract, be responsible for shipping the goods and where this is the case, it is important to know whether the seller ships on his own account as principal or as an agent for the buyer. If he ships as principal, the property or title in the goods (i.e. the ownership of the goods) will not normally pass on shipment, although it will usually do if he ships as agent (*President of India v Metcalfe Shipping Co* [1969] 3 All ER 1549).

Section 32(3) of the Sale of Goods Act 1979 provides that, unless otherwise agreed, where the goods are sent by the seller to the buyer by a route involving transit by sea, under circumstances in which it is usual to insure the goods, the seller must give such notice to the buyer as may enable the buyer to insure the goods during the sea transit, and, if the seller fails to do so, the goods shall be deemed to be at his risk (i.e. that of the seller) during such sea transit. Thus, delivery to the carrier, (the shipping line), will not necessarily pass the risk from seller to buyer in FOB contracts. Where the seller makes the contract of carriage, it must be reasonable in terms of the nature of the goods to be carried and other circumstances. If it is not reasonable and the goods are lost or damaged in the course of transit by sea, the buyer may decline to treat the delivery to the carrier as a delivery to himself, or may hold the seller responsible in damages (s. 32(2), Sale of Goods Act 1979).

There are three types of FOB contract, as identified by Devlin J in the case *Pyrene v Scindia Navigation Co* [1954] 2 QB 402. These are:

- classic;
- additional services; and
- strict.

Although the FOB contract has many variants, the basic elements of delivery, property and risk are common to them all. Under a Strict FOB contract, the obligations are weighted more to the buyer than to the seller. The buyer's main obligations are to:

- nominate an effective ship for the purposes of loading;
- give advance warning to the seller to be ready with the ship;
- select the port of shipment (i.e. loading).

The seller's main obligations are limited to the shipping of contract conforming goods (goods which correspond with the order made).

Shipment to destination FOB contract

A Shipment to Destination FOB contract is frequently used when the buyer is small and has no presence in the port of FOB origin. The contract of sale will then provide that the seller conducts certain activities on behalf of the buyer, unlike a strict FOB contract where it will be the buyer's responsibility to carry out these activities. The seller will arrange for:

- the carriage and insurance of the goods to their destination for the buyer;
- nominating an effective ship for the purposes of loading, or a substitute vessel if the original nominated vessel is not available;
- choosing when during the shipment period the seller will be shipping the goods form the appropriate chosen port of loading.

The above form of contract is similar to the seller's obligations in a CIF (Cost Insurance Freight) contract, but there are two major differences between the two forms of contract.

The first difference concerns the nature of delivery. Under a CIF contract, delivery is constructive, (by documents) whereas under an FOB contract, delivery is the physical presence of the goods on board ship (as evidenced by the arrival of the goods themselves, rather than the presentation of the documents pertaining to the shipment).

The second difference relates to the capacity in which the seller performs various tasks according to the contract concerned. Under a CIF contract, everything which the seller undertakes for the buyer is done within a principal-to-principal relationship, with clear responsibilities assumed by both seller and buyer. For example, the seller cannot arrange the insurance, because he will then be in breach of contract, unless a frustrating event such as destruction of the goods occurs to mitigate the circumstances. Under an FOB contract, however, the seller only ships on board the goods conforming to the contract, acting for and on behalf of the buyer. Everything else the seller does will be in his capacity as the buyer's agent.

There is also a requirement that the buyer must give the seller notice of when the nominated vessel is scheduled to arrive at the port of destination, otherwise the seller will not know when the buyer may call for the shipment during the shipment period. Failure to give such notice will be a major breach of contract since such a term is a condition of the contract, so the buyer will be able to rescind it.

A CIF contract

A CIF contract is a contract by which the seller agrees to sell goods at a price which includes the *cost* of the goods, the *insurance* premium required to insure the goods while in transit, and the *freight* (cost) of transporting the goods to their destination, strictly defined as the port of destination, thus employing the use of the INCOTERM CIF (Cost Insurance Freight) to named port of destination.

The seller's obligations under a CIF contract are heavier than those of the buyer. The seller has dual obligations to:

- *The goods.* The seller must either ship or buy goods already afloat which are contract conforming. Also, the seller must arrange for the insurance of the goods to their CIF destination;
- *The documents.* The seller must tender certain documents to the buyer.

The documents in question are:

- the invoice;
- the Bill of Lading;
- the insurance policy.

Once the seller has performed the obligations in relation to the goods and the documents, along with any additional obligations mentioned in the contract, he has fully performed and fulfilled his obligations under a CIF contract and is then entitled to receive payment, regardless of what may happen to the goods after shipment, as the seller does not guarantee that the goods will reach their destination. Any loss or damage to the cargo is to be claimed against by the buyer.

The primary intent is for the seller to transfer the goods referred to in the contract of sale to the buyer. The secondary intent is to cover the seller in the event of the goods being lost, destroyed or damaged along the way. Because the seller has transferred his rights to the buyer through the Bill of Lading, the buyer can sue the carrier for the loss, as the buyer has rights under an insurance policy for the goods.

Once the seller has performed his obligations under the CIF contract, then the buyer must pay the seller against the documents once they are submitted, often against a Bill of Exchange. In due course, when the goods arrive, the buyer must accept them. This is the case *even if* the goods are lost or destroyed by the time the documents are submitted. The buyer must still accept the correct documents and pay against them, even though he or she knows that the goods are lost.

The duties of the seller are to:

- ship goods of the description contained in the contract under a contract of affreightment which will ensure the delivery of the goods at the destination detailed in the contract. Undertakings in the contract concerning time and place of the shipment are nearly always treated as conditions. Thus, the buyer may reject the goods if they are shipped too late or too soon, or even in contravention of conditions such as non-allowance of trans-shipment or by a shipping line other than that stipulated in the contract, especially as defined under the terms of a letter of credit;
- arrange for insurance which will be available to the buyer;
- make out an invoice for the goods;
- submit the documents without delay concerning the transaction to the buyer in exchange for the price, so that the buyer will know the amount of the freight he must pay as part of the price, and so that he can obtain delivery of the goods if they arrive, or recover compensation for their loss if they are lost or damaged during the voyage;
- ensure that the electronic equivalent of the Bill of Lading has been correctly raised and replaced by equivalent electronic data interchange (EDI) message where seller and buyer have agreed to communicate electronically.

The seller must also pay any costs relating to checking and verification operations, such as quality control and inspection, measuring, weighing and counting, which are deemed necessary for the purpose of delivering the goods to the buyer according to the buyer's stipulation. Furthermore, the seller must provide at his own expense all packaging required for the transport of the goods arranged by him. This must be marked appropriately.

The seller must also render every assistance in obtaining any documents or equivalent electronic messages issued or transmitted in the country of shipment and/or of origin which the buyer may require for the import of the goods and, where necessary, for their transit through any country prior to arriving at their final destination.

In a CIF contract, the buyer or his agent may repudiate the contract by:

- refusing to accept the documents if they do not conform with the contract; and
- rejecting the goods on delivery if following inspection they do not comply with the details of the contract.

The risk passes in a CIF contract when the goods are shipped and the buyer will still have to pay for the goods if they are lost on the voyage, although he will have the insurance cover, which is passed to the buyer at the point of loading the consignment over the ship's rail. The property in the goods (i.e. title to, or ownership of, the goods) does not pass until the seller transfers the documents to the buyer and the latter has paid for them (*Mirabita v Imperial Ottoman Bank* [1878] 3 Ex D 164). If the goods have been shipped, but the documents have not been transferred, there is a conditional appropriation of the goods to the contract which will not become unconditional until the buyer takes up the documents and pays for them. In this respect, a CIF contract is a contract of the sale of documents, the delivery of which transfers the property and the possession of the goods to the recipient. However, a CIF contract is seen as a sale of goods because it details the transfer of goods in due course, and for this the Sale of Goods Act of 1979 applies. The Carriage of Goods by Sea Act [1992] also applies, in that section 2 provides that the person or party who is entitled to delivery of the goods "shall have transferred to and vested in him all rights of suit under the contract of carriage as if he had been a party to that contract".

However, as long as the proof of delivery, transport document or equivalent electronic message is fully valid, the buyer must accept this document in accordance with the terms of delivery if the document is in conformity with the contract.

The seller can either arrange shipment of the goods with an agent or supplier if he cannot ship them personally, as long as he arranges the shipment, or the buyer can buy a cargo on its way to the CIF destination—he may buy the goods while they are *afloat* and in transit. However, these goods must fit the description as found on the documents and must be shipped on the correct date, otherwise the buyer can reject the goods or the documents. The seller's obligations will only be discharged if he can show that:

- he could not ship the goods; and
- the goods could not be bought afloat because they were outside the contract period.

Place of shipment clauses within a contract are usually condition-type terms. CIF will always be a destination term, naming a specific port of destination, but sometimes contracts will also state the *origin* of the goods. The time of shipment is also a conditional term when it appears in a contract. This is regarded as part of the description of the goods. Failure to ship on time gives the buyer the right to reject both the documents and the goods.

If there has been a contractually agreed route to carry the goods, then it will become a condition-type term of the contract and must be complied with, as it becomes an implied term of the contract. Equally, if the vessel is to call at other ports before arriving at its agreed destination, the terms of the CIF contract must state such a means of shipment. Similarly, where trans-shipments may occur, the CIF contract should state whether trans-shipments are allowed, or whether the shipment must be loaded on to a vessel sailing *directly* for the named port of destination, without the need for trans-shipments on the way, such as the UK to India via Antwerp, or China to the UK via Rotterdam/ Europoort.

1.5.5 A CFR contract

A slight variation of the CIF contract is the CFR contract (Cost & Freight), where the seller must arrange for the goods to be sent to a port of shipment which is named in the contract. The seller must also meet all costs and freight charges for such transactions, but does not arrange insurance for the goods. This is carried out by the buyer. If the seller should arrange insurance on behalf of the buyer, then this must be paid for separately. The only obligation that the seller has is to notify the buyer that the goods are in transit. This action will then enable the buyer to arrange his own insurance, with the goods being shipped and carried at the buyer's risk.

2 THE FINANCIAL ASPECTS OF CARGO MANAGEMENT

2.1 Shipping Costs

A major element in the shipping process is not simply the physical movement of the consignment on the high seas, but also the costs associated with such movements.

There are several types of cost associated with the maritime carriage of cargo. These can be categorised as:

- voyage costs;
- crewing costs;
- stores and victualling costs;
- vessel maintenance costs;
- port costs;
- freight rates.

All these must be taken into consideration when calculating the cost of transporting a cargo from one port to another, as the costs of not only the carriage of the cargo, but also the operation of the vessel carrying the cargo must be taken into account.

The cost of running the vessel is the first element to be considered, as without the vessel, nothing can be moved by sea. The actual cost of operating a ship can be calculated as an annual cost per deadweight (dwt) per annum, based on the following formula:

$$C = \frac{OC + PM + VC + CHC + K}{DWT}$$

Where: C = Cost per dwt per annum
OC = Operating cost per annum
PM = Periodic maintenance provision per annum
VC = Voyage costs per annum
CHC = Cargo handling costs per annum
DWT = Ship deadweight

All the above should also be calculated per ship per year.

It should be noted that because operating, voyage and capital costs do not increase in proportion to the deadweight of a vessel, using a bigger ship reduces the unit freight cost. This is borne out by considering the relevant comparative costs of container vessels over the past several decades. With each generation of container vessel, the efficiency of each class of vessel has increased, especially given the technology on board the vessel coupled with the reduction in crew numbers (nowadays between 13 and 18 per container vessel) as well as the total capacity for the number of containers carried with relation to the weight/displacement of the vessel, although there will come a time when the efficiency of a vessel reaches a peak and cannot be maximised further.

The breakdown of costs for the operation of a vessel such as a bulk carrier in the year 2004 can be broken down as follows:

Table 4: Costs of operation 2004

Operating costs (US$2m per annum)	Periodic maintenance	Voyage costs (US$3.1m per annum)	Capital costs and repayments: (US$3.4m per annum)
• Crew (32%); • Stores and lubricants (11%); • Repairs and maintenance (16%); • Insurance (30%) • Administration (12%)	Specific cost (approx US$0.3m per annum)	• Fuel oil (47%); • Diesel oil (7%); • Port costs (46%)	• Interest/dividend; • Debt repayment

Operating costs

These are the ongoing expenses which are connected to the day-to-day running of the vessel, other than fuel, which is included in voyage costs. They include allowances for day-to-day repair and maintenance costs, which do not include major dry-dockings and refits. These operating costs account for approximately 25% of total costs, and their principal component elements are:

$$OC = M + ST + MN + I + AD$$

Where:

M = Manning cost
ST = Stores
MN = Routine repair and maintenance
I = Insurance
AD = Administration

Crew costs

These include all direct and indirect charges incurred by the crewing of the vessel, including basic salaries and wages, social insurance, pensions, victuals (food and refreshments) and repatriation expenses. The level of manning costs for any vessel is governed by two factors, namely the size of the crew and the employment policies adopted by the owner and the vessel's flag state. In many cases, the state where the owner resides is not necessarily the state where the vessel is flagged and registered. For example, the owner of the vessel may be based in Greece, but the vessel is registered and flagged in the Bahamas, showing Nassau as its port of registration. The reasons for this are often associated with cost, owing to legal and fiscal attractions of registration in certain locations throughout the world. Indeed, in many cases, crews are recruited on an agency basis from least-cost origins, especially from countries where wage levels are much lower than in the developed countries of Europe and North America.

Another significant cost of operating a vessel, accounting for approximately 11% of operating costs, is that of expenditure on consumable supplies. These fall into three categories—general stores, cabin stores and water and lubricants. General stores include spare parts, deck and engine-room equipment. Cabin stores cover the various domestic items used aboard ship, while the largest element is lubricating oil.

Repairs and maintenance

These account for some 12% of all costs, and cover all outside charges associated with maintaining the vessel to the standard required by company policy, the classification society and the charterers of the vessel who choose to inspect it. These costs can be split into two main categories: routine maintenance and breakdowns.

Insurance

This can account for some 37% of the operating costs of a vessel, depending upon its size and nature. In many cases, however, this figure may vary between 15% and 40%. A high proportion of marine insurance costs is determined by the insurance of the hull and machinery (H&M), which protects the owner of the vessel against physical loss or damage, and is obtained from a marine insurance company or through a broker using a policy backed by Lloyd's Underwriters. The other form of insurance is protection and indemnity (P&I), which provides cover against third-party liabilities such as damaging a jetty, wharf or oil pollution. Further insurance may also be taken out to cover against war risks, strikes and loss of earnings, although with the increased threat of international terrorism and piracy on the high seas, such risks are becoming increasingly expensive to cover.

General costs

This includes charges to recover shore-based administrative and management charges, communications, owners' port charges and miscellaneous costs. These overheads include liaison with port agents and general supervision, although in many cases the shipping line may sub-contract the day-to-day management of port-based activities to specialist agencies for a pre-determined fee. Indeed, many shipping lines prefer to use local agencies for this, rather than operating their own offices and personnel at the port.

Voyage costs

These can be defined as the variable costs incurred in the undertaking of a particular voyage. The main elements are fuel costs, port, harbour and light dues, tugs and pilotage and canal charges, where appropriate, especially in the case of the Manchester Ship Canal in the UK, and the Kiel Canal in Germany.

These costs are represented as:

$$VC = FC + PD + TP + CD$$

Where: VC = Voyage costs
FC = Fuel costs for main engines and auxiliaries
PD = Port and light dues, etc.
TP = Tugs and pilotage, etc.
CD = Canal dues (e.g. Panama Canal, Suez Canal, Kiel Canal, Manchester Ship Canal)

Fuel costs

These are perhaps the single most important element in voyage costs, accounting for some 47% of the total cost. The fluctuation in fuel costs has naturally influenced the whole state of voyage costs, as bunkering is by far and away the most important element in the operation of the vessel. As fuel costs have risen, so the drive towards more fuel-efficient vessels has increased, although the costs of fuel are inevitably passed on to the cargo shipper, usually by way of the Bunker Adjustment Factor (BAF).

Port charges

These represent another major component in voyage costs and include various fees levied against the vessel and/or cargo for the use of the facilities and services provided by the port. Charging practices may vary significantly from one port to another, but in general they fall into two distinct categories—port dues and service charges. Port dues are levied on the vessel for the general use of port facilities, including docking and wharfage charges and the provision of the basic port infrastructure, including lights and buoys marking the channels into and out of the port by sea. The actual charges may be calculated in four different ways, based on the:

- volume of the cargo;
- weight of the cargo;
- gross registered tonnage of the vessel; or
- net registered tonnage of the vessel.

The service charge covers the various services used by the vessel in port, including pilotage, towage and cargo handling.

Canal dues

These are mainly seen as those charges payable for transiting the Suez and Panama Canals, although similar dues exist for the use of the Kiel Canal in Northern Germany and the Manchester Ship Canal in Northern England.

Cargo handling costs

These are the costs of loading and unloading cargoes, and represent a significant component in the total cost equation. Cargo handling costs can be represented in the following way:

$$CHC = L + DIS + CL$$

Where: CHC = Cargo handling costs
$\quad\quad\quad$ L = Cargo loading charges
$\quad\quad$ DIS = Cargo discharge costs
$\quad\quad\quad$ CL = Cargo claims

The other element of the cost factor is the Unit Cost Function, defined as follows:

$$\text{Unit cost} = \frac{LC + OPEX + CH}{PS}$$

The unit cost of transporting a ton of cargo in a particular vessel depends on several factors. These are the:

- capital cost of the ship (LC); plus
- cost of operating the ship over its commercial life (OPEX); plus
- cost of handling the cargo (CH); divided by
- tonnage of cargo it is capable of carrying (PS).

As the size of the vessel increases, unit costs generally decrease because capital, operating and cargo handling costs do not increase proportionally with the cargo capacity. Indeed, the increased efficiency of port handling of cargo may see the unit cost decrease owing to the relative ease of loading and unloading containers on and off a ship, regardless of the number of containers that vessel may carry. Only where the port is less capable of handling large numbers of containers is the unit cost less likely to decrease. Indeed, the cost of handling small consignments is larger than that of carrying large shipments, as economies of scale prevail in maritime economics.

The level of these costs may be reduced by investment in improved ship design, to facilitate rapid cargo handling, along with advanced shipboard cargo handling gear (often found only on specific forms of geared carrier). The costs associated with the loading of such a vessel can be reduced, given the vessel's own onboard crane and handling facilities. However, because of the limited sailings of such vessels, there is a greater likelihood of charges incurred for storing materials on the quayside prior to loading, as there is usually a need to group cargoes on the quayside prior to loading them aboard such a vessel.

Another charge, the conservancy charge, covers the quayside space taken up by cargoes of a loose or containerised nature, both for incoming and outgoing cargoes. These charges account for the time a cargo is left on the quayside prior to being loaded aboard vessel or after being unloaded from the vessel and are calculated by commodity and per tonne of the relevant commodity and are usually passed to the ship's agent, who in turn passes the cost on to the shipper, along with other charges for Terminal Handling including crane operating charges for the loading and unloading of the vessel. These charges will appear on the invoice sent by the freight agent to the shipper (Buyer or Seller of the consignment) on behalf of the ship's agent.

Overall, port and cargo handling charges account for a sizable chunk of the costs incurred by a vessel and its owners, and often influence which ports the vessel visits as part of its schedule. The greater the number of ports visited within the vessel's schedule, the higher the costs incurred. The reduction in ports of call concerning the schedules of the freighters sailing from the Far

East to Europe has resulted from the view by certain operators, including Maersk Line, that certain ports are not seen as being as viable as others when it comes to operational viability concerning loading and discharging of containers, and this includes the Port of Felixstowe in South-East England. Given that Felixstowe lies on the opposite side of the North Sea to the European Ports of Antwerp and Rotterdam, then the justification for the removal of the UK ports from the list of ports served by the deep sea vessels lies in the fact that for a container vessel to call at a UK port would mean deviating from an otherwise direct path up the eastern side of the North Sea out of the Channel area, and would thus add significant costs to the voyage, costs which could otherwise be avoided and simply be absorbed in a feeder operation between the European Ports and the UK. Another more practical solution is for inbound vessels to call at the European Ports on the eastern side of the North Sea, and then proceed across the sea to the east coast UK ports before continuing south back to the Far East. In this way, a more circular kind of route can be arranged, thus facilitating calls at UK ports without the need for expensive deviations from an otherwise continuous route through European waters.

2.2 Freight Rates

The supply of marine transport is influenced by freight rates. This regime is the ultimate regulator which the market uses to motivate decision-makers to adjust short-term capacity on board cargo vessels, as well as to find ways of reducing their long-term freight costs. In the shipping industry, there are two main pricing regimes, namely the freight market and the liner market. Liner shipping provides transport for small quantities of cargo for many customers and is basically a retail shipping business, mainly focused around the container market. The container market is the main means by which such quantities of goods are shipped from one part of the world to the other, especially in groupage or consolidated container loads. The liner company is a common carrier, accepting cargo from any customer at prices set out in the rate book, seen as the freight tariff guide. This guide details prices for that carrier or for the liner conferences, where several carriers collectively pool their resources to serve several high-density routes, usually from the Far East into the European Ports. At one time, the main conference network operated on the North Atlantic routes, but investigations by the UN Trade Organisations discovered a price-fixing cartel which did little to help competitiveness on these routes, especially for the lesser-developed nations, and thus the liner conference system of the North Atlantic in the 1970s and 1980s involving the likes of Nedlloyd and Hapag-Lloyd was curtailed in its original form, although it was later restructured in the form of the TACA (Transatlantic Conference Agreement) (illustrated in Appendix 5). There is a keen competitive nature for maritime trade around the world, and this helps to maintain stability within the freight rates sector. In contrast to the liner sector, bulk shipping is a wholesale business, as it sells its services in large quantities, by contract to a much smaller number of industrial customers at individually-negotiated prices, especially where the chartering of vessels for the carriage of one-off consignments or a specified number of voyages to carry a fixed quantity of bulk cargo, such as iron ore.

In both cases, the pricing system is central to the supply of transport. In the short term, supply responds to prices as ships change their operational speed and move to and from layup (the time when a ship lies at a berth in an inactive state), while liner operators adjust their services. In the longer term, freight rates contribute to the investment decisions which result in the scrapping and ordering of ships, although in an age where technology moves forwards in leaps and bounds, the cycle of ordering and scrapping ships has more to do with the need to maintain the cutting edge when it comes to the operation of cost-efficient vessels.

Freight rates are determined by the cost required to operate a vessel, although they are also governed by the world markets in commodities. These costs are governed by the formula:

$$\text{Fixed Costs (FC)} + \text{Variable Costs (VC)} = \text{Total Cost (TC)}$$

The cost per ton to break even (B/E) is, quite simply, the total cost divided by the number of tons carried. Thus,

$$\text{Break-even (B/E) rate per ton} = \frac{\text{Total cost}}{\text{Tons carried}}$$

Under favourable business conditions, it is possible to add a profit margin to the formula as follows:

$$\text{Quoted rate per ton} = \frac{\text{Total costs} + \text{Profit}}{\text{Tons carried}}$$

The freight market is the adjustment mechanism linking supply and demand. Ship owners and shippers negotiate to establish a freight rate which reflects the balance of ships and cargoes available in the market. If there are too many ships, the freight rate is low. Conversely, if there are too few ships, the freight rate is high. This can be stated another way. Given the fixed number of vessels sailing the high seas, where the volume of cargo shipped from one part of the world is high, the freight rate is also high. Where the volume of cargo shipped from another part of the world is low, the freight rate is low. This would explain the disparities between the freight rates for the shipment of a container load from the Far East into Europe compared with the freight rates for a shipment of a container load from Europe to the Far East.

The cost of production of many items is far cheaper in China and India than it is in Europe, so as a result companies in Europe import huge quantities of products from China and India. Consequently, the demand for container shipments out of the Far East is high, which also means that space on any container vessel leaving the Far East is at a premium, despite the number of large container vessels leaving the Far East ports in any week. Therefore, the box rates for shipments from the Far East are approximately US$1800 for a 20-foot container, and US$2500 for a 40-foot container.

An additional charge is being imposed by the shipping lines on top of the normal freight rates for all imports from Asia into the UK, where a container vessel calls directly at a UK port inbound from the Far East. Because of the severe imbalance in world trade, the number of containers being deposited at UK ports is increasing at a huge rate and this is resulting in severe container congestion, with vast areas inside port confines being taken up by increasing numbers of containers which have not been returned to the Far East. This congestion has resulted in the lines belonging to the FEFC (Far East Freight Conference) imposing a surcharge of US$145 per TEU (Twenty Foot Equivalent Unit), or US$290 per 40-foot container, on all containers used for the purpose of importing goods into the UK, as from 1 December 2007.

In the other direction, however, the supply of exports to the Far East and India from the European Union is much lower, especially in terms of finished or consumer goods. Europe has lost much of its export potential, so there is far less demand for the shipment of full containers from Europe to India and the Far East. In reality, the vast majority of the container business for voyages out of Europe to the Far East is the relocation of empty containers from Europe to the Far East to be re-used for inbound shipments, although some sectors, such as food and drink, including the Scotch whisky sector, still maintain significant success in these areas. Therefore, the shipping companies are clamouring for shippers in Europe to fill the empty containers with export consignments with goods destined for the Far East and India. Given this disparity in trade, the export rates for a container out of the European port network destined for the Far East can be as low as US$300, given a clear surplus of containers on the route. In short, the following matrix can be used.

Table 5: The EU/Far East container matrix

Containers	*Supply*	*Demand*
Far East–Europe	Low	High
Europe–Far East	High	Low

Consequently, where demand is high, the freight rate is high. Where demand is low, the freight rate is low.

The making of freight rates has changed significantly in recent years as a result of the development of multi-modalism, especially in the sea freight sector. The rate is no longer based on one carrier on a port-to-port basis; it also involves two or three carriers providing a dedicated door-to-door container service featuring one overall composite rate and the sea/land bridge from the Far East to both North America and Europe using several gateway ports and a series of rail-based or road-based shipments to inland destinations. An example of the composite freight rate would be:

- Hong Kong—Felixstowe (container ship);
- Felixstowe—Birmingham (container on road chassis).

The freight rate would be from Hong Kong direct to Birmingham on a DDU (Delivered Duty Unpaid) basis, with the cost of the inland UK road haulage separated out for import VAT purposes. Import customs duty would still be calculated on the segment of the journey (i.e. the sea freight voyage from Hong Kong to Felixstowe) as a CIF landed cost (Cost Insurance Freight) basis.

The tariff raised for a consignment can embrace a number of elements other than the sea and inland transport. These are:

- tariff sea freight rate;
- bunker adjustment factor (BAF);
- currency surcharge (Currency adjustment factor, CAF);
- container loading charge;
- container unloading charge;
- terminal handling charge;
- demurrage charge (where the container is delayed at the port);
- wharfage charge;
- cargo conservancy dues (raised by the port for cargo passing over the quay);
- documentary processing fee;
- customs clearance charge;
- freight forwarder's commission fee;
- delivery/collection charge;
- trans-shipment charge (where the container is trans-shipped via another European port);
- customs import duty;
- import VAT (17.5% in the UK).

Although most of the charges are small, they accrue to a larger amount when added to the overall freight charges. The average freight and duty cost payable by the trader (the importer) can amount to as much as 33% of the purchase cost of the imported consignment, based on an Ex Works price. Although the import VAT can be reclaimed, it still means that the logistics cost for the consignment adds a considerable margin to the overall import cost of the purchased consignment. Thus, a consignment costing US$100,000 Ex Works price from the Far East can cost up to US$133,000 on import into the UK.

Not all freight costs are standard. There are specific costs for large items, such as heavy engineered products, or high-value items such as antiques or alcoholic goods, or dangerous/ hazardous cargoes such as chemicals. The ultimate freight rate, mode of transport and route will be much more influenced by the export sales contract and the international terms of delivery contained therein.

There are several factors which determine the freight rate, especially where consolidations take place as opposed to full container loads (FCLs), which are simply classed as box rates. These are:

- competition between carriers and operators;
- the nature of the commodity, its quantity, size, period of shipment and overall cubic measurements/dimensions/value;
- the origin and destination of the cargo;
- the overall transit cost;
- the nature of packaging and convenience of handling;
- the vulnerability of the cargo to damage and pilferage;
- provision of additional facilities to handle and accommodate the cargo, such as heavy lifts or specialist handling devices aboard vessel;
- the mode of transport (container ship, general cargo ship);
- actual routing of cargo consignment, especially where specified by a letter of credit.

The weight and measurement dimensions of the cargo matter significantly, especially where consolidated containerised cargoes are concerned. The aim of the freight forwarder or NVOCC is to accommodate as many cargo consignments in the same container on a groupage basis, so they need to be fully aware of the dimensions and weight of each of the cargoes concerned. For this reason, they will require this information from the shipper in advance of loading, to establish how many other loads can be accommodated inside the container and the cost for each individual shipment. The basis for such calculations concerns the maximum potential revenue to be gained, based on either the volumetric weight or the actual weight, depending upon which is greater. The formula used for sea freight is:

$$1 \text{ cubic metre} = 1000 \text{ kg or } 1 \text{ metric tonne}$$

Thus, where the dimensions of the consignment are:

2 metres (length) × 1.5 metres (breadth) × 1 metre (height), = 3 cubic metres = 3,000 kg (3 metric tonnes).

The weight is 2,000 kg = 2 metric tonnes.

The volumetric weight (3,000 kg) clearly exceeds the actual weight (2,000 kg), so the former figure will be used to calculate the freight rate for the consignment, as it takes up more space inside the container.

The freight forwarder hires in the container at the standard box rate for the route concerned, then proceeds to fill it with several individual consignments. The money made on the freight rates based on the volumetric weight measurement for each individual consignment loaded into the container will exceed the normal box rate for that container. This is where the consolidator will make his money.

For Ro-Ro trailer movements based on short-sea ferry transport, the principle is the same. The consolidator aims to completely fill the trailer prior to despatching it so he hires in the trailer at a standard trailer rate for the short-sea ferry crossing, and then proceeds to gain revenue by consolidating loads within that trailer. The only difference between trailer loads and sea freight container loads is that the formula used for road trailers is 3 cubic metres = 1,000 kg or 1 metric tonne.

In the original calculation, therefore, the consignment weighed 2,000 kg (2 tonnes) but measured 3 cubic metres. In this case, the actual weight is greater, given that 3 cubic metres = 1 tonne (1,000 kg). Therefore, the trailer consolidator will calculate the freight rate based on the actual weight of the consignment, which is 2 tonnes. This is partly to do with the maximum weight allowed per road trailer, not only for ferry operations, but also for road transport restrictions. The UK Road Haulage Association (RHA) has strict guidelines and regulations for road trailer operators, and these apply as much to Ro-Ro maritime operations as much as they do to the road sector, given that the vehicle ferry is considered a maritime extension of the road network.

2.3 Terms of Trade

The principle of "terms of trade" is normally associated with the subject of international economics. However, it can be used to refer to the issue of the worldwide shipment of commodities by sea. Terms of trade refers to the quantification of international trade by the application of the calculation of exports divided by imports. The resulting figure thus describes whether the country exporting the commodities in question is seen as enjoying a trade surplus, insofar as the term of trade will exceed 1. The term of trade is calculated thus:

$$\frac{\text{Exports } (X)}{\text{Imports } (M)}$$

Where X > M, the resulting calculation is greater than 1. Thus, where:

$$\frac{X}{M} > 1$$

the country may be seen to enjoy a trade surplus.

However, where

$$\frac{X}{M} < 1$$

the country is incurring a trade deficit.

This formula can be translated into the marine cargo sector. Where the shipping line is transporting large quantities of cargo by maritime means in one direction and carries less in the other, then the direction of trade works in the same way as the above formula. Thus, in the trade between the Far East and Europe, where

W = Westbound;
E = Eastbound.

$$\frac{W}{E} > 1, \text{ consequently } \frac{E}{W} < 1$$

since the quantity and value of westbound shipments greatly exceeds that of eastbound shipments.

This formula can be expanded to show that where W = P(rice) × Q(uantity) (W) and E = P × Q (E):

$$\frac{\Sigma\ PQ(W)}{\Sigma\ PQ(E)} > 1$$

for all commodities carried aboard vessel in each direction.

For example, suppose that a shipping line carries a total of £16 million of cargo westbound over a particular year between the Far East and Europe and only carries £10 million of cargo in an eastbound direction between Europe and the Far East, the calculation is:

W = 16
E = 10

$$= \frac{16}{10} = \textbf{1.6} \text{ as far as trade from the Far East to Europe is concerned,}$$
making a trade surplus.

However, since the shipping line is also carrying cargoes in an eastbound direction, then formula becomes:

$$\frac{10}{16} = 5/8 = \textbf{0.625}, \text{ thus incurring a trade deficit detween Europe and the}$$
Far East.

Ideally, shipping lines would be seeking to achieve a term of trade on both directions of greater than 1, as this maximises revenue for the shipping line. Where the term of trade is lower than 1, the shipping line is incurring an effective trade loss on its trade in an eastbound direction between Europe and the Far East, thus compromising its revenue potential. Successive yearly figures would thus exacerbate the issue of trade imbalances, showing that many container shipping lines are effectively engaged in one-way revenue-earning traffic. This can be further reinforced by the use of a specific year, such as the year 2000, as a base rate, to show that in each successive year beyond this base year, the terms of trade in favour of exports from the Far East to Europe increased significantly each year, as exemplified by the following table, with figures in tonnes:

Table 6: Westbound–Eastbound trade

Year	2003	2004	2005	2006	2007
West	914,241	1,017,098	1,031,868	1,211,359	1,426,755
East	282,973	316,607	377,664	426,947	497,203

Table 7: Terms of trade, Westbound traffic

Year	2003	2004	2005	2006	2007
T/Trade	3.23	3.21	2.73	2.83	2.87

Table 8: Terms of trade, Eastbound traffic

Year	2003	2004	2005	2006	2007
T/Trade	0.31	0.31	0.37	0.35	0.35

Source: Far East Freight Conference—FEFC

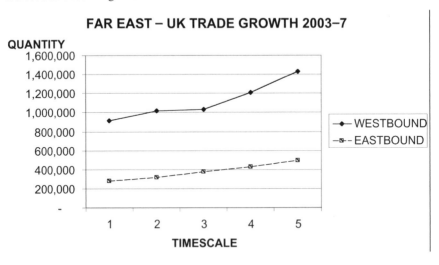

Figure 5.1: Graphical illustration of Westbound/Eastbound traffic

The figures speak for themselves, but the resulting terms of trade will show a surplus in favour of westbound traffic as opposed to a deficit for eastbound traffic.

2.4 Ro-Ro Freight Rates

Where conventional deep-sea freight requires a complex cost structure to account for all costs involved in the process, the Ro-Ro ferry market is less complex. There is no physical loading of cargoes across the ship's rail, neither is there the requirement for complex port activities. Although ferries may be chartered by other companies, they will be chartered on a bareboat basis, being operated by the crews employed by the chartering company. Vessel operating costs remain within the same overall cost structure, but as far as cargo loading and unloading costs are concerned, the process is kept simple. Trailers are usually filled inland, on a consolidation basis, although full trailer loads are common in some sectors, such as the carriage of hazardous cargoes or the transport of a specific general consignment which completely fills the trailer. Here, the trailer is loaded inland, is driven to the port and driven aboard vessel. In some cases, the booking of space aboard the vessel is arranged well in advance, especially where hazardous or dangerous cargoes are concerned, but in many other cases, the driver of the trailer may well contact the ferry company on his way to the port and arrange the ferry crossing on an *ad hoc* basis. Whereas the vessel name and voyage must be stipulated on an Ocean Bill of Lading, the ferry crossing is not stipulated on a CMR consignment note used for trailer movements. The ferry crossing is booked and paid for an a separate basis and the cost of the ferry journey is included in the overall cost, which is passed on to the shipper as part of the amount included in the consignment note, usually on a freight prepaid or freight collect basis. In the case of freight collect, the freight cost is passed by the carrier or the freight forwarder to the buyer. In the case of freight prepaid, the freight cost is passed to the seller, who then includes the freight costs in the overall invoice.

The freight rates charged to the international freight forwarder to convey the vehicle and/or trailer on the vehicular ferry are based on the length of the trailer/vehicle and whether it is empty or loaded, accompanied or unaccompanied. Further charges are levied for excessive width, and/or height, as outsize measurements could impede the loading of other vehicles close to the trailer once on board the ferry, or necessitate the vehicle being loaded in another part of the ferry, for example on the upper vehicle deck in the case of ferries with open vehicle deck space at the vessel's stern. Special rates usually exist for declared valuable cargoes. Rebates are given to hauliers and agents who arrange substantial quantities of trailer or vehicle traffic annually to a ferry operator on a particular route, such as Hull-Rotterdam, Hull-Zeebrugge or Dover-Calais. These rates are exclusive of customs clearance charges, which are in any case not applicable for intra-EU traffic where the cargoes concerned originate in an EU country and are being transported to another

EU country. There is keen competition among ferry operators, particularly concerning freight rates and fringe benefits, such as free cabins or meals, or free passage for drivers.

The actual freight rate for trailer movements on ferry services is based on the cubic measurement or physical weight of the cargo, whichever produces the greater revenue. This is related to the classification of the commodity, especially where dangerous or hazardous goods are involved, and must be classified under the categories of the IMDG (International Movement of Dangerous Goods) Code and the origin and destination of the cargo. The cargo volumetric measurement

$$3 \text{ cubic metres} = 1{,}000\text{kg} = 1 \text{ metric tonne}$$

is used for all trailer shipments. The calculation is based on the weight/ measurement option, applying whichever is largest, the actual weight or the volumetric weight based on the consignment's dimensions. Rates are very competitive, particularly compared with air or express freight rates within the European Union. To improve vehicle crew utilisation in an age of rising transport costs, an increasing number of the larger road haulage operators dispatch their vehicles unaccompanied on the vehicle ferry, especially where overnight or longer crossings are involved, particularly on the North Sea networks. This enables the driver to deposit his trailer at the ferry terminal and collect another one waiting there, having arrived at the terminal from the ferry. It avoids driver costs being incurred and enables better vehicle control to be achieved with improved reliability and lower cost. Once the trailer has been driven off the ferry at its destination port, it is collected by another driver and is driven to its inland destination.

Port costs are kept to a minimum. The ferry company still has to pay harbour and light dues, as well as berthing costs, to the port authority, but there are few loading/unloading and handling costs involved. Either the driver of the trailer drives the trailer aboard the vessel, or, as in the case of unac-companied trailers, the port authority arranges for its own tug drivers to do this. In the latter case, the port authority will charge the trailer haulage company a handling charge for the use of their trailer tugs, along with any costs relating to the storing and parking of the trailer at the port prior to loading aboard vessel. These costs are then included in the overall freight costs, and are passed directly by the freight forwarder to the buyer or seller.

The Ro-Ro ferry market is a large market, especially around the waters of Northern and Southern Europe, where an increasing demand for trailer activity means that large ferries now operate on high-density routes, especially in the Baltic and North Sea regions. Demand for these ferry services is high, and the tonnage of ferries on such routes has risen significantly. Although freight rates on these routes fluctuate according to demand, there is a general cost applied to trailer movements across Europe which includes ferry crossings using the North Sea or Channel routes, which are the most densely-used in Europe. The expansion of the European Union has created larger amounts of intra-Euro-pean trade, especially using road trailers, and the Ro-Ro ferry is considered to be an extension of the European road network, although as an instrument of maritime carriage, it has a significant importance in its own right.

The cost structure for ferry operations may be seen as follows:

Table 9: Cost structures for ferry operations

Vessel operating costs	Voyage costs	Freight costs
Crewing; Bunkering; Stores; Maintenance; Insurance.	Fuel costs; Harbour and light dues; Berthing costs.	Haulage costs; Fuel for vehicle tractor; Trailer loading/ unloading; Port storage/parking; Tug propulsion onto and off ferry (where appropriate); Documentary fee.

Overall, the Ro-Ro market is simpler to operate than the deep-sea market, because of its straightforward and integrated form of operations. It now takes account of most intra-European maritime transport operations and accounts for a sizeable proportion of the overall maritime trade conducted within European waters. Given its integrated nature, it facilitates significant cost reductions in the movement of freight by integrated means, especially in the form of trailer movements. The ferries themselves have dramatically increased in size over the past several decades. The original ferries of Fred Olsen Line on the route out of North Shields, North Tyneside, to Norway weighed in at some 9,000 gross tonnes; today, the MV *Queen of Scandinavia*, owned by DFDS Seaways and operating the route from North Shields to Bergen and Stavanger, weighs in at some 34,000 tonnes, alongside the other DFDS vessels operating from North Shields to Ijmuiden, in the Netherlands.

The same is true of the P&O Ferries services across the North Sea between Hull and Rotterdam and Hull–Zeebrugge. The first vessels on the route in the late 1960s and early 1970s, the *Norwind* and *Norwave*, weighed some 4,000 grt; the present ferries on the Hull-Rotterdam service, the *Pride of Hull* and *Pride of Rotterdam*, weigh some 60,000 tonnes, with the two vessels on the Hull-Zeebrugge route, the *Pride of York* and *Pride of Bruges*, weighing some 31,000 tonnes. The freight-deck capacity of the vessels *Pride of Hull* and *Pride of Rotterdam* is 3,345 lane metres, with a separate deck for cars and caravans. However, in that time, the cost of carrying freight on board these super-ferries has also increased, given the fluctuation in fuel costs both for road transport and for ferries.

2.5 Bulk Freight Rates

Bulk shipments are calculated per metric tonne measurement. Since bulk commodities are carried as an overall load and are not divided up into single units, as with trailers or containers, the price is calculated on the basis of the metric tonne, thus working out at the number of metric tonnes carried multiplied by the price per metric tonne. Furthermore, bulk freight rates are often governed by the means of shipment, often incorporated in the charter agreement which includes the charter of the vessel, namely a bulk carrier. In general, the charterparty specifies how freight is to be paid, when and by whom. Usual terms would normally be:

- Payable on signing and releasing Bills of Lading;
- 90% payable five days after signing and releasing Bills of Lading. The balance of 10% would be payable within 30 days of discharge with demurrage/despatch calculation/settlement;
- Payable before breaking bulk (BBB) (i.e. before the commencement of discharge of the bulk load from the vessel).

Under these conditions, freight is therefore payable for the full load as arranged in conjunction with the charter of the vessel for the carriage of the consignment in question. In the case of a voyage charter, the freight cost will be for the specific voyage of the vessel carrying the bulk load. Where a time charter is involved, the payment may be made in several ways:

- staged amounts agreed in advance of the shipment;
- quantity of bulk cargo carried per voyage;
- by other prior arrangement between the seller and the buyer.

In each case, freight is dependent upon the terms of trade (the INCOTERMS, generally on an FOB (free on board) or CIF (cost insurance freight) basis) although other terms such as DES (delivered ex ship) or DEQ (delivered ex quay) may also be used. In the case of breakbulk, then a term other than FOB or CIF may be used, as the inference is that the entire bulk load is to be landed off the vessel before it is divided into individual smaller loads for each of the buyers included in the contract of shipment. Once the appropriate INCO-TERM has been agreed, then the arrangement to carry the freight may be made.

The method of freight payment is usually specified "Free in and out trimmed" or FIOT. Other alternatives exist, such as FIOSpT or "Free in and out spout trimmed" and FIOST "Free in and out stowed and trimmed". These terms mean that the cost of loading and discharging is free to the owner who only pays the port charges. This is used to distinguish this form of freight from liner or gross terms where the owner pays both sets of charges. Sometimes these terms are referred to as "Freight in full of all port charges, pilotages, consular fees, light dues, trimming, lighterage at loading/discharging ports", which means that the owner of the cargo pays the port charges and any other specified expenses.

Ownership of the cargo depends on who has title (ownership) over the Bill of Lading and at what point it is transferred from seller to buyer. In many cases, the ownership of the cargo passes from seller to buyer during the vessel's voyage, especially where a voyage charter is concerned. In an FOB contract, the seller may pick up the loading charges and the buyer will pick up all discharging costs.

Freight is usually calculated and paid on the basis of the weight as recorded on the Bill of Lading, although this may vary depending upon the charter involved. In dry cargoes, this weight should remain constant throughout the voyage, whereas with wet cargoes, there may be some loss of moisture and hence reduction in weight as the voyage progresses. In other cases, the freight is paid on a "lump sum" basis, requiring the charterer to utilise the dead-weight and cubic capacity of the vessel and load as much cargo as possible in accordance with stowage requirements. In this respect, it shifts the responsibility of maximising the cargo from the owners to the charterers.

There is also a clause which states that freight is "deemed earned on shipment, ship and cargo lost or not lost", even though it is actually paid later. This clause can be varied to read "the freight shall be deemed earned as cargo is loaded on board and shall be discountless and non-returnable vessel and or cargo lost or not lost". This clause therefore places the freight risk on the charterer by making the freight earned and payable irrespective of carriage and delivery of the cargo, thus accounting for the conditions normally associated with the INCOTERMS FOB and CIF. It is therefore prudent for the charterer of the vessel and cargo to take out insurance on both the cargo and the freight. A further clause exists which allocates responsibility for the payment of duties and taxes on the CIF value of the cargo at the point of discharge on arrival at the port of destination. The clause will usually state "Freight and cargo taxes to be for charterer's account", because the recipient, buyer or importer, is ultimately responsible for the payment of all import duties and taxes liable on the consignment.

2.6 The Freight Futures Market

The global freight futures market is concentrated on the Baltic Exchange, located in the City of London. In 1985, the world's first freight futures market was established, giving owners and charterers the ability to protect themselves from fluctuating global freight rates, as exemplified by the volatility of the bulk trades market. The Baltic International Freight Futures Exchange (BIFFEX), based in London, opened for trading. However, the most important part of the trading operation was the Baltic Freight Index. This index is produced by a panel of shipbrokers around the world, and gives their assessment of the market value of a collection, or basketful, of dry cargo routes and trades. Today, the Baltic Index produces more than 40 daily route assessments, a sale-and-purchase index, forward prices, fixture lists and market reports. Even considering present-day activities, the Baltic Exchange is no stranger to futures markets, as it has had a coarse grain futures market since 1929. Main crop potatoes, pig meat, live cattle, soya meal and early potatoes markets were sited on its trading floor in the 1970s and 1980s. However, the Financial

Services Act of 1988 brought all these individual activities to a close and forced all the "Baltic" futures markets to unite under the banner of the Baltic Futures Association, re-siting them at the London Commodity Exchange. Baltic Exchange members are at the heart of world trade and arrange for the ocean transportation of industrial bulk commodities from producer to end-user. The bulk freight market relies on the co-operation of shipbrokers, ship owners and charterers to ensure the free flow of global trade.

The freight market is huge and complex with ship owners, vessel operators and charterers at the mercy of fluctuating freight rates. Global events can have an impact on the cost of sea transport and anyone moving bulk commodities operates in an extremely volatile environment. Maritime trade is vital in enabling the global economy to function. The world relies on a fleet of vessels with a cargo-carrying capacity of 960 million deadweight tonnes to carry every conceivable type of product. Figures produced by the United Nations show that more than 7.1 billion tonnes of trade was transported by sea in 2005 (Source: UNCTAD), thus making world trade dependent upon the availability of adequate global shipping capacity.

Vast amounts of fuels, foodstuffs and fertilisers, construction materials and other raw goods are transported by sea. Half of these are energy-related, namely oil, coal and gas. Container traffic accounts for just over 10% of maritime trade by weight, but is much higher in terms of value. The growth of the global economy has experienced a huge increase in the volume of maritime cargo over the past 30 years. Figures, released by the Baltic Exchange, illustrate this:

- World Maritime trade for 2005 reached 29,045 billion ton miles.
- The cargo-carrying capacity of the dry bulk fleet is 346 million dwt.
- A record 645 million tonnes of iron ore was transported by sea in 2005.
- The average age of the world fleet on 1 January 2006 was 12.3 years.
- Greece, Japan and Germany are the world's top shipowning nations.

(All figures derived from the Baltic Exchange)

The freight market is subject to a wide range of external variable factors, but it is fundamentally driven by the following issues:

- *Fleet supply*. The number of types of vessel available, including how many vessels are being delivered and how many scrapped.
- *Commodity demand*. Levels of industrial production. Success of grain harvests. Imports of coal by power stations. Performance of the steel industry.
- *Seasonal pressures*. The impact of the weather on the shipping markets from the size of harvests to ice in ports and river levels.
- *Bunker prices*. With bunker fuels accounting for between one-quarter and one-third of the cost of operating a vessel, oil price fluctuations directly affect ship owners and operators.

- *Choke points.* This factor can particularly affect tankers, with almost half of the world's oil passing through a handful of relatively narrow shipping lanes, such as the Straits of Hormuz, the Malacca Straits, the Strait of Dover, the Bosphorus and the Suez and Panama Canals. Any closure of these vital channels, due to conflict, terrorist attack or collision in overcrowded shipping lanes, would change the entire world's supply patterns.
- *Market sentiment.* Since perhaps as little as half of the demand side is known in a timely manner, market opinion and trends affect the freight market just as much as the actual supply and demand of ships and cargoes.

In April 2008, the Baltic Exchange Index hit a record high level, up 395 following a low in January 2008. The volatility of the freight derivatives market has led to interest in freight derivatives from investors outside the shipping world. The international investment bank UBS is setting up its own index, the "Blue Sea Index", as from May 2008, which will take into account factors such as shipping supply and demand, alongside commodity prices and the important issue of port congestion, all factors which can lead to significant fluctuations in the freight market.

2.7 Tonnage Tax

The principle of gross tonnage tax concerns the taxation of the maritime sector based upon its operating revenues. The tax refers to the level of corporation tax levied upon the company's profits based on the operations of its maritime fleet of vessels, and how it is levied.

Tonnage tax is an alternative method of calculating corporation tax on company profits by referring to the net tonnage of the ship or ships operated. The profit subject to tonnage tax replaces both the tax-adjusted commercial profit or loss on a shipping trade and the chargeable gains made or losses incurred on tonnage tax assets. Other profits of a company subject to tonnage tax are taxable in the usual way, based on the actual revenue generated by the company. The tax applies to any company within the scope of corporation tax which operates qualifying ships that are "strategically and commercially managed in the UK" (ships under UK control) thus enabling such a company to take advantage of the tonnage tax regime.

A company is regarded as operating a ship owned by it or "chartered" to it under a Charterparty Agreement, if it is:

- used by the company; or
- time or voyage chartered-out; or
- bareboat* chartered-out to another UK group member or, in some circumstances, bareboat chartered-out to a third party where there is short-term over-capacity and the charter does not exceed three years.

* *The term "bareboat" means that the vessel is chartered out without any additional services such as crew, navigation services and the like. All these elements must be supplied by the company chartering in the vessel, which infers additional operating costs incurred by that company.*

A qualifying ship must be sea-going (i.e. it is certificated for navigation at sea by a competent authority of any country) of at least 100 gross tons, and used for:

- carriage of passengers at sea; or
- carriage of cargo at sea; or
- towage, salvage or other maritime assistance carried out at sea; or
- transport by sea in connection with other services of a kind necessarily provided at sea.

Certain types of ship are excluded from this operation. These are:

- Fishing vessels or factory ships;
- Pleasure craft, such as private yachts (this does not include cruise liners, which do qualify as they are commercial passenger vessels);
- Harbour or river ferries;
- Offshore installations, such as oil and gas offshore platforms;
- Tankers dedicated to a particular oil field;
- Non-qualifying dredgers;
- Non-qualifying tugs;
- A vessel whose main purpose is to provide goods or services normally provided on land (e.g. floating hotel, houseboat or supermarket).

All qualifying tugs and dredgers must be registered in one of the ship registers of any of the EU Member States.

Table 10: UK Tonnage Tax Rates

For each complete 100 net tons up to 1,000 grt	£0.60
For each complete 100 net tons from 1,001 to 10,000 grt	£0.45
For each complete 100 net tons from 10,001 to 25,000 grt	£0.30
For each complete 100 net tons above 25,000 grt	£0.15

The daily profit is multiplied by the number of days operated (for a normal year, 365 days). A similar calculation is carried out for each ship operated by the company. The total for all ships is the company's profit for tonnage tax for the accounting period.

Example 1:

For 365 days, the profit subject to tonnage tax of a company operating a 250 ton supply vessel would be **£438**.

This is calculated by (1–250 grt = 200 [2 complete units of 100 tons]) / 100 = 2 × 0.60 × 365 = **£438**.

At the full rate of corporation tax of 30%, the tax payable would be **£131.40**

Example 2:

For 365 days, the profit subject to tonnage tax of a company operating a 30,000 ton bulk carrier would be:

(0–1,000 grt = 1,000)/100	=	10 × 0.60 plus
(1,001–10,000 = 9,000)/100	=	90 × 0.45 plus
(10,001–25,000 = 15,000)/100	=	150 × 0.30 plus
(25,001–30,000 = 5,000)/100	=	50 × 0.15 = 6 + 40.5 + 45 + 7.5 = £99

£99 × 365 = £36,135

Thus, the profit for tonnage tax would be £36,135 for the accounting year.

At the full rate of corporation tax of 30%, the tax payable would be £10,840.50.

It should be noted that as the vessel tonnage rises (e.g. to 150,000 grt), the calculation for the first three levels of the table remains the same. Only the last level, rated at £0.15 per 100 tons in excess of 25,000 grt, differs.

Thus, for a container vessel of 150,000 grt, the yearly profit tonnage tax would be:

$$6 + 40.5 + 45 + (1250 \times 0.15) = 6 + 40.5 + 45 + 187.5 = 279$$

$$279 \times 365 = £101,835 \text{ profit}$$

At the full rate of UK corporation tax of 30%, the tax payable for the year on that vessel would be: £30,550.50.

This figure accounts for the vessel's operation over the period of one calendar year. It takes no account of the number of containers carried as carriage revenue over that period. It should be noted that if the profit is based on actual revenue (the profit made from the carriage of a specific number of containers per year based on the cost of a slot charter per container on board vessel) that profit could differ substantially from the profit calculated according to the tonnage tax principle. Equally, the figure does not take into account considerations for bunkering costs, crewing, supplies to the vessel, vessel maintenance costs, voyage costs—including port and light dues and port berthing charges—figures which would normally have to be taken into account in the operation of any vessel, not just in terms of normal ownership, but also in terms of chartering, be it on a time or bareboat basis. It is based entirely on profits based on the vessel's operation, regardless of how much revenue it actually makes, as opposed to the operating costs associated with that operation. What should also be considered is that profits earned by a shipping company may fluctuate from year to year, thus affecting the annual amount of corporation tax due, whereas the tonnage tax is fixed depending upon the number of vessels and does not take into account such fluctuations.

The actual profits covered by a tonnage tax profit include those from:

- core qualifying activities in operating its own ships;
- other necessary ship-related activities integral to the above;
- qualifying secondary activities;
- qualifying incidental activities, not exceeding 0.25% turnover from qualifying core and secondary activities;
- distributions from overseas shipping companies (which only operate qualifying ships);
- loan relationship profits and foreign exchange gains, which could otherwise be classed as trading income;
- gains on the disposal of tonnage tax assets.

Secondary activities include:

- support services to other vessels in the group;
- the carriage of cargo or passengers beyond the sea-leg of an inclusively-priced journey;
- administration and insurance services;
- embarkation and disembarkation of passengers;
- loading and unloading cargo;
- excursions for passengers where the cabin remains available to the passenger;
- normal sales and services to, and entertainment of, passengers;
- similar services to third parties where there is use of surplus capacity;
- reciprocal arrangements with third parties;
- not being part of the operation of a port.

Certain special rules apply to the following activities:

- vessels supplying services at sea, where only the transport element is subject to tonnage tax;
- "offshore activities" carried out in the UK sector of the continental shelf, but excluding offshore supply services, towage, salvage, anchor handling, carriage of liquids or gases, safety or rescue services, and the carriage of cargo in connection with dredging which is subject to normal tax rules;
- transitional provisions on capital allowances;
- transitional provisions on chargeable gains;
- ring-fencing of tonnage profits from non-tonnage tax profits or losses, especially finance costs;
- leasing companies owning vessels, to which a special regime of capital allowances applies;
- corporate partnerships;
- legal avoidance.

Vessel-operating companies can enter the tonnage tax regime by elec
an initial period of ten years, which can then be renewed for a further ten
at any time prior to its expiry. Entry can be backdated, or postponed for up
two years in certain circumstances where HM Revenue & Customs agree.

It is important that prior to entering the tonnage tax scheme, companies
determine whether there would be any significant advantage in entering the
scheme, as opposed to being subject to corporation tax based on a conventional means of calculating profit and loss. Given fluctuations in the business
of shipping, there is no guarantee that a ship's operating viability remains the
same from year to year. The shipping market remains at best uncertain, and at
worst volatile, with operating costs rising on a regular basis, mainly due to
bunkering costs. These must be taken into account when calculating annual
profits, so there is no guarantee that the tonnage tax is beneficial to every
company.

2.8 Import Duties and the Tariff

Cargo management also encompasses clearance through customs, both for
export and import purposes. At the point of import, this clearance involves
liability for customs import duties, although certain commodities and products are rated at zero duty in several countries according to the worldwide
Harmonised System (HS). However, the process of marine cargo management still requires the importer to ensure that the goods to be imported are
declared properly, according to the correct value, description and tariff commodity code relating to the product or commodity concerned. The importer
is responsible for the import as the ultimate declarant, even if he appoints a
clearing agent to submit the declaration to customs on his behalf.

Customs import duty is paid at the time of import and is governed by the
following costs:

- Purchase cost;
- Freight cost;
- Cargo insurance.

This total cost amounts to the landed import cost based on the CIF (cost
insurance freight) cost of the imported consignment. It is therefore essential
that the importer submits the correct shipment cost figures for the consignment to the clearance broker at the time and point of import, to ensure that
the correct amount of import duty is paid, along with any other local taxes
such as VAT or sales tax, based on the above information plus the correct tariff
commodity code. The correct shipping documents, (Bills of Lading or sea
waybills) must be submitted to the clearing agent along with the purchase
invoice for the consignment, as well as details of the insurance premium paid
on the consignment. These documents enable the clearing agent to submit an
entry (customs import declaration) to the national customs authority, and pay

nt of import duty and local tax on the imported

l purpose of the customs tariff is to detail every item,
red article which will be imported into a country and
m import duty percentage rate (a percentage rate of
e value of the goods concerned). Every country
world has a customs tariff, but in some cases, there is a
common customs tariff in a trading bloc such as the European Union or the
South American MERCOSUR. In both of these cases, there is a common
customs tariff for each bloc as they both comprise a customs union (a customs
tariff common to all Member States). In the case of the NAFTA (Canada, the
United States and Mexico), a free trade area exists between all three Member
States, but each country retains its own national customs tariff and import
duty rates which vary from country to country. In the case of the European
Union, the tariff encompasses the Brussels nomenclature.

The structure of the main body of the tariff details all the tariff commodity
codes, and separates them in accordance with the worldwide Harmonised
System (HS), approved by the World Trade Organisation (WTO). It comprises 99 chapters, which are subdivided into different headings depending
upon the nature of the commodity or product concerned. Thus the first set of
chapters deal with live animals, followed by meat, vegetables and fruits.
Further chapters deal with chemicals and compounds, plastics, rubber, tex-
tiles and clothing, base metals, and these are followed by chapters dealing with
machinery and automotive products. The last few chapters deal with items not
included elsewhere, such as sports equipment, toys and games, antiques and
furniture, firearms and other weapons. Nothing is spared, although there are
areas which are seen by the customs authorities as being vague in description
and which often require special classification rulings.

Each tariff commodity code comprises a set of eight digits, split into two sets
of four. There is also a further set of two digits which act as a suffix depending
upon the use of the product or commodity concerned, for example in civil
aircraft or ships. Although the harmonised system has brought much of the
worldwide tariff system of commodity codes into a common structure, it has
not totally unified the system. Each country maintains its own level of import
duty rates, but also has an independent means of classifying items within its
own national tariff structure. This is achieved by using the first six digits of the
tariff commodity code as a common worldwide benchmark. The last two
digits of the eight-digit code may, however, differ radically from country to
country. Thus an item whose tariff code is found in the European Customs
Tariff may have an entirely different tariff code in the US Customs Tariff
depending upon the last two digits of the eight-figure code. In the US and
Canada, an item such as Women's Knitted Jerseys of Cashmere has a code of
6110 1210, whereas the applicable code in Mexico is 6101 1201. The US *ad
valorem* import duty rate of this particular item is 4%, but the Mexican

equivalent is 35%. In the EU, the commodity code is 6110 1290, and the rate is 12%. The following example shows the differences between tariff codes and import duty rates throughout the world.

Further elements are included in the tariff such as how the goods are to be quantified in the import declaration. These require the measure of weight/mass in kilograms (kg), but other specifications include:

- number;
- pairs (shoes, socks etc.);
- litres (liquids etc.);
- metres (lengths of items such as ropes, steel coils, wire, tubes etc.).

It is essential for the importer to have some basic idea as to the commodity codes to be used for a regular set of imports as this will condition the importer into ensuring that the correct tariff information is communicated to the clearing agent every time an import is to be cleared through customs. This can be gained by the importer themselves, or by requesting it from their freight agent.

It should not be assumed that the import duty rate used one year will stay the same. In general, the tariff rate will not increase from one year's end to the next, but it may decrease, in accordance with decisions made by the World Trade Organisation to progressively reduce tariffs on certain types of industrial goods over a succession of years until they reach zero-duty rate (i.e. they are duty-free). This is the case with many items including computers (HS Code 8471) and other electronic goods. Other items will follow suit, and it is intended that by the year 2005, many items included in the customs tariff will have reached duty-free status.

2.9 The Influence of Payment Terms on Marine Cargo Management

Much of the process of marine documentation depends not only upon the contract of carriage determined by the shipper, but also is influenced by the terms of payment between seller and buyer. There are two specific terms where such influence applies, namely Cash Against Documents and the Documentary Letter of Credit.

Cash against documents

The term "cash against documents" is used where the seller pays for the carriage of the goods by sea under a CIF (Cost Insurance Freight) contract, obtains the Ocean Bills of Lading, and sends them to the buyer's bank. The negotiable Ocean Bill of Lading is a document of title signifying ownership, or title, over the goods, and therefore cannot be passed to the buyer unless the buyer has paid for the goods, or made an agreement with the seller through the bank to pay at an agreed future date. Since the buyer cannot claim the consignment off the vessel without a valid original copy of the negotiable Bill of Lading, it needs to be able to obtain the Bill of Lading from the bank, along with the other documents pertaining to the consignment. The only way the buyer can do this is by arranging immediate payment from their account to the seller. In reality, once the documents have arrived at the buyer's bank, the bank notifies the buyer of their arrival and requests payment instructions. Once the money has been paid for the consignment to the seller, the bank releases the documents, including the Bill of Lading, to the buyer, and the consignment can then be claimed once it arrives at the port of destination. As long as the Bill of Lading is "clean" (no damage has occurred to the consignment before or after it was shipped) the buyer will accept the consignment without any problem. If, however, the Bill of Lading is "claused" (damage occurred to the consignment before it was loaded aboard vessel) the buyer has the right to reject the consignment.

This kind of contract and payment term can only take place with a CIF contract, as the buyer effectively takes charge of the consignment once it is unloaded from the vessel. The main principle is that once the Bill of Lading is issued, it is sent to the buyer's bank while the consignment is still on the high seas. As long as this is the case and the Bill of Lading arrives at the buyer's bank before the vessel enters port, then the Bill is still valid and can be used as collateral between seller and buyer in the sale. The result is that the consignment is sold while still on the high seas, and is already the property of the buyer when the vessel docks at port. This form of sale is commonplace, and is still a guarantee for both parties that the contract can be enforced. It also means that once the buyer has the Bill of Lading, they can claim the cargo from the shipping line through their freight forwarder or clearing agent, and ensure that customs clearance is effected speedily and efficiently without any reason or need for delays at the port of destination, which could result in unnecessary demurrage costs.

Documentary letter of credit

The documentary letter of credit is a form of payment from buyer to seller on conditional terms, with all such terms expressed in the letter of credit when it is raised and issued by the buyer's bank on behalf of the buyer. In most cases, letters of credit refer to maritime shipments, and require many conditions to be fulfilled by the seller in terms of maritime shipments for the contract to be honoured and payment effected. Such terms refer to the manner of shipment, in particular the arrangement of the shipment, and how it is managed.

The terms included in the letter of credit are governed by a system known as the Uniform Customs and Practice for Documentary Credits, presently Series 500 (UCP 500), but in the process of amendment and update to Series 600. In the UCP 500, Articles 23–26 cover sea freight shipments, and stipulate the conditions acceptable for the application of a letter of credit and its fulfilment.

Article 23 covers Marine/Ocean Bills of Lading, and deals with the following issues:

- The signature or authentication of the Bill of Lading;
- The requirement for "shipped on board" bills;
- Identification of the vessel;
- The port of loading and the port of discharge;
- The number of originals of the Bills;
- The terms and conditions of carriage;
- Trans-shipment conditions and whether trans-shipment is allowed.

Article 24 covers sea waybills and covers the following conditions:

- signature and authentication of the waybill;
- indication that the goods have been loaded on board the vessel;
- identification of the vessel;
- the port of loading and discharge;
- the number of copies of the waybill.

Article 25 covers Charterparty Bills of Lading, and deals with the same issues as detailed above, except that it also requires the following details:

- The indication that the Bill is subject to a Charterparty contract:
- The name and details of the party chartering the vessel, and their representative or agent.

Article 26 covers multimodal transport documents and includes the details of the maritime transport within such arrangements. It also covers the same elements as detailed in the previous Articles, and applies the same guidelines in terms of requirements to cover such forms of transport.

The overall purpose of the UCP 500 provisions and definitions concerning sea transport is to ensure that the contract of carriage is correctly undertaken by the seller, as it assumes that the seller will be made responsible for the arrangement of the carriage of the consignment, usually implying that any of the maritime-related INCOTERMS from CFR onwards are being used. It requires the exporter to ensure that all aspects of the shipment are correctly undertaken, be they logistics or documentary, and that all Bills of Lading are deemed "clean", signifying that no damage has occurred to the consignment prior to it being loaded aboard vessel. In this respect, a letter of credit may also be used to ensure that payment is made by the buyer to the seller while the consignment is on the high seas, and that the documents will be obtained by the buyer before the vessel arrives at the port of destination, although in most cases the letter of credit allows for a defined credit period before the beneficiary receives their money. As long as the seller has correctly complied with all the terms of the letter of credit, then payment can be effected smoothly and efficiently without any delays.

3 MARINE INSURANCE

Marine insurance is another of the most important elements of the process of carriage of goods by sea. It is the means by which the ship owner and the shipper have the ability and capacity to be indemnified against the risk of wreck, damage or loss to both the vessel and its cargoes. Vessel insurance was covered earlier in the text, as it refers more to the vessel's operation and the costs associated therewith, but cargo insurance is a very detailed affair and demands more attention at this point.

Marine insurance can be defined by the *Marine Insurance Act (1906)* in the following way:

"A contract of marine insurance is a contract whereby the insurer undertakes to indemnify the assured in a manner and to the extent thereby agreed, against marine losses, that is to say, the losses incidental to marine adventure."

Since a marine adventure covers the carriage of cargo by sea, then the insurance contract covers both the vessel and the cargo it carries from one country to another. Cargo insurance, therefore, is a vital part of the whole essence of the carriage of cargo by sea, as it covers for any loss or damage incurred to the cargo while it is in the care of the maritime carrier.

3.1 Lloyd's of London

Much of the cargo insurance market is governed by Lloyd's of London, and is underwritten (guaranteed) by a series of Lloyd's underwriters and insurance agents. Given that there are no fixed rates in marine insurance, the actual premium for a particular vessel and its cargo is assessed on the basis of the incidence of losses in that particular trade and the risks that the vessel transporting the cargo and the cargo itself are likely to experience during that particular voyage (deemed to be the "marine adventure").

Lloyd's is a society of underwriters which has its origins in the late 17th century, when ship owners, merchants and underwriters met at Edward Lloyd's coffee house in the City of London. Edward Lloyd provided the facilities for the clientele of his coffee house to undertake the business of marine insurance, although he had no personal involvement in this business and consequently had no responsibility or liability with respect to the risks underwritten. His profession, after all, was as the proprietor of a bustling coffee house and he allowed his clientele to undertake the honourable business in which they were engaged without interference. The business of insurance grew and Lloyd's was eventually incorporated by Act of Parliament in 1871. Today, the Corporation of Lloyd's performs the same function as that of Edward Lloyd over 300 years ago, insofar as it provides the premises and the necessary services for the underwriting members, known as "names" grouped in "syndicates" to conduct the business of underwriting. The corporation is controlled by a council comprising 28 members, who elect a chairman. The corporation itself incurs no responsibility whatsoever with respect to the business accepted by the underwriting members, although there have been occasions when severe losses incurred by some underwriters with respect to various valuable claims made against them in recent years have shaken the very commercial foundations of the corporation. The gist of the function is that business is placed at Lloyd's and not with Lloyd's. Today, the business underwritten includes non-marine, motor and aviation insurance, as well as marine insurance.

The capacity (the financial strength) of each syndicate is based on the collective wealth shown by its underwriting members. Each syndicate is managed by a managing agent, who appoints the active underwriter and supporting staff of the underwriting box of the syndicate in the Underwriting Room at Lloyd's. The underwriter, who is also a Lloyd's member, sits at the underwriting box of the syndicate and accepts risks on behalf of his members who bear the proportion of their particular share in the syndicate. Each member receives his particular percentage share of all premiums and pays the same percentage of all claims emanating from the risks for which he or she has received premium. Each member has a separate and unlimited liability with respect to the risks written on his or her behalf by the underwiter of the syndicate, hence the massive claims which have cost some underwriters dear in the past resulting from several calamities, such as the disasters concerning the oil tankers *Exxon Valdez*, *Erika* and *Prestige*. No doubt the claims as a result of the grounding of the container vessel *MSC Napoli* will also cost certain Lloyd's underwriters a considerable amount of money. Larger risks are placed with a number of underwriters in the market, each accepting a proportion (usually a percentage) of the sum insured. The underwriters also work with Lloyd's brokers, who generally act on behalf of the assured (the company requiring the insurance policy). The brokers act as intermediaries, and many are large international organisations employing several thousand people worldwide.

In most ports around the world, it is possible to find a Lloyd's agent. These may be individuals or companies appointed by the Corporation of Lloyd's to serve the maritime community in their area. Like the corporation appointing them, they have no powers of underwriting. Their main duties are:

- protecting the interests of underwriters according to instructions which may be sent to them;
- rendering advice and assistance to Masters of shipwrecked vessels;
- reporting information regarding all casualties which occur in their district and information as to arrivals and departures of vessels to Lloyd's;
- appointing surveyors to carry out inspections of damaged vessels and granting certification of seaworthiness when called upon to do so by Masters of vessels which have suffered damage;
- notifying London of all relevant information which may come to their notice;

- surveying or appointing surveyors when called upon by consignees of cargo or by underwriters to survey damage and issuing reports stating the cause, nature and extent of all damage.

3.2 Principles of Insurance

The basic principles of insurance are specified in the Marine Insurance Act 1906 and are as follows:

- insurable interest;
- utmost good faith (*uberrimae fidei*);
- indemnity; and
- subrogation.

Insurable interest

The Marine Insurance Act 1906 states that a person has an insurable interest in a marine adventure (any shipped goods or other maritime-related moving items exposed to maritime perils) where he or she stands in any legal or equitable relationship to the adventure or insurable property at risk therein in consequence of which he may:

- benefit by the safety or due arrival of the insurable property; or
- be prejudiced by its loss, or by damage thereto, or by the detention thereof; or
- incur liability in respect thereof.

Insurable interest is the financial interest of a person in the subject matter insured. They are, or stand to be, the owners of the property to be insured and stand to gain financially by being the owners of the goods, in the sense that they will sell the consignment for a profit. Thus, the insurable interest of the cargo owner is not the goods—the subject matter insured—but his financial interest in such goods and, accordingly, he should insure those goods to the extent of that interest.

However, a person does not necessarily have to own the goods to have an insurable interest in them. A warehousekeeper can have an insurable interest in goods stored in his warehouse, regardless of who owns those goods, on the grounds that they are in his care and custody. An underwriter who insures goods has an insurable interest insofar as, if they are lost or damaged by one of the perils such goods are insured against, he will be obliged to pay the claim made against him under the policy concerned. The Marine Insurance Act provides that the person entering into a contract of marine insurance must have an insurable interest or an expectation of acquiring one—that they expect to take delivery of the goods at some foreseeable time in the future. This effectively covers the case of a buyer in a CIF contract who acquires his interest when the title to the goods purchased is transferred to him sometime after transit has commenced from the seller's premises, usually somewhere on the high seas.

Concrete proof of insurable interest is not required at the time of creating an insurance contract and policy. However, if a claim is made, it is necessary for the assured to be able to show that he had an insurable interest at the time of loss, usually by production of a copy of the Bill of Lading, which is seen as the document of title and therefore confers ownership of the goods on the assured. Cargo insurance arranged with respect to CIF contracts of sale is usually based on what is known as "lost or not lost" conditions, which means that the assured may recover any loss, even though he may not have acquired his interest in the goods until after the actual time of loss. This is because the insurance policy is passed form the seller to the buyer at the point the cargo is loaded over the ship's rail at the port of loading, even if the seller arranged the actual insurance policy on behalf of the buyer.

The most common forms of insurable interest in cargo insurance are:

- ownership of the goods;
- charges of insurance (Premium);
- freight.

Ownership of the goods

The cargo owner has an insurable interest in the goods since he will benefit by their safe arrival or be prejudiced by loss of or damage to the goods. Ownership usually involves two parties, the seller and the buyer, or the consignor and consignee. The insurance requirements of these parties will depend upon the terms of the contract of sale.

The premium

The assured has an insurable interest in the premium paid with respect to any insurance he may arrange on the consignment. In cargo insurance, the sum insured reflects the cost of the goods plus the cost of insurance, usually calculated as follows:

$$(\text{Cost of goods} \times 110\%) \times 0.4\%$$

Freight

This is the cost of transporting the goods from the consignor's premises to the consignee's premises, and is either prepaid (freight prepaid) or payable at destination (freight collect). In most cases, advanced or prepaid freight is not returnable even if the goods are lost and not delivered. The freight prepaid, therefore, is at the risk of the cargo owner and, as in the case of premium, is added to the value of the goods, especially for CIF import-landed cost purposes, which must also include the insurance premium cost for the cargo.

Consequently, the sum insured reflects the cost of the goods plus the cost of insurance (premium) plus the cost of transportation (freight).

The insurance cover is also influenced by the INCOTERMS used to ship the goods from the seller's premises to the buyer's premises. In an EXW contract, the buyer is entirely responsible for all aspects of the transportation of the consignment, and is therefore equally responsible for the insurance of the cargo from the seller's premises to their own premises.

Under a FOB contract, the seller arranges insurance for the cargo from their premises up to the point of loading the consignment over the ship's rail and on to the vessel. From the point of loading over the ship's rail, the buyer becomes responsible for arranging all other insurance up to the point of delivery of the consignment to their premises.

A CIF contract places the responsibility on the seller for arranging the transport of the goods from their premises to that of the buyer and paying for the freight involved. In reality, the CIF contract transfers the responsibility and risk for the cargo to the buyer at the point of loading over the ship's rail, despite the fact that the seller is responsible for payment of the freight and insurance up to the port of destination.

3.3 Utmost Good Faith (Uberrimae Fidei)

The Marine Insurance Act 1906 states that a contract of marine insurance is a contract based upon the "utmost good faith" (*uberrimae fidei*), and if this is not observed by either party (the insurer or the insured) the other party may avoid the contract. In other words, if the party seeking to arrange an insurance contract does not notify the insurer of the true nature of the subject of the contract (the cargo, especially where it is of very high value or is of a hazardous or dangerous nature) the insurer may seek to render the insurance policy null and void should they subsequently discover its true nature.

It would be neither practical nor possible for underwriters to verify the accuracy or completeness of information submitted to them with respect to a risk to be insured. They have to rely on the other party—the proposer of the policy or the broker acting on behalf of the proposer—to observe the principle of utmost good faith which means a full disclosure of all material circumstances relating to the risk before the contract is concluded. A material circumstance is one which would influence a wise or cautious underwriter as to the desirability of the risk. Where there is a non-disclosure of a material circumstance, either wilfully or otherwise, the underwriter may avoid the contract. The underwriter may also avoid the contract if the broker is guilty of misrepresenting the risk during the negotiations to arrange the contract. In some cases, the contract making the policy may still go ahead, but the underwriter may refuse to pay the claim on the grounds that there has been a non-disclosure or misrepresentation at the time of placing the insurance, although this misrepresentation or non-disclosure would have to be proved, even in a court of law where necessary.

3.4 Indemnity

The purpose of insurance is to protect the insurable interest of the of the assured whereby, in the event of loss of or damage to the subject matter insured (the cargo, resulting from an insured peril) the assured is placed in the same position that they enjoyed immediately before the loss occurred. This principle is called "indemnity", in that the assured is being indemnified against the loss of the cargo.

While replacement of the item concerned is the normal means of effecting indemnity in some types of insurance, it would not be practical for marine insurers to replace ships and cargoes. The manner of indemnity is, therefore, a cash settlement. The value of this settlement is the insurable value and the basis for its calculation is specified in the Marine Insurance Act 1906. In the case of cargo, it is the prime cost of the goods, plus the incidental costs of shipping and insurance upon the total amount.

3.5 Subrogation

Subrogation is the corollary of indemnity insofar as its application prevents the assured from defeating the principle of indemnity by recovering his loss from more than one party. For example, a containerised cargo may be lost overboard from a vessel in the Bay of Biscay, notorious for its adverse weather conditions. Under an "all risks" insurance policy, the assured would be entitled to indemnity from their underwriters. They would also have recourse against the carrier. While they may lodge claims against both, they may not recover and retail amounts of money resulting from each claim from both underwriter and carrier as this would defeat the principle of indemnity and could ultimately be seen as a form of fraud. In practice, the underwriter, on payment of the claim for the damage, would automatically be subrogated to all rights and remedies the cargo owner had against the carrier and could, accordingly, exercise these rights either in their own name or that of the assured for a recovery against the amount paid by them under the insurance policy. In other words, the underwriter would submit a further claim against the carrier to recover the amount paid to the assured. Ultimately, the rights of subrogation pass to the underwriter on payment of any type of claim. However, where the claim is in respect of a total loss, the underwriter is additionally entitled to proprietary rights with respect to whatever may remain of the insured goods and, accordingly, may dispose of these goods as is seen appropriate, retaining the entirety of any proceeds even though the value of these proceeds may exceed the amount of the claim paid.

The contract of carriage will clearly state which party is responsible for arranging the insurance for the goods being supplied, together with the point at which responsibility for the cargo changes from seller to buyer. It is this point which determines which party has the responsibility and the right to claim from the carrier under any insurance policy affecting the carriage of the cargo concerned. This point will be reflected in the International Commercial Term (INCOTERM) applied to the contract. It is thus important that insurance cover for the consignment is in force for the entire journey being undertaken, including any loading, unloading and temporary storage. Therefore, insurance cover for the consignment should take into account the following:

- transportation of the consignment to the seaport of departure;
- the period during which the goods are stored awaiting shipment or loading;
- the time whilst the consignment is on board vessel, or on a road trailer embarked on a Ro-Ro vessel;
- the off-loading and storage on arrival at the seaport of destination, or other specified place;
- transportation to the buyer's premises.

Where the supplier is responsible for arranging insurance, the insurance certificate or policy will be sent with the shipping documentation as evidence of cover. Insurance cover arranged by the supplier may end when the goods are landed at the port of arrival, especially under the provisions of a CIF contract, which can lead to problems such as the following:

- cover required for the transit of goods from the port of arrival to the buyer's premises;
- goods arriving damaged or incomplete at the port of arrival may lead to disputes between seller and buyer. Unless the goods are inspected immediately upon arrival, it may be difficult to prove where the loss or damage occurred;
- settlement of claims may be delayed if insurance is arranged by an overseas insurer.

However, these problems can be resolved by several mechanisms, including:

- extension of the seller's marine insurance cover to the ultimate destination, with the buyer assuming responsibility for the insurance premium relating to the period after arrival at the port of destination;
- separate insurance cover being arranged by the buyer covering the final stages of the transit, although this may not resolve demarcation disputes;
- the buyer taking responsibility for insurance from the supplier's premises to the ultimate destination.

3.6 General Average

General average is defined as "the loss arising in consequences of extraordinary and intentional sacrifices made or expenses incurred, for the common safety of the ship and cargo". The term usually refers to the issue of a cargo being jettisoned over the side of a ship to ensure the safety of the vessel and crew and other consignments aboard vessel. However, it has also come to refer to the issue of the indemnity for a lost cargo owing to damage or destruction of that cargo while on board vessel based on the pooled financial premiums relating to other cargoes on board vessel. Examples of general average include jettison of cargo, loss of cargo, destruction of cargo, damage to cargo, etc.

The principle of general average revolves around the pooling of all insurance premiums for all cargoes carried aboard vessel. This financial resource is then used to indemnify a cargo owner should their cargo be subject to damage or destruction while on board vessel, or is lost at sea for whatever reason, such as containers being washed overboard in the height of a storm, as is often the case. Rather than a specific claim being lodged against the carrier for a specific reason, especially where the carrier can show that they were not responsible for the mishap which resulted in the loss of the specific cargo, then it is more common to seek redress by claiming compensation based on the collective pooled resources resulting from the total of all the insurance premiums raised for each cargo on board vessel at the time. Given the number of containers carried by vessels today, then the sums of money raised as a result of such premiums will adequately serve to indemnify the owners of any individual cargo lost through any mishap, such as the case of the cargoes lost as a result of the inferno aboard the container vessel *Hyundai Fortune* off the Yemeni coast.

In the event of a shipowner declaring a general average loss occurring, each party in the voyage must contribute in proportion to their interest in the maritime venture. This naturally involves shippers who may not have suffered any damage or loss to their cargo. The cargo is only released when the shipper or importer has given either a cash deposit or provided a general average guarantee given by the insurers, usually involving the signing of a general average bond which confirms that the importer will pay his general average contribution following the average adjuster's assessment.

CHAPTER 6

COMPLIANCES AND CONTROLS

1 CUSTOMS MARITIME CARGO REPORTING AND CONTROLS

It should be noted that, for the purposes of this book, reference is made to customs procedures in the UK, as this is where the book has been written. However, under the EU Customs Harmonisation Principles laid down by the EU, most customs procedures described in this chapter can be broadly related to those procedures used elsewhere in the EU. However, customs procedures elsewhere in the world may differ, and this book bears no responsibility for procedures used elsewhere, other than only the basic principles involved in the process of submitting customs cargo declarations for both import and export purposes.

In the UK, HM Customs & Excise, the government department responsible for indirect taxation, merged with HM Inland Revenue in May 2005 to form an expanded Revenue Department called HM Revenue & Customs (HMRC). Although the main activity of the newly merged department is the levying of national taxes, both direct and indirect, its other primary function is that of the economic defence of the realm from a maritime point of view.

Although the role of HM Customs & Excise (now HM Revenue & Customs) has changed significantly in the recent past because of the progressive use of electronic procedures, the powers of the department concerning the control over incoming and outgoing vessels has not. The Customs & Excise Management Act 1979 gives officers of the department the power to intercept, board and search vessels as required in the course of their duties, especially in cases where they have reasonable grounds to suspect a breach of the C&E Management Act.

Although the Waterguard (the waterborne means of customs patrol found at most major UK seaports in the past) has largely disappeared in its original and traditional form, the waterborne function has not, with several modern armed vessels now used to combat smuggling around the UK coastline. The vessels are part of the Marine and Aviation Agency within HM Revenue & Customs, and operate in various regional maritime sectors around the UK. The officers on board these vessels have the power to intercept and board any vessel entering the 12-mile limit (as sanctioned by CEMA 1979) suspected of attempting to contravene the C&E Act in any way, especially concerning the smuggling of taxable or prohibited goods, such as cigarettes, drugs and weapons. If such goods are found, not only may the crew of the vessel be arrested and the offending goods seized, but the vessel itself is liable to be impounded and disposed of by the department.

Customs controls are those controls exercised over the process of international trade with relation to specific control over the following areas:

- import of goods (personal or commercial);
- export of goods (personal or commercial);
- illicit trade (i.e. smuggling);
- prohibitions and restrictions of the import and export of certain commodities and products;
- trade statistics;
- duties and indirect taxes.

Customs control starts at the baseline defining the area of internal sea, but they also control ports, harbours and wharves which may serve the purpose of international trade. Every seaport must seek the approval of the national customs authority prior to becoming operational, and it thus becomes a customs port. The Commissioners of Customs & Excise are empowered by section 19 of the Customs & Excise Management Act 1979 to appoint any area of the United Kingdom as a customs port and to appoint boarding stations for customs officers to board ships (originally known as the Waterguard). However with the changes in import and export procedures to allow for more electronic-based regimes, the facility for boarding ships has decreased to a bare minimum, if not zero, allowing for little or no waterborne customs control over inward or outward shipping movements.

The ports comprise the "internal and territorial waters of Her Majesty's dominions" and extend inland up to the "mean high water line". The Commissioners also appoint "approved wharves" for the loading or unloading of cargoes (Customs & Excise Management Act 1979, s. 20).

Customs officers have a general power to board ships inside the limits of a customs port (s. 27). They may have access to every part of a ship, and any goods found concealed or undeclared are liable to forfeiture and seizure. The ship itself can also be seized, especially where illicit trade in drugs is concerned (s. 28). A ship which is constructed or adapted or simply used for the purposes of concealing or smuggling goods may itself be forfeit and seized by Customs Officers in UK waters (s. 88), generally by way of securing the "writ of assistance" to the ship's mast.

A report must be made by every ship, other than authorised regular shipping services such as cross-Channel or North Sea Ferry Services, arriving at a customs port from any place outside the UK, or vessels carrying uncleared goods (goods not in UK/EU free circulation and thus duty-paid) brought in that vessel from any place outside the United Kingdom (s. 35), including third-country (non-EU) goods which have crossed the EU under community transit (CT) conditions (undeclared up to the point of entry into the UK).

The Ship's Report, Importation and Exportation by Sea Regulations 1981 (SI 1981/1260 amended by SI 1986/1819) specify that a report (the Customs Cargo Report—CUSCAR, generally comprising the ship's cargo manifest) must be made immediately to a boarding officer if he requests it. Otherwise, the report must be made within three hours of the ship reaching her place of unloading or loading, or within 24 hours after entering the limits of the customs port if she has not then reached that place. There must be no interference with goods after the ship has come within UK internal waters until a report is made. On arrival, a ship must immediately be brought to the boarding station, unless public health regulations require her to be taken to a mooring station pending examination and clearance to dock. Goods imported by sea must be landed at an approved wharf. If chargeable or dutiable goods are unloaded from ship without payment of the appropriate duties and taxes, or prohibited goods are imported, or imported goods are concealed or otherwise not correctly declared, they are liable to seizure and forfeiture (s. 49). With the move from manual to electronic import declarations, however, there is little evidence of customs landing or import controls at the port, as there is intense pressure on the Port Authorities to ensure that containerised consignments are moved from the port to an inland destination as quickly as possible, especially given the limited space available at the port for the detention or storage of goods.

No ship may depart from a port on a voyage to an eventual destination outside the UK unless clearance has been obtained. A customs officer may board a cleared ship while she is still in UK waters, and require documentary production of her clearance. A ship departing from a customs port must bring to at a boarding station if required (s. 64). Consignments for export and store must be loaded at an approved wharf and must be correctly declared, using the new export system (NES) electronic procedures. The ship can only be cleared for departure once the customs CHIEF computer has given clearance for all goods declared for export to be loaded aboard vessel and those goods have been correctly loaded and recorded on the ship's cargo manifest, including manifests concerning the shipment of consignments to the North Sea Continental Shelf.

Although it is accepted that a regime exists for Customs cargo reporting in line with the requirements laid down by the Customs & Excise Management Act 1979, the information contained in such reports may not be enough to satisfy the customs CHIEF (Customs Handling of Import & Export Freight) computer or officers perusing such details. Containers unloaded from aboard ship will be classified in either of two categories—FCL (Full Container Load) containing cargoes pertaining to one single importer—or LCL (Less-than-Full Container Load) containing a variety of consolidated or grouped cargoes pertaining to a variety of importers. Whereas an FCL will define the exact nature of the cargo, which can then be easily defined and declared by the clearing agent, an LCL will simply be defined to HM Customs & Excise as

"Groupage" or FAK (Freight of all Kinds). At the point of reporting, it will thus be impossible for the examining officer, or the CHIEF computer, to define the nature of each consignment carried within the container until such time as the clearing agent makes the individual customs import entry declaration for each deconsolidated consignment. By this time, the container may well have left the port for a determined inland destination, and will not have been examined by an officer of HM Customs & Excise other than if it has been subjected to an x-ray at the port, in which case a full out-turn of all consignments may be required. Given this lack of control, there is no certainty that an officer would pick up any irregular details pertaining to cargoes, such as the illegal import of drugs, firearms, weapons of mass destruction or even illegal immigrants.

The issue of the exemption of authorised regular shipping services from customs reporting regimes (JCCC Papers (04)10 and (04)27, HM Customs & Excise 2004) gives rise to anomalies in the reporting of cargoes. It is very likely that these vessels are not only carrying goods of EU origin, but also consignments under community transit (CT) customs control (goods which are not in EU free circulation and are hence uncleared). They may also be carrying consignments on a consolidated basis—consignments grouped together in one consolidated trailer load, for which there are only brief summary details referring to the consolidation, not necessarily for each individual grouped consignment. There is a clear need for customs to know what these consignments are and where they are to be cleared through customs controls, as national revenue is at stake. There is a significant risk that since vessels pertaining to authorised regular shipping services (including ferry services from Norway such as the sailings of DFDS and Fjord Line into the River Tyne) are not required to report to customs prior to, or on arrival at a UK customs port, their cargoes will not be reported to customs in a way which enables them to establish the nature and status of the consignments. In one case, however, an anomaly exists concerning the now-terminated DFDS sailings between Gothenburg (Sweden) and the UK via Kristiansand (Norway), as the voyage was essentially an intra-EU sailing (UK–Sweden) with a non-EU intermediate stop (Norway). The rules that apply to such authorised services also apply to those sailings between Norway and Denmark, also operated by DFDS and Fjord Line. Indeed, there is a real risk that if a vessel was carrying consignments or passengers of a nature deemed a threat to national security, or the economic security of the nation, these could pass unnoticed into national territory without any form of verification or checks.

However, because a vessel sails within EU territorial waters between the ports of two Member States does not imply that the information about its cargoes is automatically passed from the despatching party to the receiving party. Although electronic facilities enable a seller to communicate with a buyer about the consignment of goods to be shipped, as far as commercial documents such as invoices or packing lists are concerned, this information does not necessarily correspond with that contained on loading lists or ship's manifests, or even Bills of Lading or waybills, which generally reflect upon the information in the former sets of documents. Indeed, it is very likely that the information contained in either of these documents only exists in abbreviated form, and may prevail in a greater sense with the advent of electronic Bills of Lading presently being introduced under the revisions to the Carriage of Goods at Sea Acts and the Hague-Visby and Hamburg Rules. Hence the inability of HM Customs & Excise to maintain full controls over the information submitted by shipping agents or shipowners pertaining to customs cargo reporting, despite the requirements for vessels other than those operating on authorised regular services to submit reports to the customs authority prior to or upon arrival in a UK port. This scenario shows that although information pertaining to cargoes may be known by the trader, be it import or export, it is not necessarily known or communicated by either freight agents, NVOCCs (Non-Vessel-Owning Common Carriers), port agents, liner agents, shipowners or Customs officials, despite the rules laid down by the Carriage of Goods at Sea Acts of 1971 and 1992 pertaining to the responsibilities of shipowners, shipping agents and the Masters of vessels. This would also suggest the possibility of a vacuum in information transparency and accessibility as far as the carriage of goods on the high seas is concerned. There is an urgent need to review the level and detail of cargo information pertaining to any vessel sailing into, or within the confines of EU Territorial Waters, especially as this information may concern the insurance principle of *uberrimae fidei* (utmost good faith) and also issues of national security which could be prejudicial to the wellbeing or security of the national state.

Due to the reduction in personnel in HM Revenue & Customs the Department has requested certain UK port authorities to report activities which may be deemed to be suspicious, irregular or untoward in any way. Furthermore, the resource reductions have resulted in HMRC centralising its import/export control operations in regional centres, at a distance from the seaports, and only sending officers to examine containers when deemed necessary. All import and export declarations are now submitted electronically to central entry processing units rather than to a port-based EPU. However, the port authorities themselves are under severe pressure to ensure that all consignments are moved swiftly out of the confines of the port and on to their respective inland destinations. The limitations posed by the summary information the port authority itself may receive from an incoming vessel imply that it is not possible for the port authority to inform HM Customs & Excise concerning the movements of every vessel and the nature of its cargo, especially when the individual shipping agent or the freight clearing agent receives the information about the cargo to be cleared through customs. Indeed, HM Customs & Excise places more reliance on the freight and shipping agents and the importers to declare information pertaining to each cargo rather than the seaport itself. Information pertaining to arrivals and departures from a specific port is limited to that port alone; no other port in the UK or the EU is able to gain access to such information, as the present reporting system only takes place between the vessel and the port concerned.

Given the freedoms enjoyed by the Member States of the European Union in moving goods as long as consignments originate within the EU, there are no controls on their movement. This implies that an EU-registered ship sailing from, for example, a port on the Baltic bound for a UK port will require no customs controls assuming that its cargo originates within the EU. However, it should be noted that the vessel may carry cargoes originating outside the EU (from Russia or elsewhere). Unless that cargo is individually reported as being in separate containers or trailers, or the vessel itself is registered outside the EU, the cargo may not be declared on the CHIEF customs computer when it arrives in the UK port. The underlying risk is that undeclared cargo may "slip through the net" on arrival in the UK and may either be misdeclared or not declared at all, thus posing a substantial risk not only to the national revenue and hence the economic wellbeing of the nation, but also a threat to national security if it were subsequently discovered that the cargo was weapons or chemical in nature. As the level of customs presence at the UK ports has diminished, so the risk and threat to national security of unsolicited and undeclared imports has increased. If the vessel carrying goods between two EU ports is not registered in an EU port, then the documents for all the goods on board must be accompanied by a T2L form. This confers EU free circulation status on these goods, and ensures that they will not be subject to EU customs import duty and VAT when they are unloaded from the vessel and declared through customs at the port of import.

Only if cargoes are declared at the point of entry into the distant EU state under community transit (CT) status, and are then shipped via the EU port of dispatch to the relevant UK port, will the consignment be declared on the ship's manifest to HM Customs & Excise at the point of arrival at the UK port. A full import declaration can be made in this way, and the consignment properly discharged out of customs control. However, there is still a duty of care on the part of the forwarder to ensure compliance with customs regulations, and in the case of community transit status this means that a T1 customs control document must be issued for the consignment's transit across the EU up to the point it is unloaded from the vessel and is declared to customs. Once the full import declaration has been made, the T1 is discharged and the carrier's liability for compliant carriage of the consignment is equally discharged.

As previously mentioned, most of the administrative and documentary control activity is conducted from distant entry processing units and centralised control functions elsewhere in the country. Actual port-related activities are conducted on the basis of officers travelling to a port when required (e.g. random checks made on passengers disembarking from cruise liners or container scans). Otherwise, all declarations for cargoes, ship's stores, pas-

sengers and crew are being transferred to electronic facilities. These procedures are detailed below.

1.1 Customs Export Requirements

The export element of customs control, especially with regard to maritime
movements, has become more automated with the implementation in 2002 of
the NES (new export system), although a submission of the full cargo manifest
to customs by the ship's agents prior to the vessel being cleared for sailing is
required. In this respect, the cargo manifest is based on the load list for each
consignment, coupled with the raising of NES export declarations by the
clearing agent/freight forwarder. However, the submission of each set of
documents rests with different parties, as the following summary shows:

- the cargo manifest is submitted to customs by the ship's agents or the
  port agents;
- the NES declarations are submitted by the freight agents;
- the Bills of Lading are raised by the carrier (the shipping line).

The Bills of Lading are submitted by the shipping line to the freight forwarder
responsible for arranging the shipment. Copies may also be held by the ship's
agent, who submits the cargo manifest on behalf of the line to customs. Cases
arise where there is uncertainty over who is responsible for the loading of cargo
aboard vessel, owing to the absence of a specific INCOTERM in the contract
of delivery. In some cases, Bills of Lading are not submitted to a freight agent,
and consequently no cargo manifest is submitted to customs concerning the
specific consignment. Customs are therefore unaware that the consignment
has been loaded aboard vessel and has not been correctly declared. In the case
of hazardous or dangerous cargoes, this could prove disastrous in the event of
an accident aboard vessel or a collision. The trader (the exporter or importer)
could ultimately be held liable for the consequences of such an accident. A
further consequence of a failure to correctly declare a consignment to customs
is that the trader is liable for VAT on the value of the consignment and a civil
penalty on the grounds of a false declaration being made to customs.

It is worth noting the following procedure concerning the issue of NES
export declarations since the procedures involved influence how quickly a
vessel can be cleared for departure:

- The NES pre-shipment advice declaration (PSA) is entered into the
  CHIEF customs computer and a declaration unique consignment ref-
  erence (DUCR) is raised for the individual consignment.
- The computer acknowledges the declaration and clears the consign-
  ment for movement to the port of loading.
- The consignment arrives at the port and the DUCR is input into the
  CHIEF computer.

- The CHIEF computer selects one from three possible clearance routes:
  - Route 6: electronic clearance without examination;
  - Route 1: Documentary check;
  - Route 2: Consignment examination.
- On satisfactory checks being made, especially in cases of either Routes 1 or 2, the CHIEF Computer clears the consignment for loading aboard vessel.
- The departure message is sent to the agents signifying that the vessel is ready to depart.
- The final message is sent to the agents signifying that the vessel has sailed and that the cargoes have left UK and EU waters.

In all instances of loading aboard vessel, it is imperative that all steps are taken to ensure that all cargoes are correctly entered on shipping documentation so that correct export declarations can be raised and submitted to customs in advance of the cargo being loaded aboard vessel, as well as the cargo manifest being submitted to customs prior to departure. Theoretically, failure to correctly declare a cargo to customs could result in a refusal to allow the loading of the cargo aboard vessel. In reality, few physical checks of export cargoes are made at the port owing to a lack of physical resources and manpower. However, in the European Union, the exporter is required by law to have a valid hard copy of the export customs declaration (Commission Regulation 2454/93, Articles 205.3 and 288) for each export made to a destination outside the European Union.

With most reporting mechanisms now being carried out electronically, the structure of the maritime reporting regime with regard to customs controls has also changed. Although customs still maintain control over all seaports, there is no longer the same degree of physical presence at many seaports. The CHIEF customs computer relies on the details of the DUCR to ensure that the correct details of each consignment have been entered by the exporter or, more likely, the freight agent. However, in cases where the consignment is shipped Ex Works (EXW) and especially in a groupage arrangement, the exporter is very unlikely to see a copy of the export declaration. In many cases, a DUCR may not be raised by the clearing agent as the consignment is part of a larger consolidated consignment arranged by the overseas buyer. The only declaration raised at export will be the master UCR which covers the whole LCL groupage container load. In this respect, the details shown on the declaration will show the agent/consolidator as the exporter, so their VAT details will be entered, rather than those of the individual exporters whose consignments are contained in the consolidation. There is no compliance for each exporter and this not only distorts statistical information pertaining to export consolidations, given that the customs authority places full responsibility for an export at the door of the exporter, but also masks and distorts information concerning the true contents of the container at the time of export. Such omissions contravene US Customs regulations under the CT-PAT initiative and also compromise safety regulations concerning the carriage of cargoes by sea, especially concerning the nature of the FAL 2 cargo manifest and its requirements under the IMO FAL Convention.

All export declarations for maritime cargo and ship's stores are now electronic. Many EU countries have implemented electronic export declaration procedures. The UK implemented its own electronic export regime, the NES (new export system) in 2002 for all seafreight export declarations. The CUS-CAR cargo manifest is submitted electronically by the port agent to customs in advance of the vessel being loaded (especially for shipments destined for the US, where cargo manifests must be submitted to US customs officers based in the UK 48 hours prior to the vessel's departure under the US CT-PAT initiative). The NES export declaration is submitted to the customs CHIEF computer as a pre-shipment advice (PSA) once the cargo is ready for shipment (usually no more than 24 hours before the consignment is due to be loaded aboard vessel). This declaration is acknowledged by the computer. Once the consignment has been loaded aboard the container and reaches the port of loading, another message (the arrival message) is entered by the agent into the CHIEF computer stating that the consignment has arrived at the port and awaits clearance instructions. The computer issues the appropriate message (Route 6 automatic clearance/Route 1 documentary check etc.) for the export consignment in question. Once the consignment has been cleared, the consignment is loaded aboard vessel and a Route 7 departure message is issued by CHIEF. A further Route 8 message clears the vessel to sail and departure is completed. At this point, the Marine Bills of Lading for each export consignment are issued to the party arranging the shipment.

The same electronic initiative which controls inward IMO FAL declarations is also used for outward movements. The suppliers of ship's stores must also submit electronic declarations based on the UN/EDIFACT Inventory Report (INVRPT) for all ship's stores loaded aboard vessel prior to its departure. These declarations can be submitted online in the same way that inward ship's stores declarations are submitted at the time of the arrival in port of the vessel. Thus, the electronic arrangement of customs export declarations is as follows:

- NES export declaration (exporter/freight forwarder/port agent);
- IMO FAL Form 2 cargo manifest (CUSCAR);
- IMO FAL Form 3 ship's stores declaration (Ship's master, supplier or agent).

However, given that an IMO ship's stores declaration requires a signature by either the ship's Master or the agent, there is still the need for a hard copy to be made available to a customs officer where required. The same is true of both the FAL Form 2 cargo manifest and the NES declaration. A hard copy of the export declaration plus supporting departure messages must be kept by the exporter for presentation to a customs officer where and when required for VAT zero-rating or Excise suspension purposes.

1.2 Imports/Arrivals

The vessel notifies the port of its impending arrival. The FAL 2 cargo manifest (in its IMO electronic UN/EDIFACT CUSCAR format) is submitted electronically by the port agents representing the shipping line to the CHIEF computer. The port agents also submit the IMO FAL forms detailing the following information:

- ship's stores still on board vessel (INVRPT);
- crew lists and effects;
- passenger lists.

Based on this electronic information, an officer may decide to travel to the port to board a vessel and examine the crew details.

One system which has facilitated the electronic submission of the cargo manifest is FCPS, an electronic cargo processing system originally developed by the Port of Felixstowe in the 1980s under the Maritime Cargo Processing (MCP) banner. It facilitates the submission of the cargo manifest to the port authority and customs to enable customs to select in advance containers which require examination or scrutiny on unloading from the vessel. It also enables the port authority to move containers from the vessel in a short space of time and facilitate customs and port clearance by the freight forwarders or clearing agents by streamlined means. The system also facilitates electronic import clearance direct to the CHIEF customs computer. However, the system still relies upon the accuracy of the information supplied on the cargo manifest. This may not show the exact details of every cargo contained in any container, especially groupage/consolidated LCL container loads. Only information which is also used for the purpose of the issuing of a Bill of Lading will be found on the cargo manifest. This information may be insufficient for customs purposes and may result in greater numbers of containers being selected for scrutiny at the port of arrival.

The freight agents submit online import declarations directly to the CHIEF computer. This sends back an acknowledgement along with the calculation of import duty and VAT in the form of an entry acceptance advice. Each import declaration represents the cargo in each container, which may be detailed on the CUSCAR cargo manifest.

The drawback of the increase in tonnage and size of the new super post-Panamax container vessels (8,000–11,000+ TEU) means that the cargo manifest for each vessel becomes larger. The computer systems required to analyse the information therein require constant updates to cover the increased volume of information or they may take some time to absorb all the relevant information. In many cases, the containers listed on the cargo manifest will only be detailed as groupage or consolidated loads, without defining the exact details of each individual cargo. Given the sheer volume of container information in each manifest, it is too cumbersome a task for the customs computer to analyse each cargo at the time the manifest is submitted, although containers are selected at random for scanning and examination at the port. Any cargo examined as a result of the container scan is scrutinised based on an individual declaration submitted by the clearing agent which was identified by the CHIEF Computer on a Route 2 (full examination) basis.

In theory, the Marine Bill of Lading issued for every consignment should equate with the details on the cargo manifest, although for consolidations there are two types of Bill of Lading—the Master Bill of Lading and the House Bill of Lading. In many cases, especially under Ex Works (EXW) consolidation conditions, the Master Bill of Lading is issued for the full consolidation (assuming that the whole container load is destined for the same buyer), but the House Bills referring to each individual consignment may not necessarily be issued to the buyer as the whole container load is to be delivered to the buyer's premises. The House Bills should be issued, however, for the sole purpose of declaration to the customs authority at the point of import, as a declaration must be submitted to customs for each consignment within the container.

Because of the sheer volume of containers arriving in port at any time, it is impractical to deal with clearance of those containers once they have been unloaded off the vessel and on to the quay. There are thus three specific stages in the clearance process:

- pre-declaration to customs and clearance by electronic means prior to the vessel's arrival at port;
- removal of the container to an inland clearance depot for cargo deconsolidation and clearance;
- removal to the trader's premises (where customs-approved).

Any port examinations on containers (usually where an X-ray is required) are notified by customs in advance of the container being offloaded from the vessel, usually once the customs computer has perused the cargo manifest by CUSCAR means. All other containers will be automatically cleared unless an examination of the cargo or its documents is required. Where this occurs, the examination can take place either at the port or at a nominated ERTS (enhanced remote transit shed, usually part of an inland clearance depot). Once cleared, the consignment can then be delivered to the customer more easily.

This set of procedures is designed to ensure the speedy and efficient removal of the containers from the port. As sterling has strengthened in recent times (and the US Dollar has weakened), the volume of import cargo has increased, especially from the Far East, with vessels queuing up to enter the ports in the South-East of England. The volume of import cargo traffic coupled with the congestion is already evident at these ports, so it is more likely that consignments entering the UK from overseas will have to be trans-shipped via a continental port such as Antwerp or Rotterdam/Europoort on feeder container vessels, which take up less space at the port berths and can accommodate container loads in smaller, more manageable volumes.

Despite the increasing reliance on electronic reporting and declarations for customs purposes, there is still a requirement for documentary evidence to support any electronic declaration. All parties involved in either import or export maritime activities must maintain a set of documentary records relating to every shipment. These requirements are based on the liability for either VAT or Excise duty and require the supplier of anything loaded aboard vessel, be it exporters or ship's chandlers, to show proper accurate documentary evidence for compliance and control purposes.

2 THE DUTY OF DISCLOSURE, DANGEROUS GOODS AND PORT INFORMATION

2.1 The Duty of Disclosure

The issue of disclosure revolves around the following considerations:

- How much information is conveyed by the shipper to the carrier, the ship's Master, and hence the authorities at the port of destination?
- The accuracy of the information conveyed to the above.

Disclosure affects information pertaining to several elements of the maritime framework. These are:

- vessel;
- crew;
- cargo;
- cargo insurance;
- passengers;
- marine environment.

Certain legal areas are also covered by the element of disclosure. These include:

- SOLAS;
- Carriage of Goods at Sea.

The Hague Rules, modified by the Hague-Visby Rules, confirmed the need for a shipper of goods to provide accurate information to a carrier about two main issues: the description of cargoes, as well as their nature (hazardous or dangerous), which could affect the safety of the vessel and its crew, and could thus affect the issue of damages resulting from any accident. The Hague-Visby Rules consolidated such information in the issuing of Ocean Bills of Lading and sea waybills and the consequent responsibilities upon each party involved in the raising of such documentation. The new UNCITRAL Convention

(A/CN.9/WG.III/WP.39) adds a specific duty and obligation on shippers to provide the information that carriers need to comply with state regulations. Article 27 of the Convention states that the shipper must provide information, instructions and documents to the carrier in advance of the loading of the cargo aboard ship. It continues by dealing with the shipper's liability for breach of the duty to supply information required by the carrier to satisfy government requirements. The view, recorded in UNCITRAL Report A/CN.9/552, is that the shipper's liability should be based on fault, except for situations covered by subsection (b) of draft Article 27 of the UNCITRAL Convention. In the same way that carriers are subject to absolute duties of compliance, demanding more than just the exercise of reasonable care in providing information to the relevant authorities, so shippers (and their agents) must provide carriers with accurate and complete information about their cargoes.

If the information provided by the shipper to the carrier is incorrect or inadequate, then the information provided by the carrier to the authorities at the port of destination must equally be incorrect or inadequate. A practical example of this is the description in cargo manifests of consolidated or grouped cargoes in less-than-full container loads (LCLs) as "Said to Contain . . . " or "FAK—Freight of all Kinds". In this way, the whole issue of marine reporting and controls may itself be severely compromised. The US CT-PAT (customs-trade partnership against terrorism) scheme has forbidden the use of such terms, and requires the shipper to describe and account for the cargoes loaded aboard all ships destined for any US seaport and to ensure that they are absolutely certain as to the nature, description and accuracy of all cargoes loaded aboard a container at the time of despatch. Such erroneous or vague information such as FAK or other generic information used to describe LCL shipments can, at the very least, result in the submission of false declarations to the customs authority of destination. To a greater degree, it could also compromise the validity of the cargo insurance policy or even the marine insurance policy covering the vessel itself under the principles of *uberrimae fidei*. At worst, it could lead to the compromise of national security or, should some form of catastrophe befall the vessel, the port of arrival, or perhaps the marine environment adjoining the port. This issue is covered in greater detail below.

2.2 Hazardous or Dangerous Cargoes and the IMDG Code

The Safety of Lives at Sea (SOLAS) Regulations concern the requirements by ship's Masters and shipowners to ensure, that all necessary Health and Safety Regulations covering the ship's crew are maintained and obeyed. On ships carrying general commercial cargoes or passengers, these Regulations refer to general practice under normal commercial activities, but the Regulations become more stringent on ships whose cargoes are primarily of a hazardous or dangerous nature. The Regulations about the reporting of such vessels to shore-based authorities are also more stringent. Ships carrying these cargoes are not only obliged by Regulation to report to the British and French Authorities under the Channel Navigation Information System (CNIS), but they are also required by law to report to the port authority of their destination prior to arrival at the port, so that appropriate measures can be taken to ensure their safe berthing and unloading, as well as their safe passage into national waters.

Cargoes subject to such requirements are:

- hydrocarbons (petroleum);
- liquefied natural or petroleum gas;
- other liquefied gas;
- chemicals;
- explosives.

In the case of bulk cargoes carried at sea, this requirement is clearly necessary, as there could be a disaster should an accident occur either at sea or in port. The oilspills resulting from the *Erika* disaster on the French coast proved extremely damaging to the coastline, as did previous disasters resulting from the grounding of the tankers *Torrey Canyon, Amoco Cadiz* and *Erika*. Other international disasters include the grounding of the tanker *Exxon Valdez* off the Alaskan Coast some years ago, which destroyed the local marine environment.

The same risks exist for hazardous or dangerous cargoes carried in containers alongside more general containerised cargoes on deep sea or feeder vessels. However, given the documentary regimes requiring the issuing of Dangerous Goods Notes for the carriage of such cargoes coupled with the interests of the insured parties concerning such marine ventures under the insurance principle of *uberrimae fidei*, the Master of the ship and the shipowners should be well aware of the risks. Indeed, there are strict rules within the framework of the Law of Carriage of Goods at Sea (Carriage of Goods by Sea Act (1971)) and the Hague-Visby Rules (Article IV, Rule 6) concerning where and how such consignments must be stowed on board ship and the liability of the carrier for such cargoes. For the purposes of Ro-Ro carriage of hazardous or dangerous consignments, strict rules are set out in the CMR Convention of 1956 (Articles 6(f) and 7), concerning the exact details to be included in the CMR consignment note and the duties and responsibilities of the shipper when both notifying the carrier of the nature and description of the consignment, especially its classification under the International Maritime Dangerous Goods (IMDG) code, and the liabilities incurred should the cargo be damaged or cause damage to the vessel while in carriage. In this respect, it is the express duty of the shipper to inform the carrier of the nature of the consignment so that adequate provisions may be made for the safe stowage of the consignment in either a container or a trailer aboard vessel in a position which is likely to minimise the risk of damage to the container, trailer or the vessel itself, as well as minimising the risk of compromise or prejudice to the ultimate safety of the vessel and its crew.

Under the rules of marine reporting, all ships carrying any kind or quantity of dangerous or hazardous goods must report to the port of destination prior to arrival at the port, usually 24 hours in advance of the vessel's arrival at port, to allow for special provisions for the berthing and unloading of the vessel upon its arrival at port where hazardous or dangerous cargoes are concerned. However, certain cargoes are declared to customs, the carriers and the insurers in such a fashion as to disguise their true nature, either because of the risk of the liability of higher insurance premiums or because of the desire of their owners to hide their true nature from national authorities. The buyer or the seller of such consignments has a duty of disclosure to inform the carrier of the full and true nature of the cargo being carried, although there are occasions when this duty is not exercised. It is also stated in the Hague-Visby Rules, Article IV, Rule 6, that if cargoes of a hazardous or dangerous nature are carried without the prior knowledge of the carrier, if the carrier discovers their true nature they may destroy or land the cargo at any place and hold the owner of the cargo liable for damages or expenses incurred in such action. However, if the carrier is unaware of the nature of the nature of such cargoes and fails to report the vessel's movement to the port of destination in advance under the hazardous goods rules, then the carrier may be held liable for not informing the port authority accordingly and running the risk of endangering the port, its personnel and other vessels in the vicinity.

The transport of dangerous and hazardous goods is covered by the IMDG code, which has been adopted by the IMO. The IMDG Code was developed as a uniform international code for the transport of dangerous or hazardous cargoes by sea, and was designed to cover such matters as packing, container traffic and stowage, with particular reference to the segregation and isolation of incompatible substances, where the potential contact of such substances could lead to severe accidents or could prejudice or compromise the safety and security of the vessel and her crew.

The development of the IMDG code dates from the 1960 Conference of the Safety of Life at Sea, which recommended as its outcome that governments should adopt a uniform international code for the transport of dangerous and hazardous cargoes by sea to supplement the regulations contained in the 1960 International Convention for the Safety of Life at Sea (SOLAS), which eventually became a full set of international regulations in 1974. A resolution adopted by the 1960 Conference stated that the proposed code should cover such matters as packing, stowage aboard vessel and container traffic in general, although in 1960, container traffic was still in its infancy, the first containers having been carried by maritime means in 1956 along the East Coast of the USA. The full IMDG code, resulting from a working group of the IMO Maritime Safety Committee which began to prepare it in 1961, was adopted by the fourth IMO Assembly in 1965, although since its adoption it has undergone many changes, both in appearance and content, to maintain pace with the ever-changing needs of industry as well as the overall maritime transport of goods, especially with the ever-increasing use of sea containers to transport cargoes worldwide.

Amendments to the code originate from two sources. These are:

- Proposals submitted directly to the IMO by Member States.
- Amendments which are required to take account of and provide for changes to the United Nations Recommendations on the Transport of Dangerous Goods, which set the basic requirements for all transport modes.

Amendments to the provisions of the UN Recommendations are made on a two-yearly cycle, and approximately two years after their adoption by the UN, they are adopted by the authorities responsible for regulating the various transport modes, which in the case of the UK is the Department for Transport (DfT). In this way, a basic set of requirements applicable to all modes of transport is established and implemented, thus ensuring that difficulties are not encountered at intermodal interfaces, such as the transport of containers by both sea and road, and equally the transport of cargoes by trailer using both road and sea means, especially where Ro-Ro maritime transport is involved.

For classification and definition purposes, the IMDG Code is divided into seven parts contained in Volume 1:

- general provisions, definitions and training;
- classification;
- consignment procedures;
- construction and testing of packagings, international bulk containers, large packagings, portable tanks and road tank vehicles;
- transport operations.

Volume 2 of the Code contains Sections on:

- dangerous goods list;
- limited quantities exceptions;
- proper shipping names;
- glossary of terms;
- index.

The application of the IMDG Code (now amended version 2006), is mandatory, but it also contains provisions of a recommendatory nature which are stated in chapter 1.1 of the Code. The classification of a cargo into its applicable category according to the provisions of the IMDG code is the direct responsibility of the shipper or consignor, regardless of who is arranging the shipment according to the International Terms of Delivery (INCOTERMS), or by the appropriate designated competent authority where specified in the code. This can include a freight agent, where that agent has been specifically empowered as the competent authority by the shipper or consignor/consignee.

Although the IMDG Code applies in general to ships carrying bulk cargoes of a hazardous or dangerous nature, it also applies to vessels carrying more general and varied containerised cargoes, amongst which may be cargoes of a dangerous or hazardous nature. The Code also refers to the responsibilities of agents and traders in ensuring that cargoes are correctly described and declared to the shipping line prior to loading aboard vessel. The need exists, therefore, for agents and traders trading in hazardous or dangerous goods to be equipped with an up-to-date copy of the IMDG Code at all times, to allow for changes in the Code as well as for the overall purpose of compliance with the regulations pertaining to the carriage of dangerous goods by sea.

The shipowner or operator will only accept and handle dangerous goods by prior written arrangement and then only on the express condition that the shipper provides a full and adequate description of the cargo to be shipped. If this arrangement is accepted, a special stowage order, often referred to as a dangerous goods form, will be issued which indicates to the Master of the vessel that the cargo conforms to the prescribed code of acceptance laid down by the ship owner or operator. The shipment will not take place until a special stowage order, which is the authority for shipment, has been issued by the ship owner or operator, given that the dangerous or hazardous cargo must be stowed in a specific location as far from the vessel's accommodation quarters as possible. Furthermore, the shipper must fully describe and classify the cargo, and ensure that it is correctly packed, marked and labelled. This can be achieved through the services of a freight forwarder.

Before dangerous goods can be authorised for shipment, the following information is required:

- name of sender/consignor;
- correct technical name of the dangerous/hazardous goods to be carried;
- class of dangerous/hazardous goods, as given in the IMDG code;
- flashpoint (if applicable);
- UN number to identify the substance;
- details of outer packing;
- details of inner packing;
- quantity to be shipped in individual packages and in total;
- additional information for radioactive materials, explosives and consignments in bulk (tank containers, road tankers etc.).

The Dangerous Goods Authority form will have a reference number and will also show the sailing details, including the ports of departure and destination for which the consignment is authorised, plus the following details:

- the hazard class;
- UN number;

- Labels;
- Key number (in case of emergency);
- any special instructions.

On the arrival of the goods at the port of loading, the consignment and the authority to ship are submitted to the master of the vessel for ultimate approval prior to customs clearance and loading, although in reality, the customs export declaration will have been submitted in advance of the consignment being despatched to the port of loading. The dangerous goods note (DG note) issued for the consignment must also be completed, along with a container vehicle packing certificate and these documents must accompany the goods.

2.3 Port Information

Every seaport needs to know about the vessels entering and leaving it at any time. The main reasons concern requirements for the following activities:

- vessel berthing;
- cargo handling;
- vessel and cargo clearance;
- specific requirements for dangerous or hazardous goods;
- vessel and cargo security;
- port state controls.

Information is generally conveyed to the port authority, in particular the harbour master and the port administration, by the shipping agents who receive prior information concerning the vessel and its cargo well in advance of the vessel's arrival. Unless the vessel is carrying dangerous or hazardous goods, the agent is only required to report its arrival a few days before it actually arrives, although in many cases a schedule of vessel arrivals is created in advance. Where hazardous or dangerous cargoes are concerned, the vessel is required to report to the port at least 24 hours before arrival, so that adequate provisions can be made for unloading at a suitable location. Where there are a lot of vessel movements in and out of port each day, then a detailed schedule of all vessel movements for a specific week will be required to create an organised control schedule well in advance, so that suitable berthing and unloading space may be arranged.

The information received by any port from any vessel is complex, although it may be used by different parties. In general, such information includes:

- the vessel's intended destination;
- the port of departure;
- the nature of the vessel (passenger/cargo);
- the size of the vessel;
- the flag of the vessel;
- the ownership of the vessel;

- the nature and identities of the crew;
- the nature of the cargo (cargo manifest);
- passengers (passenger manifest);
- estimated time of arrival.

All this information builds up a picture of any vessel sailing within or into UK territorial waters, but will only be privy to a specific port (i.e. the port of arrival). Once that information has been received, it will be used by a variety of authorities and organisations. These may include:

- the port authority;
- health & safety authorities;
- HM Customs & Excise;
- ships' agents and brokers;
- freight forwarders.

As the information is somewhat specific in its nature and subject to the Data Protection Act, it will not and cannot be disseminated to other parties not included in such activities unless absolutely required (in the case of dangerous or hazardous goods, where Coastguards or Port Health Authorities may require such information in the interests of the safety of the public). Indeed, certain information pertaining to the reporting of cargo may not directly reach the port authority unless the cargo is hazardous or dangerous, in which case the port authority needs to know specific details about the cargo and the ship as laid down in the various pieces of maritime legislation and regulations.

3 CARGO STOWAGE AND LOADING

Cargo stowage is a vital element to the subject of marine cargo management. Even in the days prior to containerisation, there was a need to ensure that goods were loaded in such a way as to correctly balance the vessel, so as to avoid risk if the cargo shifting should the vessel encounter heavy or rough seas in stormy weather conditions. With the change to containerised transport in the 1960s, the need became evident to create a regime where containers could be loaded aboard vessel in such a way as to minimise the risk of imbalances which would lead to the vessel becoming too heavy at either the bow, the stern or amidships. In the case of incorrect loading, the following problems could arise:

- *Front-heavy* The bow of the vessel would sit lower in the water, and would ship more water as a result of waves crashing over the bows in rough seas.
- *Too heavy amidships* The vessel could risk breaking its back in heavy seas.

- *Stern-heavy* There could be a great risk of instability from the point of amidships to the bows.

Further instability would occur if either side of the vessel were more heavily loaded than the other, thus inducing a list to either port or starboard.

Further risks could also be imposed as a result of the failure to ensure that hazardous or dangerous cargoes were isolated from each other, especially where two kinds of dangerous cargoes would react adversely if located adjacent to each other. Furthermore, risks to the safety of the vessel and its crew would be increased in cases where hazardous or dangerous cargoes were located close to the accommodation quarters on a cargo vessel, as in the case of the container vessel *Hyundai Fortune* in 2006. The essence of the issue of stowage, therefore, is to ensure that cargo is loaded aboard vessel in such a way as to avoid such risks and ensure that the vessel is correctly balanced prior to leaving port.

The International Maritime Organisation (IMO) developed a Code of Safe Practice for Cargo Stowage and Securing. This was subsequently approved by the Maritime Safety Committee in May 1990, before being finally adopted by the Assembly in November 1991. There have been several amendments to the Code since its adoption, the most recent being incorporated in the 2003 edition of the Code.

The Code has seven chapters and 13 annexes, each dealing with various aspects of cargo stowage. These are arranged as follows:

Chapter 1 – General
Chapter 2 – Principles of safe stowage and securing of cargoes
Chapter 3 – Standardised stowage and securing systems
Chapter 4 – Semi-standardised stowage and securing
Chapter 5 – Non-standardised stowage and securing
Chapter 6 – Actions which may be taken in heavy weather
Chapter 7 – Actions which may be taken once cargo has shifted
Annex 1 – Safe stowage and securing of containers on deck of ships which are not specially designed and fitted for the purpose of carrying containers
Annex 2 – Safe stowage and securing of portable tanks
Annex 3 – Safe stowage and securing of portable receptacles
Annex 4 – Safe stowage and securing of wheel-based (rolling) cargoes
Annex 5 – Safe stowage and securing of heavy cargo items such as locomotives, transformers etc
Annex 6 – Safe stowage and securing of coiled sheet steel
Annex 7 – Safe stowage and securing of heavy metal products
Annex 8 – Safe stowage and securing of anchor chains
Annex 9 – Safe stowage and securing of metal scrap in bulk
Annex 10 – Safe stowage and securing of flexible intermediate bulk containers
Annex 11 – General guidelines for the under-deck stowage of logs

Annex 12 – Safe stowage and securing of unit loads
Annex 13 – Methods to assess the efficiency of securing arrangements for non-
standardised cargo

The above chapters and annexes account for all aspects of cargo stowage
aboard every type of cargo vessel in existence, and also take into account every
kind of cargo itself, other than bulk loads of either a wet or dry nature, as such
loads are more evenly distributed throughout the vessel's cargo holds. There
are specific chapters referring to the carriage of containers and also Ro-Ro
vessels. These are Chapter 2 (containers) and Chapter 4 (Ro-Ro vessels).

Chapter 2 refers in particular to the specific means of cargo distribution
throughout the container vessel and places responsibility on the master of the
vessel to ensure that great care is taken in planning and supervising the
stowage and securing of all cargoes aboard vessel to prevent cargo sliding,
tipping, racking or collapsing (Section 2.2.1).

Furthermore, the cargo must be distributed in such a way as to ensure that
the stability of the ship throughout the entire voyage remains within acceptable
limits so that the hazards of excessive accelerations are reduced as far as
possible (Section 2.2.2). Cargo distribution should be such that the structural
strength of the vessel is not adversely affected (Section 2.2.3). Section 2.9
states that where there is good reason to suspect that a container into which
hazardous or dangerous goods have been packed or loaded does not comply
with the provisions of the 1974 SOLAS regulations or the IMDG code, the
unit (the container, should not be accepted for shipment).

Chapter 4 deals with the carriage of certain specific cargoes such as road
vehicles and road trailers, especially on Ro-Ro ships such as vehicle ferries.
Points must be provided on these vessels for the purpose of securing trailers
while the vessel is in motion and road vehicles intended for transport by sea
must be provided with arrangements for their safe stowage and securing. This
arrangement includes road trailers carrying their own cargoes and special
consideration must be given to the height of the trailer and its centre of gravity.
Furthermore, the master of the vessel has the right not to allow a road vehicle
on board unless he is satisfied that it is suitable for the intended voyage and
that it is provided with at least the securing points specified in Section 5 of the
Annex to Resolution A.581(14). This gives details of the lashing and securing
points required for the purposes of securing road vehicles and trailers.

In general, the master is made totally responsible for the safe stowage and
securing of all cargoes aboard vessel, although in reality there is a load master
at the port terminal whose role it is to supervise and control the loading of all
cargoes aboard vessel. The loading schedule is arranged prior to the vessel's
arrival in port, according to the number of containers being loaded aboard
vessel and their respective weights and where they should be located with
respect to other containers already loaded aboard vessel. The load plans are
often arranged by the shipping agents, these are conveyed to the port authority
in readiness for when the vessel arrives and is to be loaded. Similarly, great

care must be taken to ensure that the vessel's load line (the "Plimsoll Line", named in the 19th century after its inventor, Samuel Plimsoll), is not exceeded. The load line gives various measures for the levels of acceptable loading according to the time of year ("winter" and "summer" load lines) as, should the acceptable level of load be exceeded, the safety of the ship could be compromised, which would incur the risk of a heavy fine being imposed on the vessel's master. To this extent, the ship's cargo officers must ensure that the vessel is not overloaded beyond the appropriate load line depending upon the time of year and the density of the water drawn by the vessel.

The lines shown on the load line represent the various levels which cannot be exceeded with respect to the density of water at a particular time of year, as shown by the indicators on the diagram. In general, the vessel will be loaded to a point above the lines concerned, to allow for variations in sea conditions. The main mark is the summer load line, which is calculated in relation to the ship's length, its gross tonnage, the type of vessel and the number of super-structures, the amount of sheer and the minimum bow height.

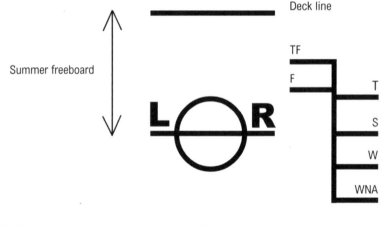

TF	Tropical fresh water	WNA Winter, North Atlantic,
F	Fresh water	for vessels < 100m in length
T	Tropical sea water	LR Letters indicating the registration
S	Summer, sea water	authority (here, the Lloyds Register)
W	Winter, sea water	

Figure 6.1: The Load Line, or Plimsoll Line

The differences between fresh and sea water limits are influenced by the displacement of the vessel dependent upon whether it is sailing in fresh or sea (salt) water. Sea water has greater density owing to the amount of salt and other minerals, which then gives greater buoyancy to the vessel and enables it to ride higher out of the water. Consequently, a load in a vessel which reaches the sea-water mark on the load line means that the vessel sits somewhat higher out of the water than it would if it were sailing through fresh water, such as the Panama Canal. Therefore, where vessels are sailing through sea water and fresh water conditions, the line to be obeyed on the load line markings is the winter sea water line, not the fresh water line, as the fresh water line allows for less buoyancy owing to a lower water density in fresh water conditions. Similarly, tropical sea water and summer sea water are lighter than winter sea water. This means that vessels leaving northern ports destined for southern waters (especially the Asia–Europe routes) can only load up to the winter sea water mark, as the loads on board will result in the vessel riding lower in the water once it reaches warmer waters due to lower water density.

There are several examples where these loading conditions need to be taken into account, and these include the following routes:

- Atlantic Ocean to Pacific Ocean via the Panama Canal/Gatun Lake.
- Irish Sea to Manchester Ship Canal.
- Atlantic Ocean and St Lawrence Seaway to the Great Lakes.

Whereas the oceans and seas are salt water, the Panama Canal/Gatun Lake, Manchester Ship Canal and the Great Lakes networks are all fresh water. This means a substantial difference in load limits when the vessel is transiting these areas, or moving between sea and fresh waters.

When loading certain cargoes, such as ore or oil, the vessel is liable to adopt a sagged position, especially where the heavier loads are located towards the bow and the stern, where loading is uneven or unbalanced, or where the vessel sags amidships owing to a concentration of heavier loads at the centre of the vessel. Where the vessel is sagging, the apparent mean draught will be less than the actual mean draught and such a situation does not permit overloading. Indeed, in these circumstances the loading plan for the vessel should be reviewed and the problem alleviated by shifting some of the load to a more even pattern throughout the vessel, although in the case of bulk cargoes this may be more difficult to achieve. The aim of the exercise is to ensure an even loading throughout the ship to achieve complete stability while the vessel is in motion on the high seas. Many accidents have occurred because of incorrect loading which led to an imbalance aboard the vessel and an inherent instability which meant that the vessel listed significantly to either port or starboard in a violent storm. In some cases, loading the vessel with the heavier loads being located amidships has led to the vessel breaking her back and foundering under heavy sea conditions. In other cases, there was insufficient attention paid to the location of containers aboard vessel, which ultimately led to an inferno because hazardous and dangerous cargoes were too close together on board vessel. There is also the rule that hazardous or dangerous goods should never be located below deck in limited spaces, where there is more risk of prejudice to the vessel's safety and its integrity. The greater the length of the ship, the greater the propensity for severe forces being exerted on the vessel's hull by the waves during choppy or rough sea conditions, especially when the vessel is heavily-laden. The increased deadweight in terms of the cargo exacerbates these forces and can lead to a shortening of the vessel's lifespan, resulting in premature heavy maintenance costs, especially during refits or dry-dock inspections, or even a premature departure for the breaker's yard. Such has been the case for several container vessels, especially owing to accidents or damage sustained as a result of encountering stormy sea conditions, as in the case of the container vessel *MSC Napoli* in the Channel in January 2007.

Another case of cargo and container damage occurred on the night of 25/26 February 2007, when the UK-registered short-sea container feeder vessel *Annabella* was sailing across the Baltic Sea en route from the port of Antwerp to the port of Helsinki. She had loaded with containers in the port of Rotterdam between 21 and 23 February 2007, before proceeding to the port of Antwerp for further loading of containers. From Antwerp, she proceeded up the North Sea coast and through into the Baltic Sea. During the night of 25 February, off the Swedish island of Gotland, she encountered heavy seas which resulted in severe rolling. In the early hours of 26 February, sea and weather conditions improved, and when checks were made on the vessel's cargo, it was found that seven 30-foot containers stowed lower down in Bay 12 of Hold 3 had collapsed under the weight of the upper containers, several of which contained butylene gas and were therefore classed under the IMDG code as hazardous cargoes. It was discovered later that no account had been made on the stowage programme of the 30-foot containers given their intermediate size, which was not accounted for in the port loading software. The result was an assumption that the 30-foot containers would be capable of supporting the weight of the larger and heavier containers located above them, which was, in reality, not the case. This anomaly in the loading pattern meant that no account was made for the greater weight resting upon the smaller containers below deck, with the result that, during the period of heavy seas when the vessel was rolling and pitching in the Baltic Sea, the vessel's violent movements caused an instability in the container lashings, and this, coupled with the disparities in container sizes, resulted in the lower containers collapsing under the weight of the upper containers. The software used for the stowage planning had not recognised the existence of 30-foot containers, and when these details were changed to 40-foot container dimensions, the computer was not alerted to the difference. Furthermore, there was no stability information available concerning the *Annabella*, and the containers were duly loaded without taking into account the differences in container sizes. The net result was an inherent instability concerning the differences between the container sizes on board vessel in Hold 3, with the result that the collapse of the containers occurred while the vessel was negotiating the heavy seas. The resulting investigation by the Marine Accident Investigation Branch (MAIB) of the Maritime and Coastguard Agency (MCA) highlighted the anomalies and errors in the system, in particular the failure of the computer software used to plan the loading and stowage of cargoes aboard the vessel to account for the differences in container sizes.

Another hazard to the correct loading and stowage of sea containers aboard vessel is the phenomenon known as "parametric roll". On modern container ships, containers may be stacked several levels high above deck, although they are supposed to be securely lashed and secured. However, the design of container ships requires an aqua-dynamically-designed hull, especially beneath the waterline, to allow for increased operational service speeds. This streamlined hull beneath the waterline is combined with a full hull above the waterline designed to accommodate the maximum number of containers possible, along with the minimum practical space allowable for a super-structure. The end result is a vessel which, in calm weather, has no problem negotiating the average slight ocean waves, but, when encountering rough seas, is more susceptible to violent rolling from side to side owing to a higher centre of gravity caused by the disparity in hull construction.

This phenomenon is an extreme form of lateral roll which is not encoun-tered by other vessels. Indeed, so violent is the propensity to roll in heavy seas that on many occasions, several containers have been wrenched away from their secure fastenings and have fallen off the vessel into the ocean, with other containers remaining aboard vessel being badly damaged by the violent motion of the vessel. Academic studies are underway in various universities to understand the phenomenon and to attempt to reduce its prevalence, but as long as container vessels require aqua-dynamic streamlining below the water-line, the propensity for such an effect prevails. The problem is exacerbated by the numbers of levels of containers stacked above deck on any container vessel.

Were the vessel to simply hold containers below deck in the container holds, then the problem would probably not arise owing to the lowering of the centre of gravity on the vessel. But as the number of containers stacked above deck increases with the need to use as much space aboard vessel and above deck as possible, so the centre of gravity rises to a point where the vessel could risk becoming top heavy, or at the very least losing its overall lateral stability. It is this effect which increases the risk of violent rolling in heavy seas and increases the risk of the vessel capsizing or at least shedding some of its precious cargoes. Heavy seas are almost a certainty at some times of the year and there is a greater risk of this occurrence in such adverse sea conditions, especially in some parts of the world, such as the Bay of Biscay, where rough conditions are seen to be more prevalent than elsewhere. As long as containers are stacked several levels high on container vessels, the propensity towards the prevalence of parametric roll remains equally high.

A possible solution to the problem is to ensure that heavier container loads are placed within the hull section of the vessel, below deck, with lighter loads located above deck. In this way, the collective weight of the heavier container loads serves to lower the centre of gravity and lessen the effects of violent rolling in rough sea conditions. It serves to provide an efficient form of ballast, to maintain a better equilibrium on the vessel and so ensure that greater lateral stability is achieved. In turn, this lateral stability reduces the risk of parametric roll and so reduces the risks to the safety of the vessel when encountering adverse weather conditions. As long as the collective weight is evenly distributed throughout the length of the vessel's container holds, the effects of such cargo distribution are less likely to damage the vessel's integral construction and lead to structural damage or worse the structural failure of the vessel's hull.

4 THE IMO FAL CONVENTION AND THE ISPS CODE

4.1 The FAL Convention

The original Convention on the Facilitation of International Maritime Traffic was agreed by all the governments subscribing to the International Maritime Organisation (IMO) in 1965 and has remained in force ever since. Its purpose is to simplify and reduce to a minimum the formalities, documentary requirements and procedures on the arrival, stay in port and departure from port of all commercial ships engaged in international voyages. It refers in general to those ships and shipping lines not included in the schedule of Authorised Regular Operators (those shipping lines involved in Ro-Ro short sea operations within European waters, and also excludes warships and pleasure vessels).

The Convention refers the following details to the summary declaration to the port authority and to the national customs authority:

- cargoes;
- crew's effects;
- crew members;
- passenger lists;
- ship's stores;
- general declarations;
- maritime declarations of health.

The purpose of the regime is to enable both the port of arrival and the customs authority to assess the contents of the ship without the need to scrutinise the ship in minute detail once it arrives, and to clear it through all relevant national controls in the shortest time possible.

In the *General Declaration*, which must be dated and signed by the ship's master or the shipping agent, the information required by the appropriate authorities is as follows:

- name and description of vessel;
- nationality of vessel;

- registry details;
- tonnage details;
- master's name;
- name and address of vessel's agent;
- brief description of cargo;
- number of crew;
- number of passengers;
- brief details of voyage;
- date and time of arrival or departure;
- port of arrival or departure;
- location of vessel in the port.

The FAL 2 Cargo Declaration for arrival purposes contains details of the ship and the ship's master, as well as the ports of arrival and departure, and details of both the cargoes and shipping documents (e.g. Bills of Lading) as well as the destination of any cargo remaining on board following the unloading of cargo at the port in question. For departure purposes, the declaration must contain details of the cargo loaded aboard, and details of all the shipping documents (Bills of Lading) associated therewith. Cargoes of hazardous or dangerous goods should be included, but should also be declared separately on specific declarations.

The Crew Declaration details the crew and their respective ranks.

The Passenger Declaration details the names and addresses of all Passengers aboard ship, their point of embarkation and point of disembarkation.

The *Maritime Declaration of Health* provides information required by Port Health Authorities concerning the state of health of all persons aboard vessel, be they crew or passengers, during the voyage and on arrival at port.

The Cargo Declaration, Crew Effects Declaration and Ship's Stores Declarations are subject to scrutiny by the national customs authority and allow customs officers to board ship while in port and verify the details of the declarations. It should be pointed out that all vessels while in port are subject to customs controls, and thus may not leave port without customs clearance.

The Convention also allows for facilities by the port to clear cargoes and passengers off ships, and to ensure that all clearance formalities are conducted as swiftly and efficiently as possible, in order to avoid unnecessary delays.

It should be noted that the IMO FAL Declarations for the crew of a vessel do not substitute and are not substituted by the formalities laid down by either the IMO ISPS Code or national customs import declaration requirements, but are complementary to them, thus resulting in additional bureaucracy for vessels and port authorities alike. Although the element of security is contained in both regimes, different levels of security apply depending on the specific regime required. It would appear that with the introduction of the ISPS regime, the shipping lines, agents and port authorities have become increasingly embroiled in greater amounts of administration in dealing with the respective FAL and ISPS regimes. This has inevitably led to an overlap in the requirements of each regime.

The FAL forms are still generally completed in manual format, although the initiative now exists to translate all the forms into electronic format using EDI (Electronic Data Interface) technology. In a booklet published in 2001 (FAL.5/Circ.15, February 2001), the IMO recommended that the FAL regime be converted into electronic transmission by vessels and agents using the EDI regime, which was also being introduced into other reporting facilities, especially customs declarations. It was decided that all the FAL forms could be transmitted in electronic format using EDI, and that other documents of a manual nature could be dispensed with by the appropriate public authorities. The EDI system would allow for the download and derivation of a hard copy format of the appropriate FAL form, which could be stored on computer and printed off when required as documentary evidence.

The electronic declarations are designated in UN/EDIFACT format as follows:

- FAL Form 1—IMO General Declaration (CUSREP);
- FAL Form 2—IMO Cargo Declaration (CUSCAR);
- FAL Form 3—IMO Ship's Stores Declaration (Inventory Report Message—INVRPT);
- FAL Form 5—IMO Crew List (PAXLST);
- FAL Form 6—IMO Passenger Declaration (PAXLST);
- FAL Form 7—IMO Dangerous Goods Manifest (International Forwarding and Transport Dangerous Goods Notification Message— IFTDGN).

It should be noted that there is no EDI equivalent of the FAL Form 4, the crew's effects declaration. Also, FAL Forms 5 and 6 have been integrated as one single crew and passenger list, simply referring to all persons aboard vessel, crew and/or passengers.

The CUSCAR cargo manifest, presented by the shipping line or the agents to customs at the time of the ship's arrival in port, is seen as a major issue by shipping lines, customs and coastguard alike, because of its sheer bulk. It may be transmitted separately from the FAL summary form, but is seen by many as an encumbrance rather than an advantage. The brief summary of the cargo manifest as a FAL Form 2 does not detail all cargoes in depth, and the ship's manifest has always been seen as a separate document, issued by the shipping line to the ship's master at the time of sailing. With the introduction of the new, huge super post-Panamax container vessels of the size of 7,000 TEU (Twenty-foot equivalent unit) plus (at present 8,000 TEU+ vessels are being constructed and introduced into service) the sheer volume of information provided on the cargo manifest is in many cases too much for the average computer to cope with, and even in ZIP format, provides problems in terms of download and analysis of cargo information. A further problem emerges concerning the information provided per container, where consolidated group-age cargoes are described in the Bill of Lading as "Said to Contain . . . " or "Freight of all kinds", statements now outlawed by the United States. This scenario leaves wide open the possibility of omissions in information presented to customs, coastguards and port authorities concerning each individual cargo, especially where cargoes of a dangerous or hazardous nature are concerned. These issues are addressed in a later section of Part II of the study. Customs in the UK has already admitted that it is unable to fully scrutinise all details of the existing CUSCAR manifests for several reasons:

- it leaves all import declarations to the trader—the importer, or the clearing agent;
- it prefers to ensure that all cargoes leave the port of import as quickly as possible;
- it cannot distinguish cargoes based on a consolidated entry in the manifest;
- there is too much information to digest from the present reports from the large container ships.

The UK customs computer can, however, select individual containers or their covering documents for examination, or it can identify specific containers for scanning at the port of arrival. There is a system in place which enables customs to make random checks on containers being imported for the purpose of security, examination of goods, and the prevention of illegal smuggling and illicit trade. However, this process is entirely random, and does not necessarily prevent every aspect of anomaly, fraud or illicit trade, except where specific traders, through a history of non-compliance, are targeted for the purposes of regular scrutiny by the department.

With the increasing passing of responsibility for the accuracy of customs declarations to the trader or the agent, it would appear that customs are no longer able or even willing to spend vast amounts of resources in examining cargo manifests, and would only scrutinise details on a purely random basis, or on the grounds of prior information referring to the suspect nature of a specific container. Indeed, most examinations of containers at the port by customs are conducted through the container scans undertaken on a random basis. The cargo manifest will be transmitted to the port authority and hence derived and downloaded in theory by the various agents clearing import consignments carried by all incoming ships. In reality, most import clearances are still undertaken by the clearing agent based on the clearance instructions given by the importer in the form of specific documentation, such as invoices, packing lists and Bills of Lading.

4.2 The International Ship and Port Security Code (ISPS)

As shown in this text, maritime cargo security encompasses a variety of issues, but refers in different ways to different aspects of the maritime sector. In order to enhance maritime security for both vessels and ports, through amendments to SOLAS Chapters V and XI, the IMO introduced in 2002 the International Ship and Port Facility Security (ISPS) code, which came into force in July 2004. Alongside the implementation of the code, International Ship Security Certificates (ISSCs) are issued to each ship able to satisfy the Maritime Security conditions laid down by the IMO. Other technical co-operation and co-operative work is being carried out with other UN organisations such as the International Labour Organisation and the World Customs Organisation.

Chapter XI of the SOLAS has been split into two sections: XI-1 and XI-2. The newly created Section XI-2 deals with special measures to enhance maritime security, and includes a requirement for ships and shipping companies to comply with the ISPS code. Chapter V of SOLAS also made the requirement for all vessels over 300 grt to install the AIS facility, now compulsory in all such vessels. These requirements form a framework through which ships and port facilities can co-operate to detect and deter acts which pose a threat to maritime security, although the regulatory provisions do not extend to the actual response to security incidents, or to any necessary clear-up activities following such an incident.

The ISPS Code deals with the following activities for both ports and vessels:

- enabling the detection and deterrence of security threats within an international framework;
- establishing roles and responsibilities;
- enabling the collection and exchange of security information concerning vessels, crews, passengers and cargo;
- providing a methodology for assessing security;
- ensuring that adequate security measures are in place;
- gathering and assessing information;
- maintaining communication protocols;
- restricting access; preventing the introduction of unauthorised weapons, etc;
- providing the means to raise alarms;
- implementing vessel and port security plans, and ensuring that training and procedural drills are properly conducted.

In practice, the ISPS Code requires all ships to have a recognised and competent security officer, as well as a recognised security office in each shipping company, including its address and contact details. The Master of the ship must report all necessary security details, including details of its complement and identification, to the port authority on or prior to arrival at the port of destination. Action Checklists are maintained by both the port authority and the vessel concerning such security measures, although these do not include the monitoring and inspection of cargoes other than the mandatory reporting of hazardous or dangerous cargoes. Any inspection of cargoes, especially in the container sector, is usually carried out at the time and point of loading the container at the trader's premises, although in many cases such inspection is kept to a minimum because of time constraints. Indeed, it is often the case that there is no inspection carried out to ensure that all consignments have been loaded, an anomaly which can result in discrepancies between the physical consignment and its associated documentation. There is, therefore, a significant reliance on the documentation, rather than the consignment itself, for the purposes of shipment, and there are many cases where the details of the consignment as described on the documentation do not relate to the actual consignment itself.

The main implication of the ISPS Code for the port sector is that all ports must maintain a full security regime with reference to the entry and exit of personnel, vehicles and cargoes. While it is recognised that there needs to be a free flow of movement in terms of the management of cargo activities between vessel and quayside, there is still the need for a substantial form of control to ensure that unauthorised personnel are not allowed within the confines of the port operational area and that all unauthorised cargo movements are prevented. The procedure for checking all cargoes into the port is carried out by electronic means and all cargoes are monitored up to the point of loading aboard vessel. All container movements are recorded and each container is allocated its own space at the time of arrival prior to loading aboard vessel. Any clearance formalities for customs purposes are carried out at this stage, and these are generally undertaken electronically, with clearance being given by messages sent electronically to both the agent and the port authority. As the loading sequence commences, each container is removed from its bay at the terminal and is loaded by crane aboard the vessel. The port authority must ensure that all consignments held within the port area are accounted for and that all records concerning movements of cargoes are correctly maintained. Similarly, all movements of consignments from the port by road (imported cargoes) must be correctly and full monitored in accordance with both ISPS and customs requirements, and that all customs clearances have been carried out prior to a consignment being released from the port to the trader. In general, all customs clearances are carried out in advance of the vessel docking and any examinations or container scans are carried out on a specific basis to keep delays to a minimum. Where automatic electronic clearances are made, the authorisation for removal is given to the agent prior to the container being off-loaded from the vessel, thus ensuring that onward transport can be quickly arranged, and the container transported quickly and efficiently out of the port in the minimum of time.

Although much of the information relating to international cargo movements is maintained by the shipping lines or their agents, there is still the need for these organisations to work closely with the port authority, not only to ensure that the ISPS regulations are adhered to, but that there is a constant flow of information between all parties concerned to facilitate the smooth operation of loading and unloading vessels at the port. The electronic nature of the flow of information via EDI format means that paperwork is kept to a minimum wherever possible and that there is a common network of information available to shipping lines, their agents and the port authority.

CHAPTER 7

ROLES AND RESPONSIBILITIES

1 PERSPECTIVES FROM BRIDGE AND SHORE

1.1 A View from the Bridge

The state-of-the-art marine freighter bears little relationship to its forebears in terms of the technology of its control systems. Gone are the telegraphs between bridge and engine room and the conventional wheelhouses with their huge steering wheels. Everything is controlled today by complex on-board computer systems, from steering and navigation to engine control and position monitoring. Once the vessel is underway and out of the harbour confines, the vessel's master selects the autopilot based on the vessel's integrated inertial GPS navigational system and the vessel is guided across the ocean by automatic means, without the need for a conventional helmsman. Even the marine propulsion systems have changed, from the combinations of conventional stern-mounted screws linked to huge marine engines and bow-thrust mechanisms, to bridge-controlled azymuth propulsion systems, where the propulsion systems can revolve through 360 degrees. These are connected to smaller, more efficient diesel engines by an adjustable link mechanism, which eliminates the need for a conventional rudder steering mechanism. The one main link with more traditional times is the vast array of Admiralty Charts ranged across the available desk space, although even this is giving way to the ECDIS computerised charts. Today's control systems rely heavily on a mixture of GPS, VTS, AIS and conventional radar systems. From port of departure to port of destination, the vessel monitoring process from a navigation point of view revolves around the following systems:

- Leaving port—VTS/AIS;
- Open sea—AIS/GPS;
- Entering port approaches—AIS/VTS;
- Port arrival—VTS.

The VTS systems allow for the close monitoring of vessels within port approaches and port areas themselves, while AIS allows for the monitoring of vessels throughout their voyage and indeed while the vessel is in port, as long as the AIS transponder is switched on. The drawbacks with any of these systems is that they identify the ship, but not its crew, its cargo or complement of passengers. Equally, the AIS system is still subject to a slight delay between the time the transponder emits the signal and the time this registers on the system and registers the ship's position.

All this may be good insofar as it exists, but it does not tell the full story. There are considerable gaps in the whole process, mainly because of the issue of cargo reporting and these gaps are the issues of the greatest importance, owing to the risks posed by unreported cargo and other security considerations. Other risks also prevail, in particular the lack of monitoring of vessels outside the remit of the VTS and AIS systems, which could have an adverse effect on the security and safety of vessels covered by these systems. Despite the evident technological tools available to the ship's master and his crew, the view from the bridge may still be obscured by many external factors beyond his control.

The synopsis of procedures concerning the voyage of a cargo vessel may loosely be categorised as follows:

- the ship's agent and the freight forwarders verify specific documentation (e.g. Dangerous Goods Notes etc.) to ensure compliance with IMO requirements;
- the cargoes destined for loading aboard vessel are declared to customs by electronic input;
- customs clearance is given for the consignments to be loaded aboard vessel;
- the ship is loaded at port with the cargoes (containers);
- Bills of Lading are issued for all cargoes loaded aboard vessel and the cargo information is also entered on the cargo manifest;
- a copy of the ship's manifest is given to the ship's master by the ship's agent (the port agent) and a further copy of the manifest is also submitted to customs;
- the ship's master notifies the port and the customs authority that all cargoes are loaded aboard vessel;
- the ship is given clearance to sail;
- the Master maintains contact with the port VTS concerning the ship's movement out of the port, through the Channel and into the open sea;
- the ship maintains electronic contact with other vessels and land through the use of the AIS system.

The ship sails across the ocean to its destination. Upon the approach to the port of destination, the following action is undertaken:

- the vessel's agent notifies the port of destination of the arrival of the vessel;
- the ship notifies the port of destination 24 hours in advance with details of the ship, its crew and any hazardous or dangerous cargoes aboard vessel in accordance with the IMDG code, and its intention to dock;
- the ship enters national territorial limits and notifies the port of details of its crew, its stores and any other information required by the national authorities;

- the ship maintains contact with the port through the VTS system from the time it enters the port approaches and proceeds to enter the port;
- a copy of the cargo manifest is submitted by the port agent to the port authority and the customs authority prior to the ship's arrival at port;
- the ship's master submits a FAL declaration to customs of all details of crew and stores on board;
- the ship's master gives a detailed report to the port authority complying with the regulations set down by the ISPS Code.

Although details of cargo reporting may have been covered earlier, they still have an overall bearing upon the safety and wellbeing of both the vessel and its crew. It should be noted that the ship's Master can only report details of the cargo if he is fully aware of that cargo aboard vessel according to the cargo manifest. In many cases, the cargo may only be known by its groupage description (a generic description of the consolidated cargo in a LCL container load) and not by details of each individual consignment within that consolidated cargo. This absence of information may not yield vital information, such as the hazardous nature of an individual cargo, or whether such a cargo was [in]correctly stowed aboard vessel. It is this lack of information which may mask a much greater risk to the ship, its crew and its location depending upon the location of other vessels close by (e.g. within the confines of port approaches) or where adverse weather conditions such as fog may be prevalent. It is this anomaly which may prejudice or compromise the safety and security, not only the ship and its crew, but also the safety of the surrounding environment including the port itself. There is a further risk if the exact nature of the crew is not fully known, concerning their professional competence to crew the vessel or even their nationality or motives for being aboard vessel at the time of the voyage.

A major problem arises where the buyer (the importer) arranges groupage shipments and has the cargo consolidated at a point in the country of departure under an Ex Works (EXW) basis. Given that the buyer initiated the transport of the various consignments, the shipping line will still issue both a Master Bill of Lading for the LCL groupage shipment as well as a set of house Bills of Lading, but may not necessarily issue the house Bills to the buyer unless specifically requested. Thus, the exporter may never receive a copy of the house Bills of Lading relating to their consignment since they did not arrange the shipment. Nor will the exporter receive a copy of the export customs declaration for that consignment, assuming that an individual export declaration is physically raised by the freight forwarder, which may not be the case in the event of a consolidated consignment. In many cases, this does not happen. There is thus no audit trail available to the exporter to show that their particular consignment was shipped. Furthermore, where a groupage consignment simply shows "Freight of all kinds (FAK)" or a generic description such as "cosmetic products" or "automotive equipment", there is no specific means of verifying the individual consignments grouped within the container in question, as there may be the risk that no specific house Bills of Lading were raised for each individual consignment as far as the exporter is concerned. Furthermore, this lack of detailed information will also reflect on the cargo manifest issued to the ship's Master and to customs at the point of export.

The problem is compounded by the fact that the forwarding agent notifies the port agents about the cargo once the shipment has been arranged for loading aboard vessel. The freight forwarder is responsible for sending full details of the cargo to the port agent for the latter to incorporate the details of the consignment and the container in which it is loaded on the cargo manifest. The port agents are responsible for dealing with all affairs relating to the vessel while it is berthed at port, including the loading and unloading of the vessel and the liability for conservancy and port handling charges. It is thus the responsibility of the port agent to ensure that the ship's master is made aware of all cargoes loaded aboard vessel and that all hazardous or dangerous cargoes are notified in advance to the master of the vessel to ensure compliance with port regulations, SOLAS regulations and the general regulations concerning the correct stowage of all cargoes aboard vessel. If a freight forwarder does not submit the correct information concerning cargoes, especially those of a groupage or consolidated nature, to the port agent, the freight forwarder could be made liable for any accident or damage which could occur as a result of the failure to inform the port agents or the ship's Master or even the port itself of the nature of the cargo being loaded aboard vessel. In reality, the responsibility for correctly divulging information pertaining to the cargo lies with the exporter. If the exporter does not inform the freight forwarder of the true nature of the consignment, the rest of the chain of reporting is severely prejudiced, including the ramifications for insurance of the cargo in question.

In short, neither the ship's master nor the shipping line nor the port authority may be entirely knowledgeable about the crew of the vessel or its cargo. Although the ISPS Code goes a long way to tightening up security measures aboard vessel as well as providing information about the crew, it only covers that which is known or is divulged in the company's interests. In the case of the ISPS Code, there are, however, likely to be cases where although the crew's nationality may be known, other information about each crew member may not be known because of the withholding of personal information by certain crew members for personal or other reasons. Furthermore, there is no internationally-binding code obliging the exporter or the freight agent to correctly declare all freight being loaded into a container and in this way the cargo considerations are completely divorced from the issues of the nature of the vessel's crew. Even the recently introduced ISO 28000 and 28001 standards allow the trader to compile and implement their own set of checklists and procedures concerning cargo security and do not dictate the exact details of such procedures. The underlying principle is still one of *uberrimae fidei*. Thus, in an age of information technology and access to information, the data held by the shipping line pertinent to the cargo on any of its vessels may only be as accurate as the organisation inputting that information to the shipping line, such as a freight agent. With large-scale cargo consolidations, the risk of inaccuracy and increased risk on this basis is greatly increased. A ship will not report in to either a seaport or a control centre overlooking a narrow strait concerning the nature of its cargo if it is not aware of any hazardous or dangerous cargo on board, especially since the 24-hour reporting mechanism in place at many ports, especially those in the UK, is still voluntary and is not fully mandatory. The ship is entirely at the mercy of the shipping line's agents and the freight agents responsible for shipping cargo consignments. This level of uncertainty only adds to the risk of accidents or catastrophes occurring as a result of marine accidents, and thus severely compromises marine safety for the vessel, its crew and other cargoes aboard the vessel.

1.2 A View from the Shore

The aspect of maritime reporting is naturally important from the perspective onboard vessel. However, from the port perspective, there are many issues which beset port and landward activity which need to be addressed on a long-term basis, mainly as a result of recent maritime legislation which affects worldwide maritime activities.

The EU Directives covering vessel monitoring and tracking have meant that more sea lanes must be covered by some form of VTS system. The waters around southern Scandinavia are being increasingly brought under some form of VTS activity, the most recent being the Storebaelt (Great Belt) within Danish territorial limits. Invitations to tender have also been submitted for the purpose of the provision of a VTS system to cover the Oresund, between Denmark and Sweden. And yet, there are still many sea areas, including much of the coastal waters surrounding the UK, which are not yet covered by an interactive VTS system similar to that at the Strait of Dover. Only the AIS system is being actively used around all UK waters and even this is only effective if the vessels have their AIS transponders switched on. There are various AIS websites for public use and these are in some ways the only way in which many organisations can monitor maritime activity around the UK coast. However, there is no fully-integrated VTS system for the whole of the UK and every port manages its own affairs concerning vessel control activity. Indeed, there are still major ports in the UK which are not yet equipped with a VTS system, inferring that they have little, if any, monitoring or control facility over inward and outward vessel movements, despite the incidence of marine accidents close to their domains. Ports do not divulge information to other ports for a variety of reasons and there is therefore no way of knowing a vessel's circumstances without being located at the port of arrival or departure. In short, the UK system of vessel control is severely fragmented, with information concerning a vessel's movements restricted to the authorities located at the vessel's port of arrival, unless it is passing through the Strait of Dover, in which case, that information is also known to the MCA's CNIS operations. Other than this, only the vessel's agents will retain information concerning particular vessels, their cargoes and their movements, and they will only convey that information to the port of destination.

Such information concerning the vessel's cargo is also becoming less manageable because of the increasing sizes of vessels. The latest vessels entering service with shipping lines such as Maersk, CMA CGM and COSCO (China Overseas Shipping Company) are well in excess of 100,000 grt and can carry some 9,000–10,000+ TEUs (Twenty-Foot Equivalent Units). The increasing number of containers carried aboard vessel inevitably results in a greater difficulty in managing such information as the compilation and transmission cargo manifests, as well as the problems associated with the loading and unloading of containers at any port visited. This additional burden of loading and unloading will also result in increased pressure on the ports to mange their infrastructural facilities, which inevitably leads to increased congestion of land-based traffic entering and exiting the ports.

Another area of concern stems from the fact that, in the UK, the Maritime & Coastguard Agency (MCA) has already rationalised its structure to the point that it no longer maintains the number of coastguard stations around the UK coastline that it once did. Many of the MCA operations are not even controlled from coast-based stations, but are managed from inland-based centres. Even MCA operations concerning the North Channel, the Firth of Clyde and the Scottish West Coast are controlled from one building based at Gourock, on the upper reaches of the Firth of Clyde, far removed from such sea areas. It is assumed that in the event of a maritime emergency or incident, all operations can be controlled from this one centre. It has been confirmed by the MCA Office on the Clyde that it does not even use a VTS system for these areas, but relies on the AIS systems and information available. This approach is hardly contributing to compliance with the VTMS Directives issued by the EU Commission.

It is appreciated that legislation is designed to formalise and direct activities in a variety of sectors, but there are occasions where such legislation has led to increasing burdens upon those activities leading to questions being asked concerning the efficiency of those operations. The ISPS code has been introduced by the IMO and is being implemented by all ports worldwide. However, the smaller the port, the more difficult it is to incorporate the code's requirements within an already stretched scope of resources. Larger ports find it less difficult to comply with the regulations, as they already have a security-based system within which to operate. Small ports have to find the resources to incorporate such changes to their operating structures, and this inevitably leads to greater expenditure and other strains on such resources, as well as the burden of added levels of bureaucracy required to administrate such changes and activities. Add to this any port-based activities associated with the impact of the IMDG Code on HAZMAT movements and VTS requirements, and the system moves closer to overload. Additional burdens may now be placed on the system by the introduction of ISO 28000 and ISO 28001 standards, and this will inevitably stretch already limited resources yet further.

In summary, the main codes, regulations and standards which a port must adhere to include the following:

- VTS (seaward);
- AIS (seaward);
- ISPS (landward and seaward);
- IMDG (landward and seaward);
- SOLAS (seaward);
- FAL (landward);
- ISO 28000/28001 (landward).

Other issues, such as port state controls and the presence of both MCA and customs are also prime issues in port management, as these controls refer equally to both vessel and cargo security. The port authorities are now so enmeshed in such regulations that they appear to need to spend more time complying with such regulations than in actually managing maritime activities. However, despite such regulations and controls, it is often the case that the port's harbourmaster is the last point of contact concerning the arrival of a vessel, as the shipping agents will already have arranged berthing formalities with the port authorities in advance and the vessel does not necessarily report its arrival until it passes through the breakwaters and enters port, thus negating in part the whole rationale behind the reason for many of the regulations concerning vessel movements and port controls.

The question must ultimately be asked as to whether the smaller ports will be able to maintain their operations for much longer in the light of the implementation of such regulations and the inevitable costs associated with such changes. As the threat of terrorism and the general concerns over maritime security increase, so too does the requirement for increasing levels of security at the ports. This inevitably costs time, effort and money, and many of the smaller ports are finding it difficult to keep up with the necessary changes imposed as a result of such requirements, especially as in general they do not receive financial aid from nation al authorities for the implementation of such changes. Even the larger ports are required to adopt more stringent measure with regard to both port, vessel and cargo security, especially under the requirements of the ISPS code, and this is creating an atmosphere of radical change within the port environment, from both a landward and a seaward perspective, as well as an increasing level of bureaucracy associated with such changes.

1.3 The Role of the Shipping Agency

Much of the mechanism relating to the reporting of the vessel and its cargo revolves around the role of the ship's agent. The agent represents the shipping line in most ports and deals with all aspects of the ship's entry into port and the time it spends at the berth, as laytime for unloading, loading and maintenance. The agent is also responsible for communication with the port authority concerning the berthing of the vessel, the stevedoring arrangements for unloading and loading activities, the provision of ship's stores and the administration of and documentation for, all such activities. It is also the duty of the agency to inform the harbourmaster of the arrival and departure of all vessels they represent and in so doing, inform the harbourmaster and hence the port of all hazardous cargoes or problems with the vessel. The submission of this information depends upon how much information the master of the vessel holds concerning the cargo. Normally, the cargo manifest and the mate's receipt will give this information, but in cases of consolidations, the information pertaining to a cargo may be less than detailed or at worst inaccurate. The larger the vessel, the greater the volume of cargo carried aboard the vessel. The greater the volume of cargo, the greater the amount of documentary information required pertaining to that cargo. With the introduction of 10,000+ TEU container vessels, the greater the risk that this documentary information is less accurate or detailed on the grounds of the sheer volume of information required for the ship's manifest. And with this risk, there is a greater probability of a risk of danger owing to the lack of awareness on the part of both the ship's master and the agent of all hazardous or dangerous cargoes, or any other items potentially deemed as being prejudicial to the safety of the vessel, its crew or the port itself. Indeed, it is becoming evident that certain ports in Europe, including the UK, may not be able to handle such vessels, such is their size as well as the quantity of their containerised cargo.

It is the responsibility of the agent at the port of loading to ensure that the correct information is given to the vessel's master concerning the cargo being loaded aboard vessel, as the cargo manifest containing such information must agree with both the Bills of Lading and the mate's receipt, which is duly stamped and signed by the master or the mate. If the information should be lacking in any way, then it is the direct responsibility of the agent at the port of loading to shoulder any liability resulting from loss or damage in the event of an accident or a disaster befalling the vessel during the voyage or on arrival at the port of destination. In this respect, a great degree of professional responsibility is required on the part of the agent, along with a considerable knowledge of the rules and procedures involved in vessel management. In many cases, larger agency companies have offices in a variety of port locations and deal with a wide range of vessel and freight-related activities, ranging from chartering through port and liner agency to freight forwarding and customs clearance.

2 THE SHORT-SEA SECTOR AND THE "MARINE MOTORWAY"

The issues raised to date have largely concerned deep-sea traffic on a global basis, and in general refer to containerised and bulk movements. However, a further area requiring scrutiny concerns the short-sea sector, especially shipping movements within the Nordring (North Sea and Baltic) vicinity and the Mediterranean area. Both are major maritime areas in terms of their importance, and both are used by a mixture of container, bulk cargo and Ro-Ro (Roll-On, Roll-Off) trailer and passenger vessel movements. The container and bulk cargo operations are similar in many ways to the deep-sea operations, as such movements are not necessarily frequent between the ports in the region, and refer to specific cargo loads. This said, the feeder services linking the North Sea ports with the deep-sea vessel movements out of the larger container ports are conducted on a very regular basis, with most feeder services out of Rotterdam, Antwerp and Felixstowe to the smaller ports operating on a weekly or twice-weekly basis at very least, as are those in the Mediterranean region from ports such as Genoa. The primary regular sailings in the North Sea and Baltic region, as well as others in the Mediterranean region, however, concern Ro-Ro ferry operations, with sailings several times a day in many cases, and on a daily basis in others. These services are conducted by ferry companies classified as authorised regular operators, which are authorised by the maritime authorities in the countries where they operate to avoid the normal reporting requirements on the grounds that their ferries will be expected in port on a regular scheduled basis. These regular sailings are commonly referred to as the "marine motorway" because of their frequency coupled with the fact that they carry large numbers of road vehicles as part of an integrated journey from seller to buyer by road, a facility often seen as a marine extension to the extensive road network throughout Europe.

There are indeed many operators who believe that a ferry service is simply an extension of a roadway out to sea. It is often forgotten that a specific regime exists for the carriage of cargoes by such means of transport over and above that which exists for road haulage which requires a specific form of documentation to account for all consignments carried by trailer on board vessel. However, such information pertaining to the vessel carrying such trailers is not necessarily included on the shipping document pertaining to the overall trailer journey, such as an international consignment note (CMR). It should also be noted that the same principle of the marine motorway also applies to the container feeder services operating in the North Sea area as well, since their services operate several times per week between ports, where specific sea freight documentation is required, namely a Marine Bill of Lading or a sea waybill.

However, an absence of a reporting requirement does not absolve such operators from ensuring that information pertaining to their cargoes is correct and accurate. There is still the need for the master of a feeder vessel or a

Ro-Ro Ferry to be absolutely certain as to the nature of the cargoes aboard vessel. In the case of feeder services, this requirement is an extension of the reporting and documentary requirement for the deep-sea element of the operation, as the cargoes aboard the feeder vessel will doubtless be trans-shipped at the intermediate port to a larger vessel for shipment to elsewhere in the world, or vice versa. The rules and problem issues applying to the trans-port of hazardous and consolidated cargoes therefore apply as much to feeder vessels as they do to their larger counterparts.

In the case of Ro-Ro traffic, however, the rules pertaining to cargo doc-umentation are more vague and less well-controlled. Within the European short-sea regime, there are more simplified rules concerning the issue of shipping documentation than for deep-sea traffic, as there is no requirement for Bills of Lading. The cargoes carried are generally transported by road trailer, which is loaded aboard vessel as a unit, with or without its haulage tractor unit. The trailer will have been loaded at an inland point, and will be driven to the port of loading where it is driven aboard vessel. Upon the arrival of the vessel at the port of destination (Europoort Rotterdam) it will be driven off the ferry and on to its final destination elsewhere on the European con-tinent. This integrated journey, including the ferry sailing, is covered by one single document, the consignment note (CMR). Although the ferry sailing is included as part of the movement, it is not necessarily specified on the document, although a separate note may be issued to the carrier for the maritime sector of the journey as evidence of contract of carriage by the ferry operator. Where the road carrier is an integrated part of the combined move-ment including the ferry operation, such as DFDS, then the maritime sector of the journey is an automatically assumed part of the overall operation.

The CMR consignment note is raised by the carrier according to the instructions of the trader arranging the shipment. This document may cover a single trailer load, or it may cover a consolidated trailer shipment. Depend-ing upon who arranges the shipment according to the relevant INCOTERM, the information provided on the CMR will be detailed or otherwise. In the case of consolidations, it is often the case where the information contained on the master consignment note covering the whole consolidation is very vague and generic. For such intra-European movements, it is generally the case that only two INCOTERMS are used (i.e. EXW (Ex Works) or DDP (Delivered Duty Paid)).

Where the consolidated shipment is arranged by the buyer on an Ex Works (EXW) basis, the information on the CMR may well be very limited and generic and may not accurately reflect the details of all the individual consign-ments loaded into the trailer. In the case of the movement of hazardous goods by trailer, this lack of information could prove in itself dangerous, as the risk of accidents aboard vessel is heightened by the very fact that the documentary information pertaining to such cargoes is lacking and could compromise the safety of the lives of the crew and passengers aboard vessel, as well as the integrity of other cargoes carried on the same vessel. Where the carriage of a consignment is arranged by the seller on a DDP basis, the risks of this omission of information are decreased, as the seller may well ensure that greater attention is paid to the correct recording of essential information on the CMR, as they require some form of proof of shipment.

The terms EXW and DDP are the most common terms used for road transport, as they reflect a direct integrated movement, and they are often referred to as "Freight Collect" and "Freight Prepaid" respectively, given the inference of the party responsible for the arrangement and payment of carriage of the consignment. Both terms refer to integrated journeys involving possibly two forms of transport, although the terms used do not reflect the complexity of such movements, accounting simply for a door-to-door integrated movement by trailer. The process of movement is simplified, and in the case of a ro-ro ferry journey, simply involves the use of a freight forwarder who in turn books a space aboard the next available ferry for a journey across an expanse of water such as the North Sea or the Channel. In many cases, the ferry crossing may only be booked at the last minute for reasons of convenience or cost, and is not therefore reflected in the original journey arrangements agreed between the shipper and the freight forwarder. Indeed, the shipper may never be aware of the actual route taken buy the trailer until its arrival at the destination (i.e. the buyer's premises).

Two comparative diagrams of this arrangement can be seen as follows:

Delivered duty paid

Figure 7.1: The DDP Route

Ex works

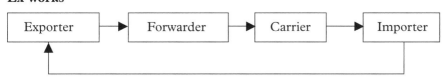

Figure 7.2: The EXW Route

Note how, in the first diagram, the exporter arranges the shipment and ensures control over that shipment. In the second diagram, however, the exporter has absolutely no control over the shipment, as the buyer arranges everything, including the documentation. Under the terms of Ex Works, the buyer is not legally bound to send any proof of shipment, including the CMR, to the seller. Under maritime rules, this arrangement gives little control by the seller over how the consignment is being shipped by maritime means and means that the maritime carrier is entirely at the mercy of the arrangement between the buyer, the freight forwarder and the carrier. If the buyer arranges the consolidation and gives little information to the forwarder concerning the nature of each cargo included in the consolidation, then the forwarder will in turn give little information to the carrier (and hence the shipping line) concerning the consolidation, hence the elevation of the risk with regard to the maritime shipment.

In this way, there are increased risks concerning the safety of the ferry and its complement, especially under the SOLAS Convention. Many cargoes are carried by ferries without the full knowledge of the master as to their nature, as the vessel's cargo manifest will not contain full information concerning these cargoes. In this respect, the risks to short-sea maritime safety are as great as those concerning deep-sea shipments and require addressing in terms of marine reporting in the same way as those pertaining to deep-sea operations. The simplification of regulations concerning short-sea shipments have in some ways prejudiced and compromised reporting requirements in terms of safety and compliance with international trade controls even more than the requirements for deep-sea traffic, with the result that in many cases, short-sea traffic may be seen as a greater risk than its deep-sea counterpart.

3 PERCEIVED ANOMALIES IN MARINE REPORTING

In assessing the principle of marine vessel and cargo reporting, several anomalies arise which require addressing in the maritime sector. These include:

- requirements of the national maritime authority;
- the reporting of the vessel to the port of destination;
- the reporting of the vessel in restricted international waterways;
- the details included in the report;
- shared responsibility between the owners of the vessel and the agents.

3.1 Requirements of the National Maritime Authority

Each national maritime authority has its own national or supranational marine reporting requirements, as in the case of the European Union. Those requirements are based on the legislation passed by the national government, or, in the case of the EU, Directives issued by the Commission in Brussels. In the case of the EU Vessel Reporting and Monitoring Directives, each Member State takes its own action based on its interpretation of the Directive. In the case of Denmark, a VTS system already exists covering the Storebaelt, the Strait passing though Danish national territory, but a system has yet to be implemented in the Øresund, the Strait separating Denmark and Sweden. Conversely, a mandatory Vessel Reporting System covering the Strait of Dover is jointly operated by the UK and French authorities, whereas there is no system whatsoever covering the North Channel, the Strait separating Scotland and Northern Ireland. All shipping movements through the North Channel are monitored at a distance by the AIS system used by UK coastguards, and even this does not physically control or monitor vessel movements. It merely shows the vessel movements through the Channel on a computer screen at a considerable distance from the Strait, in the coastguard building at the other end of the Firth of Clyde. This situation is detailed in a case study at the end of the text.

3.2 The Reporting of the Vessel to the Port of Destination

Unless the vessel's owners have their own representation at a port, it is normal practice for the vessel's agents at the port to report the arrival of the vessel to the port authority, although this practice is not necessarily carried out within the requirements set out in EC Directive 2002/59. This report will give details of the vessel, some general details of its cargo and the berth, dock or wharf required for the purposes of unloading and loading. To this extent, some general details of the cargo are included, especially as the cargo manifest for the vessel must be submitted to the customs authority for the purposes of cargo examination by customs should the need arise. However, with the increase in size of container vessels, the complexity and size of the cargo manifest has also increased. Besides which, although the 24-hour reporting rule applies for all vessels entering port (or at least an inbound report once the vessel has left its port of departure, assuming a voyage of less than 24 hours), the agent does not always report the arrival of the vessel to the harbourmaster, even in the case of the vessel carrying dangerous or hazardous (HAZMAT) cargoes. It is to be expected that as part of any reporting mechanism, the ISPS rules at Security Level 1 pertaining to the security arrangements for the vessel itself are obeyed when the vessel enters port. The rules pertain to the security plan of the vessel and those responsible for the vessel's security. It is often the case that the harbourmaster only receives information concerning the vessel's arrival via the port authority once the agent has already notified the port authority. In theory, however, the port harbourmaster will have a list of vessels expected to arrive at the port some time before their actual arrival, as the agent will have made arrangements for the docking of the vessel some time in advance of the vessel's arrival, usually some weeks. It is the express duty of the agent to complete a declaration (the agent's declaration) to the port prior to the vessel's arrival, giving all relevant details of the vessel concerned. However, this declaration assumes all known facts are correct; it does not account for any sudden change in the vessel's condition or circumstances, such as accidents aboard vessel, problems with the vessel itself or its cargo.

In brief, therefore, it is the responsibility of the ship's agent to declare the vessel's arrival to the port authority well in advance of that arrival, and to ensure that all information about the vessel and its crew and cargo is known to the port and other authorities accordingly. However, the normal 24-hour reporting rule is not often obeyed, implying that certain information may not be transmitted to the port authorities in the acceptable manner. There are many instances where the harbourmaster is the last point in the chain of contact to know of the vessel's impending arrival at port. The port authority itself will however already be well aware of the vessel's arrival, having been informed by the vessel's agent well in advance of the vessel's arrival.

3.3 The Reporting of the Vessel in Restricted International Waterways

When a vessel is entering restricted international waterways such as the Strait of Dover, the Oresund or the Storebaelt, it is the duty of the master of the vessel to notify the international authorities of each country bordering the strait in question concerning the vessel's passage through the Strait. In this case, it is not the task of the vessel's agent to do this, as the vessel may not be calling at a port near the Strait in question. It is the direct responsibility of the master of the vessel to carry out this task. However, such reporting may not always be undertaken, as the use of AIS may simply pick up the vessel on radar and monitor it through the strait in question. Only where a mandatory vessel reporting system exists will the master be obliged to report the vessel's presence and intentions as part of its sailing plan, especially where the vessel may be carrying hazardous or dangerous cargoes. In this respect, a more proactive control regime such as VTS (vessel traffic systems) facilitates a greater control over the vessel in question by allowing the constant monitoring of and contact with the vessel while it remains within the domain and scope of the control system. The drawback of the VTS regime is that it does not take account of details of vessel's cargo or its crew. As with the AIS system, it simply identifies the vessel and its registration details. Because of the VHF radio channel frequencies available for contact between the vessel and the monitoring authority, contact with the vessel's master may be maintained by radio link. However, the purposes of the VTS system is to monitor and track the vessel's movement. Although the VTS operator may issue guidance to the master of the vessel for the purposes of navigation through a channel within a restricted waterway, the system used does not actively intercept that vessel for security purposes, nor does it request details on the contents of the vessel. The information provided will refer to the identification of the vessel and its destination. In this respect, there is a distinct difference in the responsibility for the identification of the vessel depending upon whether the vessel is passing through a strait of international water or whether it is calling at a port in the area. It is this distinction which determines which party (the vessel or its agents) should declare the vessel's presence to the authorities.

3.4 The Details Included in the Report

The reports for the arrival of a vessel at port or its passage through a restricted international waterway differ radically in their content and detail. Details of the vessel's cargo, however general, are required for the vessel's arrival at a port, whereas these are not required at present for the purposes of a vessel's passage through a restricted international waterway. A report for a vessel passing through a strait deals solely with the identification of the vessel, whereas this information is increased to include general details of the vessel's cargo when it arrives at a port, partly as the vessel is entering national customs territory when it arrives at the port and is therefore required to declare all items it carries, including details of the crew, passengers, stores and cargoes, according to the international IMO FAL regulations. Cargo reports are usually of a more detailed nature, given that the cargo manifest should give full details of all cargoes carried aboard the vessel. This document is also supported by the mate's receipt, which is the document showing that the master of the vessel is certain of all the cargoes carried by that vessel. This set of documents should also be supported by all Bills of Lading relating to the cargoes aboard vessel, although in cases of consolidations, FAK (Freight of all kinds) or "Said to Contain", this is often not the case. To this extent, cargo manifests and other reports may be scant in the details they provide, which does not give rise to adequate security of cargo or even the safety or security of the vessel itself. Even in an age of increasing tonnages of cargo vessels, there is still the need for detailed reports of the cargo of any vessel and this detail should be known by any relevant authority whether a vessel is passing through a strait or entering a port. In this way, such details can be passed between the authorities concerned in order to allow for the full transparency of any maritime reporting regime.

3.5 Shared Responsibility between the Owners of the Vessel and the Agents

Ultimately, the owner of the vessel is responsible for the safety, security, upkeep and well-being of the vessel at all times, although it devolves a certain degree of that responsibility to the agents when the vessel enters port. However, the owners of the vessel equally devolve the responsibility of the reporting of the vessel to different parties depending upon the circumstances of the vessel at a particular point in its voyage. The sailing plans are the responsibility of the master and the crew, as well as any charter parties using the services of that vessel. The reporting mechanisms required for sailing through restricted international waters are the responsibility of the master of the vessel, while the responsibility for declaring the vessel's arrival at a port are devolved to the ship's agent at the port in question. In this respect, the vessel's owner takes little responsibility for the vessel's activities, other than those basic legal responsibilities required of the owner. The rest is split between the vessel's master, the agents and perhaps the vessel's charterer.

There is a requirement, therefore, for a degree of collective responsibility relating to all parties involved, concerning who should accept responsibility for what function. It is unfortunate that the use of electronics for the purpose of vessel monitoring does not allow for in-depth scrutiny of information relating to both the vessel and its contents. Various rules pertaining to the responsibility for various degrees of reporting functions are often overlooked in the interests of expediency, and often do not account for the complete situation concerning the presence of a vessel in a specific location, especially in an international strait or on the approach to a port. If information is not required or specifically requested, it will not be divulged. A major area of anomaly concerns how much information should be divulged by the operators of a vessel, the vessel's agents or the vessel itself. The net result is that between all these considerations, there is no standardisation in the detail or the amount of information available to the maritime authorities from any vessel. It is ultimately this anomaly which needs to be addressed, to achieve a complete control over not only a vessel's movements but also what it carries, for overall security purposes.

There are therefore several anomalies in the present marine reporting structure which can at any time give rise to breakdowns in communication between any vessel and the national authorities. Many of the anomalies refer to the level of perceived basic or essential information required by each of the authorities against the actual information available, as well as the incompatibility of various existing systems with each other, but the main area of concern is to what extent maritime security is being prejudiced by the lack of essential information pertaining to not only the vessel itself and its sailing intentions, but also the cargo it carries and the lack of accurate information pertaining to that cargo. If such details, such as cargo or passengers, are not adequately reported, then safety or security issues could be severely compromised. In an age of insecurity and uncertainty, such failure to fully report any information relating to the vessel or its cargo engenders an increasing level of risk, which may in turn compromise the level of national security for any nation concerned.

3.6 Cargo Fraud

There is an increasing amount of fraudulent activity concerning the international shipment of cargoes, usually with regard to full container loads, and where, upon import, the container is found to contain either nothing at all or contents which bear no relationship to the shipping documentation. Indeed, in certain cases, the containers simply do not arrive at their destination, and appear never to have been shipped in the first place. The February 2007 edition of the magazine *Shipping Today and Yesterday* reported a case where steel shipments from North Africa supposedly bound for the Indian subcontinent were in fact false. The Bills of Lading associated with such shipments contained a series of discrepancies, including incorrect container numbers, and were deemed to be false. It was also ascertained that intermediaries were involved in the operation, and were themselves victims of the fraud on various occasions. Other scams have involved the sale of timber from the Far East to customers in Europe, except that although the Bills of Lading were made out to the consignees, the timber never arrived. In fact, it never existed, and the victims of the fraud had already parted with large sums of money as part of the deal. In other cases, containers supposedly loaded with clothing were despatched from the EU to the United States. When the containers arrived, they were found to contain sand. It transpired that the consignments had been switched en route between the despatching warehouse and the port of export. The term *caveat emptor* applies very much in these cases, and it is vital that the buyer ensures that the documentation relates exactly to the shipments concerned, as well as ensuring that adequate insurance against loss is taken out against the transaction. In cases where short shipments are concerned, i.e. where the contents of the container upon import are found to be less than the quantities stated on the invoices and Bills of Lading, then the buyer must do all that is necessary to ensure that either the balance of the quantity is shipped as soon as possible, or that compensation or reimbursement is obtained in lieu of the discrepancy, including any refund of Import Customs Duties on items not shipped. It is unfortunate that in cases where containers are not examined until they reach the buyer's premises and where all duties were paid at the point of import into the country, there is little right of redress for the buyer other than to present evidence of non-shipment or short shipment to the authorities in the hope that the matter can be equitably addressed and resolved.

3.7 Implications of the "Erica", "Prestige" and "Hyundai Fortune" Disasters

In 2002, the tanker *Prestige* split apart during a fierce storm off the North-West Spanish Coast and her cargo of crude oil was lost into the sea. A similar fate befell the tanker *Erica* off the French coast, in ways similar to the loss of the tanker *Amoco Cadiz* off the French Coast in the early 1980s. The SafeSeaNet system was implemented by the European maritime authorities to try to avoid the repetition of such disasters. The notion of the system is to maintain an information base on all commercial vessels and the risks they pose to the maritime environment. However, the basis for the SafeSeaNet initiative was the risk posed primarily by vessels designed to carry bulk hazardous cargoes especially carriers of crude oil and chemicals, so the regime was designed around the dissemination of information concerning the nature and state of these vessels. The SafeSeaNet initiative has been partly responsible for ensuring the reduction in illegal spillages of oil as a result of tank cleaning at sea, along with other legislation passed over the past few years. However, there was no provision made for the mandatory reporting of such vessels when approaching national territorial waters other than the customary 24-hour reporting rule when the vessel approaches its port of destination. The VTS systems presently in operation are only designed to provide an information-based system as well as monitoring the progress of any vessel within the scope of the VTS system. There is, as such, no proper reporting system in operation requiring a vessel to report into the national authorities on its approach to national territorial waters, other than the US and Canadian 96-hour reporting regimes in operation.

The case of the container vessel *Hyundai Fortune* reinforces the need to establish a regime requiring the master of a commercial vessel to be fully aware of all his cargoes, especially in the case of container vessels, and to be able to report this information in advance of entering national territorial waters. On 21 March 2006, a fire broke out aboard the 5000 TEU container vessel *Hyundai Fortune* while sailing through the Gulf of Aden, on her way to the Suez Canal and the European Ports. Just after midday, an explosion ripped through the lower cargo area and hull of the vessel and aft of the accommodation area, sending between 60 and 90 containers falling into the ocean. The explosion caused a massive blaze which spread through the stern of the vessel, including the accommodation area in the vessel's superstructure. As a result of the fire, secondary explosions occurred in seven containers above deck, which, it was discovered later, were full of fireworks. This fact was not known to the vessel's master at the time of the disaster, but was only discovered later as a result of extensive investigations into the vessel's cargo. It was also ascertained that as many as one-third of the vessel's complement of containers were damaged by the inferno. Every container aft of the accommodation area was either incinerated or lost at sea. It has been conjectured that the latter, larger explosions which crippled the vessel were caused by the detonation of the fireworks as a result of the heat resulting from the initial blaze. In this case, the requirements set out in the IMDG code had clearly not been obeyed, and this breach could be used to bring severe liability to bear on the shipping line or its agents.

The main element of the issue concerns the knowledge of the cargo by the master of the vessel. It would appear that the containers holding the fireworks were all in close proximity to each other. Under the rules of stowage aboard vessel, any containers known to contain hazardous or dangerous cargoes must not be stowed together in a place close to the management of the ship or its accommodation area. They must be stowed well apart from each other, away from the areas of accommodation, and their presence must be known and understood by the vessel's master, as in accordance with the SOLAS Regulations it is the master who must ensure that all steps are taken to reduce the risk of spillage or destruction or the risk of threat to other cargoes or even the vessel itself, while the cargo is in transit. In the case of the need to report the vessel's impending arrival at a port or even the vessel's presence in limited waterways such as the Strait of Dover or the Storebaelt, the risk of disaster is increased where the master of the vessel is not aware of certain cargoes aboard vessel, especially those of a hazardous or dangerous nature. If such a disaster had occurred in areas of water more limited than the Gulf of Aden, such as the Strait of Dover, the results would have been even more catastrophic, especially as there would have been no specific report issued to the UK or French maritime authorities concerning the hazardous nature of the cargoes aboard vessel. Previous incidents in the Strait of Dover have reflected similar circumstances, where a collision occurred between two vessels and the resulting fire aboard one of the vessels resulted in the release of toxic vapours. One of the contributory factors of this fire was that certain containers of hazardous chemicals had been stowed in the forward area of one of the vessels, and these containers were damaged in the collision. The possibility of absence of knowledge of these cargoes by the master of one of the vessels may have contributed to a lack of information reported to HM Coastguards at Dover, coupled with a failure by one of the vessels to adhere to its correct separation lane.

Vessel reporting must be based on the risk posed by the vessel and its cargo to the maritime environment and the region which it is approaching. The higher the risk, the greater the need for a robust mandatory vessel reporting system imposed by either a national or a supranational government. A simple dissemination of existing known information concerning a vessel or its whereabouts is insufficient. There is the need for commercial vessels to physically report into a national authority prior to entering national territorial waters and state its sailing plan, its cargo and its intended port of destination. In this way, decisions can be taken earlier concerning how to handle, monitor and control the vessel's movements prior to its entry into port, as well as making adequate provision for its safe arrival at port and security concerning the unloading or discharge of its cargo. Although provisions are presently made for the arrival of the vessel at port by the shipping agents, these provisions are made upon the level of knowledge available concerning the cargo of the vessel, and do not necessarily account for the actual details of the cargo which may not always be known by all parties concerned, details which may compromise the safety and security of the vessel and its cargo, as exemplified by the disaster on board the *Hyundai Fortune* in March 2006.

4 AUTOMATIC IDENTIFICATION SYSTEM (AIS)

The Automatic Identification System (AIS) is an electronic system enabling an observer to view and track the movements of several vessels at any one time projected on a computer screen. It can thus be used by shipping lines and cargo operators to track the movements and locations of vessels carrying specific cargoes. The vessel's identification, direction, speed and heading may be monitored throughout a period of time, and by clicking the computer mouse on a particular vessel, its identification information can be accessed immediately. Manoeuvring and other accurate navigation information can also be accessed simultaneously and can be related from both ship and shore to other vessels in the vicinity. The AIS is a shipboard broadcast system which acts like a transponder, operating in the VHF Maritime Band, that is capable of handling well over 4,500 reports per minute and updates as often as every two seconds, and can be accessed by ship and shore alike.

The information broadcast includes:

- the Unique Referenceable Identification Number of the Vessel;
- navigational status, including "at anchor", "moored" and "under way using engine";
- rate of turn—Port or starboard;
- speed over ground;
- position accuracy;
- exact latitude and longitude;
- course over ground relative to North;
- true heading—0–359 degrees;
- time stamp—the exact time the information was generated.

In addition, the Class A AIS system broadcasts the following information every six minutes:

- the Vessel's Unique Identification Number;
- IMO number;
- international radio call sign;
- the name of the vessel;
- type of ship/cargo—exact details of cargo, especially cargo manifests, are not given;
- dimensions of ship to nearest metre;
- location on ship where reference point for position reports is located;
- type of position fixing device (GPS to undefined);
- draught of ship;
- destination;
- estimated time of arrival at destination.

The AIS system allows for the monitoring and tracking of the vessel by electronic means from the moment it leaves port throughout its voyage, or at least through the part of its voyage which can be monitored by the system, which in theory is the whole voyage as long as the vessel has its transponder system switched on throughout the voyage. Indeed, the system allows for the vessel to be identified while it is still in port. In some ways, the system bears certain similarities to the satellite-based Global Positioning System (GPS) used by most if not all the global commercial and military maritime sector. AIS is being implemented on both vessels and ports, as well as with the CNIS at Dover, in accordance with the 2004 Vessel Tracking and Monitoring Directive and is proving extremely useful in tracking and monitoring vessels on their voyages.

Although AIS has been a mandatory measure for all commercial vessels since the end of 2004, its functions are still somewhat limited. The system must now be installed in every merchant ship over 300 grt, and is being used by many ports, with other ports in the process of developing and installing the system for their own use. However, at present, the system only allows for the vessel to be identified concerning its general characteristics such as name, IMO registration number, dimensions, tonnage, flag and owner. The AIS website identifies all such vessels shown within the monitoring scope of the website areas and accesses not only their identification information but also pictures of the vessel where available, enabling the viewer to establish the nature of the vessel and to deduce its function. However, cargoes and contents of each vessel recorded on the system are not included in the information provided.

However, ships under 300grt are not yet included on a mandatory basis in the system, nor are leisure craft such as yachts and pleasure-cruisers, although initiatives exist to extend the use of AIS to smaller vessels. This may be seen as a major issue, since much of the marine activity around the coastlines of both the UK and the European Union concerns the movements of both small commercial craft and leisure craft, both coastwise and internationally. To this extent, there is a vacuum in the information available concerning the relation-ship between the movements of merchant ships and the movements of leisure craft, especially in cases where the movements of the latter may be seen as encroaching upon the movements of the former. Furthermore, AIS applies to merchant ships—it appears not officially to refer to warships or submarines of any national navy which, in any case, are not subject to commercial maritime traffic requirements other than passage through certain international Straits such as the Strait of Dover and the Oresund between Sweden and Denmark.

However, warships and other vessels used by government departments involved in maritime protection such as fisheries may be fitted with AIS, to monitor the movements of other vessels, especially fishing vessels. Fishing vessels used in deep waters are already fitted with passive AIS, enabling them to detect other vessels in the vicinity without displaying their own position. In the interests of fishery protection, particularly in the areas bounded by the European EEZ, such fishing vessels are monitored by the fishery protection vessels of each EU maritime nation, in order to enforce the maintenance of strict fishing quotas laid down by the EU as part of the common fisheries policy. Those fishing vessels deemed to be contravening the quota regulations may be boarded, arrested and escorted to the nearest port. In this respect, AIS may be used for governmental monitoring purposes as well as general mon-itoring within the commercial sector. It should also be noted that vessels used by government agencies for these purposes will often have their own AIS systems switched off for some of the time, to avoid being detected by commer-cial vessels for a variety of reasons, especially those relating to security. Naval vessels, customs vessels and fishery protection vessels fall into this category, as they are operating at sea on activities relating to matters of national security, and require a level of secrecy as part of their operations.

Information pertaining to the movements of commercial vessels is available to all parties with access to computerised facilities. The AIS Internet website allows anyone with an interest in any particular vessel located in a specific area included on the internet-based facility to access information pertaining to its whereabouts at any point in time. Two specific AIS websites can be found at:

- www.lloydsmiu.com
- www.aisliverpool.org.uk

and they can be accessed by online registration of the person with their e-mail address and brief description of their activities and/or occupation. Once registration has been completed, the viewer may access a whole variety of worldwide locations included in the AIS web portal. The AIS Liverpool website only covers UK maritime territory, but is still very comprehensive in its scope, affording a significant view over all vessel movements around the UK coastline. It is also free of charge to users, and offers a wide range of access to related maritime links.

However, as a security measure, the AISLive website is divided into two formats:

- general information (website free of charge);
- specific information (website payable by subscription).

Unlike the AIS Liverpool website, the free AISLive website does not give specific details of ships, on the grounds that the users will be of a more amateur nature and will not be using the system for professional reasons. Such users are also not seen to be verified for security purposes so cannot gain access to specific information on vessels and their true position at the time of access of information. The information provided on the free website portal thus takes into account a delay of some two hours in the vessel's position between the reporting of its position and the time its location is shown on the AIS display.

The payable website displays up-to-date information of a more accurate nature, although in reality this information may still be slightly out-of-date by up to two minutes. However, the exact information relating to the vessel's identity and nature may be accessed on the payable website, thus allowing the user (usually a shipping professional or a national authority such as the coastguard or customs) to access up-to-date information on the vessel, its route and its identification details.

The AIS Liverpool website at www.aisliverpool.org.uk shows details of vessel movements in considerable detail, including a tracking device to show the historical movements of vessels over the previous hours, as well as up-to-date details of all shipping located in all UK maritime areas. It also has links to other European AIS websites for various locations, including the Netherlands, Sweden and Norway.

The AIS system can be used to target a specific vessel and show its IMO details, dimensions and tonnage, as well as its active status at the time of perusal (moored, at anchor or underway using engine). For vessels underway, their course and speed will be shown, along with their destination. The AIS system allows for the monitoring of the vessel's course and position while the vessel is within the domain of the AIS area covered on the website. The AIS screens are divided into particular sectors, for example Solent, the Strait of Dover, the North Sea, the Channel and the Irish Sea. By clicking on any of these areas, it is possible to gain more detailed and accurate information concerning the movement and location of a particular vessel. The more accurate image will also show the movements of other vessels in the area. This enables the viewer to establish the location of a specific target.

Such information is without doubt a useful tool to any authority or individual seeking to monitor the movements of vessels within the geographic scope of the AIS domain, and is a valuable tool alongside the existing monitoring controls used by authorities such as the CNIS facility at Dover or port authorities. It is to be assumed that most users of the AIS website system are doubtless quite innocent in their motives for information access, and are either shipping enthusiasts or maritime professionals. However, the ease of use of the system and its availability to the public at large may render the movements of vessels monitored within the AIS website domain vulnerable to the less-than-honourable attentions of such people whose nature and motives for accessing the AIS website may be somewhat deceptive and undesirable, such as terrorists or the traffickers of illegal contraband. Crews of vessels, ship-spotters, marine enthusiasts, port authorities, national authorities and commercial organisations are one thing; international terrorists and the traffickers of illegal goods and immigrants are another. Internet access is available to all, but there is a need to monitor the usage of such systems to ensure that the motives of the user are justifiable and are for purely benevolent or professional purposes, as well as maintaining the integrity of the Data Protection Act. Although in principle the nature of the system is admirable, insofar as it provides instant access to information pertaining to the movements of all applicable participating vessels, it is not totally watertight and secure in that it allows access by anyone registered on the website to maritime information pertaining to all such vessels, nor is it sufficiently far-reaching in providing total information pertaining not only to information concerning the vessel itself but also the nature of its contents, be they passenger or cargo. And, as pointed out by various users, the information contained on the database is not always completely accurate, either because of delays in the transmission of information or because of inaccurate data on the vessel itself.

It should be noted that, in some ways, AIS is a historic tracking device. The history of vessel movements can be shown on a graphic display and this in turn can be used to show a succession of vessel movements within a given scope of maritime activity. Although the system does not relate to a vessel's sailing plan or even its contact with maritime authorities, a good picture can be derived concerning how any vessel may be tracked throughout a segment of its voyage.

The other advantage of the system is that it denotes the types of vessels in the area, shown by the colour schemes depicting each type of vessel. In theory, any area covered by an advanced and detailed AIS system will therefore show the historic movements of all commercial vessels within a given timeframe, enabling the operator to track all movements in that area and thus derive sailing patterns for all such vessels. Certain other shipping line websites, such as ACL, enable the shipper to track each of the ACL vessels while they are in transit.

Other AIS sites, such as AIS Holland (www.aisholland.com), enable the shipper or vessel operator to identify and track vessels entering and leaving the Maas/Rijn estuary at the port of Rotterdam. Given the density of traffic activity and relative congestion within the Rotterdam waterways, it can be seen just how necessary a vessel tracking and monitoring system is in the area, both for port control purposes as well as for commercial tracking and monitoring purposes.

For the shipper and the shipping line, vessel tracking is a requirement in an age of heightened security. There is a need at all times to know a vessel's location, as well as its date of departure and its estimated date and time of arrival at the port of destination. Considering also the needs of the shipper, this device also enables the shipper to plan shipping movements and cargo deliveries, in order to plan production scheduling and order fulfilment. For the shipping line, the AIS device enables them to accurately track any of their vessels while in transit and to guarantee vessel departures and arrivals to their customers at any time, thus also guaranteeing quality of overall service.

CHAPTER 8

AWARENESS AND VIGILANCE

1 THE AUDIT TRAIL

The audit trail is vital to any aspect of the marine cargo management process. It is pointless for an export trader to make a consignment ready for shipment without maintaining any proper records of how the consignment was actually shipped, especially where the buyer arranges the overall shipment. In the age of increased levels of risk and [in]security, there is a far greater requirement for a high level of vigilance and compliance in the marine cargo sector, given the risk of terrorism and piracy, as well as marine accidents and mishaps. The planning of any maritime shipment is vital and requires a lot of attention.

The basic information required to issue instructions to the freight agent to commence the expedition process for any consignment by maritime means are as follows:

- the nature and description of the goods, including the first four or six digits of the tariff commodity code;
- details and categories of the hazardous nature of the consignment (if hazardous or dangerous);
- the weight of the consignment;
- the cubic dimensions of the consignment;
- the destination of the consignment;
- the means of transport of the consignment;
- the International Commercial Terms of Delivery (INCOTERMS) to be used;
- cargo insurance details.

Documentary details will also be required for the shipment, namely:

- commercial invoice;
- packing list;
- certificate of insurance (or details of policy reference);
- dangerous goods note (if hazardous or dangerous).

The audit trail commences with the exporter. The exporter must supply sufficient information to the freight forwarder to ensure the safe and efficient carriage of the consignment to its destination (the buyer) regardless of who actually arranges the shipment. In this respect, the use of the INCOTERMS is immaterial. There is still a joint and several responsibility and liability on the part of both exporter and importer to ensure that all information pertaining to the shipment is fully divulged to the agent, to ensure the safe and expedient carriage of the shipment. Shipments do not move on their own. Someone must pay the ferryman. The audit trail is vital in ascertaining both the responsibility of the shipper and the information provided concerning the nature of that shipment. This audit trail must include information which could be seen as prejudicial to the safety of the vessel and her crew, such as the nature of the consignment in the case of hazardous or dangerous cargoes. Cases such as the sinking of the vessel *Estonia* in the Baltic Sea in September 1994 and the subsequent investigations concerning her loss have shown that discrepancies in reports concerning her condition at the time of her sinking could cover up a multitude of sins. There are still reports circulating that certain elements of the cargo she was carrying may not have been known to the vessel's Master and the crew for a variety of reasons. Other cases of accidents such as aboard the container vessel *Hyundai Fortune* reveal that information concerning the cargo, which would be vital to the means by which the cargo should be stowed aboard vessel, was not given to the Master.

Vessel and crew safety relies on a fully-transparent audit trail. Without it, the risk of accident or compromise to vessel safety is greatly increased. If the audit trail is correctly implemented, that risk reduces and the voyage becomes a much more straightforward affair. Insurance is equally compromised by an insufficient audit trail and this in turn could prejudice the validity of many insurance policies should it be later found that the principles of *uberrimae fidei* were not applied.

An example of a typical marine cargo audit trail from supplier to customer would be:

- full container load (FCL) under DDU arrangements;
- consignment made ready for shipment at seller's premises;
- the seller completes the export cargo shipping instructions (ECSI) form;
- the seller contacts the freight forwarder to arrange the shipment to the buyer;
- the freight forwarder contacts the shipping agent to arrange a sea container;
- the container is sent to the seller's premises;
- the container is loaded in accordance with the load list;
- the cargo manifest is arranged by the shipping agent;
- the export declaration is raised and submitted to customs;
- the container is despatched to the port of loading;
- the container is cleared for loading and is loaded aboard vessel;
- the completed cargo manifest is handed to the Master of the vessel;
- the vessel sails from port;
- the Bills of Lading are raised and are passed to the shipper;
- invoices and shipping documents are sent to the buyer;
- the vessel arrives at the port of destination;
- the buyer's agent arranges unloading and clearance of the container;

- the import declaration is raised by the clearing agent and is submitted to customs;
- the container is unloaded from the vessel and is cleared through customs;
- the container is driven to the buyer's premises and is unloaded at the premises.

These stages may seem detailed and complex, but this is the ideal audit trail including the documentary process for an FCL.

The LCL process involves a slightly different audit trail, but nevertheless requires absolute vigilance. This time, the process involves the free carrier (FCA) term of delivery.

- the consignment is made ready for despatch by the seller, who notifies the buyer;
- the buyer issues the export cargo shipping instructions (ECSI), based on the information provided by the seller;
- the buyer arranges consolidation of the consignment with other consignments at a place of loading through a Freight Forwarder/ NVOCC;
- the forwarder/NVOCC arranges the shipment of the consolidated container through the shipping agent;
- the seller arranges transport for the consignment to the place of consolidation (e.g. an inland clearance depot (ICD));
- the consolidator (the NVOCC) arranges the container load list according to the information provided for each consignment to be consolidated;
- the consignment is loaded into the container at the ICD according to the load list and the export declarations for all loads in the container are submitted to customs;
- the cargo manifest for the container load (LCL) is raised;
- the consignment is despatched to the port of loading;
- the container is cleared and is loaded aboard vessel;
- the completed cargo manifest is submitted to the Master of the vessel;
- the vessel is cleared and sails from port;
- the Bills of Lading for the container are issued by the shipping agent;
- the shipping documents and invoices are sent to the importers;
- the vessel arrives at the port of destination;
- the shipping agent arranges unloading and clearance of the container;
- the container arrives at an inland clearance depot (ICD);
- the clearing agent submits the import declarations for each consignment to customs;

- the consignments are cleared through customs;
- the consignments are despatched to the Importers.

The LCL process requires an even more complex audit trail, as all the consignments are consolidated into one container, and the documentation concerning the container load must ensure that each consignment is correctly and accurately recorded and accounted for. There are many occasions when each individual consignment within a sea container are not correctly detailed, which can lead to problems with shipping documentation, customs declarations and even container security. It is therefore vital that every shipment is correctly documented when it is loaded into a container in readiness for international shipment. This allows all parties involved in the shipment process to track the container effectively and ensure that full and complete documentary evidence exists for all consignments loaded within that container.

The difference between FCL and LCL shipments is that where an FCL shipment usually comprises one single unitary load destined for a single buyer, an LCL shipment comprises many different shipments, possibly from different exporters and each possibly destined for different importers. In some cases, however, a single importer may arrange the shipment of several consignments from different suppliers but loaded into the same container on an LCL basis using the FCA term. This being the case, the importer will still require separate sets of shipping documentation to be raised, each set of documents covering each individual consignment within the consolidated LCL shipment, and with separate customs declarations, both export and import, for each individual consignment. In this way, the audit trail would be more transparent and thus more complete. Both supplier and customer would be able to show how a specific individual consignment was loaded into the container and thus arrived safely at its destination with a trail relating to all pertinent shipping and Customs Documentation.

Given that most container shipments are undertaken on a multi-modal basis, there is a need on the part of the shipper to know exactly how the container is being shipped. This means that they must have full details of all modes of transport to be used, as well as obtaining all the relevant documentation pertaining to the shipment, especially the copies of the Through Bill of Lading, showing all details of the transport used, including the marine vessel and shipping line. All necessary steps must be taken to ensure that all the information required to raise the Bill of Lading is correct, and that the true cost of the door-to-door shipment is also fully accounted for. From the point of view of the importer, the costs relating to the multi-modal shipment must be correctly broken down into both international freight costs and domestic haulage costs, as import duty is only calculated on the part of the journey up to its entry into the country of destination on a CIF (cost insurance freight) basis. The additional inland haulage costs are added on for VAT or local tax purposes, and these must be itemised separately. In terms of haulage costs from the point of loading the container, these costs may be added to the international carriage costs for the purpose of freight costs to the point of unloading off the vessel.

For trailer loads, the process is less detailed, but nevertheless requires an audit trail. For full unitary trailer loads, the shipper must ensure that they have a copy of the consignment note relating to the shipment, with all details of the cargo aboard the trailer, including, where possible, the details of the means of international transport, namely the vehicle ferry used as well as the ferry operator. In the case of consolidated loads, details must be obtained by the shipper of the following:

- the carrier (i.e. the ferry company) used for the international shipment;
- the consignment note relating to the shipment, and issued by the carrier or freight forwarder;
- details of the journey;
- the name of the vehicle ferry used;
- the ferry operator.

The consignment note acts as proof of shipment, as well as evidence of the contract of carriage and the receipt for the consignment by the carrier, and must detail the ferry operator, as under the system of carriage of goods by sea, the responsibility for notifying the ferry operator of the nature of the cargo aboard vessel lies with the shipper, through their appointed freight agent, and all details of the cargo must be supplied to the ferry operator accordingly.

In the case of shipments to offshore oil and gas fields, standard shipping documentation such as Bills of Lading is not necessarily issued. In such instances, the shipper requires a copy of the cargo manifest relating to their consignment on board vessel, and, if available, an endorsed copy of the Mate's Receipt. This documentation will be issued by the vessel operator, and must be issued once the vessel has been loaded.

2 ISO 28000/ISO 28001 AND SIX SIGMA

2.1 ISO 28000/ISO 28001

As well as initiatives introduced by organisations such as the IMO and the World Customs Organisation (WCO), the International Standards Organisation (ISO) has endeavoured to introduce a series of international standards implementing the individual Codes such as ISPS requiring all worldwide port authorities and shipping lines to implement ISO standards to maximise their security potential and thus minimise levels of security risk in the international supply chain. The ISO 28000 initiative has been introduced to apply a security standard to the International Supply Chain, by implementing a set of procedures and checklists for all exporters and importers when shipping consignments of goods overseas. The standard requires each exporter to ensure that all consignments being exported are subjected to a series of checks prior to the goods being packed and containerised for security purposes, based on a security risk assessment, and in the form of a security management system. The purpose of the implementation of such a set of procedures is to anticipate any potential risk and reduce or eliminate it at the point of the goods being despatched from the exporter's premises. The drawback in the system is that it refers to the actual goods themselves and the ability of the exporter to control the shipment. It does not necessarily relate to the details contained in the documentation accompanying the consignment.

However, the initiative does include details concerning both upstream and downstream movements, which cover responsibility for the integrity of the cargo and ensuring that adequate steps are taken to account for every item being included in the cargo being shipped. This would include supervising the loading of vehicles, trailers and containers, and ensuring that an account is made on the load list pertaining to the vehicle load, of every item scheduled to be loaded aboard that means of transport.

Downstream refers to the actions, processes and movements of the cargo in the supply chain that occur *after* the cargo leaves the direct operational control of the organisation, including, but not limited to, insurance, finance, data management, and the packing, storing and transferring of cargo. Downstream thus refers to the despatch process for the goods when they are no longer in the custody of the organisation in the supply chain, e.g. the exporter.

Upstream refers to the actions, processes and movements of the cargo in the supply chain that occur *before* the cargo comes under the direct operational control of the organisation, including but not limited to insurance, finance, data management and the packing, storing and transferring of cargo. Upstream thus refers to the arrival process for the goods before the organisation (the importer) in the supply chain, takes custody or possession of the goods.

Much of the issue concerning upstream and downstream operations concerns the extent to which the shipper is fully aware of the nature, description and quantity of the consignment being shipped. On many occasions, little attention is paid to the consignment at the time of loading aboard vehicle at the seller's premises, hence the problems which can arise concerning the accuracy of manifests and shipping documentation. Under ISO 28000/1, it is the express responsibility of the seller to ensure that adequate supervision is exercised over the despatch process, to the point of tallying off the load list referring to the vehicle load prior to its despatch.

One of the main points of ISO 28000 is the security management system. It states the following:

- an organisation must establish, document, implement, maintain and continually improve an effective security management system for identifying security risks and controlling and mitigating their consequences;
- an organisation must define the scope of its security management system;
- where an organisation outsources any processes affecting conformity with these requirements (including Ex Works shipments), the organisation must ensure that these processes are controlled, and that the necessary controls and responsibilities of such outsourced are identified within the security management system.

Under the Ex Works (EXW) principle this may be a vague area, as the exporter bears no responsibility for the actual shipment. However, within the security management system there are five main action elements:

- policy;
- security risk assessment and planning;
- implementation and operation;
- checking and corrective action;
- management review.

This implies that a constant self-corrective action plan should be drawn up by the organisation and adhered to at all times. This suggests that more responsibility should be placed on the organisation to ensure that it does have control over all its shipments, both inward and outward. In itself, this is a worthy solution, and it can be used effectively, depending upon the transparency of information provided by all parties in the shipping process. Indeed, much of the process behind the ISO 28000 and 28001 benchmarks has also been included in the Authorised Economic Operator (AEO) status initiative being implemented by HM Revenue & Customs, which will apply as much to shipping agencies as much as it does to the shippers themselves, and indeed the AEO status is included in the provisions of ISO 28000/1.

According to ISO 28001 (ISO 28001, section 3.3), the Authorised Economic Operator (AEO) is a party involved in the international movement of goods in whatever function that has been approved by or on behalf of a national customs administration as complying with WCO (World Customs Organisation) or equivalent supply chain security standards. AEOs can include exporters, importers, manufacturers, brokers, carriers, consolidators, intermediaries, ports, airports, terminal operators, integrated operators, warehouses, and distributors. Indeed, any organisation concerning with the manufacture, supply, handing and movement of goods on an international basis may seek to be approved as an Authorised Economic Operator (AEO).

Any assessment of security risk, audit trails and accountability takes into account all aspects of transport, including ocean shipping, short-sea shipping,

Ro-Ro and inland waterway transport, as well as the other forms of international transport. It details all aspects of handling, including:

- loading;
- manufacturing;
- storage (including intermediate storage);
- transfer;
- unloading;
- consolidation/groupage;
- deconsolidation/breakbulk.

It also concerns the level of competence and training of company employees, as well as the handling or processing of information about cargo or transport routes.

2.2 Six Sigma

The whole process of ISO 28000/1 bears a similar relationship to that of the Six Sigma process, which is a statistical means of quality control and which can be successfully applied to the logistics sector.

The Six Sigma process can be defined as:

- **Define**
- **Measure**
- **Analyse data**
- **Implement changes**
- **Control the Process**

or **DMAIC,** for short. In reality, the organisation which is content to work within the 3–4 Sigma scale will encounter a problem level of between 25% and 40% or errors requiring addressing in a process, a figure which allows for considerable deviation and also does little to reduce wastage levels or even address total quality issues. Working towards a Six Sigma level will reduce this to below 0.01%. The actual table used to define the Sigma level (process capability) of any organisation is based on the level of defects per million opportunities (each transaction). It seeks to control the level of allowable defects (if any defective operation can ever be seen to be allowable) as most organisations will seek to reduce their defect acceptance level to zero wherever possible. In the international logistics and transport sector, especially relating to the subject of marine cargo management, it also disciplines the shipper into ensuring that all consignments are subject to a rigorous control regime and that every container and its contents loaded aboard vessel can be monitored and controlled at every stage, including the accuracy of the details of the manifest, the load list and the Bill of Lading referring to the contents of the container.

Table 11: Probability of defects of different Sigma Levels

Sigma level (Process capability)	Defects per million opportunities
2	308,537
3	66,807
4	6210
5	233
6	3.4

Although this system is primarily to increase quality levels, in production processes it can also be used in the service sector equally effectively, especially in terms of the enhancement of security within the supply and logistics chain, especially as the issues of supply chain security and the efficiency of cargo management are more prevalent than ever before given the need to provide a quality-driven cargo shipping service in an age of increasing competition and cost-efficiency on the high seas.

The use of such controls within the six sigma process can include:

- the number of correct reports issued in advance of the arrival of all vessels in port per month, compared with the number of actual reports submitted;
- the number of correct reports issued in advance of the arrival of all vessels in port per month, compared with the number of actual arrival of vessels;
- the number of correct cargo reports issued per manifest, compared with the number or actual entries on the manifest.

The analysis of such data will yield the number of successes against the number of actual reports, and will enable the authorities concerned to tighten up their procedures to ensure that all vessels arriving at any port must adhere to the reporting requirements set out at the very least by EC Directive 2002/59/EC. In many cases, the harbourmaster may not know about all movements of vessels into and out of the port prior to those involved with berthing the vessel and handling its cargo. According to EC Directive 2002/59/EC, the vessel should submit a report to the port of arrival giving all its essential details, including cargo, prior to its arrival. The information should therefore be submitted by the vessel to the harbourmaster as well as to the port VTS operators in advance of its arrival, as well as by the vessel's agents at the port, a situation which does not happen with the required frequency.

This means that any organisation maintaining control over the security of its shipments will ensure that it will rarely, if ever, encounter problems relating to those shipments, as it will seek to ensure that all information relating to shipment documentation is correctly completed and recorded and that it has full access to such information and documentation. This effectively rules out the present principle of Ex Works (EXW), and pushes it more towards free carrier (FCA) or further along the INCOTERMS chain.

It should be pointed out that the six sigma process works on the basis of six sigma (six standard deviations) from the average calculated as the mathematical mean of any process, and that the closer an analysis comes to six sigma, the closer the process comes to perfection, as a six sigma measurement allows for virtually no imperfections in a system. Indeed, the six sigma approach may work better than the ISO 28000 approach for a security management system.

ISO 28001 refers to customs controls and how containers are packed and loaded aboard vessel. It refers not only to the consignment in terms of physical checks made prior to export, but that the cargo manifest refers to and agrees with the consignments within the container. Again, the information may not be sufficient enough to satisfy all requirements, in that agents still apply generic terms to consolidations, rather than necessarily recording all exact details of each consignment within the container. Only with the CT-PAT initiative has some attempt been made to itemise in detail all consignments entering the United States and Canada from overseas by maritime means. However, the same rules have yet to be applied to other countries, especially the European Union. The adoption by the WCO of a standard unique consignment reference (UCR) for all imported and exported consignments is only part of the solution. In many cases, the UCR may only refer to a consolidated load, and does not necessarily refer to all consignments within that consolidation. There is still the risk that the information provided on either the Cargo Manifest or the Bill of Lading may bear little relation to the cargo actually loaded into the container and aboard vessel, and this may still emanate from the fact that the party arranging the shipment made the decision to consolidate every cargo loaded aboard the container, and simply instructed the agent to provide a basic set of information, rather than exact details of every load therein. This arrangement of the shipment also depends upon the Term of Delivery (the INCOTERM) used and thus is open to considerable interpretation and discretion on the part of either buyer or seller.

The other main reason for customs involvement is the move away from the examination of consignments at the port, and towards self-regulation by the trader. The AEO initiative is partially designed for this purpose. Any trader wishing to be approved by customs for such status, namely a privileged fast-track form of clearance of consignments through customs, will have to ensure strict compliance with a series of regulatory requirements partly based on the ISO 28001 initiative, and aimed at ensuring greater degrees of security and compliance in terms of information supplied by the trader to the customs authority through electronic means. The electronic form of declaration has taken over from the traditional approach to examinations and clearance internationally, and in turn customs frontier resources have been reduced, especially with regard to port controls. In the UK, it is expected that the AEO status is to be initiated in 2007, and to be fully achieved after 2010.

Although ISO 28000 and ISO 28001 go a long way to highlight the risks in the supply chain and attempt to address and reduce this risk, they do not answer all the questions. The increasing size of container vessels and hence the increased amounts of cargo carried inevitably mean that more information for these cargoes is required, especially on an electronic basis. There is thus a higher risk that such information may not be sufficiently scrutinised to ensure that all cargoes are properly screened prior to entry into another country and cleared through border controls. The emphasis is on moving the container through the port to the trader's premises as quickly as possible, with the minimum of delays for examination on the way. Inevitably, there is the risk of corner cutting, and the fact that computers do not always make the correct decision. There is a risk that some information will drop through the net, and hence the risk of accidents or threats of terrorist attack increases, especially where the Master may still be unaware of the nature of all the cargoes aboard vessel because of omissions by the agents who inputted the original information for each cargo at the time of loading aboard vessel.

3 DOCUMENTARY AND PROCEDURAL REQUIREMENTS

3.1 Commercial Documentation

The process of compliance in cargo management starts with the instruction given by the shipper to the freight agent to ship the consignment, usually in the form of the Export Cargo Shipping Instructions (ECSI). These instructions are used by the agent to arrange a container for the purposes of shipping the cargo. The agent will contact the shipping line to arrange the necessary container and have it transported to the exporter's premises or a suitable place of loading or consolidation. If the original shipping instructions are incorrect or lacking in appropriate information, so any documentation may also be incorrect. When a vessel is to be loaded, it is imperative that all the information about the cargoes to be loaded aboard vessel is available and correct. If it is not, the vessel, its crew and indeed other cargoes may be at severe risk, with regard to safety or security. The process of loading cargoes into containers, then loading these containers aboard vessel demands a specific regime, which must be monitored and checked at all times. It is also important to ensure that the correct HS tariff code is inserted on any commercial documentation, as this not only affects the export declaration to customs, but also is inserted on the cargo manifest for input into the customs computer at the points of both export and import, for the purposes of customs cargo reporting.

Basic documents such as commercial invoices and packing lists are absolutely vital in this process, as these documents determine the validity and applicability of all other documentation associated with the shipping process, including customs declarations. Both the invoice and packing list must contain the correct information primarily concerning details of the consignor, the consignee, the description of the cargo and its weight and dimensions, as well as whether the cargo is either dangerous or hazardous. In the meantime, the shipper issues shipping instructions to the freight agent, instructing the agent to ship the consignment to its destination. The commercial documentation is then raised, which must reflect the details of the consignment as contained in the shipping instructions. On the basis of the instructions to ship, the agent arranges the shipment through the shipping line or their appointed agents, who then raise a cargo manifest containing the details of the shipment and the container(s) used to transport the consignment. The manifest contains details of the container number(s), the description, weights and dimensions of the consignment being shipped. The details on the shipping instructions and the commercial documentation are also used by the forwarding agent to raise an export customs declaration. Once the container has been loaded aboard vessel and the vessel has sailed, the shipping agent or shipping line will raise the appropriate Bills of Lading for transmission to the shipper.

In this respect, the accuracy of the details of the shipment and the way in which it is shipped depend upon the combination of the commercial documentation and the original shipping instructions. If either set of documentation is wrong or has discrepancies, then the shipping documentation will also have discrepancies and the carrier holds the right not to ship the consignment according to the rules set down by the Carriage of Goods by Sea Acts of 1971 and 1992.

Therefore, complete accuracy is required for the following documents raised by the shipper:

- commercial invoice;
- packing list;
- certificate of origin (where required);
- export cargo shipping instructions (ECSI);
- dangerous goods note (where required).

It is the express responsibility of the shipper to ensure that all documentation is correct and accurate prior to issuing shipping instructions, to ensure basic compliance with the rules and regulations concerning the carriage of goods by sea.

3.2 Logistics Documentation

Given the differences in transport and logistics documentation depending upon the method of transport by either deep sea means or by Ro-Ro vessel, the requirements and responsibilities for the carriage of consignments also change. Deep-sea traffic revolves around the use of the Bill of Lading, whereas Ro-Ro traffic uses the CMR consignment note, which does not imply the same legalities and strict functions as does a Marine Bill of Lading. A Marine Bill of Lading is based on the details contained on the cargo manifest and hence the export shipping instructions, whereas a CMR consignment note is based more often on a despatch note, especially as the consignment is not strictly being exported, especially in the case of shipments to and from other countries within the European Union. However, according to the regulations laid down by the 1956 CMR Convention, there is still a need for the carrier of the consignment to fully and properly notify the master of the Ro-Ro vessel of the nature and size of the load being carried aboard the trailer which itself is being loaded aboard the Ro-Ro vessel, as the law pertaining to the Carriage of Goods by Sea applies while the trailer is aboard ship en route to its ultimate destination. In this case, the law concerning the carriage of goods by sea applies as much to Ro-Ro shipments as it does to deep sea container or bulk shipments. Therefore, all the documentation relating to the shipment must be accurate and correct at the time of issuing, otherwise a breach of either the CMR Convention or the Carriage of Goods by Sea Acts will occur and render the carrier or the shipper liable. In the case of full trailer or container loads, the issue of inaccuracies and discrepancies is less likely, except in cases of blatant and flagrant fraud. However, in the case of consolidated loads, there is a greater risk of discrepancies or the sheer absence of necessary information pertaining to the consolidated load.

3.3 Roles and Responsibilities of the Importer and Exporter

The importer or exporter is responsible for all transactions made in the course of its business, be they national or international. In an era of cost-cutting, downsizing and outsourcing, many corporate responsibilities have been devolved to outside contractors, especially the logistics and transport sector, leaving only the absolute basic or essential responsibilities within the company itself. Such responsibilities include sales and accounts functions, as well as manufacturing functions wherever appropriate. Export functions are split between the sales function and the accounts function depending whether the matter concerns obtaining an export order or securing payment. The import function, if it ever exists, is split between the purchasing section and the accounts payable section, which in reality often belong to the same overall accounts function. This is where such corporate responsibility ends. All other functions, including that of logistics, are devolved to outside contractors such as freight agents. It is also often the case that the company concerned has little or no idea whatsoever about the actual role of the freight agent, and assumes that it can simply pass the whole logistics process over to the agent without any reason for communication other than to pay the bill from the agent when it arrives.

Such reliance on other parties is, to say the least, extremely short-sighted. The actual responsibility for importing or exporting which is placed on the importer or exporter is, in reality, very substantial, and cannot be taken lightly. For the purposes of customs clearance in either importing or exporting, the freight agent acts on behalf of the importer or exporter, and cannot be held directly responsible for the actions of either party. The freight agent acts on the express instructions of the importer or exporter, and ships or clears the consignment accordingly. It is often the case where what appeared to be lucrative deals between buyer and seller have become nightmares because the seller did not properly negotiate the deal based on common internationally accepted terms of delivery, otherwise known as INCOTERMS. Freight and duty costs were not taken into account, and the resulting burden had to be borne by the seller, thus completely eliminating any profit which might have been gained. Thus an exporter cannot simply tell a freight agent to ship a consignment without ensuring that both parties (the exporter or importer) are aware of who takes responsibility for the shipment and who will pay the freight charges. In the event, the importer is liable for all import duty and tax payments whether or not they take responsibility for the shipment of the consignment. In this respect, the common opt-out for the exporter is to use the INCOTERM "Ex Works", which implies that the importer will take complete control over the whole shipping process. If, however, the exporter is proficient in the exporting process, then a variety of terms become applicable, from FOB (Free on board named port of shipment) through CIF (cost insurance freight named port of unloading or arrival) to DDU (delivered duty unpaid direct to the importers' premises). Given the complexity of these terms and the different implications they hold, then the exact term of delivery to be used must be included in the transaction at the time of negotiation. The term EXW implies the exporter does nothing more than make the consignment ready for shipment, whereas the term DDU implies that the exporter arranges everything related to the shipment of the consignment up to the point of delivery to the customer's premises, with the customer doing no more than pay import duty and any other associated taxes. All other terms fall between these two with respect to both responsibility for shipment, payment of freight costs and accepting the risk of shipment.

But the logistics element is only part of the international transaction equation. There remains the question of tax liability on the part of importer and exporter alike. An exporter does not pay taxes to export goods from the UK, but must prove to HM Customs & Excise that the consignment has indeed been exported. In the case of goods consumed in the UK, VAT is liable on such sales. In the case of goods exported to the rest of the European Union, VAT is zero-rated since the consignment will become liable for VAT upon importation into another Member State at its VAT rate. In the case of goods exported to a non-EU country, VAT is exempt on the exported consignment, since the importing country may not have a VAT regime or equivalent.

Whichever the export destination, the exporting company must obtain a Certificate of Shipment to prove that the consignment was exported. If this cannot be produced, then HM Customs & Excise can take the view that there is no evidence that the consignment was indeed exported, and can thus charge the company VAT on that consignment. The certificate of shipment must be obtained from the freight agent, since the agent would clear the consignment through customs controls and would therefore retain all documentation related to the shipment.

For the importer, the responsibility becomes greater still. All imports from non-EU countries into the UK are liable for the payment of import duty to HM Customs & Excise. Import duty can only be waived on three basic conditions:

- duty-free status as dictated by the customs tariff;
- preferential duty-free status according to preference agreements between the EU and other countries (on production of a valid certificate of origin or movement certificate);
- import duty relief authorisation approved by HM Customs & Excise.

Unless any one of the above conditions can be satisfied, the import consignment concerned is liable to import duty being paid to HM Customs at the time of importation. Although the clearing agent may pay the import duty plus VAT at the time the consignment is imported, this will only be done on behalf of the importer and will be charged ultimately to the importer's account. The agent is thus not responsible for the payment of import duty and VAT on their own account. Ultimate responsibility for import duty and VAT liability lies with the importer. Thus the importer holds the responsibility for instructing the clearing agent how to clear the import consignment through customs controls and what information is necessary to ensure a declaration fully compliant with customs procedures. Unfortunately, many importers have little or no idea as to what information is required for the purposes of customs clearance. Many importers have never seen a customs tariff, let alone used one. They assume that the clearing agent is fully conversant with such information, and that all they need to do is to tell the agent that an import consignment is expected imminently. End of story? No. The agent is employed to act on the importer's behalf, and requires a considerable amount of information concerning the exact details of the consignment, including its description, value and quantity. It is also preferable that the importer has some basic idea of the tariff commodity code concerned to ascertain the exact import duty rate to be applied. In many cases, however, the ignorance of the importer in such matters means that the agent has to resort to their own copy of the customs tariff to supply such information.

Even assuming that the agent has been furnished with all appropriate information to clear the consignment properly, the importer is still required to obtain copies of all relevant associated import documentation from the clearing agent for their own filing system. If a national customs authority sees the need to challenge an import at any stage following clearance of the consignment in question, they will approach the importer for any appropriate information, not the agent. If the importer cannot produce such information, then the importer is liable for any penalties associated with such matters as determined by the national customs authority under any national customs legislation pertinent to the country concerned. If the importer has total access to such documentation relating to the import in question, then at least there is a better chance that the importer can successfully argue a case with HM Customs should a problem arise. As far as the European Union is concerned, the other main reason for the importer to retain all records relating to an import consignment is that for VAT purposes it is necessary for the importer to maintain adequate records of all import transactions. VAT is paid on all imports other than foodstuffs and other zero-rated or exempt items, and thus it is essential for every importer to maintain copies of all import documentation to prove the validity of each transaction for the purposes of VAT records.

3.4 Role and Responsibility of the Freight Agent

The role and responsibility of the freight agent differs from country to country. In the UK and many other parts of the world, the freight agent has a variety of roles, from international forwarder to temporary storage holder of goods to customs broker. This combined role allows for an integrated package of services to be offered to the customer, be it importer or exporter. The personnel within the offices of a freight agent will be expected to undertake a variety of roles, from completion of import and export declarations and freight forwarding documentation to arranging shipments with air or sea carriers and monitoring the storage of goods on the customer's behalf. The total logistics concept has become more commonplace with the passage of time, with some freight forwarding companies having become more specialist or more global in their sphere of operations. The larger and more global the freight logistics company, the more likely the capacity of the company to ship any type of consignment to any part of the world, albeit at an appropriate cost to the importer or exporter.

In the United States, however, the role of the freight agent differs sharply from its counterparts in Europe. Forwarding agents are responsible for the forwarding and shipment of goods. Customs brokers are responsible for the clearance of import or export goods through customs, and may also take on the role of importer of record (i.e. the responsibility of importing on behalf of a variety of customers). Such customers may have negotiated a transaction with an overseas seller, but do not take direct responsibility for the import process given its complexity. They will pass such responsibility to an authorised customs broker who will import the goods on their behalf, clear the consignment through US Customs and may store the goods for a limited period until the customer is ready to take delivery of the consignment. Although the customs broker specialises in customs clearance, they must pay an annual bond fee to US customs to hold a licence for such a role as well as becoming an importer of record.

In the UK, no such distinction exists. There is no such thing as a definitive customs broker or importer of record in the UK, as the relationship between freight/clearance agent and the UK customs authority differs greatly from that in the United States. There is no licensing system in the UK to govern the proficiency of UK forwarding agents, and nor is there likely to be one. The reality is that in the UK any person or groups of people may establish a freight forwarding company, no matter how proficient or incompetent they may be. Instances have arisen in the UK of forwarding agents failing to represent their principals (the importer) in an acceptable or professional manner, with regard to the processing of import or export documentation. Such action or failure by the agent to act in accordance with the wishes of the importer has resulted in several importers being penalised by HM Customs & Excise for incorrect import declarations or associated documentation.

The occasional error by a clearance agent can be foreseen and acted upon. This is usually as a result of an inadvertent lack of communication between the importer and the agent, or an oversight in the information being supplied to HM Customs for the purposes of an import clearance. Incompetence, on the other hand, is unacceptable, especially on the part of a clearance agent, given the responsibility of making a false declaration to HM Customs & Excise. HM Customs make it abundantly clear that it is the express responsibility on the part of the importer or exporter to ensure that they procure the services of a reputable agent when seeking to clear import or export consignments through customs controls.

There is therefore a definitive business relationship between importer/exporter and the freight agent. This relationship may be based on an infrequent set of international transactions, or it may be ongoing on the basis of a continual series of shipments within the scope of the international supply chain. The freight forwarding agent exists to perform the functions of international logistics which the importer or exporter cannot and therefore is expected to perform such a role in as professional a manner as befits their status, acting as intermediary between the importer or exporter and customs.

3.5 The Role of the Shipping Agent

The role of the shipping agent is to ensure that the consignment is correctly loaded aboard vessel and that all information pertaining to the consignment is correctly recorded and documented for maritime purposes. The shipping agent represents the shipping line, so it is the duty of the agent to ensure that all matters concerning the loading of the vessel and its safe voyage are dealt with properly and efficiently. In this respect, the shipping agent is reliant upon the shipper, be it exporter or importer, and the freight agent, to ensure that all the necessary information concerning the consignment has been submitted, and that the cargo is correctly loaded. Any problems concerning the clearance and loading of the consignment must be reported to the freight agent and shipper if there is a need for the submission of additional information to resolve such problems.

3.6 Assumptions, Perceptions and Communications

The previous sections have outlined the roles and responsibilities of the respective parties involved in the process of international trade. Each party has its own defined responsibility, and such responsibilities are sanctioned by the legislative process as detailed in the C&E Management Act 1979. But it is also evident that the Act is only known to members of HM Customs & Excise, and is not widely appreciated in the commercial sector, which would undoubtedly explain the multiplicity of problems that are encountered by the commercial sector when dealing with HM Customs & Excise. There is an inherent fear on the part of the commercial sector when faced with a problem concerning Customs & Excise matters, which appears to stem from five main sources:

- a lack of knowledge or ignorance of Customs & Excise regulations;
- a refusal by the importer or exporter to admit to the existence of a problem;
- a fear that if a problem is admitted to HM Customs, then more problems will emerge as a result;
- an incapacity or lack of understanding on the part of the importer or exporter to be able to solve the problem;
- an inherent lack of willingness on the part of the importer or exporter to seek help, especially when it is most needed.

These issues are, regrettably, endemic throughout the importing or exporting community, and much of the issues concerned have arisen as a direct result of corporate downsizing or outsourcing of importing or exporting technicalities to outside contractors without retaining any expertise relating to such issues within the company itself.

Such ignorance of basic procedures allows for a large number of assumptions when relating to the international process. Such assumptions are often mutual between importers or exporters and freight agents. The importer or exporter assumes that the freight agent is responsible for many activities and has all the appropriate information available, whereas the agent may equally assume that the importer or exporter has all the relevant information to ensure speedy and efficient customs clearance of all consignments. Equally, in the process of international shipping transactions, the importer or exporter perceives that the freight agent can do everything, and that the importer or exporter needs do little or nothing, expecting that the whole operation will perform like clockwork.

This is not so. The respective roles and responsibilities of each party dictate that each performs its own part of the bargain to ensure that the right information is conveyed in order to undertake the transaction of clearing imports or exports through customs control. A vital part of this exercise lies in clear and understandable communication between one party and the other. The importer or exporter conveys the necessary information to the agent concerning the means by which they require clearing a consignment through customs. The agent completes the appropriate documentation according to the information provided, and duly undertakes the clearance. If, subsequent to the import or export clearance, customs discovers that some of the information provided on the declaration was incorrect, they will challenge the importer or exporter, not the agent, since the agent carried out their instructions.

There is thus no room for assumptions or perceptions in the process of import or export declarations. Accurate communication is vital in the process, and such communication cannot depend or rely on assumptions of any kind. Every piece of information essential for correct declarations to be made must be conveyed prior to the declaration being carried out, since after the event such information communication is useless. It is futile to explain to customs when they are knocking on the door seeking unpaid revenue that the company did not have the information at the time, or did not know that such information was required at the time of submitting the customs declaration. Customs will not accept such arguments or excuses under any circumstances whatsoever. And the importer or exporter must pay as a result.

If, however, the importer or exporter accepts all necessary responsibilities and ensures that they are fully conversant with all necessary customs procedures, then such mistakes are less likely to arise. Companies which are in full control over their logistics and customs requirements stand a better chance of being able to address problems should they arise, or will at least be able to seek the appropriate advice where and when necessary. Not every company may be able to solve all problems related to importing or exporting activities, especially where customs are concerned, but they will at least know where to seek assistance in resolving such issues. Customs is not in a position to help every company all the time, but they can give and are willing to give basic information to the public when required and when asked the right questions. If the problem is of a more complex nature, then extra help may be required from other sources in the form of business advice or staff training. The advice given by business consultants is not given free of charge as opposed to that given by customs. Given that the role of customs officers has become more limited over the passage of time, a certain level of investment in business or consultancy advice can, over the long term, be far more valuable than having to spend money in penalties or liabilities to customs as a result of not taking advice earlier.

Two case study scenarios serve to illustrate this anomaly, and are described as follows. They also concern the shipment of engineered automotive products.

3.7 Case Study 1

The first scenario concerns shipments of automotive products from a company in the UK to automotive customers elsewhere in the European Union. The customer arranges the shipments, as it also receives automotive products from other suppliers, also in the UK. The consignments are collected individually from each supplier on an Ex Works (EXW) basis, and are delivered to a central consolidation point somewhere in Eastern England, where they are consolidated into a trailer and are loaded at an East Coast port aboard a Ro-Ro vessel bound for the continent. The documentation raised by the consolidator only relates to the consolidated load, it makes no mention of each consignment within that consolidation. The documentation raised for the consolidated shipment is issued to the customer under the Ex Works basis and no documentation is sent to the supplier. The consolidator states that should the supplier require any form of documentary evidence of shipment, the documentation will cost a significant sum of money to issue. The only means of verification that the consignments arrive at their destination is by a monthly schedule of receipts raised by the customer. The supplier has no way of knowing how the consignment was shipped, and aboard which vessel as required by the CMR consignment note.

3.8 Case Study 2

The second scenario involves the same suppliers in the UK. The consignments are once again arranged by the customer on an Ex Works (EXW) basis, only this time the customer is based in the United States. The customer arranges the collection of individual consignments from the supplier's premises, and has them delivered to a centrally located consolidator based in the Midlands. The consolidator consolidates the consignments into a sea container, and despatches the container to the port of despatch. The consolidator is not authorised to complete export declarations and only raises an overall consignment note for the container. The Bills of Lading are arranged by the agent at the port of despatch, who also raises the export customs declaration for the container load. Because of the lack of information concerning each individual consignment within the consolidated container load, both the Bills of Lading and the export customs declaration only refer to the consolidated load and not its constituent individual consignments. The documentation only refers to "automotive parts", yet this information is accepted by the US customs automated manifest system (AMS), and the container is cleared for loading aboard vessel. Similarly, there are no individual export customs declarations for each individual consignment within the consolidation, so the supplier receives no documentary evidence of shipment whatsoever. Under the regulations of the European Union Commission, the lack of a customs declaration for each consignment is considered a breach of the regulations, and is thus considered an offence under customs law, as well as a breach of the law concerning the carriage of goods by sea, in this case referring to the carriage of goods by deep-sea means, as the supplier receives neither a copy of the export customs declaration nor copies of the individual Bills of Lading for the consignment being shipped.

In both cases, the company would fail to attain the requirements specified under both ISO 28000 and ISO 28001, as there are insufficient provisions in place to minimise the security risk of the shipment of such consignments. Indeed, there is little in the way of a definitive audit trail to establish the logistics security for the movement of such consignments.

It is vital for both exporter and importer to receive copies of the shipping documentation, as this ensures that cargoes can be correctly verified and tracked using a proper audit and documentary trail comprising accurate information. As shown by the above examples, it is impossible to track a consignment only on the basis that the customer supplies information from the supplier once the consignment has been received and entered into the customer's system. Regulations concerning export compliance state that both parties need to be aware that a consignment has been correctly shipped and that there is a documentary trail to reflect this. Similarly, the carrier requires sufficient information from the shipper concerning each individual cargo consignment to ensure that under the law of the carriage of goods by sea, the carrier is adequately informed concerning the nature of the shipment and its full description as required by the law.

The process of the issuing of marine deep sea shipping documentation can be detailed as follows:

- ECSI;
- load list;
- cargo manifest (FCL/LCL);
- stowage plan;
- mate's receipt;
- Bills of Lading.

It should be noted that the Bill of Lading is the last shipping document to be raised and issued. This is because the document is usually of the nature of a Shipped On Board Bill of Lading, so can only be issued once the cargo has been loaded aboard vessel and the vessel has sailed. Up to this point, several other documents must be raised by the carrier, namely the load list and cargo manifest, which detail the contents of the container. The mate's receipt is given to the Master of the vessel by the ship's agent for approval and endorsement once loading of the vessel has been completed. Once these documents have been raised and have been approved by the Master according to the stowage plan of all cargoes loaded aboard vessel, then the vessel awaits clearance to sail. The Bills of Lading are issued once the vessel has sailed.

In the case of Ro-Ro vessel movements, Bills of Lading for each consignment aboard vessel are not issued. The manifests for all cargoes loaded by road trailer aboard vessel will refer to the Consignment Notes (CMR) issued by the road carrier. It is imperative that these documents are in order, as any discrepancies can lead to the Master of the vessel refusing to allow the loading of a trailer aboard vessel should there be any suspicion or inference that any of the information relating to the cargo loaded into that trailer is incorrect or uncertain, especially in cases of hazardous or dangerous goods, which could risk compromising the safety of the vessel, its crew and its passengers. Even within the scope of Ro-Ro short-sea movements, the rules and regulations concerning the maritime carriage of goods still apply and these must be complied with at all times.

3.9 Customs Documentation

As well as logistics and shipping documentation, Customs documentation is a vital part of the shipping process, and must be accurate in every way. The Customs declaration, be it for export or import purposes, must be totally accurate, as Customs law (Customs & Excise Management Act 1979, s. 167(1)) states that if a declaration is not accurate or even made at all, this is an offence, and the declarant is deemed to have submitted a false declaration, making the declarant liable to summary prosecution.

In the above cases, although a formal declaration is not required for intra-EU shipments, the supplier is required to hold sufficient dispatch records to show that the consignment has been exported in the form of some kind of shipping documentation or a certificate of shipment issued by the carrier. Where shipments are carried on short-sea container vessels between two EU ports, such as on a feeder service, a T2L document is required for the consignment in question to show that it is of EU origin, and is thus in EU Free Circulation. In the case of fully international shipments to non-EU destinations, there is a need for a customs declaration for both exported and imported consignments. In this way, the issue of consolidations has no bearing whatsoever on whether there should be an export declaration for either the consolidated load or each individual consignment within the consolidation. The law states that there is a need for an individual export and import declaration for each consignment, whether consolidated or not, and this means that for every export consolidation, there is a need for an individual export declaration for each individual load in the form of a declaration unique consignment reference (DUCR), as well as an overall declaration for the overall consignment on the basis of a master consignment reference (MUCR). These details must appear on the declaration itself when it is being submitted to the customs computer at the point of lodgement. In the case of trans-shipments from the

UK via another EU port such as Antwerp or Rotterdam, then a further copy of the NES export declaration must be sent with the consignment to the port of trans-shipment, where it must be endorsed and stamped by the customs authority at the port, and this copy must then be returned to the UK, with a copy for the exporter and a copy for the central community transit office of HM Revenue & Customs (HMRC) at Harwich, Essex. This procedure is required as the consignment is under community transit customs-controlled conditions from the moment it is exported from the UK until it is loaded on board the deep-sea vessel at the port of trans-shipment, and is shipped out of the European Union.

3.10 The Export Declaration

The declaration must reflect and represent all aspects of the consignment, and, in the case of UK export declarations, must include the following details:

- consignor;
- consignee;
- declarant (where different form the exporter, as in the case of the clearing agent);
- TURN (trader's unique registered number);
- description of the consignment;
- tariff commodity code (TTCN);
- customs procedure code (CPC);
- unique consignment reference (UCR);
- details of licences (where appropriate);
- port of loading;
- destination.

Although there may be slight differences from country to country concerning the exact details required on a typical export declaration, the essential information required remains the same. In the case of the European Union (EU), the systems by which both export and import declarations are submitted electronically to customs have been harmonised as part of the SAD-H declaration harmonisation initiative, with the same information required for submission in each of the EU member countries.

Once the declaration has been submitted to the customs computer and has been acknowledged by the computer, the consignment may be transported to the port of loading. The shipping agent or representative of the shipping line at the port then inputs the basic information regarding the consignment into the computer, including the UCR, and the computer decides what action must be taken. This is usually automatic electronic clearance to load, although a documentary check may be required. Using the US-based AMS system, this also means submitting the information at the same time into the AMS prior to loading the container aboard vessel. Assuming clearance of the consignment, the container may then be loaded aboard vessel, and a further message to this effect is submitted to the customs computer, also using the UCR. Once this procedure has been carried out for all containers being loaded aboard vessel, the vessel is cleared for departure, and the computer issues a further message notifying the agents of this clearance. This final message is seen as the absolute proof of clearance and can be used for compliance purposes to show proof of despatch and export.

The overall procedural summary is thus:

- Submission of export declaration to the customs computer in the form of a pre-shipment advice using the creation of a unique consignment reference (UCR);
- acknowledgement and acceptance by the customs computer;
- movement of the consignment to the port of loading;
- submission of arrival message (goods arrived at port) by the agent in the form of the UCR;
- electronic clearance to load authorised by customs computer (Route 6);
- consignment loaded aboard vessel;
- departure message issued by computer;
- vessel clearance message issued by computer;
- vessel sails.

This procedure ensures that all necessary steps have been taken to ensure export compliance, and that all customs regulations and requirements have been satisfied. It should be noted, however, that the clearance process allows for examination of the cargo by an officer should it be deemed necessary to verify the details of the consignment. Although this can be carried out at the trader's premises, it can also be effected at the port of despatch, which often means opening the container at the port for an examination to be carried out. The same is true of the AMS systems, where a US customs officer could carry out similar checks if required. If a documentary check is required, a full set of export documentation (minus the Bill of Lading but including a copy of the manifest referring to the individual consignment in question) must be presented to the examining officer, who then checks the information for accuracy and identifies any discrepancies in the documentation, should they exist. The officer then makes the decision whether to delay the consignment pending clarification of information, or whether to release it for shipment. Once the consignment has been released, a further message is submitted to the customs computer acknowledging clearance following examination. The consignment can then be loaded aboard vessel. It is thus important for all information pertinent to the declaration and clearance to be submitted in advance of the vessel arriving at port, as there is always a deadline time for containers to be received at the port of loading prior to the vessel being loaded to allow for delays in clearance as well as the receipt and full acknowledgement on the port computer of all consignments to be loaded aboard vessel. Because of the deadlines imposed on the receipt of cargoes at the port, the customs declarations must be submitted well in advance, in order to allow sufficient time for full clearance by the customs computer. There are often delays to loading caused by failure to clear, usually because the customs computer requires more information about the consignment itself. These delays are often caused by the lack of information submitted by the shipper concerning the consignment, leading to incomplete declarations being submitted to the customs computer. It is therefore vital that the shipper ensures that at the time of submission of the export declaration, all information pertaining to that declaration is correct at the point of entry.

3.11 The Import Declaration

The import declaration works in the same way as the export declaration, except in reverse, in that it is used to declare an imported consignment to customs for the purposes of import duty and tax purposes, as well as other controls such as licensing and quotas. The transport documentation plus the commercial invoice give details of the consignment itself, namely the following information:

- the importer;
- the declarant (the clearing agent);
- the description of the consignment;
- the origin of the consignment;
- the value of the consignment;
- the correct tariff commodity code;
- the freight cost;
- the insurance cost.

Other details, such as import licences or preferential certificate details, must also be included on the declaration where required. The accuracy of the declaration depends upon the above information provided, since import duty and national tax will be calculated and levied against that consignment at the point of import, for payment by the importer, and thus it is vital that all information used for input into the declaration is correct, including details of the container used to import the goods, as well as all freight and insurance costs, which, when added to the purchase invoice cost, give rise of the CIF (cost insurance freight) import landed cost value for import duty purposes. The declaration also acts as proof of import, for the purposes of auditing, and must be made available should an audit be carried out on either an internal or external basis. All freight and insurance details must be itemised separately from the purchase cost details, as these are required as evidence under the CIF principle.

3.12 Penalties

There are inevitable penalties, both commercial and fiscal, when errors are made, especially concerning documentary matters. In cases where erroneous commodity codes are used, the penalty is a demand by customs for additional import duty to be paid. Where insufficient information is used to input the details of the consignment into the US AMS and Canadian ACI customs computer systems in advance of loading the consignment aboard vessel, the computer can reject the information and thus delay loading, until sufficient accurate information is provided to clear the consignment for loading.

In cases where documents are not submitted in time, or where the information provided on the Bill of Lading is incorrect, then the consignment will be held in a warehouse operated by the shipper or Port Authority until the matter is resolved. The time spent for storage of the consignment is called *demurrage*, and can amount to a significant sum of money, depending upon the number of the days incurred as a result of the delay. The costs incurred are determined by fixed storage rates dependent upon the amount of space occupied by the consignment. Given the sums of money involved, it is in the interests of the shipper to ensure that any problems concerning the consignment are resolved as quickly as possible.

The most common causes of demurrage are:

- delays in customs clearance;
- failure to present documents;
- vessel delay;
- discrepancies in documentation;
- procedural delays.

Such problems can, however, be avoided by the following means:

- correct documentation, checked at the point of issue;
- timely presentation of documentation;
- correct means of presentation of documentation;
- correct shipping procedures;
- forward planning.

Certain other issues can be more difficult to avoid, such as vessel delays, but in general such issues can be communicated between buyer and seller should they be anticipated, such as adverse weather conditions or port congestion. However, issues such as customs delays are less likely to be anticipated, such as container scanning or examination of documents or cargoes, as these matters are governed by the customs computer and cannot be foreseen in advance. However, demurrage costs, although generally incurred by the agent, must be passed on to the shipper, as the problems which often cause demurrage arise as a result of failure by the shipper to correctly carry out their part of the transaction, thus rendering the shipper liable to pay for such issues.

3.13 US and Canadian Cargo Requirements

Following the tragic events of 11 September 2001, the United States Government introduced a legislative means by which all incoming cargoes would be screened and vetted prior to their loading aboard vessels bound for the United States, and all cargo manifests raised for the cargoes to be carried by vessel leaving for the US to be submitted electronically to US authorities at least 24 hours prior to the vessel being loaded. In reality, the time required is 48 hours, on the grounds that the manifest must have been cleared by the US authorities some 24 hours before the vessel has even arrived at the port where the consignments will be loaded. If the correct information pertaining to the cargoes being vetted was not available the system implemented would not allow the cargo to be loaded aboard vessel, and any vessel containing cargo which was not correctly described could be turned away from a US port or arrested by US Coastguard officials. As detailed earlier in this text, the terms "Freight of all Kinds" and "Said to Contain . . . " are not be allowed to describe consignments on a Bill of Lading under the rules issued by the US Customs & Border Protection Agency. Furthermore, officials from the US Customs service would be located at all ports where trade with the US was carried out and would have the power and the right to inspect containers and their cargoes where required to do so. These actions were embodied in the CT-PAT (Customs and trade partnership against terrorism) initiative and the US Trade Act of 2002.

The US administration also introduced an electronic system which allowed for the vetting and screening of all cargo manifests raised by the agents prior to the loading of the vessel at the port of despatch, known as the automated manifest system (AMS). This system is used to assess the information on the container and its contents submitted by the shipping agents some 24 hours prior to the container being loaded aboard vessel by the computer of the US Customs Authority. If the information provided is not deemed to be correct, permission to load will be denied by the US electronic system. It should be noted that the AMS system only operates for consignments entering the United States, but not for consignments exported from the US to overseas destinations. The European Union operates no comparative system, implying that there is little check made on containerised consignments at the time of loading prior to them being despatched to EU destinations.

According to the US Customs and Border Protection Agency (CBP), the AMS is a multi-modular cargo inventory control and release notification system. AMS interfaces directly with customs cargo selectivity and in-bond systems, allowing faster identification and release of low-risk shipments. In reality, it gives US Customs the power to interrogate and identify any cargo bound for the US prior to it being loaded aboard vessel in the despatching country, and also gives US Customs the power to stop any cargo from being loaded which they deem to present a problem. AMS is also designed to speed the flow and entry processing and to provide participants with electronic authorisation to enable cargo to be released by customs prior to its arrival in the US. The US import agent or customs broker is still required to submit a formal import customs entry to customs, but this can be done before the cargo vessel arrives at its US port of destination. AMS also reduces the reliance on paper documents and thus speeds the processing of manifest and waybill data.

Although the AMS is designed to provide a more secure and speedy means of cargo clearance, it also requires the exporter, the forwarding agent, the shipping agent and the importer to maintain a more robust means of procedural and documentary compliance concerning the shipment of consignments to the United States. It therefore means that all traders shipping consignments from the UK to the US must ensure that all necessary information is contained not only on the shipping documents but also on the cargo manifest. Failure to do so would result in delays to the cargo being loaded aboard vessel on the grounds that the AMS system could reject the information submitted to the computer owing to incomplete details concerning the cargo.

US importers are required to communicate the following requirements to their overseas locations as well as their overseas suppliers:

- the shipper's name and address;
- consignee, owner of the consignment or owner's representative name and address (in the case of "to order" shipments, the name of the ultimate consignee, owner or owner's representative will be required);
- piece count, the count of all items within the consignment, both in the container and at the lowest external packaging unit (e.g. cartons instead of pallets);
- precise and accurate cargo description and quantity;
- harmonised tariff schedule (HTS) number to the six-digit level.

The Canadian advance cargo information system (ACI) works in exactly the same way as the US AMS system. It was applied and implemented by the Canada Border Services Agency (CBSA), the successor to the Canadian customs department, in the wake of the US terrorist attacks, given the volume of cross-border container traffic between Canada and the US that was originally unloaded at a Canadian port. As with the AMS system, it requires all shippers exporting goods to Canada to pre-lodge the manifest concerning all cargoes loaded into containers at least 24 hours prior to the container being loaded aboard vessel and came into effect in April 2004. Marine carriers, (shipping lines) or their agents are thus required to electronically transmit cargo and conveyance data to Canadian customs at least 24 hours prior to the loading of the cargo aboard vessel in the foreign port. Freight forwarders are also permitted to transmit certain electronic cargo information, as they have direct electronic access to the Canadian customs computer. Provided the cargo or conveyance (the container) does not pose any health, safety or security threats to the authorities, Canadian customs will authorise the loading of the goods on the Canada-bound vessel. Cargo or containers considered to be high risk are held for examination by customs authorities in the foreign port, until they have been cleared for loading subject to customs and security requirements. Where consignments are being shipped via a Canadian port to an onward US destination on a multimodal basis, then electronic submissions must be made to both the Canadian ACI and US AMS systems at least 24 hours in advance of the consignment being loaded aboard vessel.

In all the above issues, bulk shipments are exempt. The advanced manifest system requirements refer to all containerised cargoes, both FCL and LCL, as these are pre-loaded into containers and must be fully accounted for and declared prior to loading aboard vessel. For containerised cargoes, the AMS and ACI requirements apply to all US and Canadian seaports, all commodities and all shippers. By using the automated manifest system regimes, both the US and Canadian governments have implemented a means of assessing risk for individual containerised shipments before they are loaded to a vessel at the port of loading. The greatest protection to US and Canadian ports is to prevent suspicious cargo from being loaded at the port of origin. Therefore, both the US CBP and the Canadian CBSA require all manifest information prior to cargo loading for all containerised shipments. Once that information has been scrutinised and approved electronically, the cargoes may then be loaded aboard vessel.

Further steps were taken in 2006 to increase security measures concerning containers arriving at US Ports. The 9/11 Commission Recommendations Act (also known as the SAFE Port Act) was signed, requiring all containers shipped to the US to be scanned at the port of departure prior to being loaded aboard vessel. This measure is designed to be enforced by 2012, and means that all ports exporting container loads to the US must comply with this law, despite the added cost and inconvenience to the shipper which this measure may cause. It also means that the port scanning devices will be used for both incoming and outgoing containers, especially concerning trade with the United States.

3.14 The WCO SAFE Framework of Standards

Alongside the initiatives concerning the US CT-PAT regime implementing the AMS and the ACI systems, the World Customs Organisation (WCO) introduced its own initiative, agreed in Brussels in June 2005, to establish a global system of security rendering the whole regime of cargo movements both transparent and accountable, and facilitate a safer world trade regime, entitled the "Safe framework of standards". The document also included the customs initiative to create the authorised economic operator (AEO) regime, whereby companies involved in frequent international trade activities would be able to apply for a specific authorisation to operate a simplified import and export declaration regime based on their history of compliance with customs import and export requirements. This authorisation would allow such traders to use fast-track export and import clearance procedures, thus resulting in savings of both time and costs. The AEO regime was initiated in 2007, with companies being invited to apply for the authorisation.

Although the essence of the AEO regime is largely concerned with overall customs compliance, it requires the shipper to maintain complete control over their inward and outward shipments, particularly in the maritime cargo sector. This means that the shipper must maintain complete control over the management of all maritime cargo shipments, concerning both documentation and procedural issues.

The SAFE Framework has several principles:

- to establish standards providing supply chain security and facilitation at a global level to promote certainty and predictability in the supply chain process;
- to enable integrated supply chain management for all modes of transport;
- to enhance the role, functions and capabilities of customs to meet the challenges and opportunities of the 21st century;
- to strengthen co-operation between national customs administrations to improve their capability to detect high-risk consignments;
- to strengthen customs/business co-operation;
- to promote the seamless movement of goods through secure international trade supply chains.

There are four core elements within the SAFE Framework. These are:

- The harmonisation of the advance electronic cargo information requirements on inbound, outbound and transit shipments.
- Each country joining the SAFE framework commits to employing a consistent risk management approach to address security threats.
- The requirement that at the reasonable request of the receiving nation, based upon a comparable risk targeting methodology, the sending nation's customs administration will perform an outbound inspection of high-risk containers and cargo, preferably using non-intrusive detection equipment such as large-scale X-Ray machines and radiation detectors.
- The definition of benefits that customs will provide to businesses which meet minimal supply chain security standards and best practices.

There are two pillars within the SAFE Framework:

- customs-to-customs;
- customs-to-business.

Each pillar involves a set of standards which are consolidated to guarantee ease of understanding and rapid international implementation. Like the US and

Canadian initiatives, the framework is designed to provide better security against terrorism and increase the contribution of customs and trade partners to the economic and social well-being of countries. It is designed to improve the ability of customs to detect and deal with high-risk consignments and increase efficiencies in the administration of goods, thereby expediting the clearance and release of goods, as well as, in the words of the document setting out the principles of the SAFE framework, securing and facilitating legitimate global trade, along with the facilitation of the modernisation of global customs operations. A further aim is to improve revenue collection and the proper application of national laws and regulations.

The establishment of customs-to-customs network arrangements is designed to facilitate the efficient exchange of accurate information which is supposed to place customs administrations in the position of managing risk on a more effective basis. This network would enable customs to more easily detect high-risk consignments and to improve their controls along the international supply chain, thus leading to a more efficient allocation of customs resources. Such supply chain controls would thus enable the customs administration of an importing country to request the customs administration of the exporting country to carry out controls earlier in the supply chain, for example examinations of export consignments before they are loaded aboard vessel, either at the shipper's premises or at the port of loading.

One of the main elements of the SAFE framework as far as the shipper is concerned is the submission of advance electronic export goods declarations to customs at export prior to the goods being loaded on to the means of transport, such as a sea container, in effect consolidating and developing the existing electronic export declaration systems used, *inter alia*, by shippers in Canada and the UK. The UK electronic export declaration system, the so-called "new export system", was introduced in 2002 and now covers all exports to non-EU destinations from the UK. Where simplified electronic export declarations are submitted at first instance, these would have to be followed up at a later stage by supplementary declarations as required by the national legislation. Similarly, the carrier or their agent would have to submit an advance electronic cargo declaration to customs at export and/or at import. For maritime containerised shipments, the advance electronic cargo declaration would have to be lodged prior to the consignment or container being loaded aboard vessel, and would be followed up by a supplementary cargo declaration as stipulated by national legislation.

Similarly, the same procedure would be carried out at the import stage, in that an advance import goods declaration would be submitted to customs prior to the cargo being landed at the port of destination. In the case of a simplified declaration, this would be followed up by a supplementary declaration for the purposes of calculation of import duties and other local taxes. The proposed "authorised supply chain" procedure would allow for the possibility to integrate the export and import information flows into one single unified declaration for export and import purposes, which could be shared between the customs administrations concerned.

Time limits for the pre-lodging of goods and cargo declarations by both shippers and carriers would be imposed by each national customs authority. These would be as follows for maritime shipments:

- containerised cargo (including multimodal transport): at least 24 hours before loading at the port of departure;
- bulk/Break-bulk: at least 24 hours before the arrival of the consignment at the first port in the country of destination.

The *authorised supply chain* is a concept under which all participants in an international trade transaction are approved by customs as observing specified standards in the secure handling of goods and relevant associated information, including export, import and shipping documentation. Consignments passing from origin to destination entirely within such a chain would benefit from an integrated cross-border simplified procedure, where only one simplified declaration with minimum information would be required for both import and export purposes.

In essence, the new framework simplifies the supply chain process, but it requires all parties to the process to be absolutely compliant in all their related activities, especially concerning the shipment of consignments. There is a need for a clear audit trail, as well as the complete transparency of information, to facilitate the smooth and efficient flow of information and the equally efficient means for shipping goods and facilitating quick and efficient clearance through all customs controls at the point of export and import.

CHAPTER 9

SUMMARY AND APPRAISAL

The process of marine cargo management is both complex and time-consuming. It is also definitive, precise and exacting. It involves a variety of means of maritime transport and shipment, although if it is carried out correctly and accurately, it will save a great deal of unnecessary delay and inconvenience to all parties concerned. It is also tightly regulated, and requires a strict duty of care on the part of carriers and shippers, as well as due diligence by all parties concerned. However, with the introduction and implementation of electronic systems, it has become easier for shippers and carriers to manage the marine cargo flow process. The use of electronic means for both documentary and procedural processes has resulted in a smoother and more efficient flow of information, as well as providing a better and more manageable audit trail and tracking process with regard to ensuring that cargoes are transported efficiently from one part of the world to another, as long as the correct information is used. However, there is still a need for knowledge and awareness of regulations and processes for cargo management on the part of shippers, agents and carriers, and this involves ensuring that all aspects of the maritime shipping process are understood and applied correctly. Failure to understand and carry out the correct procedures can lead to costly—and often tragic—mistakes, as illustrated by accidents aboard vessel. Many accidents have occurred to vessels en route because of a breakdown in the cargo management process, as well as various maritime disputes because of a failure to understand basic shipping principles. Knowledge of this process is vital, despite its relative complexity. This is why there are so many facets and perspectives to the business of marine cargo management, and why in many ways it is impossible for one person to know and manage the whole process. In this way, there are also different professions engaged in the business, all specialising in different aspects of the cargo management process. However, a basic knowledge of the principles of cargo management is required by most people involved in the process of international business, as this enables each party involved in the overall process of the international supply chain to communicate effectively with other parties involved in the process elsewhere.

Cargo management is controlled internationally by a series of Conventions and Regulations made and imposed by international maritime authorities. The rules and regulations are created for a prime purpose—to ensure that maritime cargo is carried safely and efficiently. However, there is evidence that such rules are either overlooked or ignored by many commercial entities concerning the carriage of goods be sea. The general principle and practice is that the shipper leaves all aspects of the expedition of goods to the agent, who in turn leaves the actual carriage of the goods to the carrier. The shipper, in many cases, has little or no knowledge of how the process of cargo management takes place, and in many cases does not want to. The international rules concerning the carriage of goods, however, impose ultimate responsibility for the cargo on the shipper, whether this is the seller or the buyer, and in many cases the process of international payments, especially where letters of credit are concerned, also requires a duty of care on the part of the exporter to furnish the correct documents to the buyer. In many cases, however, the seller/exporter has little idea as to how goods should be shipped and prefers not to be involved in the carriage process, especially as most exporters have devolved such responsibilities to the freight agent and the carrier. The freight agent, however, is literally that—an agent, and is not responsible for the generation of information concerning the shipment. That responsibility rests with the shipper, and only the shipper, either the exporter or the importer, whoever arranges the carriage of the consignment, although both exporter and importer have a clear and distinct duty of care to ensure that the correct information concerning the consignment is conveyed to the freight forwarder, the clearance broker and the carrier.

9.1 Factors in the Marine Cargo Management Process

The process of marine cargo management is influenced by several factors. These include:

- details of the consignor;
- details of the consignee;
- the destination of the cargo;
- the international terms of delivery (INCOTERMS) to be used:
- the description of the cargo;
- the nature of the cargo (general, hazardous etc.);
- when the consignment is required for delivery;
- the cost of shipping and overall transportation;
- the size, weight and dimensions of the cargo;
- the availability of a vessel or a sailing;
- the identification of the shipping line to be used;
- the route to be taken;
- the specific ports to be used (especially where the INCOTERMS stipulate this);
- the time taken for shipment;
- insurance considerations;
- documentary requirements and considerations;
- international and national legal, economic and political requirements;
- customs clearance and duties.

None of the above factors are mutually exclusive. All of the above factors need to be taken into account when arranging a shipment, be it within the European framework or overseas, and in many cases are prerequisites when letters of credit are used for payment purposes, thus making them preconditions in terms of shipment compliance. There is equally inevitably a cost attached to any shipment, and this too depends upon all the above factors. The more lax or badly-organised the cargo management process is arranged, the greater the cost will be, usually as a result of avoidable delays and possible mishaps.

The planning of every maritime shipment is vital. In many cases, consignments are loaded into a vehicle by the exporter, without any form of consideration as to what arrangements for shipment have been made, and even what documentation is required, especially where Ex Works (EXW) shipments are involved. Where the exporter does arrange the shipment, the actual arrangements are left to a freight forwarder to undertake, and the exporter takes little responsibility other than raise an invoice and a packing list. The stark reality is that the exporter, as the shipper, is responsible for ensuring that the correct shipment instructions are issued to the freight agent, and that all necessary information concerning the cargo is conveyed through the appointed freight forwarder to the carrier to ensure the efficient despatch and expedition of the cargo. Failure to do so can result in the possible risk of disaster or damage, or at very least, expensive delays to the shipment of the cargo and its arrival at its intended destination. It is an unfortunate fact of present-day cargo movements that the shipper often has little or no idea as to how the international logistics process functions, or even wishes to, as long as the cargo is delivered safely to the customer, hence the view of the shipper that such matters are the responsibility of the freight forwarder and the carrier. However, the freight forwarder and carrier are only as good as the information concerning each cargo allows them to be. The shipper has a strict duty of care to ensure that the correct details of the cargo are conveyed to the carrier and thus the shipper is required to have some knowledge, however basic, of the shipping process, as they are deemed responsible for ensuring that the information relating to the cargo at the time of loading is fully correct and in order.

However, where an auditable and manageable process exists, the results are worthwhile. In an age of the electronic transfer of information and greater efficiency of freight transport, the process of cargo management is not seen as being rocket science. It takes a reasonable amount of acquired knowledge, as well as a reliance on expertise from the professionals who deal with cargo movements on a daily basis. It also requires knowledge of rules and regulations, especially given the need for increased levels of vigilance and security. And ultimately, the responsibility lies on the shoulders of the shipper, be it the exporter or the importer. The carrier acts solely as the means by which a cargo is transported from one place to another. The carrier relies upon the information provided by the shipper to carry the goods without problems. The failure to provide that information may result in all kinds of problems, both for the shipper and the carrier, so there is a need to manage the whole process of cargo movement in a transparent, auditable and efficient manner. The absence of vital information concerning specific cargoes has often resulted in disaster, along with the inevitable investigation. There is no excuse for the withholding of essential information concerning a cargo and indeed certain accidents or disasters relating to the carriage of goods can be attributed to negligence on the part of the shipper in not conveying sufficient information to the carrier concerning the nature of the cargo concerned. Ultimately, blame can be laid at the door of the shipper, should it be proven that the shipper failed to inform the carrier of the true nature of the consignment. Ultimately, any party injured by the failure to correctly carry out the transaction of the movement of goods, be it seller or buyer, can resort to legal means to gain satisfaction if the need requires. Although legal action is often seen as the last resort, it can result in substantial damages or compensation being awarded to either party. However, the carrier can only be held liable for loss or damage if it can be proven that the carrier failed in their duty to ensure that the cargo was carried safely. Where the shipper is at fault for a failure to convey the correct information concerning the cargo to the carrier, then the shipper is held liable for any subsequent loss or damage to the cargo. In this respect, the carrier is still fully reliant upon the shipper for the correct details of the cargo being carried.

As far as security and customs requirements are concerned, the implementation of the US AMS and Canadian ACI systems has done much to discipline both shippers and carriers into ensuring absolute compliance concerning the maritime shipment of cargoes. Quite simply, if the information concerning the cargo is not submitted to the computer, clearance will not be given for the cargo to be loaded aboard vessel. This means that there is no longer any excuse concerning the issue of generic terms such as FAK or "Said to Contain", as under the US and Canadian systems, these terms are no longer allowed. There will hopefully come a time when such terms are outlawed worldwide.

The WCO SAFE Framework will require the information for all cargoes to be submitted by the carrier to the computer of the customs authority in the country of destination prior to the cargoes being loaded aboard vessel. This will mean that the details of all containers and their cargoes, whether full or consolidated loads, must be entered into the computer at least 24 hours prior to the loading of the vessel. The same rules will apply worldwide as presently apply to consignments destined for either the United States or Canada, especially those concerning the phrases "Said to Contain" or "Freight of all Kinds", which will be outlawed by all countries. The phrase "Said to Contain" implies that there may be doubt as to the authenticity or accuracy of the information provided with relation to the cargo loaded into the container. This in turn implies that neither the shipper nor the forwarder may have taken adequate steps to supervise the loading of the container. Hence, the carrier may equally not be certain as to the contents of the container at the time of loading aboard vessel. This is quite simply unacceptable and this has been acknowledged by the World Customs Organisation (WCO). In an age of political uncertainties and increased levels of maritime security, there is greater need than ever to ensure that all information pertaining to maritime cargo is fully available and is totally accurate. Although full container loads (FCL) are less of a problem than consolidated loads there is still the need for a supervisor to be present at the loading of any container, to ensure the accuracy of all the documentation relating to the contents of the container and that a full tally is made of all consignments being loaded into the container.

The situation is even more critical concerning the loading of consolidated consignments into Less-than-full container loads (LCL). At present, generic descriptions are used for the purposes of the raising of consolidation or Master Bills of Lading, generally using the term "Said to Contain", but this situation is no longer acceptable. As with FCLs, a supervisor must be present at the loading of a consolidated container and must ensure that a full and complete tally is made of all consignments being loaded into that container. This used to be the case at most consolidation and groupage depots, in the main inland clearance depots, where the loading of each container was supervised by a member of the staff of the depot, and the load lists presented to HM Customs & Excise (in the case of the UK) for approval and clearance prior to the container being locked and sealed for its onward journey. In an age of stream-lining and distance operations, this practice has regrettably diminished, and it is high time that the practice of loading supervision was revived. Failure to do so and a continuation of present streamlined short-cut practice will result in delays to export shipments as the computer of the authority of overseas destination will reject the information at first instance because of lack of acceptable detail. Such rejection of information may well lead to delays in loading the container aboard vessel, and even non-loading aboard the allocated vessel because of delays. Such delays are becoming more common, given the lack of cargo information available. It is the express duty and responsibility of the shipper to ensure that such situations can be avoided. However, one of the main problems concerning the duties of the shipper is that in many cases there is nobody in the company responsible for logistics arrangement and control and this lack of expertise often leads to a breakdown in communication as well as a failure on the part of the shipper to understand the maritime logistics process, especially when communicating information concerning the cargo and its nature with either the freight forwarder or the carrier. Whereas at one time every exporting company would have a member of staff concerned with logistics, especially international logistics, in an age of cost-cutting and outsourcing, such personnel functions have become an expensive luxury to many companies with the result that a downsizing policy has led to the outsourcing of such functions, with a total reliance by the shipper on freight forwarders to ship consignments worldwide, without ensuring some level of logistics competence within their own organisation.

9.2 Common Errors in Cargo Management

Many errors can occur as a result of a failure to supervise and monitor cargo loading into the container and account for all consignments to be loaded into the container by documentary means. These include the following:

- discrepancies between actual consignments, manifests and Bills of Lading;
- short shipments;
- wrong descriptions of goods;
- conflicting or inconsistent cargo information;
- absence of specific consignments;
- damage to consignments while in transit;
- no proof of loading (load list).

Further errors include the following, especially in cases of Ex Works (EXW) arrangements:

- failure to raise export declarations, especially in the case of consolidated consignments;
- failure to issue a unique consignment reference (UCR);
- failure to raise house Bills of Lading;
- no evidence of shipping documentation held by the exporter;
- no evidence of hard copy export declarations;
- no proper export cargo shipping instructions (ECSI) or shipping notes.

Supervision of cargo loading is vital to ensure compliance with security and control measures. This supervision should be carried out by either a member of staff of the exporting company, or a representative for the freight forwarding company arranging the shipment. Equally, the responsibility of the provision of all information concerning the cargoes themselves rests firmly at the door of the shipper. Even under Ex Works (EXW) terms, the exporter is still responsible for the export declaration of the consignment and must ensure that they have sufficient detail about the consignment being exported and how it is to be shipped, despite the fact that the importer, or buyer, may be the party actually arranging the shipment. Ignorance or lack of knowledge of the rules is no excuse and cannot be admitted or accepted by any authority. The shipper has a distinct duty of care to ensure that the consignment is correctly loaded into a container and is accounted for before the container doors are shut. Failure to do this can lead to the carrier refusing to carry the consignment owing to lack of knowledge of the contents of the container in question. The circumstances behind the *Hyundai Fortune* disaster in 2006 clearly illustrate the need for vigilance and due diligence on the part of the shipper and the freight forwarder regarding the reporting and loading of cargoes inside containers and on board vessels. It would appear that the carrier had little or no idea that immediately behind the accommodation quarters on the container vessel *Hyundai Fortune* were six containers loaded with pyrotechnics (fireworks). If the master of the vessel had known about these containers, it is highly unlikely that he would have allowed the containers to be stacked together, and so close to the vessel's superstructure, let alone over a sensitive part of the vessel, namely the engine room. The master has the duty of signing off the cargo manifest prior to the sailing of the vessel, and indeed in extreme circumstances, the master may refuse to allow the loading of a cargo if he is unsure as to its nature or description, in accordance with the SOLAS Convention and the IMDG rules. In such cases, especially under the IMDG rules, containers loaded with dangerous goods must be stowed as far way from the superstructure and, for that matter, the engines and propulsion mechanisms, as possible. In this case, it would appear that there was a complete breakdown in information relating to the stowage of these containers at the point of loading, and there may even be the possibility that the carrier may not have been made fully aware of the contents of these containers. Even a simple case of the dimensions and weights of containers being unknown by the computer at the time of loading of the vessel may lead to disaster, as in the case of the *Annabella* in 2007, where the computer programmed with information concerning the loading and stowage of containers aboard the vessel did not recognise the dimensions of several containers, namely a series of 30-foot containers, and the details had to be amended to 40-foot dimensions. It is thus the prime responsibility of both the shipper and the freight forwarder to ensure that all information concerning both the container and its contents is fully conveyed to the carrier in advance of arrival at the port of loading to ensure efficient and compliant loading aboard vessel and safe carriage of the consignment from the port of loading to the port of destination, as well as ensuring that all adequate steps are taken to ensure that the computer used for loading control purposes is programmed with the correct information from the very outset.

There is no absolute rule on how cargoes should be moved by maritime means, as there are many facets to the process of marine cargo movement, from loose cargo through bulk shipments and deep sea containerised cargo to short-sea Ro-Ro trailer cargo traffic. Each method of shipment has its own rules, processes and arrangements, and each method also is also seen as a discipline in its own right. Furthermore, each method of movement has its own cost and time structure, depending upon the complexity or simplicity of the movement, and these factors may influence the shipper in which method of shipment to use, hence the need for meticulous planning on the part of the shipper prior to actually arranging the shipment itself.

However, the carrier also needs to ensure that they undertake and fulfil all parts of any agreement to move cargoes from one point to another by maritime means. There is a definite duty of care on the part of the carrier to ensure that all necessary steps are taken to guarantee the safe and secure delivery of a consignment to the customer. The marine sector is still by a long way the principal means of shipment of cargoes worldwide. It is appreciated that time and cost constraints often dictate how cargoes are to be moved, but there is ultimately a price to be paid by the shipper for the movement of any cargo. The less standard the cargo is, the greater the cost will be. The cost also increases depending upon the dimensions or weight of the cargo, as for consolidation purposes the freight cost is calculated on the basis of actual weight or volumetric weight, whichever is greater. The one caveat for any shipper is that to ensure the success and efficiency of the shipment, meticulous advance planning is required to move that shipment, given all the stages that exist in the process of the movement of a cargo by sea. This process is not an overnight affair. It can take days or even weeks to manage and complete. Marine cargo management is a science, although it is not rocket science. It is very much a case of obedience of accepted rules and regulations, and it revolves around a series of basic and accepted principles. As long as all the principles are adhered to, marine cargo management can work very efficiently. Although technology has changed over the ages, the basic principles, methods and regulations of the movement of goods by sea have not. They remain as prevalent as ever, and will always be required.

Most cargo taken to and from UK shores is carried in vessels owned and operated outside the UK, with all the major container carrier lines and the international ferry operators owned by overseas interests. Not one of these carriers is now owned form the UK. However, it would be too simple to say that everything pertaining to the UK maritime sector is overseas-owned. This is not true. The family silver has not been entirely sold off as yet. A small amount still remains in the family vaults. Several UK ports and a few shipping companies are still UK-owned, such as Forth Ports and Peel Ports, BP Tankers, James Fisher and Caledonian MacBrayne, but the vast majority of the maritime sector has been sold off to overseas interests. The UK has, to a large extent, lost the basis of its proud maritime heritage, mainly in the name of a quick financial fix. But there is a huge difference between a financial fix and an economic future. The nature of the UK's economic status lies in the maritime sector. The unfortunate fact is that in the past fifty years, the national maritime heritage which made the UK a great nation has been progressively eroded to the point of virtual non-existence. The maritime resources which the UK once boasted have been drained away or sold off to the highest bidder. The main source of UK wealth generated in the maritime sector is made in the City of London, with the maritime exchange, insurance and charter markets. Indeed, the vast majority of the global maritime freight sector as a commodity is traded on the floors of the London markets.

There is no one reason for this decline. The decline in the British shipyards stemmed from a mixture of industrial unrest in the shipbuilding sector coupled with the cheaper costs of constructing vessels overseas, the increasing size of deep-sea vessels, and eventually the inability of many yards throughout the world, especially in the UK, to construct the larger vessels of the present day. The need for rationalisation in the container market has resulted in an increasing number of mergers and acquisitions of shipping lines throughout the world, resulting in the mega-carrier organisations of the present.

In an economic crisis, the UK would become totally reliant on outside forces to maintain its maritime links, a situation never known before. The overseas-owned deep-sea cargo and ferry services would become a vital necessity to the nation. However, a nation cannot live on past traditions. It has to adapt to meet a world of constant change. Unfortunately, the cost of adaptation as far as the UK has been concerned has been too great to bear, and the UK maritime sector has suffered as a result. The UK is no longer the great maritime nation it once was, despite its efforts to maintain a shipping industry. In these respects, Britannia no longer rules the waves. Indeed, the UK is now forced to rely on economic lifelines provided by other nations, rather than providing its own lifelines to other nations. UK maritime resources have been severely drained over the years, with a near-total reliance on other countries to provide the services it so badly needs.

It is a tragedy to imagine that a once-proud maritime nation has been reduced to near-total reliance upon nations once thought of as far less powerful in status and indeed which have been soundly defeated by UK naval forces in times gone by. And much of this change in ownership has been carried out in the fickle name of financial expediency. It is perhaps this financial "quick fix" which has, to a large extent, cost this country its economic maritime future. The ports, shipyards, and the shipping lines—all have either disappeared or have been sold off, mainly to overseas bidders, the rest consigned to oblivion and the history books. The rest of the decline in the UK shipping sector can be attributed to the complex changes in the maritime cargo sector, especially with the rapid rise in the container sector, which left much of the UK cargo sector behind, other than P&O Containers, which for some time competed successfully against the overseas container carriers, until it was first merged with Nedlloyd and finally swallowed up by the gigantic Maersk Line. In time, the risk is that the UK becomes a slave to overseas powers that own and control the maritime lifelines on which the UK relies. Britannia no longer rules the waves; the waves now rule over us.

CARGO DOCUMENTATION

CMR CONSIGNMENT NOTE

LETTRE DE VOITURE INTERNATIONALE **CMR** INTERNATIONAL CONSIGNMENT NOTE

No 24382

.... Pays/Country

1 Expéditeur (nom, adresse, pays)
Sender (name, address, country)

2 Destinataire (nom, adresse, pays)
Consignee (name, address, country)

3 Prise en charge de la marchandise / Taking over the goods:
Lieu / Place

Pays / Country

Date   Heure d'arrivée / Time of arrival   Heure de départ / Time of departure

4 Livraison de la marchandise / Delivery of the goods:
Lieu / Place

Pays / Country

Heures d'ouverture du dépôt / Warehouse opening hours

5 Instructions de l'expéditeur
Sender's instructions

6 Transporteur (nom, adresse, pays, autres références)
Carrier (name, address, country, other references)

7 Transporteurs successifs / Successive carriers

Nom / Name

Adresse / Address

Pays / Country

Reçu et acceptation
Receipt and Acceptance   Date   Signature

8 Réserves et observations du transporteur lors de la prise en charge de la marchandise
Carrier's reservations and observations on taking over the goods

9 Documents remis au transporteur par l'expéditeur
Documents handed to the carrier by the sender

10 Marques et numéros Marks and Nos	**11** Nombre de colis Number of packages	**12** Mode d'emballage Method of packing	**13** Nature de la marchandise Nature of the goods	**14** Poids brut, kg Gross weight in kg	**15** Cubage m3 Volume in m3

Numéro ONU / UN Number

Nom voir 13 / Name see 13

Numéro d'étiquette / Label Number

Groupe d'emballage / Packing Group

(ADR) / (ADR)

16 Conventions particulières entre l'expéditeur et le transporteur
Special agreements between the sender and the carrier

17 A payer par / To be paid by:

	Expéditeur / Sender	Destinataire / Consignee
Prix de transport / Carriage charges		
Frais accessoires / Supplementary charges		
Droits de douane / Customs duties		
Autre frais / Other charges		

18 Autres indications utiles / Other useful particulars

19 Remboursement / Cash on delivery

20 Ce transport est soumis, nonobstant toute clause contraire, à la Convention relative au contrat de transport international de marchandises par route (CMR)
This carriage is subject, notwithstanding any clause to the contrary, to the Convention on the Contract for the international Carriage of Goods by Road (CMR)

21 Etablie à / Established in _____ le / on _____ 20..

24 Marchandises reçues / Goods received

Heure d'arrivée / Time of arrival   Heure de départ / Time of departure

Lieu / Place   le / on ____ 20..   20..

22   **23**

Signature ou timbre de l'expéditeur / Signature or stamp of the sender

Signature ou timbre du transporteur / Signature or stamp of the carrier

Signature et timbre du destinataire / Signature and stamp of the consignee

Partie non contractuelle réservée au transporteur / Non-contractual part reserved for the carrier

OCEAN BILL OF LADING

P&O Containers

B/L No.
Booking Ref.:
Shipper's Ref.:

Bill of Lading for Combined Transport shipment or Port to Port shipment

Shipper

Consigned to the order of

Notify Party/Address   (It is agreed that no responsibility shall attach to the Carrier or his Agents for failure to notify of the arrival of the goods (see clause 20 on reverse))

Place of Receipt   (Applicable only when this document is used as a Combined Transport Bill of Lading)

Place of Delivery   (Applicable only when this document is used as a Combined Transport Bill of Lading)

Vessel and Voy. No.

Port of Loading

Port of Discharge

Marks and Nos; Container Nos;	Number and kind of Packages; description of Goods	Gross Weight (kg)	Measurement (cbm)

Above particulars as declared by Shipper, but not acknowledged by the Carrier (see clause 11)

Received by the Carrier from the Shipper in apparent good order and condition (unless otherwise noted herein) the total number of quantity of Containers or other packages or units indicated in the box opposite entitled **"Total No. of Containers/Packages received by the Carrier" for Carriage subject to all the terms and conditions hereof (INCLUDING THE TERMS AND CONDITIONS ON THE REVERSE HEREOF AND THE TERMS AND CONDITIONS OF THE CARRIER'S APPLICABLE TARIFF) from the Place of Receipt or the Port of Loading, whichever is applicable, to the Port of Discharge or the Place of Delivery, whichever is applicable. Before the Carrier arranges delivery of the Goods one original Bill of Lading, duly endorsed, must be surrendered by the Merchant to the Carrier at the Port of Discharge or at some other location acceptable to the Carrier. In accepting this Bill of Lading the Merchant expressly accepts and agrees to all its terms and conditions whether printed, stamped or written, or otherwise incorporated, notwithstanding the non-signing of the Bill of Lading by the Merchant.

Place and Date of Issue

IN WITNESS of the contract herein contained the number of originals stated opposite has been issued, one of which being accomplished the other(s) to be void.

Number of Original Bills of Lading

For the Carrier:

As Agent(s) only.

P&OCL B.Ll 10/91

*Total No. of Containers/Packages received by the Carrier

Movement

Freight and Charges (indicate whether prepaid or collect):

Origin Inland Haulage Charge ... ...

Origin Terminal Handling/LCL Service Charge ... ...

Ocean Freight ... ...

Destination Terminal Handling/LCL Service Charge ...

Destination Inland Haulage Charge ... ...

ICS
CT B.L
April 78

IMO FAL 2 CARGO DECLARATION

		Page No.
☐ Arrival	☐ Departure	

1. Name of Ship	2. Port where report is made	

3. Nationality of Ship	4. Name of Master	5. Port of Loading/Port of Discharge

6. Marks and Nos.	7. Number and kind of packages; description of goods	8. Gross weight	9. Measurement
....	....	....	....
....	....	....	....
....	....	....	....
....	....	....	....
....	....	....	....
....	....	....	....
....	....	....	....
....	....	....	....
....	....	....	....
....	....	....	....
....	....	....	....
....	....	....	....
....	....	....	....
....	....	....	....
....	....	....	....
....	....	....	....
....	....	....	....
....	....	....	....
....	....	....	....

IMO FAL   10. Date and signature by master, authorised agent or officer
FORM 2
* Transport Document No.

Also state original ports of shipment in respect of goods shipped on multimodal transport document or through bills of lading

APPENDIX 3

CONTAINER LOAD LIST

Page No.

1. Container No.		2. Shipping Line/Operator		
3. Place of Loading	4. Date of Loading	5. Destination		
6. Marks and Nos.	7. Number and kind of packages; description of goods	8. Gross weight	9. Measurement

10. Date and signature by authorised agent or supervisor

Transport Document No.

Also state ports of shipment in respect of goods shipped on multimodal transport document or through bills of lading

275

APPENDIX 4

TRAILER LOAD LIST

Page No.

1. Trailer No./Vehicle Registration No		2. Carrier/Operator		
3. Place of Loading	4. Date of Loading	5. Destination		
6. Marks and Nos.	7. Number and kind of packages; description of goods	8. Gross weight	9. Measurement
....	....	....	....
....	....	....	....
....	....	....	....
....	....	....	....
....	....	....	....
....	....	....	....
....	....	....	....
....	....	....	....
....	....	....	....
....	....	....	....
....	....	....	....
....	....	....	....
....	....	....	....
....	....	....	....
....	....	....	....
....	....	....	....
....	....	....	....
....	....	....	....
....	....	....	....

10. Date and signature by authorised agent or supervisor

Transport Document No.

Where Ro-Ro transport is used, also state intended ports of shipment in respect of goods shipped on transport document

FREIGHT CONFERENCES 2008

FAR EASTERN FREIGHT CONFERENCE (FEFC)

ANL Container Lines Pty Ltd
APL Co Pte Ltd
CMA CGM
CSAV Norasia Liner Services
Egyptian National Shipping Co
Hapag Lloyd AG
Hyundai Merchant Marine Co Ltd
Kawasaki Kisen Kaisha Ltd ("K" Line)
Maersk Line
MISC Berhad
Mitsui OSK Lines Ltd (MOL)
Mediterranean Shipping Co SA (MSC)
Nippon Yusen Kaisha (NYK)
Orient Overseas Container Line (OOCL)
Safmarine
Yang Ming Marine Transport Corporation
Zim Integrated Shipping Services Ltd

TRANSATLANTIC CONFERENCE AGREEMENT (TACA)

Maersk Line
Atlantic Container Line AB (ACL)
Mediterranean Shipping Company SA (MSC)
Nippon Yusen Kaisha (NYK)
Orient Overseas Container Line (OOCL)

WESTBOUND TRANSPACIFIC STABILIZATION AGREEMENT (WTSA)

APL
Hyundai Merchant Marine Co. Ltd
COSCO
"K" Line
Evergreen
Nippon Yusen Kaisha (NYK)
Hanjin Shipping
Orient Overseas Container Line (OOCL)
Hapag Lloyd AG
Yang Ming Marine Transport Corporation

CONTAINER SPECIFICATIONS

Length (m)	Imperial Size (ft)	Width (m)	Height (m)	Gross Weight (kg)	Tare Weight (kg)	Payload (kg)	Usable Capacity (cu m)
6.05	20′	2.438	2.438	20320.9	1590.3	18730.6	30.75
9.12	30′	2.438	2.438	24401.2	2092.92	23308.3	46.84
12.19	40′	2.438	2.438	30481.4	2593.64	27887.0	62.92

US VARIATIONS

Length (m)	Imperial Size (ft)	Width (m)	Height (m)	Gross Weight (kg)	Tare Weight (kg)	Payload (kg)	Usable Capacity (cu m)
6.05	20′	2.438	2.591	24000	2330.0	21670.0	32.9
12.19	40′	2.438	2.591	30481.4	4150.0	26330.0	62.92

Length (m)	Imperial Size (ft)	Internal Length (m)	Internal Width (m)	Internal Height (m)
6.05	20′	5.901	2.35	2.374
12.19	40′	12.035	2.346	2.374

GLOSSARY

ACI	Advanced Cargo Information (Canadian Customs Computer System)
AIS	Automatic Identification System
AMS	Automated Manifest System (US Customs Computer System)
Authorised Regular Operator	Short-Sea Ferry Service
BIFFEX	Baltic International Freight Futures Exchange (Baltic Exchange)
CFR	Cost and Freight
CHIEF	Customs Handling of Import and Export Freight (UK Customs Computer)
CIF	Cost Insurance Freight
CIP	Carriage and Insurance Paid
CMI	Comité Maritime Internationale
CMR	Consigne de Marchandise Routière (Road Consignment Note)
CNIS	Channel Navigation Information Service
COGSA	Carriage of Goods by Sea Acts
Container Manifest	The list and description of all cargoes inside a container
CPT	Carriage Paid To . . .
CT	Community Transit
CT-PAT	Customs and Trade Partnership against Terrorism
CUSCAR	Customs Cargo Reporting
DDP	Delivered Duty Paid
DDU	Delivered Duty Unpaid
Demurrage	Port Storage costs on goods delayed for clearance
Dwt	Deadweight Tonnage
EC	European Commission/European Community
EDI	Electronic Data Interchange/Interface
EEZ	Exclusive Economic Zone
ELAA	European Liner Affairs Association
EMSA	European Maritime Safety Agency
EU	European Union
EXW	Ex Works
FAK	Freight of All Kinds

FAL	IMO Facilitation
FAS	Free Alongside Ship
FCA	Free Carrier
FCL	Full Container Load
Feeder Service	Regular scheduled short-sea container service, usually linking in with deep-sea container services
FEFC	Far East Freight Conference
FOB	Free On Board
GATS	General Agreement on Trade in Services
GPS	Global Positioning System
Grt	Gross Registered Tonnage
HAZMAT	Hazardous Materials
HMRC	HM Revenue & Customs
HNS	International Convention on Hazardous and Noxious Substances
HS	The Worldwide Harmonised System of Tariff Commodity Code Classification
IMDG	International Movement of Dangerous Goods
IMO	International Maritime Organisation
INCOTERMS	International Commercial Terms of Delivery
ISO	International Standards Organisation
ISPS	International Ship and Port Security Code
Laytime	The length of time a vessel lies idle at the port berth
LCL	Less-than-full Container Load
Liner Service	Regular Scheduled Container Vessel Service
Load Line	The lines used to denote the maximum allowed loading limit for cargo vessels (also known as the "Plimsoll Line")
Load List	The list detailing all the cargoes to be loaded inside a container
MAIB	Marine Accident Investigation Branch
MCA	UK Maritime and Coast Guard Agency
Metric Tonne	The weight of a consignment depending upon its dimensions
MSC	Mediterranean Shipping Company
Multimodalism	The practice of using two or more means of transport to move a container from one point to another (also Intermodalism)
NES	National Export System (formerly New Export System)
NVOCC	Non Vessel-Owning Common Carrier
OBO	Oil/Bulk/Ore Carrier
OOCL	Orient Overseas Container Line

Panamax	The largest size of vessel capable of negotiating the Panama Canal
Post-Panamax	Vessels larger than the maximum limit allowed to negotiate the Panama Canal
Reefer	Refrigerated Ship or Container
Ro-Ro	Roll-On Roll-Off
SOLAS	Safety of Lives at Sea
TACA	Transatlantic Conference Agreement
TEU	Twenty-Foot Equivalent Unit; the standard container size
UNCITRAL	United Nations Commission on Trade Law
UNCLOS	United Nations Convention on the Law of the Sea
UNCTAD	United Nations Conference on Trade and Development
VAT	Value-Added Tax
VLCC	Very Large Crude Carrier
Volumetric Weight	The weight of a consignment based on its cubic measurements
VTS	Vessel Traffic Services
WCO	World Customs Organisation
WTO	World Trade Organisation

FURTHER READING

For further reading, refer to the following books and websites:

Books:

August, R., *International Business Law* (Pearson Prentice Hall, 2004)

Bichou, K., M.G.H. Bell and A. Evans (eds.), *Risk Management in Port Operations, Logistics and Supply Chain Security* (Informa, 2007)

Branch, A., *Export Practice & Management* (Business Press, Thomson Learning, 2000)

Cargo Stowage and Securing (IMO, 2003 Edition)

Charlery, J., *International Trade Law* (M&E Handbooks, 1994)

Churchill, R.R. and A.V. Lowe, *The Law of the Sea* (Manchester University Press, 1999)

Collins, N., *The Essential Guide to Chartering and the Dry Freight Market* (2000)

Cudahy, B., *Box Boats: How Container Ships changed the World* (Fordham University Press, 2006)

FAL Convention (IMO, 1998 Edition)

Farthing, B. and Brownrigg M., *Farthing on International Shipping* (LLP, 1997)

Hodges, S., *Law of Marine Insurance* (Cavendish Publishing, 2001)

House, D.J., *Cargo Work* (2005)

IMO, *IMDG Code* (2006 Edition)

IMO, *IMO Compendium on Facilitation and Electronic Business* (2001 Edition)

IMO, *ISPS Code* (2003 Edition)

International Standardization Organization, *ISO/PAS 28000, Specification for Security Management Systems for the Supply Chain* (ISO: Geneva)

International Standardization Organization, *ISO/PAS 28001, Specification for Security Management Systems for the Supply Chain* (ISO: Geneva)

Kendall, L.C. and J.J. Buckley, *The Business of Shipping* (Cornell Maritime Press, 2001)

Levinson, M., *The Box* (Princeton University Press, 2006)

Lloyd's List (Informa)

Smith and Keenan, *Advanced Business Law* (Pitman Publishing, 1997)

Stamatis, D.H., *Six Sigma Fundamentals* (2004)

Stopford, M., *Maritime Economics* (Routledge, 2004)

Websites:

AIS Holland: www.aisholland.com

AIS Liverpool: www.aisliverpool.org.uk

AIS Liverpool: www.shipais.com

Baltic Exchange: www.balticexchange.com

Clydeport Port Authority: www.clydeport.co.uk

Comité Maritime Internationale: www.comitemaritime.org

EU Directive 2002/59/EC: http://europa.eu.int and also: www.mcga.gov.uk

Far East Freight Conference: www.fefclondon.com

HM Revenue & Customs: www.hmrc.gov.uk

International Maritime Organisation: www.imo.org

Lloyd's List: www.lloydslist.com

Lloyd's Loading List: www.lloydsll.com

Lloyd's MIU: www.lloydsmiu.com

Maritime & Coastguard Agency: www.mcga.gov.uk

Transatlantic Conference (TACA): www.taafc.co.uk

UNCITRAL: www.uncitral.org

Uniform Customs & Practices, Series 600 (UCP 600), available through the local Chamber of Commerce or at: www.britishchambers.org.uk

INDEX